The Collected Works
of Ann Hawkshaw

The Collected Works of Ann Hawkshaw

Edited by
Debbie Bark

ANTHEM PRESS
LONDON · NEW YORK · DELHI

Anthem Press
An imprint of Wimbledon Publishing Company
www.anthempress.com

This edition first published in UK and USA 2014
by ANTHEM PRESS
75–76 Blackfriars Road, London SE1 8HA, UK
or PO Box 9779, London SW19 7ZG, UK
and
244 Madison Ave #116, New York, NY 10016, USA

Copyright © 2014 Debbie Bark editorial matter and selection

The moral right of the authors has been asserted.

All rights reserved. Without limiting the rights under copyright reserved above, no part of this publication may be reproduced, stored or introduced into a retrieval system, or transmitted, in any form or by any means (electronic, mechanical, photocopying, recording or otherwise), without the prior written permission of both the copyright owner and the above publisher of this book.

British Library Cataloguing-in-Publication Data
A catalogue record for this book is available from the British Library.

Library of Congress Cataloging-in-Publication Data
Hawkshaw, Ann, 1812–1885.
[Works. Selections]
The collected works of Ann Hawkshaw / edited by Debbie Bark.
pages cm
Includes bibliographical references and index.
ISBN 978-1-78308-021-2 (hardcover : alk. paper)
1. Hawkshaw, Ann, 1812–1885. I. Bark, Debbie, editor of compilation. II. Title.
PR4765.H4A6 2014
821'.8—dc23
[B] 2014004997

ISBN-13: 978 1 78308 021 2 (Hbk)
ISBN-10: 1 78308 021 3 (Hbk)

Cover image of Ann Hawkshaw courtesy of Lady Alexandra Wedgwood.

This title is also available as an ebook.

Contents

Preface and Acknowledgements	xi
Biographical Introduction	xv

1842

'Dionysius the Areopagite', with Other Poems	1
Introductory Stanzas	3
Dionysius the Areopagite	6
Part I	
Part II	43
Part III	61
The Past	69
The Future	77
Wild Flowers	85
The Welsh Bard's Last Song	86
Spring to the Flowers	87
Sonnet—To America	88
Palestine	89
Land of my Fathers	90
To Fountain's Abbey	90
To a Bereaved Father	91
The Exile Song	92
The Mother to her Starving Child	93
To—— on the Death of Three of her Children	95
To—— after the Death of her Daughter	96
Lines on a Friend lost at Sea	96
The Prophet's Lament	97
Song	98
The Greek Girl's Song	99
The Captive King	100
Why am I a Slave?	102
Sonnet to——	103

1843

Life's Dull Reality	105

1847

Poems for My Children	107
Spring is Coming	110
Mary's Wish	111
The Festival of the Last of October—Scene in the Time of the Druids	112
Common Things	114
The Little Wanderers	115
Part I.—The Resolve	115

Part II.—The Avalanche	118
Part III.—The Cave in the Mountains	122
The Wind	125
Scene in the Time of the Romans	126
The City Child's Complaint	128
The First Spring Flowers	129
To Editha	130
Editha	131
The Oak Tree	132
I do not love the Night	134
Thinking and Dreaming	135
King Alfred and His Mother—a Scene in the Time of the Saxons	137
The Angel Friend	139
The Stream	140
The Poor Fly—for my little Harry	141
The Land of my Dreams	142
The History of a Coral Islet	143
The Hermit, the Chieftain, and the Child—a Tale about Happiness	145
God is Love	148
The Monk of Chester—a Scene in the Time of the Normans	149
A Talk in Furness Abbey—to J.C.H	152
A Little Girl's Wish	153
Sir Oswald's Return—a Scene in the Time of the Crusades	155
Part I	155
Part II	158
Ada	164

1854

Sonnets on Anglo-Saxon History	167
Introductory	171
I. The beginning	173
II. Progress	175
III. The Druids	177
IV. The Romans	179
V. Christianity	181
VI. Christianity in Britain	183
VII. Change	185
VIII. The Saxons.—I	187
IX. The Saxons.—II	189
X. Saxon Mythology	191
XI. Christianity received by the Saxons.—I	193
XII. Christianity received by the Saxons.—II	195
XIII. Merlin	197
XIV. Ethelbert examining the Christian Doctrines	199
XV. Ethelbert embraces Christianity	201

XVI. The great Edwin of Northumbria.—I	203
XVII. Edwin of Northumbria.—II	205
XVIII. The Thane Lilla saving Edwin.—III	207
XIX. Caedmon the Anglo-Saxon Poet	209
XX. The Chronicler	211
XXI. The Venerable Bede.—I	213
XXII. The Venerable Bede.—II	215
XXIII. The death of Bede.—III	217
XXIV. The Northmen	219
XXV. Destruction of the Abbey of Peterborough by the Northmen	221
XXVI. Under-Currents	223
XXVII. The Serf	225
XXVIII. The Serf Freed	227
XXIX. Ina resigning his Crown	229
XXX. The Pilgrim.—I	231
XXXI. The Pilgrim.—II	233
XXXII. The Pilgrim.—III	235
XXXIII. Alfred of Northumbria.—I. Retirement	237
XXXIV. Alfred of Northumbria.—II. Self-Reliance	239
XXXV. The Monastery	241
XXXVI. Ethelberga	243
XXXVII. The benighted Ceorl	245
XXXVIII. The Witena meeting at Easter	247
XXXIX. The Markman's Cottage.—I	249
XL. The Markman's Cottage.—II	251
XLI. True Workers	253
XLII. The Mother of Egbert	255
XLIII. Egbert	257
XLIV. Ethelwulph leaving the Cloister.—I	259
XLV. Ethelwulph.—II	261
XLVI. The Tomb of Ethelberga	263
XLVII. Anglo-Saxon Patriots	265
XLVIII. Alfred the Great.—I. The Child	267
XLIX. Alfred the Great.—II. Remembrances	269
L. Alfred the Great.—III. Adversity	271
LI. Alfred the Great.—IV. Releasing the Wife and Children of Hastings the Northman	273
LII. Alfred the Great.—V. Romney Marsh, Kent	275
LIII. Denulf	277
LIV. Woman.—I. Ethelfleda, the daughter of Alfred	279
LV. Woman.—II. Ethelfleda	281
LVI. Woman.—III. Ethelgiva the Nun	283
LVII. The three Pilgrims	285
LVIII. The Hero-King	287

LIX. The Thane's Fireside	289
LX. The remorse of Athelstan.—I	291
LXI. Athelstan.—II	293
LXII. Edwy and Elfgiva	295
LXIII. The Town	297
LXIV. Disunion	299
LXV. Dunstan.—I. The Boy	301
LXVI. Dunstan.—II. The Dream	303
LXVII. Dunstan.—III. The Youth's aspirings	305
LXVIII. Dunstan.—IV. The Trial	307
LXIX. Dunstan.—V. Love	309
LXX. Dunstan.—VI. The Fall	311
LXXI. Dunstan.—VII. Nature's Revenge	313
LXXII. Dunstan.—VIII. Refusing to crown Ethelred	315
LXXIII. Ethelred the Unready	317
LXXIV. Massacre of the Danes	319
LXXV. The Poet	321
LXXVI. Edmund Ironside	323
LXXVII. Canute the Great	325
LXXVIII. The Forest	327
LXXIX. Godwin.—I. Childhood	329
LXXX. Godwin.—II. The meeting with Ulfr	331
LXXXI. Godwin.—III. The Flight	333
LXXXII. Godwin.—IV. The Earl	335
LXXXIII. Godwin.—V. The Death-Feast	337
LXXXIV. Sweyne, the Outlawed	339
LXXXV. The Visit	341
LXXXVI. Editha in the Monastery at Wherwell	343
LXXXVII. Death-Shadowings.—I. Edward the Etheling	345
LXXXVIII. Death-Shadowings.—II. Leofric	347
LXXXIX. Death-Shadowings.—III. Leofric	349
XC. Edward the Confessor.—I	351
XCI. Edward the Confessor.—II	353
XCII. The Eventide.—I	355
XCIII. The Eventide.—II	357
XCIV. Harold.—I	359
XCV. Harold.—II	361
XCVI. The Mother of Harold	363
XCVII. Night after Battle	365
XCVIII. The Anglo-Saxons	367
Conclusion	368

1871
    Cecil's Own Book   369
        Part I
            The Wonderful Adventures of Hassan the Younger, the Son
                of Hassan-el-Alfi the Camel Driver   371
            The Selfish Toad   383
            The Discontented Stream   387
            Little Prince Bepettedbyall   390
            The Noontide Dream   393
            The Squirrel that forgot that it would be Winter   395
            The Ambitious Water-Lily   398
            The Fairy Gift; or, The Iron Bracelet   403
        Part II
            Change—not Death   417
            Earth's Waters   418
            The Birds of Passage   420
            Homes of the Flowers   420
            In Memoriam   422

Appendix A   425
Appendix B   451
Bibliography   457
Index of Titles   461
Index of First Lines   465

Preface and Acknowledgements

In the early 1990s Ann Hawkshaw's poetry was included in the first wave of the critical recovery of Victorian women poets led by Isobel Armstrong. Armstrong included Hawkshaw in her landmark survey of women's poetry of the Victorian period, '"A Music of Thine Own": Women's Poetry – An Expressive Tradition?' in *Victorian Poetry: Poetry, Poetics and Politics* (1993). Armstrong notes that Hawkshaw was 'an educated poet with strong working-class connections who produced orthodox-seeming work with unusual subtexts', judging Hawkshaw to be 'an impressively strong and independent writer'.[1] She comments on Hawkshaw's long narrative poem 'Dionysius the Areopagite', mentions her sonnet sequence, *Sonnets on Anglo-Saxon History*, and makes brief readings of 'Why am I a Slave?' and 'The Mother to her Starving Child'. She concludes that Hawkshaw's work 'is exceptional' (323). Hawkshaw's short lyric poems 'Why am I a Slave?' and 'The Mother to her Starving Child' are included in *Nineteenth-Century Women Poets: An Oxford Anthology* (1996), co-edited by Armstrong. The entry for Hawkshaw, which begins 'very little is known about Ann Jackson's (later Hawkshaw's) life', goes on to give a brief outline biography, noting her Manchester connections to Elizabeth Gaskell and Samuel Bamford and suggesting that she may have been a Unitarian.[2] The biographical introduction concludes by identifying Hawkshaw as the children's poet, 'Aunt Effie': 'She was best known for the children's poetry that she wrote under the name of "Aunt Effie", whose two books of nursery rhymes were brought out in 1852 and 1854' (346). The identification of Hawkshaw as 'Aunt Effie', while commonplace, is mistaken. Although several early twentieth-century educational readers and anthologies of children's poetry published in England and the United States include poems from *Aunt Effie's Rhymes for Little Children* (1852) and *Aunt Effie's Gift to the Nursery* (1854) and cite Hawkshaw as the author, or conversely, include Hawkshaw's poems under the name 'Aunt Effie', the connection of Ann Hawkshaw to 'Aunt Effie' is erroneous. The pseudonym is that of Jane Euphemia Browne, who, as Morag Styles notes in her survey of the history of children's poetry, was the 'daughter of a well-to-do landowner in Cumberland', who 'wrote books of verse […] which were much loved at the time.'[3]

Ann Hawkshaw published three volumes of poetry: *'Dionysius the Areopagite', with Other Poems* (London: Jackson & Walford; Manchester: Simms & Dinham, 1842); *Poems for My Children* (London: Simpkin & Marshall; Manchester: Simms & Dinham, 1847); and *Sonnets on Anglo-Saxon History* (London: John Chapman, 1854). A fourth volume of poems and short stories, *Cecil's Own Book*, was printed for private circulation in 1871. As the span of three decades between the first and last examples of Hawkshaw's writing suggests, her poetry offers an exceptional insight into the changing political and religious landscape of the mid-nineteenth century. Conveyed through the perspective of a woman who began life in a large family of dissenters working the land in rural Yorkshire, and who, by the time

---

1 Isobel Armstrong, *Victorian Poetry: Poetry, Poetics and Politics* (London: Routledge, 1993), 322.
2 Isobel Armstrong, Joseph Bristow and Cath Sharrock, eds, *Nineteenth-Century Women Poets: An Oxford Anthology* (Oxford: Clarendon Press, 1996), 346–8.
3 Morag Styles, *From the Garden to the Street: Three Hundred Years of Poetry for Children* (London: Cassell, 1998), 96. A discussion of the misappropriation of Hawkshaw's work can be found in Appendix B.

of her death, was titled, affluent and moved in the most influential cultural and literary circles of the age, Hawkshaw's poetry is a valuable addition to the field of nineteenth-century literary scholarship. The themes of death, religion, science, history and nation that run through Hawkshaw's poetry demonstrate her capacity for extended critical thought, as she engages with subjects at the heart of nineteenth-century cultural and religious debates whilst challenging the work of established scholars and writers.

The Collected Works brings together Hawkshaw's four volumes and reprints them for the first time, whilst the introduction fills in the biographical gaps noted by Isobel Armstrong in order for Hawkshaw and her poetry to be viewed in a literary and cultural context. An appendix of reviews and contemporary criticism of Hawkshaw's work is included, along with details of the republication of individual poems. Headnotes to each of the volumes include the date and place of publication, details of contemporary reviews and further biographical information where appropriate. Footnotes are included where clarification of an event, place, person or source would be useful. Annotations to the poems included in the original text have been reproduced in the footnotes and placed in brackets as [Poet's Note]. All other annotations are my own. In transcribing these poems I have kept the original spelling, punctuation and, indeed, capitalization of the texts, footnoting corrections where an obvious misspelling occurs, in order to remain as faithful as possible to the original publication. I have worked throughout from printed editions rather than authorial manuscripts as these have not yet been recovered and, indeed, may not be extant.

In piecing together a biography for Ann Hawkshaw I am indebted to her descendants who have offered me every help in accessing family documents from which to tease out the details of her life. My first and warmest thanks are to Lady Sandra Wedgwood, who, with her late husband Sir Martin, welcomed me into their home in the early days of my research, sharing family portraits and providing an introduction to other members of the extended family including James Caulfeild and Diane Whitehead, and Hawkshaw's great-great-grand-daughter Dr Christabel Barran. The primary sources for Hawkshaw's biography comprise the unpublished memoir of John Clarke Hawkshaw, Ann's eldest son, which was compiled in 1913 and later transcribed from the manuscript notebooks by Martin Beaumont with the original retained by Dr Barran, and Ann's brief memoir, 'Memories of My Childhood', which she began writing in Scotland in late 1856, following the death of her eleven-year-old son Oliver. The memoir is written in a bound, hardback, lockable notebook, largely without corrections; I thank Mrs Whitehead for her kind access to this valuable resource. In addition, the Hollycombe House visitors' book, covering the period from 1873 to 1935 and logging the visits of Charles and Emma Darwin, Alfred Tennyson and his son Hallam, and others to the Hawkshaws' Sussex home, was generously shared by Mrs Whitehead.

In addition to the unpublished memoirs, letters written by Ann to Unitarian and educationalist John Relly Beard, dated 1851 and 1862, and to her son Henry, written at various dates in the 1860s and covering mainly family matters, give a voice to Hawkshaw as a friend and mother. I am grateful to the Woodhouse Collection, John Rylands University Library, Manchester, and to the Staffordshire and Stoke-on-Trent Archive Service, Staffordshire Records Office respectively, for their help in accessing these letters. Thanks also to David Southern at Duke University Press, compilers of the Carlyle Letters Online, who kindly provided a copy of a letter written by Ann's husband, John Hawkshaw, to Thomas Carlyle, dated 22 January 1844, in which he enclosed a copy of Ann's volume

'*Dionysius the Areopagite*', with *Other Poems* for Carlyle's perusal. Carlyle in turn forwarded this to his mother with a covering letter, a transcript of which David kindly supplied.

My warmest thanks are extended to John Holmes at the University of Reading whose support of my work on Hawkshaw has been of immeasurable value. I would like to acknowledge and thank the Arts and Humanities Research Council for their sponsorship of the initial research into Hawkshaw's work through their doctoral award scheme. Thanks also to Anthem Press for their commitment to republish rare or scarce material; without this vision Hawkshaw's work may have remained unread for another century. Particular thanks to Tej Sood and Rob Reddick at Anthem for their guidance in bringing this project to publication.

A version of Hawkshaw's biography was first published in *British Writers*, supplement 18: my grateful thanks to Gale, Cengage Learning for their generosity in giving kind permission to reproduce the biography, with amendments and additions.[4]

---

4 Debbie Bark, 'Ann Hawkshaw', *British Writers*, supplement 18 (2012): 127–43. © 2012 Gale, a part of Cengage Learning, Inc. Reproduced by permission. www.cengage.com/permissions.

Jane James Ann
        died + 6 ↑ James Mary Eliz
               |
              5 infants
              + Sophia d. 1851

H further children of which 6 plus Jane died

Biographical Introduction

On 1 May 1885, the *Manchester Guardian* published the following obituary for Lady Hawkshaw, who had died the previous week at her London home:

> Death of Lady Hawkshaw.—We much regret to announce the death, which took place on Wednesday evening, at her residence, Belgrave Mansions, Grosvenor Gardens, London, of Ann, wife of Sir John Hawkshaw, F.R.S. Among many accomplished women who have made their home in Manchester during the past half century, none secured a deeper regard than the gifted lady whose death we now record. Lady Hawkshaw was the daughter of the Rev. James Jackson, of Green Hammerton, Yorkshire, where she was born in 1813 [*sic*]. Soon after her marriage (in 1835) her husband was appointed engineer to the Manchester and Bolton Canal and Railway, and subsequently to the Lancashire and Yorkshire Railway; and they took up their residence in the first instance in Sandy Lane, Pendleton; afterwards in Islington Square, Salford; and for some years at Broughton Lodge, Higher Broughton. It was during her fifteen to twenty years' residence in Manchester that Mrs Hawkshaw gave to the world strong evidence of being possessed of the poetic gift. If we remember rightly, some of her earliest effusions appeared in the Manchester Guardian—a corner of which at that period was supplied by the muse of some of our best-known local poets. In 1842 appeared 'Dionysius the Areopagite, with other Poems. By Ann Hawkshaw'. The little volume, which was issued by a firm of local publishers—Messrs. Simms and Dinham, of Exchange-street,—attracted considerable attention and was very favourably received both in London and the provinces. In 1847 she published another volume of verse, called 'Poems for My Children', which showed much tenderness of feeling and beauty of expression. In 1854 she published a series of 98 'Sonnets on Anglo-Saxon History', and in 1871 a series of prose and poetical sketches for children entitled 'Cecil's Own Book'.[5]

Clearly proud of her association with the city and her contribution to its cultural heritage, the obituary traces Ann Hawkshaw's rise from a clergyman's daughter to a writer who earned the respect of Manchester's literary community. In privileging her talent as a poet over her status as the wife of a leading Victorian engineer, the 1885 obituary acknowledges Hawkshaw as a poet of some note: an accolade not repeated until the recent rediscovery of her work.

By the time of her death Ann Hawkshaw had been granted an honorific title and was well positioned in late-Victorian society, yet her start in life was somewhat more modest. She was born on 14 October 1812, the second daughter of the Reverend James Jackson (1776–1849), dissenting minister of the Green Hammerton Independent Chapel in the West Riding of Yorkshire, and his wife Mary (née Clarke). Ann, their third child (Jane had been born in 1806 and James in 1809), would be followed by a further eleven children, although by the time Ann left home to be married in 1835, seven of these children had died, including Ann's beloved elder sister Jane. James Jackson had come to Green Hammerton from Allerton Mauleverer, near Knaresborough, in 1794. He was ordained on

---

5 *Manchester Guardian*, 1 May 1885, 8.

5 November 1801 and would go on to enjoy a 40-year tenure as congregational minister of the parish. At the vanguard of a religious revolution, Jackson and his fellow clergymen offered rural Yorkshire an alternative to the established church and oversaw the building of independent chapels in Green Hammerton and surrounding villages.

In the spring of 1806, the Reverend Jackson married Mary Clarke, the daughter of an agricultural family who had owned land in Green Hammerton for over three hundred years. With Mary's parents living close by, the young Jackson children revelled in the attention of their grandparents, and were free to explore the rural landscape during frequent walks and visits to neighbours. Ann's descriptions of Green Hammerton, recorded in later life in her short manuscript memoir, 'Memories of My Childhood', resonate with nostalgia for the rural idyll. 'My native village', she recalls, 'was one of the prettiest in the north of England', a 'perfect picture of rural comfort and country beauty' – especially on those fine afternoons in summer or early autumn 'when the heavy laden wagons were slowly coming up the road and the well-fed cows were returning to their pastures after milking-time'.[6] In this large clergyman's family, blessed with an abundance of life and yet touched by the reality of early death, Ann was raised under the strong and principled religious and moral influence of her father and grandfather, and the nurturing and encouraging eyes of a mother and grandmother who inspired Ann's love of reading, learning and nature. In her memoir, Ann remembers her maternal grandmother with fondness, describing her as 'a beautiful character' and admits to feeling for her 'a love scarcely second to that I felt for my mother'. With her elder sister Jane, Ann would sit sewing with her grandmother, listening attentively to her stories. Although their grandmother tended to 'dwell on her long rambles over wild heaths and moors on a horse that no one but herself would mount', the girls would steer her towards their favourite subjects, for she 'had a strong and energetic mind and could make clear and just views of life and duty'. Ann grew to admire her grandmother's free-thinking and religious independence, hearing how she 'left the Church of England in whose communion she had been brought up, and joined the dissenters', because her 'free mind turned with disgust from clergymen stained with vice of the most odious kinds, and her soul revolted at men who in meanness and dishonesty were below the peasants they professed to instruct'. Ann recalls her grandmother's small bookcase, 'filled with devotional books of that severe theology taught by the dissenters and the Evangelical clergy aroused from their lethargy by the preaching of Whitefield, Wesley, and Rowland Hill',[7] but goes on to suggest that 'Calvin's stern creed could never affect her heart, filled as it was with the gentlest of womanly affections'.[8]

'I was a very happy but a very idle child', recalls Hawkshaw. 'At six years old I could not read, nay did not know my letters and the only tears I remember to have shed were shed over the "Reading Made Easy"[9] – oh sad misnomer.' Although slow to read, Ann nevertheless took great pleasure in listening to the rhymes and rhythms of Ann and Jane

---

6 Ann Hawkshaw, 'Memories of my Childhood' (1856), unpublished. Original manuscript viewed with the kind permission of Mrs Diane Whitehead.

7 George Whitefield (1714–70): English evangelical preacher and evangelist, founder of Calvinistic Methodism; John Wesley (1703–91): English theologian and evangelist, founder of the Methodist movement; Rowland Hill (1744–1833): English preacher and evangelical.

8 John Calvin (1509–64): Christian reformer and theologian, principal figure in the development of Calvinism.

9 A reference to one of the many early nineteenth-century educational readers comprising exercises in reading and spelling, often based around stories from the scriptures.

Taylor's recently published poetry for children. Under the guidance of her mother, Ann became part of that first generation of children to learn by rote the work of the Taylor sisters. 'In my worst dunce days I could learn hymns and pieces of poetry from hearing them read over a few times', Ann recalls, 'and never thought it a hardship to stand by my Mother's knee and while she plied her needle with a book open before her taught me one of Jane Taylor's little hymns for infant minds, or one of her "Original Poems".'[10] Before long, Ann became a competent, then voracious, independent reader: 'When I did acquire the art of reading all my other amusements appeared tame in comparison [...]. I became a devourer of books; suitable ones if they were to be had, unsuitable if no others were to be got.' Her access to books was limited by circumstance; as she observes, 'The price of books at that time placed good libraries beyond the reach of persons of moderate income and reading societies had not sprung into being. However life is full of compensations, and if I had not many books to read those I had were well studied and highly prized; nature was more loved and admired perhaps than it is by young people of these novel reading days.'

Ann took great delight in her ability to read and was keen to demonstrate her skill at every opportunity. She recalls her visits to neighbouring agricultural workers Fanny and Thomas, 'a humble honest couple' who 'brought up a family of seven or eight children without any aid from the Parish though they never could have had more than twelve shillings a month'. Fanny's 'desire for information on subjects beyond the narrow sphere of her own observation was intense', remembers Hawkshaw, 'and her memory wonderfully retentive; she read well, which I believe she learned to do after she became an adult, her husband could not, but would gladly listen to her'. She continues:

> I was a great favourite with this good pair and often in my walks up and down the village called to see them; I was a prodigy of learning in their eyes, for climbing on Fanny's knee I poured out all my stories of Knowledge into her attentive ears, scraps from newspapers, anecdotes from biographies I heard my father relate at table, old tales found in some of the first numbers of 'The Lady's Magazine' some odd volumes of which I used to pour over at my Grandfather's [...], adventures of shipwrecked mariners, descriptions of volcanoes and whirlpools and monsters of the sea: my information was of the most heterogeneous sort but its truth was never questioned: 'She read it out of a book' was thought enough to silence all sceptics to the correctness of my stories, and Fanny's 'Thank you honey for coming to see us' and Thomas's aside of 'What a bairn it is' sent me home quite happy for the rest of the evening.

Looking back on these visits, Hawkshaw wryly observes that her 'vanity was often too much flattered by poor Thomas, who had less judgement than his wife'.

Whilst the value of reading and learning was instilled in Ann at home, at the age of fourteen she was sent away to school. She recalls that 'the first real sorrow I ever had, at

---

10 Ann and Jane Taylor published a number of volumes of poetry for children: *Original Poems for Infant Minds* was first issued in two volumes in 1804 and 1805, *Rhymes for the Nursery* followed in 1806, and *Hymns for Infant Minds* in 1808. Jane Taylor's poem 'The Star' from *Rhymes for the Nursery* is better known as 'Twinkle, Twinkle, Little Star'. In her memoir Hawkshaw quotes lines from 'A Child's Hymn of Praise' (*Hymns for Infant Minds*): 'I thank the goodness and the grace / Which on my birth have smiled, / And made me in these Christian days, / A happy English child.'

least so I judge now, as it remains imprinted on my memory after thirty years have gone by […], was leaving home for school – I was sent into the neighbourhood of Gomersal amidst the scenes of Charlotte Brontë's *Shirley*.' From 1826, Ann was a boarder at the Moravian School in Little Gomersal, about forty miles distant from Green Hammerton; the Moravian Church had opened a day school for girls there in 1758, converting to a girls' boarding school in 1792. This connection of landscape to literary markers is a feature of Hawkshaw's memoir: old willow trees stretching across the river where she played as a child are recalled in terms of 'poor Ophelia' in an allusion to the death of Ophelia in *Hamlet*; when describing the neighbourhood of Thorp Green, one of her favourite childhood haunts, Hawkshaw remarks: 'I think some of the scenes described in Anne Brontë's *Agnes Grey* refer to scenes she witnessed at Thorp Green; certainly the descriptions of the lanes with primrose-covered banks, or the plantation thicketed fields were taken from it.' Details of Hawkshaw's formal education are scant. However, through the thematic concerns of her poetry it is clear that she was widely read in all manner of topics and a competent researcher. The allusions to classical and biblical history in the long narrative poem 'Dionysius the Areopagite', the engagement with religious and scientific debates in 'The Past' and 'The Future' and the extensive and heavily researched *Sonnets on Anglo-Saxon History* suggest a remarkable depth of knowledge and a keen intellectual curiosity that extended beyond her school years.

At some time during the late 1820s, Ann met her future husband, John Hawkshaw. John had been born on 9 April 1811, the fifth child of Leeds publican Henry Hawkshaw (1774–1813) and his wife Sarah Carrington. Ann and John's paths most likely crossed during family visits to the village of Hampsthwaite, some fifteen miles west of Green Hammerton. Here, John's uncle on his mother's side and Ann's uncle on her father's were in business: Peter Carrington as a blacksmith, William Jackson as a farmer. Having left Leeds Grammar School at 13 to take up a local engineering apprenticeship as pupil of road surveyor Charles Fowler, John Hawkshaw had spent five years working on local turnpike schemes. In 1830, John moved to Liverpool as assistant to Alexander Nimmo, surveying a proposed railway connection from Liverpool to the Humber via Leeds. When Nimmo died in 1832, John decided to travel to South America, as engineer to the Bolivar Mining Association's copper mines at Aroa, Venezuela. By September 1834, John was forced to return from Venezuela through ill health, and on 20 March 1835 he and Ann were married, in the parish of Whixley, close to Green Hammerton.

At the time of their marriage, John was living in Liverpool, but by 1836, the Hawkshaws had relocated to Salford, where John took up an appointment with the Manchester, Bolton and Bury Canal Company. Having been invalided home from Venezuela, John continued to suffer from ill health. As John Clarke notes in his diary, the first doctor his father consulted in Manchester 'told him he had cancer of the liver', but 'not satisfied that his was such a hopeless case, he consulted another physician who told him to go home and live well, which he did, and ever after enjoyed excellent health, with one exception, that for many years he had a slight recurrence of ague once a year'.[11] Indeed, John Hawkshaw flourished in Manchester as engineer to the Manchester and Leeds Railway, capitalising on the expansion of the railway network across the North West. Aside from his considerable contribution to civil engineering, John made a valuable contribution to the field of nineteenth-century

---

11 'The Diary of John Clarke Hawkshaw of Hollycombe', vol. 1 (1913), unpublished. Transcribed from the manuscript notebooks by Martin Beaumont, original notebooks retained by John Clarke Hawkshaw's great-grand-daughter, Dr Christabel Barran.

travel writing by publishing a memoir of his trip to Venezuela. Published in London in 1838 by Jackson & Walford, the official publisher for the Congregational Union, *Reminiscences of South America: From Two and a Half Years' Residence in Venezuela* was inspired by the earlier work of German naturalist and explorer Alexander von Humboldt, whose *Personal Narrative of Travels to the Equinoctial Regions of the New Continent* (1814), detailing his South American exploration, had been an influential text for Charles Darwin on the *Beagle*. Yet as John Hawkshaw notes in the preface to *Reminiscences*, von Humboldt's account of Venezuela had been written 'when the country was a Spanish colony, and when the population was nearly double of what it is now, when there was a far greater proportion of Europeans resident there, and when the social system [...] differed much from its present state'.[12] In writing his memoir, John Hawkshaw sets out to update the 'valuable work of Baron Humboldt' and to 'afford some little information to the next inquirer' as to the 'state of the country and of society there at that time', for in 'respecting a country of which so little is known, everyone who had something to communicate should contribute his mite' (v–vii).

The personal, reflective response to the Venezuelan landscape in *Reminiscences* has much in common with Darwin's style in *Voyage of the Beagle* (1839). Rather than producing a methodical record of geological observations, John uses a proliferation of metaphors and similes to convey the unfamiliar landscape in terms that would be familiar to his English readers. The account is often humorous, and yet interwoven with a concern for social justice in the Americas and at home. For instance, he criticises the United States' continued reliance on compulsory labour, pointing to the 'strange anomaly of a people with many free institutions, and professing above all other countries to be free, dwelling with slavery at their very doors, nay, within their homes, and around their social hearths' (52). He rounds off his critique of America with a couplet from Ann's then unpublished 'Sonnet—To America':

> and hence it will be affirmed of this country, as it has been written,—
> 'Future ages on one page shall see
> The Slave's unheeded prayer—*the song of Liberty*'. (52)

The sonnet was published in full in 1842 in Ann's first collection *'Dionysius the Areopagite', with Other Poems*. The 22 poems which make up the collection were crafted during the 1830s and early 1840s, during which time the first three of the Hawkshaws' six children were born: Mary Jane Jackson in 1838, Ada in 1840 and John Clarke in 1841. Using the same London publisher as her husband, and Simms and Dinham in Manchester, Hawkshaw's debut onto the Manchester poetic scene coincided with a resurgence of poetic interest in Manchester; a revival energised by writers who sought to dispel the widely held assumption that artistic expression had succumbed to a preoccupation with free enterprise and trade. James Wheeler acknowledges this perception of Manchester as a literary wasteland in the preface to an early anthology:

> 'Manchester Poetry!' exclaim doubtless the majority of those who may chance to bestow a passing glance upon the book—
> 'Bless us! what a word on

---

12 John Hawkshaw, *Reminiscences of South America: From Two and a Half Years' Residence in Venezuela* (London: Jackson & Walford, 1838), vii.

A title-page is this!'—
and, as if satisfied in their own minds that this same town cannot produce any good thing save only such as emanates from the spindle or the power-loom, they indulge, it may be, in a slight laugh at the presumption of the editor, and go on their way rejoicing.[13]

In highlighting the presupposed antithesis between art and industry, Wheeler engages with the opposition of imaginative thought and reason, inspiration and craft that had so energised the Romantic movement; yet Wheeler suggests a flaw in the commonly held presumption that one should preclude the other. 'Perhaps of the Poetry of Manchester, until these later years, little that is favourable could be said' (xii), continues Wheeler, as 'it is only in the nineteenth century, within some dozen or twenty years of the present time, that any pretensions have been made by Manchester writers to rank among the gifted of the earth' (xiii). And yet, finds Wheeler, 'even those claims—modest and well-founded as it is conceived they have been—are met at this day [...] only with a contemptuous smile, by most of the crowd of gentlemen whose genius lies rather in the detection of an imperfect fabric than in the right appreciation of perfect poetry' (xiii). In bringing together a collection of poems from 16 Manchester-based writers, including the poetical works of a number of divines, such as the Reverend William Gaskell, husband of Elizabeth, and notable poets of the moment, such as Charles Swain and Samuel Bamford, Wheeler's *Manchester Poetry* prompted the repositioning of poetry in the city at the turn of the decade.

By the early 1840s a distinct poetic community had been established in the city. The self-styled 'Manchester Poets', or 'Bards of Cottonopolis' as they were latterly termed,[14] met at the Sun Inn, Long Millgate, locally designated as 'Poets' Corner', 'for the purpose of advancing their common interests, and creating kind and reciprocal feelings', with those gathered promoting 'the cause of literature generally, and diffus[ing] amongst its contributors and admirers mutual sympathy and respect'.[15] The first formal meeting of the Manchester Poets, on 7 January 1842, was reported locally as a 'Poetical Soiree', 'a friendly meeting of poets and friends of poetry, representing Manchester and its neighbourhood'.[16] This was followed on the evening of 24 March 1842 by a 'Poetic Festival' held at the Sun Inn and attended by some forty literary men.[17] Songs were sung, and messages read from well-wishers. Many of the poetical works had been written especially for the event, and

---

13 James Wheeler, *Manchester Poetry* (London: Charles Tilt, 1838), v–vi.
14 A term used by Thomas Swindells to describe the Manchester poets in *Manchester Streets and Manchester Men* (Manchester: J. E. Cornish, 1908), 75. For discussions of Manchester poetry see Martha Vicinus, 'Literary Voices of an Industrial Town: Manchester, 1810–1870', in *The Victorian City: Images and Realities*, vol. 2, ed. H. J. Dyos and Michael Wolff (London: Routledge and Kegan Paul, 1973), 739–61; Brian Maidment, 'Class and Cultural Production in the Industrial City: Poetry in Victorian Manchester', in *City, Class and Culture: Studies of Social Policy and Cultural Production in Victorian Manchester*, ed. Alan J. Kidd and K. W. Roberts (Manchester: Manchester University Press, 1985), 148–66; Debbie Bark, 'Manchester and Early Victorian Literary Culture', *Literature Compass* 8, no. 6 (2011): 404–14.
15 John Bolton Rogerson's preface to *The Festive Wreath: A Collection of Original Contributions Read at a Literary Meeting Held in Manchester March 24th 1842* (Manchester: Bradshaw and Blacklock, 1842), iv.
16 *Manchester Guardian*, 12 January 1842.
17 As reported in the *Manchester Guardian*, 30 March 1842.

were published after as *The Festive Wreath: A Collection of Original Contributions Read at a Literary Meeting, Held in Manchester March 24th 1842.* The importance of the Sun Inn group to Ann Hawkshaw's work is twofold. First, the 'Introductory Stanzas' to Hawkshaw's first published collection are dated 'Manchester, March 25, 1842' – just one day after the widely publicised 'Poetic Festival'. It is highly likely that Hawkshaw would have read the articles in the *Manchester Guardian* advertising the event. In debuting at this moment, Hawkshaw positions herself as part of the poetic momentum of Manchester at this time. Second, poets from the Sun Inn group were familiar with Hawkshaw's work and referred to it in their own. In the preface to his *Poems* of 1843, Samuel Bamford cites a number of poets whose work was enjoyed by the 'literati' of Manchester in the early 1840s:

> Since his last volume of poetry was published,—which is about eight years ago—the attention of the literati of Manchester, and its neighbourhood, has been justly claimed by the productions of a Swain, a Prince, a Rogerson, inhabitants of the town—of a Festus, the circumstances of whose first surprising essay in poetry, having been printed at Manchester, will one day be esteemed an honour to the town[18]—and of Mrs. Hawkshaw, whose interesting poem, 'The Areopagite' has added another name to those destined for immortality.[19]

This brief but complimentary appraisal indicates that Hawkshaw's poetry had come to the 'attention of the literati of Manchester' by the early 1840s. Another of the Sun Inn group, George Richardson, quotes Hawkshaw twice in his collection *Patriotism*, published in 1844. In each instance, Hawkshaw's poetry is included alongside other prominent contributors to Manchester's poetic scene. Using extracts from the poetry of Samuel Bamford, John Critchley Prince and Ann Hawkshaw, Richardson sets up the argument of canto 2 of the title poem, 'Patriotism', in which he addresses social injustice, the education of the poor, temperance and Christian faith. Selecting lines from Hawkshaw's poem 'The Past', Richardson draws on her invocation of poetry to rouse a sense of patriotism, countering the threat of revolutionary uprisings with the glories of England's past:

> For in the crowded street, the voice of woe,
>   The low faint cry of poverty opprest,
> Sounds like the requiem of my country's peace,
>   The dirge for her long day of glory fled;
> Harp of my country, waken ere it cease,
>   And the last spirit of the land be dead![20]

Later in the collection Richardson uses a couplet from Hawkshaw's 'Dionysius the Areopagite' ('Weeks sped their flight, and left a trace, / A withering touch on one young

---

18 Bamford refers to Manchester poets Charles Swain (1801–74), John Critchley Prince (1808–66) and John Bolton Rogerson (1809–59), and to Philip James Bailey (1816–1902), whose poem *Festus* (1839) was printed in Manchester by Wilmot Henry Jones.
19 Samuel Bamford, preface to *Poems* (Manchester: published by the author, 1843).
20 Ll. 139–44 of Hawkshaw's 'The Past', epigram to canto 2 of 'Patriotism'. George Richardson, *Patriotism, in Three Cantos, and Other Poems* (London: W. J. Adams; Manchester: G. & A. Falkner, 1844), 36.

face') as an epigram to his poem 'The Forsaken One', alongside lines from John Critchley Prince's poem 'There's Falsehood' (*Hours with the Muses*, 1842).

The publication of the *Dionysius* volume, and the favourable reviews that followed, positioned Hawkshaw locally as a poet of some note. During 1843, Hawkshaw's uncollected poem 'Life's Dull Reality' was included in a 'little volume of original poems entitled the "Athenæum Souvenir"': a compilation of poetry by Manchester poets on sale at the Manchester Athenæum Bazaar on 2 October 1843.[21] The bazaar had been 'instituted in aid of the funds of "the Manchester Athenæum for the advancement and diffusion of knowledge"', and the *Manchester Guardian* review of the event highlights Hawkshaw's 'Life's Dull Reality' as one of the poems in the volume that 'seem to us to be *amongst the gems of the book*'.[22] The poem was printed in full in the *Manchester Guardian* on 11 October 1843. Other Hawkshaw poems were republished in a variety of regional newspapers; Appendix B gives full details. In *Lancashire Authors and Orators* (1850), John Evans writes extensively on Hawkshaw's poetry and 'safely assign[s] Mrs Hawkshaw the chief seat among our present line of Lancashire poetesses'.[23]

John Hawkshaw was clearly proud and supportive of his wife's work. On 22 January 1844, he sent a copy of *'Dionysius the Areopagite', with Other Poems* to Thomas Carlyle, with the following covering letter, transcribed from the Carlyle papers:

> Islington, Salford
> 22nd January 1844
>
> Sir,
>
> I beg to forward you a small volume of poems, which I do on the part of the authoress, as some acknowledgement of the deep gratification that has been afforded to her, by reading your own writings, which, as proof perhaps, that neither have a very extensive acquaintance with the realms of literature, have only lately come into our hands.
>
> The whole have been, to both of us, as a new land, wonderful as the New World to Cortez, and are calculated, we think, to work a great change in the literature of this England of the 19th century, where more writers have been diligent, out of mud and straw, to erect all manner of grotesque images, that should attract, if by no other marks, at least by those of their frightfulness, like the gods of the East.
>
> I may add that the writer of the small volume truly feels, what is expressed in the last two lines of the sonnet written on its first leaf [*], and if you will allow it to be so presented, you will oblige her, and her husband—
>
> I am sir,
> Yours very faithfully
> John Hawkshaw

---

21 'Life's Dull Reality', in *Athenæum Souvenir; original Poems, &c., contributed by various Authors, in aid of the Funds of the Athenæum Bazaar, held in the Town Hall, MANCHESTER, October 1843* (Manchester: J. Gadsby, 1843), 3.

22 *Manchester Guardian*, 4 October 1843, 3.

23 John Evans, *Lancashire Authors and Orators: A series of literary sketches of some of the principle authors, divines, members of Parliament, etc, connected with the county of Lancaster* (London: Houlston and Stoneman, 1850), 127–32; see Appendix A for the full review.

The asterisk after 'first leaf' was inserted by Carlyle, who then enters the last two lines from the dedicatory sonnet in the bottom margin: 'Accept this gift, for at the costliest shrine / The poor may lay their gifts, and thus I offer mine.—AH.' The sonnet would appear to have been written by Ann expressly for Carlyle, but has not yet been recovered in its entirety. In a letter to his mother dated 24 January 1844, Carlyle refers to the Hawkshaws' communication and forwards Ann's book for his mother's perusal. It is unclear whether he had read the book, or simply the dedicatory sonnet: 'This morning I received by Post a very agreeable gift from a Manchester Poetess and her Husband; a book inscribed to me in really an elegant and intelligent manner.'[24] With a copy of *'Dionysius the Areopagite', with Other Poems* listed in an 1859 catalogue of Wordsworth's library at Rydal Mount, it is possible that John distributed his wife's work to other writers admired by the Hawkshaws. From John's letter to Carlyle, it is evident that the experience of reading Carlyle's works had been profound and that he and Ann were keen to read more widely. In his diary, John Clarke remembers book club meetings held at the Hawkshaws' home between 1845 and 1850: 'The meetings of a book club held at our house from time to time made an impression on me, and I can recall the gatherings now, and the books which were bought and circulated among the members and were afterwards disposed of when they had gone the round.' Regrettably John Clarke records nothing of the members or the books that they read.

With John Hawkshaw at the forefront of industrial innovation in Manchester and the surrounding area, the Hawkshaws thrived in the city, and whilst not exclusively wealthy, were certainly well positioned in society. John's election to the Manchester Literary and Philosophical Society in 1839 would have brought him into contact with many of Manchester's prominent names. John Clarke's diary notes his father's connection to scientist John Dalton, 'a friend of my father's' who 'gave him copies of his works', to cotton merchant John Kennedy and to Samuel Dukinfield Darbishire, solicitor to the Lancashire and Yorkshire Railway and a leading Unitarian. The Darbishires became close family friends of the Hawkshaws, who often holidayed at the Darbishires' home at Pendyffryn.[25] As the Darbishires were great friends of the Gaskells, it is likely that John and Ann were likewise acquainted. Although there is no extant correspondence between either Elizabeth or William Gaskell and the Hawkshaws to suggest the extent of their association, correspondence between the Winkworth sisters from 1847 shows that they met socially in Manchester. In a letter to her sister Susanna, dated 16 November 1847, Catherine Winkworth describes an afternoon tea meeting with the 'Cobdens, Leislers, Hawkshaws, Gaskells' in which, 'the principle gentlemen [...] before tea was half over [...] were deep in a discussion on the present state of the commercial world, which lasted a great part of the evening'.[26] Richard Cobden and John Hawkshaw, she notes,

---

24 A copy of Hawkshaw's letter to Carlyle, and a transcript of Carlyle's letter to his mother were kindly provided by David Southern at Duke University Press, compilers of the Carlyle Letters Online, http://carlyleletters.dukejournals.org/ (accessed 22 July 2013).
25 John Clarke's diary makes reference to 'many happy visits to the Darbishires' pleasant home at Pendyffryn', whilst Ann's letter to her son Henry, dated 27 April 1863 refers to the Darbishires accommodating Henry at Pendyffryn. The letter is part of an original bundle of letters written to Henry Hawkshaw by Ann Hawkshaw, held at the Staffordshire and Stoke-on-Trent Archive Service, Staffordshire Records Office, reference D4347.
26 Margaret J. Shaen, ed., *Memorials of Two Sisters: Susanna and Catherine Winkworth* (London: Longman, Green, 1908), 26.

were engaged in a 'regular pitched battle [...], the latter representing the railway interest, and maintaining that Parliament should never have interfered with railways at all. [...] Mr Cobden of course took exactly the opposite view' (26–7). From Elizabeth Gaskell's letters it is evident that the Gaskells' connection with the Hawkshaws continued after John and Ann had moved to London in 1850. A letter dated 26 May 1860 is addressed to Gaskell's eldest daughter Marianne, care of 'John Hawkshaw Esq, 43 Eaton Place, Belgrave Sq, London';[27] in another, written to her publisher Edward Chapman from the same address on 9 June 1860, Gaskell explains that she 'came up here suddenly on Wednesday, on account of my daughter's illness', suggesting that Marianne was staying with the Hawkshaws when she became unwell with suspected smallpox.[28] A letter to Gaskell's longstanding friend Mary Green is similarly addressed from the Hawkshaws' Eaton Place residence, dated 14 June 1860.[29] Gaskell writes again from the Hawkshaws' address on 6 June 1862, accepting an invitation to share breakfast with Lord and Lady Stanhope.[30]

The extent of the friendship between the Hawkshaws and Gaskells can only be surmised, but intriguingly, in her unpublished 'Memories of My Childhood', written between December 1856 and the first months of 1857, Ann reveals antipathy towards Gaskell as a writer – particularly with regards to *The Life of Charlotte Brontë*, first published at this time. Her initial allusion to Gaskell is indirect. In calling to mind a local farming family from her childhood, where the youngest of three sisters to have inherited their father's small estate 'had married, or rather had taken a husband to assist in the farm', Hawkshaw likens the ineffectual husband, whose 'existence as a master was [...] completely ignored by the servants and labourers', to the 'husband of a landlady or lodging-house help' or even, she concludes with a flourish, 'the husband of a literary woman!'

The context for this comment becomes clear later in the memoir after Hawkshaw's specific references to *The Life of Charlotte Brontë*. She begins by linking Gaskell's biography of Brontë to her own recollections of a childhood spent exploring the countryside around Green Hammerton: 'One of our favourite haunts was the neighbourhood of Thorp Green, then the residence of the Robinson family, one of whose members, a Lady Scott, has since obtained incredible fame by the publication of Mrs Gaskell's *Life of Charlotte Brontë*.' Hawkshaw's comment reflects the reception of the first edition of the *Life*, which was published in March 1857 and sold well enough for a second edition to be published in the April. Although initially attracting favourable reviews and publicity for its author, Gaskell's book became caught in an undercurrent of unease regarding the thinly veiled accusation of impropriety between Charlotte's brother Branwell and Mrs Robinson, the mistress of Thorp Green. On 26 May 1857 all copies were recalled under threat of legal action after Lady Scott (formerly Mrs Robinson) demanded a revision of chapter 13 of the first volume, removing all references to her alleged seduction of Branwell Brontë. Branwell had been employed as a tutor to the Robinsons' young son Edmund, and according to the first edition of the *Life*, the unnamed Mrs Robinson took a strong hold of the 'pitiable'

---

27 J. A. V. Chapple and Arthur Pollard, ed., *The Letters of Mrs Gaskell* (Manchester: Manchester University Press, 1966), 619.
28 Chapple and Pollard, *Letters*, 622.
29 John Chapple and Alan Shelston, ed., *Further Letters of Mrs Gaskell* (Manchester: Manchester University Press, 2000), 209.
30 Chapple and Shelston, *Further Letters*, 242.

Branwell, who in 'his agony of guilty love' gave 'passionate way to his feelings' at the hands of the 'profligate woman' who had tempted him 'into the deep disgrace of deadly crime'.[31]

Gaskell reluctantly agreed to make the revisions, despite standing by the accuracy of her first account. Her annoyance at the forced amendment is expressed most explicitly in a letter to her publisher, George Smith, in which she includes the following ironic preface, suggested by her friend Mary Mohl: 'If anybody is displeased with any statement or words in the following pages I beg leave to with-draw it, and to express my deep regret for having offered so expensive an article as the truth to the Public.'[32] Writing her memoir at the time of Lady Scott's rebuttal and Gaskell's retraction, Hawkshaw joins the debate by questioning 'the wisdom or propriety of making Branwell so prominent a character in Charlotte's memoirs as Mrs Gaskell has done'. Moreover, as the furore concerning Lady Scott's threatened lawsuit had only served to maximise demand for Gaskell's book, Hawkshaw goes on to consider the ethical implications: 'Since Mrs G has retracted her aspersions they say she has engaged in the notoriety that the publication of her connection with the Brontës has given her, yet she has children who cannot but feel a mother's shame, and relations to whom its disclosure to the world must be bitter.'

In this way, Hawkshaw reflects what Angus Easson has observed to be the main area of debate surrounding the reception of *The Life of Charlotte Brontë*, namely, 'whether personal detail should be made public [...] when those still alive might be offended or hurt'.[33] 'Either what she printed was a fact or not', Hawkshaw continues, before going on to invoke her earlier characterisation of ineffectual husbands and intractable wives in her description of the Gaskells: 'If not founded on sufficient credence it ought never to have been published [...]. I think it had injured both the Authoress and her husband in many quarters: I have been told that he begged her not to publish it, but she was obstinate in her resolution of doing so.'

Hawkshaw's suspicion of Gaskell's 'publish and be damned' approach to Brontë's biography is borne out by a letter written by Gaskell to her publisher before the publication of the *Life*, which seemingly reveals her intention to libel. Countering her later assertion that she believed the account to be true she writes to George Smith, 'Do you mind the law of libel? I have three people I want to libel – Lady Scott (that bad woman who corrupted Branwell Brontë) Mr Newby, and Lady Eastlake'.[34]

During their fourteen years living in the Manchester area the Hawkshaws moved several times. Living first on the breezy heights of Pendleton in Sandy Lane Terrace, the Hawkshaws then moved down into Islington Square, most likely into one of the large houses built in the 1830s for Manchester's merchants, before moving back up into the area of Broughton in 1846. When *Poems for My Children* was published in July 1847 they were living in Broughton Lodge in the Manchester suburb of Higher Broughton, in a house built by John Hawkshaw on part of the old zoological gardens. There were now five young Hawkshaw children: Mary (aged 9), John Clarke (aged 6), Henry (aged 4), Editha (aged 2) and Oliver (aged 1): John and Ann's second child, Ada, had died of hydrocephalus in 1845, a month before her fifth birthday. Despite her physical absence, Ada was still very much

---

31 Elizabeth Gaskell, *The Life of Charlotte Brontë*, vol. 1 (London: Smith, Elder, 1857), 327.
32 17 June 1857, Chapple and Pollard, *Letters*, 455.
33 Angus Easson, ed., *Elizabeth Gaskell: The Critical Heritage* (London: Routledge and Kegan Paul, 1991), 36.
34 2 October 1856, Chapple and Pollard, *Letters*, 418.

part of the family, as the inclusion of the poignant elegy 'Ada' in this collection suggests. *Poems for My Children* is an intensely personal collection that opens a window into the Hawkshaw nursery. Through the influence of their parents' teaching, and through the medium of their own imaginations, the young Hawkshaws look out from this nursery to wonder at other worlds, with their mother giving the children a voice to express their thoughts, often in conversation with Hawkshaw herself: 13 of the collection's poems are either addressed to one of her children, or made up of dialogue between Hawkshaw and her child. A handful of poems are narrated as if from the child's perspective, unmediated by an adult, drawing comparisons with Robert Louis Stephenson's *A Child's Garden of Verses* (1885) from later in the century.

Though ostensibly a poetic offering for her own children, there was much in *Poems for My Children* to entertain, educate and guide the collection's wider readership. Ann's interest in nature, particularly flowers, is evident in the thematic concerns of many of the poems. John Clarke describes his mother as a 'good botanist' who used to teach her children 'how to describe flowers on the old Linnaean system'. He recalls having a notebook in which he wrote descriptions of the flowers his mother gave him to examine, using 'rather a good little book called *Flowers of the Field*'.[35] Ann's books of reference were James Smith's *The English Flora* (4 vols, 1824–8) and John Lindley's *Ladies' Botany* (2 vols, 1837–8). Practical geology was also a feature of the family home, where a collection of minerals and fossils collected by his father attracted the eager attention of the young John Clarke. In his memoir, he recalls how the 'look of the ores of copper, often brilliantly coloured and of iron haematites, pyrites and others, became impressed on [his] memory at an early age.' As well as being informed observers of the natural world, the Hawkshaws were close to contemporary advances in science, particularly geology. As a fellow of both the Geological Society of London and the Manchester Geological Society, and a member of the British Association for the Advancement of Science, John Hawkshaw's professional interests brought him into discussion with geologists such as Adam Sedgwick and William Buckland.[36] A lithograph entitled 'Visit of Members to the Fossil Trees in the Coal Measures, near Manchester, June 1842', shows John Hawkshaw presenting the find of a huge fossil tree to a British Association for the Advancement of Science meeting in Manchester 1842. Included in the group of interested onlookers are both Sedgwick and Buckland.[37]

As well as developing her children's ability to observe and classify the world around them, Ann, like her mother before her, nurtured a love of poetry in her children.

---

35 Charles Alexander Johns, *Flowers of the Field*, 2 vols (London: Society for Promoting Christian Knowledge, 1853).

36 Adam Sedgwick (1785–1873): British geologist and mathematician, made president of the Geological Society in 1829; William Buckland (1784–1856): English theologian, geologist and palaeontologist, author of 'Geology and Mineralogy Considered with Reference to Natural Theology' (1836), treatise six of the eight Bridgewater Treatises (1833–36).

37 James A. Secord, *Victorian Sensation: The Extraordinary Publication, Reception, And Secret Authorship of 'Vestiges of the Natural History of Creation'* (Chicago: University of Chicago Press, 2000), 210. Secord notes that the lithograph had been prepared from a design by London artist Robert William Buss: 'Visit of Members to the Fossil Trees in the Coal Measures, near Manchester, June 1842', which was used as the frontispiece to James Heywood's *Illustrations of the Manchester Meeting of the British Association for the Advancement of Science, June 1842* (Manchester: Thomas Forrest, 1843).

Before they were able to read for themselves, she would recite to them the poetry of Byron and Southey. Several of John Clarke's recollections of his mother are framed with reference to the poetry that they shared: 'My mother had a very good memory and could recite long poems, such as the "Prisoner of Chillon" with ease.'[38] 'I was fond of reading poetry, choosing Southey in my early days. My mother used to recite to me "How does the water come down at Lodore".'[39] 'When I could read myself "Thalaba the Destroyer" was my favourite.'[40] In remembering a family holiday to Tunbridge Wells, John Clarke recalls carving poetry into the sandstone rocks with Ann: 'I spent much time in carving the lines which my mother quoted to me, "Oh! vain attempt to give a deathless lot, to names ignoble, born to be forgot".' It is not clear whether the opening lines to William Cowper's sonnet 'On Observing Some Names of Little Note Recorded in the Biographia Britannica' (1780) are intentionally misquoted by Ann, or misremembered by John Clarke, but the subtle shift from 'Oh fond attempt to give a deathless lot, / To names ignoble, born to be forgot' (Cowper), to the 'Oh! vain attempt' of John Clarke's recollection certainly gives a more cynical gloss to the sentiment of the sonnet, and to the practice of historiography that Cowper's poem critiques, something Hawkshaw herself addresses in her own poetry, particularly through *Sonnets on Anglo-Saxon History*.

Having worked primarily as a railway engineer in Manchester, John Hawkshaw set up as a consulting engineer and moved his practice to London in 1850, taking offices at 33 Great George Street, Westminster. John Clarke notes that 'at that time many engineers lived, or had offices in Great George Street [...]. We used to go to children's parties at their houses.' The family lived at Great George Street until 1852, when they moved to Eaton Place. Ann's correspondence with John Relly Beard, Unitarian minister, educationalist and principal of Stony Knolls High School in Manchester, where her son John Clarke had boarded, suggests that she was preparing work for publication at this time. In a letter to Beard, written in 1851, Ann writes, 'I enclose two titles if you think them suitable for your magazine, they may fill a page.'[41] Beard was founder and editor of *Christian Teacher* (later the *Prospective Review*), and *Unitarian Herald*, and although Hawkshaw's work does not appear to have been published in either the letter suggests that Ann had submitted an earlier poem to Beard for consideration, which was untitled, and that after some reflection she was 'puzzled to find a better title than 'Stanzas'. For I dislike what are called 'catching titles'. They seem to me mere claptrap.'[42]

In 1854, Ann published her third volume of poetry, *Sonnets on Anglo-Saxon History*, using London publisher John Chapman. As editor of the *Westminster Review*, Chapman championed the literary and political ambitions of a group of women intellectuals that included George Eliot, Harriet Martineau and Bessie Rayner Parkes, making him an obvious choice of publisher for Hawkshaw's ambitious and notable sonnet sequence. Sections of the sequence are overtly anti-Catholic, with several sonnets making an implicit criticism of High Church ideology: stifling and corrupt religious hierarchies are contrasted with an individual's relationship with God as experienced through the natural

---

38 392-line narrative poem by George Gordon, Lord Byron (1788–1824), published in 1816.
39 Onomatopoeic poem 'The Cataract of Lodore' (1820) by Robert Southey (1774–1843).
40 Robert Southey's epic poem, published in 1801.
41 19 August 1851, original held in the Woodhouse Collection, John Rylands University Library, Manchester, reference A2/1, shelf 22.8.
42 Ibid.

world. Taking an eclectic range of subject matter, Hawkshaw expands and elaborates the historical framework on which Wordsworth based part 1 of his poetic survey of church history, *Ecclesiastical Sketches* (1822), broadening her remit to cover aspects of history often overlooked by conventional narratives of church and state, such as the perspective of women and those oppressed by authority. Moreover, as each sonnet is faced on the page by a short prose extract from the work of prominent contemporary historians of the Anglo-Saxon period, or from early nineteenth-century translations of Anglo-Saxon texts, Hawkshaw draws attention to the practice of popular nineteenth-century historiography: in this way historians become as much the subject of Hawkshaw's work as the aspects of history that they seek to convey. Hawkshaw was clearly well read in Anglo-Saxon history. Her sources include Sharon Turner's landmark study, *The History of the Anglo-Saxons: From the Earliest Period to the Norman Conquest*, published in four volumes between 1799 and 1805, Francis Palgrave's *History of the Anglo-Saxons* (1831) and John Mitchell Kemble's *The Saxons in England* (2 vols, 1849). She also draws on Asser's *Life of Alfred*, King Alfred's translation of Bede, the English Historical Society's translation of Bede's *Ecclesiastical History* and the Bohn's antiquarian library translations of Bede's *Ecclesiastical History* and the *Anglo-Saxon Chronicle*. In attempting a reworking of national history through the medium of the sonnet, in doing so in response to a poetic tradition appropriated by Wordsworth, her generation's leading male poet, and in openly challenging a tradition of historiography likewise gendered, Hawkshaw's sonnet sequence is a significant body of work that attracted a good deal of critical attention, being reviewed both in England and America.[43]

During the 1850s and 1860s John Hawkshaw's work frequently took him abroad, with Ann often accompanying him. Ann gives details of her travels in correspondence with John Relly Beard. In a letter written from 43 Eaton Place, London, dated 23 October 1862, Ann informs Beard that she and her youngest daughter Editha are 'just on the eve of starting for Egypt: the old land', where, on the request of the viceroy, her husband will 'inspect the works of the Suez Canal'.[44] In another letter, she informs Beard that she is leaving 'with Mr Hawkshaw to Holland on the 19th where he has a great work going in "The Amsterdam Ship Canal"'.[45] Other trips include Brussels (August 1865), Brazil (August–December 1874) and New York (May–August 1876). The visit to Brazil was reported in the *Anglo-Brazilian Times* and makes particular mention of the now Lady Hawkshaw's[46] valuable support of her husband's work:

> The *Anglo-Brazilian Times* of November 7 says—Sir John and Lady Hawkshaw return in the Tiber to England, Sir John having completed his examination of the ports upon which the Government had desired his authoritative report. His staff

---

43 See Appendix A for contemporary reviews of the collection.

44 Original held in the Woodhouse Collection, John Rylands University Library, Manchester, reference A2/1, shelf 22.8. The DNB entry for John Hawkshaw mentions this trip: 'He was invited in July 1862 by Said Pasha, viceroy of Egypt, to report on the proposed Suez Canal, and spent nearly a month there. His favourable report induced Said to let the project proceed, and De Lesseps later acknowledged his debt to him.'

45 8 July (no year specified, but as John Hawkshaw worked on the Amsterdam Ship Canal from 1862, it is likely that Ann's letter is from this year). Original held in the Woodhouse Collection, John Rylands University Library, Manchester, reference A2/1, shelf 22.8.

46 In 1873 John Hawkshaw was knighted for services to engineering.

of assistants, however, remain to complete the details required for a decisive report. The *Anglo-Brazilian Times* adds—Sir John expresses himself greatly gratified with his visit to the Brazilian Empire, and speaks in high terms of the hospitality he has experienced in it and of his courteous reception by his Imperial Majesty and the Ministers. Our Polytechnic Institute naturally paid all respect to this distinguished engineer, and did itself the honour of electing him as honorary member of the society at an extraordinary meeting convened for the purpose. Doubtless, in the course of his trip Sir John's trained eye and scientific mind have found much to note, and probably some of his observations while in Brazil may yet see the light of publicity […]. In his visit to this country, at the earnest invitation of the Imperial Government, Sir John Hawkshaw has rendered a most important service to it, and the results of his commission must redound greatly to its advantage, and furnish another laurel to the wreath he has woven in his numerous commissions at home and abroad. Lady Hawkshaw accompanied Sir John on nearly all his trips to the parts examined by him, and her frank amiability and thirst for information, endeared her to all who met her. Few indeed have wakened in so short a time so much general esteem and liking as Sir John and Lady Hawkshaw have in Brazil. On the eve of departure Sir John sent a cheque for £300 to the treasurer of the Polytechnic Institute, to be invested, and the interest to be applied from time to time to give a gold medal to the student sending in the best paper of any engineering subject. No doubt the medal will be called 'The Hawkshaw's Medal', and will be looked upon in Brazil as an object of honourable commendation. ('Sir John Hawkshaw's visit to Brazil', *Freeman's Journal*, 4 December 1874, 2.)

Whilst living primarily in London, the Hawkshaws frequently escaped the city. John Clarke recalls family holidays spent with his mother, brothers and sisters on the Isle of Arran and the Isle of Wight, at Eastwear Bay near Folkestone and on Brighton Downs. Winters were usually spent out of town, with the family taking houses at Richmond: 'The Christmas of 1859–60, we were at Ham House, an old house close to the Ham Gate entrance into Richmond Park […]. There was a good library at Ham House, with many fine illustrated old books.' 'In Christmas 1860–1861, we had Camden House, lower down in the town, with a large garden along the tow-path by the river.' John Clarke remembers his father's passion for shooting, with the family holidaying in Scotland where John Hawkshaw would shoot on the moors near Pitlochry. It was during one of these holidays in the summer of 1856 that the youngest of the Hawkshaw children, Oliver, contracted typhoid fever and died. He was buried in the churchyard at Moulin, near Pitlochry. His sudden and unexpected death prompted Ann to write her brief memoir, 'Memories of My Childhood', in which grief over the death of her second child awakens memories of her own childhood growing up in Green Hammerton. Likening her retreat into introspection with the opening dream sequence of John Bunyan's *The Pilgrim's Progress*, the preface to 'Memories of My Childhood', dated 14 December 1856 and written from the Hawkshaws' home in Eaton Place, London, reveals the catalyst for Hawkshaw's remembrances:

> The isolation of soul made by sorrow has rendered me careless of what was passing around, the noise of the busy world without has been hushed […]. The scenes of the present could not be seen through the midst of tears, while those of the past have risen up around me […]. I have lived again in my childhood, my girlhood, my early married

life; the fields where I played, the flowers that I planted, the companions I loved, all have been seen once more; I did not think the store-house of memory contained so many recollections of those early days and their simple pleasures. The past three months have been the saddest of my life [...]. Fallen for a while from the stirring scenes of existence, not compelled to mingle in the crowd by the calls of society, or the claims of affection, I have conversed with my own heart and communed with the past.

Here Ann draws upon memory for consolation as she seeks solace in the past, internalising an idea of childhood as a time of 'simple pleasures' and innocence. The experience of losing Oliver leads Ann to reflect more broadly on what it means to be a mother. 'It is a blessed but a fearful thing to be a Mother!' she exclaims. 'Heaven with its splendours above her, the abyss with its terrors beneath her. Her life is multiplied but she must die many deaths.' In her sorrow, Ann turns to God, as 'He alone can know' a mother's grief, and 'He alone can comfort', drawing strength from the certainty that she will meet Ada and Oliver again in heaven: 'In your Mother's heart you both are cushioned, no years, no changes can deprive you of that home, not death, for that will reunite us.'

The loss of her children seemingly brings to mind other losses which she addresses in the memoir, framing her recollections with poetic references:

How freshly the memory of long summer afternoons [...] comes back to me even now: 'we were four', four fast friends, two are left and they from circumstances did not meet for years and now can meet but seldom; a third, my noble-minded sister, has slept beneath the grass of the little cemetery at Green Hammerton for more than twenty years, the white rose on her grave has shed its fair petals there for nearly a quarter of a century, and the forth, the youngest of the four, faded away in a tropic land and died in sight of her own shores, to which her husband brought her back too late to save her, but in time for her ashes to rest on English earth: 'It was something to see its cliffs once more / And lay her bones on her own loved shore.'

In an allusion to 'We Are Seven', the poem by William Wordsworth, published in *Lyrical Ballads* (1798), in which the child speaker includes her dead siblings in a count of her family, despite the insistence of the adult voice that the number should exclude them, Hawkshaw's 'we were four' shifts tenses to suggest that she feels keenly the absence of her dear friend and her beloved sister; the closing couplet re-genders lines from 'The Soldier's Funeral' (1824) by Letitia Elizabeth Landon (1802–38): 'But 'twas something to see its cliffs once more, / And to lay his bones on his own loved shore.' The process of memory itself prompts thought here, with Hawkshaw noting that it is 'strange that some trifling occurrence should remain woven in the roof of memory's web in bright and lasting colours, while the tints in which others were wrought have faded away.' She continues with profoundly expressed philosophical wonderings over the nature of memory:

Why should the recollection of one day when we found, we the four, a bed of sweet scented white violets on a bank on which we were sitting trying to make a basket of the pith of rushes, come back to me now, here, with the ocean before my window and not a sight or tone that tells of spring on the broad lands – I cannot tell, unless it be to keep fresh in the world-worn breast a green and healthy spot.

The references to the ocean suggest that the memoir was, at least in part, written whilst in Scotland, the place of Oliver's death and far away from her London home.

Hawkshaw's reflections on her childhood provide an insightful commentary on many aspects of rural life at a time of immense social and political change. Having left Green Hammerton some twenty years earlier, Hawkshaw returned often to visit family and her memoir is an amalgamation of these present-day observations and memories of a childhood spent in the village. Her writing engages with many pertinent areas of debate and offers a valuable insight into the changing physical, political and religious landscapes of the mid-nineteenth century. For instance, she is critical of the legacy of evangelical religion in rural communities, reflecting on how, within only two generations, well-meaning religious practices had evolved into repressive and spirit-sapping doctrines of restraint:

> I cannot but pause, and ask what has been the result of all the activity, time and money spent on evangelising (as it is called) the rural districts? At first it worked well; chapels were built, barns were fitted up as meeting houses, persons walked long distances to the 'preachings' and sang hymns as they walked home in the moonlight across the lonely fields: it was like the old times of the Reformation [...]. Unlettered peasants listened for the first time to the Word of God, and felt that there was something for them too, besides the daily toil for bread. But the next generation were placed in a different circumstance and required different treatment, and it was not there, and the effect was what might be expected. The deep reverential feelings that had filled the minds of those who had lived during the great revival of religion in England did not impress them, and its place had not been supplied by the belief of reason and principle. That culture of mind that the wants of the times demanded, and that the masses in the large cities were beginning to enjoy, did not reach to the rural districts: schools were few, and those few badly managed; books were expensive and libraries there were none; the periodicals that found their way to the villages were not of a kind to interest or instruct the young. They consisted entirely of magazines embracing the gloomy theology of Calvin, or with accounts of the visions and dreams, and special guidance of the followers of Wesley. Harmless amusements were denounced as sin, and a walk on the Sabbath was construed as Sabbath-breaking; no books except those of a strict religious kind were allowed to appear on tables on a Sunday [...], books intended, one would think, to terrify the young with a hypocritical assumption of religion, not to fire them with the love and sweetness of Christ's teaching to a life of goodness; what a prize to the children of the religious in those days was old Bunyan! His book was a treasure: many an eager childish eye was bent on it with wonder and delight, and often its perusal has taken away the tedium of the hours 'between services' and served to fill the infant mind with wondering thoughts during the long sermon of which it could understand little. These enforced observances did incalculable injury to the young; they submitted, but it was with a feel of injury, and in most cases as soon as removed from puritanical restraint they plunged headlong into vice; this was the fate of the sons, that of the daughters though less glaringly painful, was perhaps equally destructive of right and moral feeling; either they became self-righteous, stern and harsh, or discontented and soured, dragging on a monotonous existence without aim, without a hope.

The pessimistic summary of the effects of stern evangelising on communities whose access to wider influences is limited by circumstance is scathing and perceptive. Hawkshaw's solution involves the gentle, nature-based invocation of God and goodness which informs her teaching in *Poems for My Children*:

> It is much to be regretted that no simple lectures on natural history, no classes for music, or singing, were ever formed by the clergy or dissenting ministers; they would do far more good to the morals of the rural population by such means than by preaching weekday sermons and distributing religious tracts of antiquated theology and questionable morality.

Here, as with her much of her poetry, Hawkshaw's reminiscences of childhood reflect her association of God with the wonders of the natural world. There are echoes in the memoir of her earlier poem, 'The Past' (1842), in which knowledge of the natural world only serves to enhance belief in God as creator:

A blessed and wonderful thing is Christianity, that can satisfy the intellect and heart of a Newton, and yet cheer and elevate the simple cottager, to whom the stars are but specks of light, and the sun a ball of fire, wasting away at night, and kindled up again by God in the morning (these are not my imaginings, they were the very words used by a labourer in the village of my father).

> And have the wonders of creation woke
> Of adoration not a loftier strain,
>   As one by one upon the mind they've broke,
> And yet are moving on, an endless train?
>   If, when a child, thine eye was raised above,
> In wonder, to the God who spread the sky
>   With sparkling gems, how deep thine awe and love
> Who know'st them now, as worlds, and suns on high.
>   ('The Past', ll. 201–8)

Although it seems that Hawkshaw had drawn inspiration from those she had conversed with as a child, her later reflections concede, maybe curiously for one who has chosen poetry as her means of public expression, that 'there is no poetry in the dirt and disorder of those West Ridings of Yorkshire and Lancashire places as there is about the poverty of an Italian village; no projecting window throws a shadow, no vine relieves the flatness of the wall'. Yet the value of the individual lives of those villagers in Green Hammerton with whom she conversed in her youth is acknowledged in terms of the lives unseen, the inner lives which have the potential to offer an unmediated history of the times; not maybe through her pen, but as creative fodder for the 'modern novelist':

> Was it not Mr Johnson who said that if the history of the humblest individual could be truly written it would afford instruction to the philosopher? The people with whom I came into contact in my youth and whose lives passed away amidst the most unfrequented of hamlets and the loneliest of farmsteads had each a mental history which if written faithfully would instruct the dwellers of the noisy world, for

it would be the story of minds fashioned by themselves, influenced in the smallest degree by others, a moral state; but such history I cannot write, most of them now sleep under the old yew trees of the church yards, but some of them had an outward as well as an inner life that contained some portion of romance, life and death; love and hope went on in their quaint homes and made their daily life and moulded their hearts and minds, but at times this monotony was broken by dark deeds and fierce out-breaks of passion that would have formed the stock in trade of many a modern novelist.

Elsewhere, Hawkshaw uses her remembrances of the rural landscape to pass comment on the changing political and economic landscape. Having called to mind the comparatively uncultivated environs of the Green Hammerton of her childhood, where trees and flowers were left to flourish where nature had left them, Hawkshaw wryly notes, 'I dare say the clever agriculturalists of the present day would have cut down the oaks and trimmed the fences to proper economical dimensions and the banks of primroses would have been ploughed away.' Seeming to resent the commodification of the landscape, and longing to retain the inspiration of nature which had sustained her as a child, Hawkshaw states with some pride that her 'dear old Grandfather was satisfied with the returns his estate yielded under such management as his forefathers had taught him'. 'For my part', she continues, 'I am glad that so much loveliness was left for my childish eyes to look upon, and sure I am that no money could have procured for me the pure pleasure I even now enjoy in recalling the simple delight of passing long summer days of idleness amid those flowery fields.'

But although her grandfather resisted change, the village of her childhood changed: 'The Green Hammerton of 1856 is not the village of my childhood. In thirty years the tide of events that has swept over England has not left untouched that quiet little nook.' In part, the change as Hawkshaw records it is aesthetic, as 'most of the thatched farm houses and low-roofed cottages have given way to more comfortable, but less picturesque dwellings'. But more significantly for Hawkshaw, it is 'the manners of people' that 'have undergone as great a change, the distinction between class and class, employers and employed has grown wider'. Whereas once her grandfather would sit 'smoking his pipe, sitting in his black leather arm chair in the chimney corner, the old thrasher Billy on a three-legged stool opposite him, and the other men and boys at a respectful distance in the background [...], with the firelight twinkling on the pewter plates on the shelf' now 'the rough but friendly greeting between the farmer and his labourer has ceased to be heard'. This fireside scene remembered from her early childhood becomes a domestic metaphor for the political changes that she perceived then, but only began to understand as an adult: 'I remember feeling that old forms of society were being broken up, and middle-age customs disappearing when that old pewter was taken down from the place it had occupied for so many generations and white earthenware was put in its stead.' 'I know where I was standing by my Grandmother at the time she pointed out the alteration', Hawkshaw continues, 'I was insensible to all her arguments on the desirability of change; that the earthen dish could be washed in a minute, and the pewter one required half an hour of labour to make it clean and bright was nothing to me.' Though trading the labour-intensive for the utilitarian signalled progress to her grandmother and to all those tasked with household chores, for the young Ann Jackson the move away from tradition prefigured a future that she was not yet ready to embrace: 'I dreamed of the past, and did not wish one link that told of it to be broken; slowly only have I learnt to think the present better than the past.'

The 'distinction between class and class, employers and employed' which Hawkshaw observes suggests a keen interest in, and awareness of, industrial relations, and a political sensitivity which is reflected in the Hawkshaws' wider political engagement. In 1863, John Hawkshaw stood as an unsuccessful Liberal candidate at Andover: John Clarke's diary notes that his father was not returned because 'he told the electors that he would prosecute anyone who took a bribe'. In 1865 John intended to stand again, this time in Lyme Regis where the Hawkshaws had bought an estate, but as John Clarke notes, just before the election he 'found out that he was disqualified as a candidate by holding a Government appointment as engineer to the Holyhead Harbour.' 'It was difficult to find a candidate at so short a notice', John Clarke continues, 'so it was decided that I was to stand in my father's place.' The account of his canvassing says much about the need for electoral reform:

> I went down at once to Lyme Regis with Mr Batten, my father's solicitor, and made acquaintance with the inhabitants, calling on every voter [...]. Only on one of my calls was the question of politics brought forward and that was in the case of an unfortunate tradesman, who told me, almost with tears in his eyes, that he dared not vote as he wished, for in that case he would lose his trade. The most trying part of my calls was the amount of indifferent cider that I had to drink. Lyme Regis was a most corrupt borough and was very properly disenfranchised later on. The people had lived for years on smuggling and elections. Charmouth formed part of the Borough for voting purposes, and I heard after the election that there were only eleven electors in Charmouth who were not bribed, I lunched at one house where, after lunch, they asked £100 for their vote.

John Clarke lost the election by nine votes to 'Mr Treeby, an elderly man and a local builder'. The frailties of the voting system are emphasised in his account of polling day:

> The other side made some of our voters drunk, and so we lost their votes. Old Dr Hodges, the Rector, asked me to breakfast with him. He was a delightful old man, a thorough going Tory, and said he would vote for a broomstick if it put up on the Tory side. It was as well, on the whole, that I lost this election, for I do not think Parliamentary life would have suited me.

Having published *Sonnets on Anglo-Saxon History* in 1854, there is a gap of some 17 years before Hawkshaw publishes again, this time for private circulation. The events of the intervening years provided the inspiration for what would be Ann's final collection of work, *Cecil's Own Book* (1871). Comprising three short stories and ten poems and written by Ann for Cecil Wedgwood, her young grandson who had been born in March 1863, copies of the beautifully bound book, complete with illustrations, seem to have been distributed amongst Ann's wider family, to friends and to acquaintances. The circumstances of Cecil's birth are particularly pertinent to the themes addressed in the collection, which is dedicated to the memory of Cecil's mother and Ann's eldest daughter, Mary Jane Jackson Wedgwood. At some time during the early 1850s, whilst the Hawkshaws were living in London, they had become acquainted with the Darwin-Wedgwood family. With Hensleigh Wedgwood and his daughter Frances (Snow) close friends with Elizabeth Gaskell, it is possible that Gaskell made the initial introduction of the Hawkshaws to the

Wedgwoods and Darwins. In his account of a family holiday to Tunbridge Wells in 1857, Ann's eldest son John Clarke remembers how he, then 16, and his brother Henry, 14, had ridden to Tunbridge Wells on their ponies, 'staying a night on the way at Mr Darwin's house at Down. We took our night clothes and a comb and toothbrush rolled up on our saddles in front of us.' Furthermore, Mary Pugh, who had been governess to the Hawkshaw children in the early 1850s, was later employed as a governess to the children of Charles and Emma Darwin. A somewhat melancholy character, Pugh was with the Darwins at Down House between 1857 and 1859, but kept in touch with the family and visited often – even after she had left her post. Although she was later certified insane and spent her last years in an asylum, Mary Pugh remained financially supported by her previous employers, with Charles Darwin paying £30 a year for her to have a holiday and John Hawkshaw paying her asylum fees.

By the early 1860s, the Hawkshaws' eldest children, John Clarke and Mary, were romantically involved with siblings Cecily and Godfrey Wedgwood, great-grandchildren of Josiah Wedgwood, and Darwin's niece and nephew. Cecily and Mary had been at school together and were great friends. On 24 June 1862, Mary Hawkshaw and Godfrey Wedgwood were married at St Peter's Church, Pimlico. Mary fell pregnant almost straight away, yet by the following March instead of joyfully anticipating the arrival of her first child, Mary was gravely ill with her mother by her side at the Wedgwoods' home at Hem Heath, Stafford. In a letter to her son Henry, dated 27 March 1863, Ann tells him that she is 'compelled to stay here' and that she 'cannot leave poor Mary alone'.[47] The following day Cecil Wedgwood was born and only 11 days later Mary died from puerperal mania. The awful inevitability of her death is suggested in the diary entry made by Emma Darwin on 7 April 1863: 'Mary's death came.'[48]

Losing their eldest daughter in this way was a terrible blow for the Hawkshaws, who had already buried two young children. One can only imagine Ann's distress at watching her beloved eldest child die in such circumstances. In letters to her son Henry in the months following Mary's death, Ann speaks of her own illness, brought on by the trauma of losing her daughter: 'This is only the second time since my illness that I have tried to write, so you must not be surprised at my singular penmanship; my hand does not seem much under the control of my will at present' (27 April 1863). 'I cannot write much for I am still very weak' (6 May 1863). Although not mentioning Mary's death directly, Ann writes of the family's support of Godfrey Wedgwood, who 'says he needs love so much now' (27 April 1863) and who 'clings more to us than ever; he has had baby [Cecil] photographed asleep in his cot, and dear Mary's dog Jack too' (6 May 1863).[49]

Under the watchful care of his father and grandparents, the young Cecil Wedgwood thrived. Much of his early childhood was spent with his Hawkshaw relatives, particularly John and Ann at Hollycombe, their four-thousand-acre West Sussex estate, which they had purchased in 1865. Its proximity to a mainline station meant that John was only an hour and a half away from London, enabling him to move between his offices in the

---

47 Part of an original bundle of letters held at the Staffordshire and Stoke-on-Trent Archive Service, Staffordshire Records Office, reference D4347.
48 *Darwin Online*, http://darwin-online.org.uk/content/frameset?itemID=CUL-DAR242%5B.27%5D&viewtype=image&pageseq=1 (accessed 15 May 2009).
49 Extracts from an original bundle of letters held at the Staffordshire and Stoke-on-Trent Archive Service, Staffordshire Records Office, reference D4347.

City and his country estate with relative ease. Charles Darwin's diary records a visit to the Hawkshaws at Hollycombe between 7 June and 9 June 1876, with the Hollycombe visitors' book for the period showing that his wife, Emma Darwin, and botanist J. D. Hooker arrived with him. Amongst the family and friends signing the Hollycombe visitors' book are the writer Anne Thackeray, daughter of novelist William Makepeace Thackeray, who visited in January 1877, and poet laureate Alfred Tennyson and his eldest son Hallam, who visited Hollycombe in October 1882.[50] Unfortunately there are no further records of these visits, or of the extent or nature of these acquaintances. It is from Hollycombe that Ann writes *Cecil's Own Book*, undoubtedly to amuse her young grandson, but also, as the book's dedication suggests, as a memorial to her daughter: 'To the Memory of Mary, the Mother of Cecil.' In a parallel act of remembrance, John Hawkshaw built a school at nearby Wardley Green in 1869 in memory of the dead Hawkshaw children.[51] The original school building housed a rectangular stained-glass window depicting a mother and three children entitled *Fides, Spes et Caritas* (Faith, Hope and Charity). A commemorative stone replaced this shortly after the Second World War, dedicating the school 'To the Memory of Ada, Oliver and Mary.' The school was handed over to the Education Authority in 1873, the year of John Hawkshaw's knighthood. The Education Authority report from November of that year notes that 'Lady Hawkshaw and party visited' and that Lady Hawkshaw 'gave the children various exercises in singing'.[52]

As well as the beneficiary of *Cecil's Own Book*, the young Cecil Wedgwood features in several of the collection's poems and short stories, in particular through Hawkshaw's characterisations of young, motherless boys in the stories 'The Wonderful Adventures of Hassan the Younger, the Son of Hassan-el-Alfi the Camel Driver', 'Little Prince Bepettedbyall' and 'The Fairy Gift; or, The Iron Bracelet'. In these stories, Hawkshaw writes as a grandmother, weaving adventures for her grandson in the style of the Arabian Nights, Charles Kingsley's *The Water-Babies* and Lewis Carroll's *Alice's Adventures in Wonderland*. As in her other collections, nature frames the poetry in *Cecil's Own Book*. But unlike her earlier work, God is absent in nature, not simply 'unremembered' as Ann had cautioned in her poem 'The Future': 'The good may be forgotten in the great; / The moral, in the mental; and the hand / Who built and furnished all the fair estate, / Be unremembered 'mid the works He planned'.[53]

Whereas in Hawkshaw's earlier poems, each aspect of the natural world, from the tiniest drop of dew to the magnificence of the solar system, served as evidence of a benevolent and loving God, in *Cecil's Own Book* poems such as 'The Discontented Stream', 'The Selfish Toad' and 'The Ambitious Water-Lily' resonate with images of anarchic and wasteful nature. Whether the death of Hawkshaw's beloved eldest daughter – like Darwin's own loss of his daughter Annie – raised the spectre of wasteful nature to such an extent that she doubted the presence of God in the natural world can only be surmised. But there seems little doubt that having faced the death of three of her children,

---

50 Hollycombe visitors' book, covering the period from 1873 to 1935. Viewed with the kind permission of Mrs Diane Whitehead.
51 Wardley Green School is now known as Hollycombe School.
52 Val Porter, *Milland: The Book* (Milland: Milland Memories Group, 2003), 387.
53 Ann Hawkshaw, 'The Future' in *'Dionysius the Areopagite', with Other Poems* (1842), ll. 221–4; here Hawkshaw celebrates scientific progress whilst asserting her belief in God the Creator.

the comfort of life eternal spent with her children in heaven fades, leaving only earthly sadness. This sadness is most poignantly expressed in the final poem in *Cecil's Own Book*: 'In Memoriam'.

The end of Hawkshaw's poetic journey is marked by a poem which itself tells of a journey: a mother's journey through sadness and loss. 'In Memoriam' is a touching elegy on childhood death from a mother's perspective, separated from the preceding poems and stories by an illustration depicting a small child with head bowed at the foot of a memorial stone in a churchyard. Amongst the branches of the churchyard trees are the words 'In Memoriam' in a font resembling plant stems from which small shoots and blooms grow. From the final stanza of the poem it is clear that the small child in the picture is Cecil, and the grave his mother's. But the poem begins many years before, when Cecil's mother was herself a child, and when her own mother had been untouched the all-pervading fear of loss – a fear that develops over the poem's 11 stanzas. Here the poem begins:

> Once in a far-off northern home,
>   *Five* happy children played:
> They ran beside the mountain streams,
>   And through the pine woods strayed,
> Or watched the wild birds on the hills,
>   From morn to evening's shade.
>
> One made a mill-wheel in a stream,
>   Another read his book—
> Stretched on the sweet thyme-covered bank:
>   But oft away would look
> To where his youngest brother fished
>   For minnows in the brook.
>
> And ever by the brother's side
>   Kept the two sisters dear,
> And borne upon the mountain breeze
>   Their laugh came soft and clear—
> To where the mother sat—her heart
>   Had not then learned to fear. (1–18)

Even though Hawkshaw narrates in the third person throughout 'In Memoriam', the autobiographical subject matter combined with Hawkshaw's position of retrospection lends the poem an intensity of personal feeling. In setting her 'happy children' in the hills and countryside surrounding their Manchester home, and in the mountains of Scotland where the family frequently holidayed, Hawkshaw draws on the memory of an idyllic rural landscape to represent an equally idyllic childhood. Here, within hearing distance of their mother, John Clarke occupies himself with a small-scale engineering project, making a 'mill-wheel in a stream', whilst Henry reads a book and the youngest boy, Oliver, fishes for minnows, watched at the water's edge by his attentive elder sisters, Mary and Editha. Not until line eighteen does the shadow of childhood death appear, in an allusion to the loss of Ada: 'her heart / Had not then learned to fear'.

Yet in reading on, it is clear that Hawkshaw had not 'learned to fear' from the death of her first child:

> "Death is contented with that one:"
>   Such was the mother's dream,
> "That bud of beauty, will it not
>   "My other flowers redeem?"
> Oh! foolish was that mother's thought,
>   Beside the mountain stream. (25–30)

Indeed, rather than having learned to fear from Ada's death, Hawkshaw recalls her now seemingly naïve hope that in losing one child, her 'other flowers' would be redeemed. As she so poignantly acknowledges in the introduction to 'Memories of My Childhood', the experience of losing a child is part of the 'blessed but […] fearful thing' that defines motherhood. In retrospect, however, Hawkshaw knows that death was not content with one, nor two, but three of her children; far beyond the pact of motherhood that she had accepted: the allusion to foolishness suggests that she feels betrayed. In the lines that follow Hawkshaw appears increasingly sceptical about the extent to which any comfort or reason can be found in the deaths of her young, innocent and good children:

> But then these young lives were so glad,
>   Their hearts so good and pure,
> They filled one home so full of love,
>   It seemed it must endure:
> For, to fill up such void on earth,
>   What solace, or what cure. (31–6)

Stanzas on Oliver's illness and death follow next, his absence first apparent in the '*four*' children walking through the highland landscape of which they were all so fond:

> There came a change—through highland glen
>   Walked quietly but *four*,
> Or talked with whispered words, within
>   The heather covered bower,
> Or gathered for the sick boy's room,
>   Green fern or autumn flower. (37–42)

Oliver had lain ill for some five weeks with typhoid fever and peritonitis, and in remembering the last days of his life, Hawkshaw beatifies her son, recollecting his 'fair brow and sunny hair' (43), and how he bore his illness with fortitude, offering his mother comfort in the face of death: 'Upon his couch he lay, / Patient and loving to the last:— / And as he passed away, / Giving sweet words of love to her / Who wept in wild dismay!' (44–8). Reunited with the landscape he so loved, Oliver is buried in the Scottish highlands:

> Amid the scenes he loved so well,
>   There is a little grave:
> The giant hills behind it tower,—

> Before it corn-fields wave,
> And there, with bitter tears, they lay
> To rest, their good and brave. (49–54)

Hawkshaw's numerical countdown of untimely death calls to mind Wordsworth's 'We Are Seven'. And yet whereas the little girl of Wordsworth's poem holds on to the number seven in her imaginative state of family unity, Hawkshaw counts down, all too aware of the awful earthly reality of her children's physically diminishing numbers. The italicisation of '*five*', '*four*' and then '*three*' inflects Hawkshaw's incredulity at their deaths as the poem progresses.

From her sadness at Ada's death in 1845, to the 'wild dismay' of Oliver's in 1856, Hawkshaw moves towards the 'hideous dream' (59) of losing her eldest daughter in 1863:

> Time passed—and then there were but *three*:
> Who wept in speechless woe,
> The young wife-mother, must she die!—
> Oh! God,—must this be so?
> It must be but a hideous dream!
> They could not let *her* go.
>
> Beside the village church, a cross
> Tells where that dear one sleeps:
> Her boy treads gently there,—and love,
> Untiring vigil keeps;
> And years go by, of good and ill,
> But still that mother weeps! (55–66)

In the death of this 'young wife-mother', Hawkshaw's narrative of motherhood is doubly challenged: not only has she lost another child, but a mother has also been lost. Mary's death takes Hawkshaw beyond her capacity to accept the wastefulness of early death, both as a mother herself, and with Mary herself as a mother – and for the first time in the poem, Hawkshaw invokes God. But unlike her earlier work, she does not turn to God for comfort: here, 'Oh! God' is an expression of disbelief, rather than a statement of belief. Despite the hint of regeneration and hope implied in the shooting buds of the font used in the poem's title page, hope is absent in the denouement of Hawkshaw's poetic remembrance. Rather than the hope of life eternal spent with her three children in heaven, the cumulative effect of their deaths has left Hawkshaw with only earthly sadness. The absence of biographical material between 1871 and Hawkshaw's death in 1885 leaves 'In Memoriam' as Hawkshaw's final word.

The changing response to nature and death in Hawkshaw's poetry represents a loss of certainty in belief, rather than an absolute loss of faith. Even after Mary died in 1863, the church continued to be central to Ann's life. Following her death from a stroke on 29 April 1885, Sir John Hawkshaw dedicated a stained glass window to his beloved wife in the parish church of St Mary the Virgin, Bramshott, Hampshire, in sight of the Hawkshaws' Hollycombe estate. The window's pictorial images show a female likeness alongside Jesus and St Peter, accompanied by brief biblical passages from the New Testament: 'God loveth a cheerful giver' (2 Corinthians 9:7), and two passages relating to Tabitha, said to have been raised from the dead by St Peter: 'This woman was full of good works' (Acts 9:36) and 'When she saw Peter she sat up' (Acts 9:40). In light of Hawkshaw's changed perspective on death in 'In Memoriam', it is notable that she is aligned with a woman who had been brought back to an earthly life, rather than ascending to heaven. The composition of the dedicatory window suggests that both Sir John and Lady Hawkshaw acceded to the conventions of ceremonial Anglicanism, yet ended their lives reflecting on the worldly significance of death and their faith, rather than looking confidently on death and faith as the gateway to life eternal. Sir John outlived his wife by six years. He died at Belgrave Mansions, Grosvenor Gardens, London, on 2 June 1891 and was buried in an identical tomb alongside Ann in the churchyard of St Mary's Church, Bramshott.

1842

'DIONYSIUS THE AREOPAGITE', WITH OTHER POEMS

'Dionysius the Areopagite', with Other Poems was published in November 1842 in London by Jackson & Walford, and in Manchester by Simms & Dinham. The collection was favourably received and reviewed.[1] The title poem retells the biblical story of Dionysius, an elected member of the Areopagus whose conversion to Christianity in light of St Paul's teaching is briefly mentioned in the New Testament (Acts 17:34).[2] Although the poem's opening sections are loosely based on the biblical account of St Paul's teaching in Athens, the majority of the poem is an imaginative reconstruction of Dionysius's personal journey towards Christianity and his decision to choose the Christian faith over romantic love. Through the scriptural figure of Dionysius the Areopagite Hawkshaw explores doctrines of Protestantism, as she objectifies mid-nineteenth-century challenges to religious faith by looking back to the persecution of early Christians in the period shortly after the crucifixion. By challenging the account of Christian persecution given by eighteenth-century historian Edward Gibbon (1737–94) in *The History of the Rise and Fall of the Roman Empire* (6 vols, 1776–89), Hawkshaw uses the struggle between paganism and the emergent Christian church in Rome as a paradigm for the move away from the High Church orthodoxy that she observes in mid-nineteenth century Britain.

Although a religious poem, 'Dionysius the Areopagite' is not a work of pious didacticism. True to her Protestant beliefs, Hawkshaw takes her poetic inspiration from the scriptures, but unlike the poetic reinforcement of ceremonial dogmas that defined the work of the Tractarian devotional poets of the period, Hawkshaw presents a practical religion anchored in the morality of the individual, rather than in the ceremony of tradition. The polemic narrative interjections at the beginning of each of the three parts bring broad thematic concerns to the fore, which Hawkshaw goes on to explore and illuminate by focussing in on the individual experiences of the poem's characters. This tightening in of the focus is a feature of the poem's structure. Each of the poem's three parts reduces in length with part 1 made up of 1420 lines divided into eleven sections; part 2, 697 lines over five sections; and part 3, 369 lines over two sections. In this way, the structure of 'Dionysius the Areopagite' reflects Hawkshaw's wider project of producing poetry which acknowledges the authoritative foundations of conventional history but which itself chooses to focus in on an individual's experience. In taking the spiritual journey as its theme and intertwining faith with romantic love, the poem has much in common with *The Epicurean* (1827) by Thomas Moore (1779–1852), forerunner of *Marius the Epicurean* (2 vols, 1885) by Walter Pater (1839–94). Moreover, 'Dionysius the Areopagite' offers a powerful account of female

---

1 See Appendix A for the following reviews: *North of England Magazine* (December 1842); *The Gentleman's Magazine* (January–June 1843); *Court Magazine and Monthly Critic* (June 1843). John Evans reviews *'Dionysius the Areopagite', with Other Poems* and *Poems for My Children* in his survey of regional writers, *Lancashire Authors and Orators* (1850). See also note 10 for Samuel Bamford's response to the collection.
2 The Areopagus was the highest judicial court in ancient Athens.

subjectivity with Hawkshaw's polemic interjections as the poem's (female) narrator and the introduction of female characters in Corinna, Myra, Mycale and the priestess, and the dramatic emphasis placed on the relationship between them. However, there is no overriding sense of female unity in the poem, but rather an exploration of the complexities of female relationships: it is the betrayal of female friendship rather than the betrayal of romantic love that elicits powerful emotional responses in the poem's plot and subplot as Corinna is condemned to death as a Christian martyr. The poem appears to be a likely source for an early twentieth-century play, *Dionysius the Areopagite: A Tragedy*, by A. W. Langlands.[3] Written in verse, the play's eponymous hero (described in the dramatis personae as 'Dionysius, a councillor of the Areopagus, also Christian Bishop of Athens') struggles to reconcile his Christian faith with love for Krinon, who, like Hawkshaw's Myra, eschews the Christian faith. As with Hawkshaw's poem, Langlands's play considers ideas of public and private declarations of Christianity in a pagan society, with Dionysius martyred for his Christian beliefs as the play ends.

In other poems in the collection Hawkshaw engages with prevailing social and political concerns. 'Introductory Stanzas' excels in its representation of a particular moment in Manchester's literary history, as the city's aesthetic production competes with the forward motion of thrusting capitalism. In these opening stanzas Hawkshaw sets out her poetic manifesto by proposing a new aesthetic and spiritual response in order to challenge the traditions of poets such as Felicia Hemans (1793–1835) and William Wordsworth (1770–1850). Elsewhere in this first collection, Hawkshaw traces a move away from a Romantic sentimentalisation of childhood death towards the more sober realities of the Poor Law Amendment Act (1834) through the image of a mother and her dying child in 'The Mother to her Starving Child'. In calling to mind a Romantic idealisation of death and the consoling effect of memory, the mother's voice expresses the inadequacy of such a response to a death that is both political and avoidable, marking a move away from the consoling balm of Romanticism towards a more sober Victorian poetic sensibility. Hawkshaw's political voice comes to the fore once more in a group of poems in support of the antislavery movement: 'Land of my Fathers' offers a celebration of Britain's moral supremacy post-emancipation; 'Sonnet—To America' draws attention to the anomaly of the United States resisting the abolition of slavery when its own constitution sets out the principles of freedom of speech and freedom of religion in its First Amendment; 'Why am I a Slave?' presents the voice of a plantation slave in the colonies speaking movingly of their captivity. Other prominent poems in the collection are 'The Past' and 'The Future', companion poems which cast Hawkshaw as a representative voice speaking of the moment and which develop at length her desire for an appreciation of the natural world and for increased spiritual awareness. Writing in the tradition of natural theology, most probably informed by William Paley's *Natural Theology* (1802) and the more recent Bridgewater Treatises (1833–36), Hawkshaw takes up the argument for design in these poems, in which evidence of God as the Creator is enhanced, rather than demolished, by scientific observations of the natural world. By engaging with some of the most challenging philosophical questions of the age, Hawkshaw negotiates between a rationalisation of man's pursuit of knowledge and her framework of Christian faith. She urges her readers not to be seduced by scientific progress which questions God's agency, and to instead

---

3 A. W. Langlands, *Dionysius the Areopagite: A Tragedy* (London: Elliot Stock, 1910).

celebrate the wonders of a God who, as she points out in 'The Past', 'spread / The vault of heaven gave it a thousand hues, / And strewed the very ground on which we tread / With tinted cups, to hold the evening dews', and who has 'spread the sky / With sparkling gems'. In these poems Ann's upbringing in a family of religious dissenters, and her position as the wife of an engineer whose work brought her into contact with some of the leading scientists and innovators of the day, come together in a narrative perspective that looks to accommodate intellectual and scientific progress with a deeply held faith. By reaffirming Christian theology, Hawkshaw resists a move towards rational explanations of the natural world and man's place within it. By upholding her belief in God the Creator and the pre-eminence of humanity, Hawkshaw makes a notable contribution to mid-nineteenth-century assertions of faith. The assured narrative interjections that frequently punctuate her work suggest self-confidence in her own position as a writer as she makes her debut onto Manchester's vibrant poetic scene.

Introductory Stanzas

Where are the strains like solemn music stealing,
    Which erst from Cambria's ancient vallies came?[4]
Where is the heart that shrined all holy feeling?
    Remains there only now of her* a name?[5]
Is the lyre broken and the music o'er?
Oh! sweeter never woke the echoes of our shore.

And could she not bequeath her gift of song,—
    Treasure far richer than the Indian mine?
Could not those mountain winds the strain prolong,
    Which sweep o'er heights where freedom built her shrine,
Or sigh o'er many an elder minstrel's tomb?
Free winds that never fanned a conqueror's plume!

It may not be—on the dead soldier's breast
    They lay the sword and lance, and they have borne
Her lyre in sadness to her place of rest,
    And for its silence wherefore should we mourn?
For there are few would listen to the strain
Were she to wake that lyre's deep chords again.[6]

---

4 Cambria: classical name for Wales.
5 [Poet's Note: *Mrs Hemans.] Felicia Dorothea Hemans (1793–1835), English Romantic poet. Widely regarded as the foremost female poet of the Romantic period, her death was marked in literary tributes from Letitia Elizabeth Landon ('Stanzas on the Death of Mrs Hemans' [1835], 'Felicia Hemans' [1838]), Elizabeth Barrett Browning ('Stanzas Addressed to Miss Landon, and Suggested by Her "Stanzas on the Death of Mrs Hemans"' [1835]) and William Wordsworth ('Extempore Effusion upon the Death of James Hogg' [1835]).
6 In the original, stanzas 1–3 are printed on the recto, with 4–6 on the verso; the page turn marks a shift to the present, to Manchester 1842.

This is no time for song: there is a strife
   For wealth or for existence all around;
And all the sweet amenities of life,
   And all the gentle harmonies of sound,
Die like the flowers upon a beaten path,
Or music midst the noise of toil and wrath.[7]

Oh! to awake once more the love of song,
   The love of nature, and of holier things
Than crowd the visions of the busy throng:
   Alas! the dust is on the angel's wings,
And those who woke the lyre in days gone by
Wake it no more, or touch it with a sigh.[8]

*Bard of the lakes, is there not yet a tone[9]
   Slumbering within that silent harp of thine,
Is there no forest glade, no mossy stone,
   No quiet lake, nor old forgotten shrine,
Left unrecorded and unsung by thee?
Oh breathe one parting strain of thy pure minstrelsy.

Manchester, March 25, 1842.[10]

---

7 This stanza is included in John Evans' review of *'Dionysius the Areopagite', with Other Poems* in *Lancashire Authors and Orators* (1850): 'We dwell at this length in our observations upon this passage, because it introduces us to one who has proved by her writings alone that this is a time for song; for if any of our fair *literati* in Lancashire ever did show the gift of song, it is certainly in the highly gifted lady before us. Did we want a proof of the existence of the spirit of poetry in this noisy locality, we do not think we could select a more befitting one than a volume of the poems of Mrs. Hawkshaw. And we do not say this out of mere gallantry, or the courtesy that is generally expected to meet any female effort. Setting all this aside, Mrs. Hawkshaw's poetry will stand a fair critical test. Here we find none of those namby-pamby, milk-and-water sentimentalisms that are so frequently identified with the early efforts of many young authors or poetesses; all her effusions manifest something of a genuine character, something that you feel and know to be real poetry in the most enlarged acceptation of the word. You cannot peruse her effusions without being sensibly affected by the high poetic feelings they convey' (128–9); see Appendix A for the full review.

8 This stanza is included in the review of *'Dionysius the Areopagite', with Other Poems* in *North of England Magazine* (December 1842); see Appendix A.

9 [Poet's Note: *Wordsworth.] William Wordsworth (1770–1850), English Romantic poet. 'Bard of the lakes' is a reference to Wordsworth's connection to the Lake District where he was born and spent much of his life. Wordsworth was appointed Poet Laureate by Queen Victoria (1819–1901) in 1843. In calling to mind Hemans and Wordsworth in this way, Hawkshaw seems to be suggesting that a changing cultural and political atmosphere requires a change in poetic response. In doing so she carves out a space for herself as a poet within a poetic tradition that informs her poetry, but which does not eclipse it. Debbie Bark discusses Hawkshaw's engagement with her Romantic precursors in 'Poetry of Social Conscience, Poetry of Transition: Ann Hawkshaw's "Introductory Stanzas" and "The Mother to her Starving Child"', in *Poetry, Politics and Pictures: Culture and Identity in Europe, 1840–1914*, eds Ingrid Hanson, Jack Rhoden and Erin Snyder (Oxford: Peter Lang, 2013), 45–65.

10 The date of 25 March 1842 is pertinent. On the previous evening a 'Poetic Festival' had been held at the Sun Inn, Long Millgate, Manchester, attended by some forty literary men. Amongst the most prominent of local writers present were poet and engraver Charles Swain (1801–74), reedmaker-turned-poet John Critchley Prince (1808–66), poet and editor John Bolton Rogerson (1809–59), the self-styled 'Bard of Colour and Laureate of the Western Isles' Robert Rose (1804–49) and the weaver-poet and radical writer Samuel Bamford (1788–1872). Many of the poetical works had been written especially for the event, and were published after as *The Festive Wreath: A Collection of Original Contributions Read at a Literary Meeting, Held in Manchester March 24th 1842*. Locally designated as 'Poets' Corner', the Sun Inn was a popular meeting point for the Manchester poets and although Hawkshaw was writing on the fringes of this group, *'Dionysius the Areopagite', with Other Poems* had met with the approval of Samuel Bamford, who, in the preface to his *Poems* (1843) suggests that Hawkshaw, alongside Rogerson, Prince and others, had attracted the attention of the 'literati of Manchester' and were names 'destined for immortality' (see Appendix A). In October 1843 Bamford gifted a copy of *Poems* to Hawkshaw 'with the author's respectful compliments'. In locating and dating the 'Introductory Stanzas' to her first published collection in this way, Hawkshaw seems to be reflecting on what it means to be writing poetry in Manchester at this time, whilst positioning her work within Manchester's established poetic community.

Dionysius, the Areopagite

Part I.

I.

What more will be thy prey?
    Oh thou insatiate time!
Which of the earth's bright cities next,
    The temples of what clime,
Will thy foot trample into clay,
Or touch convert to ruins grey?
Thou hast crushed the gorgeous palaces
    Of Shinar's ancient plain;[11]
One shapeless mound alone is left[12]
    And thou and silence reign:—
Silence, though broken by the scream
Of the lone bittern, by that stream
O'er which there floated many a tone
Of revelry in ages gone.

All, all, at length are thine,
City, and pyramid, and shrine!
Like the red simoon's burning blast,[13]
Thy wing o'er Mizraim's land hath passed,[14]
    And Memnon's harp is silent now:—[15]

---

11 Shinar's ancient plain: the plain where the city and tower of Babel were said to have been built (Genesis 11:2).

12 [Poet's Note: All that is left of Babylon is a collection of heaps which appear like natural hills, (except that no green thing grows upon them) until the excavations shew that these heaps cover all that remains of the "beauty of the Chaldea's excellency." The principal mound is the Birs Nimrod or Burnt Mountain, supposed to be the remains of the temple of Belus.] 'Beauty of the Chaldea's excellency': see Isaiah 13:19. Birs Nimrod, or Birs Nimrud: site of ancient city of Borsippa, in Babylon Province, Iraq. Temple of Belus: occupying the site of the Tower of Babel, the temple was erected for the Babylonian god Belus. Burnt Mountain: see Jeremiah 51:25.

13 simoon: a hot, dry, suffocating sand wind which sweeps across the African and Asiatic deserts at intervals during the spring and summer (n. form of 'simoom' OED).

14 Mizraim: Hebrew name for the land of Egypt.

15 [Poet's Note: To me there is something very beautiful in the fable of Memnon greeting the rising sun with joyful strains, and lamenting its setting with mournful ones, for how often
    Do evening shades in sadness close
    O'er hopes that with the morning rose.
There are many statues that bear the name of Memnon, but that which was vocal is identified with the northernmost of the two colossal statues in the Theban plain, on the west bank of the Nile. The sounds are supposed to have been a device of the priests. Humboldt speaks of sounds that are heard, at sunrise, to proceed from rocks on the banks of the Orinoco, which he attributed to confined air making its escape through crevices and caverns where the difference

Strange land of wonders where the dead
   Have silent cities of their own,
And men of generations fled
   Dwell in their caverned tombs of stone.

Still, frail as human works may be,
   They have an immortality
That nations know not: ages yet
   Shall the dark pyramids arise,
Keeping the secret of their birth,
   'Neath Egypt's burning skies;
And many an empire pass away,
And nations crumble to decay,
Ere their last fragments mix with clay.

The shrine outlives its creed. Who piled
Yon lonely carn upon the wild?
What hands that moss-grown altar placed
In the stone circle on the waste?
History now darkly tells the tale
Of bloody rites that there were done,
By white robed druids to the sun.[16]

---

of the internal and external atmosphere is considerable. The French *savans* mention having heard similar sounds at Carnack on the east bank of the Nile; and hence it is conjectured that the priests, who had observed this phenomenon, contrived either to cause similar sounds to be heard around the statue, or to magnify the natural murmuring of the winds into supernatural meaning. It is thought that the head of the colossal Memnon in the British Museum has no claim to be considered as the vocal Memnon of Strabo, Tacitus, and Pausanias.—(See *British Museum*, Vol. I. page 266.)] Much of the wording here is a précis of sections of the entry for 'Memnon' in vol. 15 of *The Penny Cyclopædia of the Society for the Diffusion of Useful Knowledge*; a multivolume encyclopaedia edited by George Long, published by Charles Knight between 1833 and 1843. The source for the section 'Humboldt [...] contrived' is referenced by Long as taken from *The British Museum: Egyptian Antiquities* vol. 1 (1832), 266. Humboldt: Alexander von Humboldt (1769–1859), German geographer, naturalist and explorer. The couplet 'Do evening shades in sadness close / O'er hopes that with the morning rose' would seem to be Hawkshaw's, although it is similar to lines from canto 3 of 'Ellen Fitzarthur: A Metrical Tale'(1820) by Caroline Bowles Southey (1786–1854): 'And hope, that with the morning rose, / Went down in tears at evening close' (ll. 136–7).

16 [Poet's Note: The worship of the heavenly bodies is the earliest form of superstition among all people; but it is not improbable that the Druids received the worship of Baal or the sun from the Phoenicians, who traded to these islands after they formed their settlements in Spain, and who adored that deity with many cruel and bloody rites.] Druids: an order of men amongst the ancient Celts of Gaul and Britain who, according to Caesar, were priests or religious ministers and teachers, but who figure in native Irish and Welsh legend as magicians, sorcerers and soothsayers (n. 'Druid' *OED*). Baal: the chief male deity of the Phoenician and Canaanitish nations (n. 'Baal' *OED*). Phoenicians: native or inhabitants of Phoenicia, an ancient country consisting, in the

And in the forests of the west,
That cast their shadows o'er the breast
Of deep Ontario's lake, or wave
By many an Indian hunter's grave,
    Rise the green mounds of earlier time;[17]
The work of nations, who are dead,
Past like the leaves the winds have shed.

And still on Grecian hills and plains
Are roofless temples, priestless fanes,
All beautiful; as though decay
But touched them with a pencilled ray:
So autumn skies give colours bright
To forests which they come to blight.
The shrines are there, but Dorian flute[18]
And Theban lyre alike are mute.[19]
The shrines are there, but on that shore
The choral hymn is heard no more.
The fountain in the Delphian shade[20]
May spring: but she the enchanted maid
Who drank its vaporous magic, now
Sleeps with the nameless dead below.

When shall the penalty be paid,
That heaven upon thy land hath laid
For thy dark deeds? When will arise
The day-star in thine azure skies?
It shall shine out at length: it dawns
Already on thy sea washed isles,
    Where freedom, from her ancient heights,
Looks o'er the land she loved and smiles.
Oh! Phenix like, spring, upward spring,
With higher flight and stronger wing;
Bid all be wise, bid all be free,

---

first millennium BC, of a narrow strip of land on the coast of Syria (roughly corresponding to modern Lebanon) and including the cities of Tyre and Sidon (n. 'Phoenician' *OED*).

17 [Poet's Note: Both in North and South America mounds of earth have been discovered which are supposed to be the work of a people anterior to the present Indian race: there are many of these remains on the banks of lake Ontario, some of which contain fragments of pottery.— (*Penny Cyclopaedia*, Article, *America*.)] Hawkshaw's source is the entry for 'America' in *The Penny Cyclopaedia of the Society for the Diffusion of Useful Knowledge*, vol. 1 (1833), 429–48.

18 Dorian: of Doris or Doria, a division of ancient Greece (adj. 'Dorian' *OED*).

19 Theban: of or belonging to Thebes, capital of ancient Boeotia in Greece (adj. 'Theban' *OED*).

20 Delphian: of or relating to Delphi, a town of ancient Greece on the slope of Mount Parnassus (adj. 'Delphian' *OED*).

Who tread thy earth, who plough thy sea;
Thy chain is burst, oh! twine not now
The nightshade round a sceptic brow.

II.

I love the beautiful where'er
'Tis found, in ocean, earth, or air;
I love the beautiful in art,
And music's tones deep joy impart—
Awaking chords that quivering thrill,
When the sweet magic sounds are still;
I love the music of the woods,
Of waters and of solitudes;
The dash of waves along the shore,
Their rushing and their ceaseless roar;
The murmur low the streamlet makes
Creeping along through tangled brakes,
While bearing on with gentle force
The fallen rose leaf in its course:
I love the wild flower of the glen,
And in the crowded haunts of men
I can find beauty too; in faith
That conquers shame and smiles at death;
Or when affection mid the strife
And weariness and toil of life,
Smiles like a sun-beam on a scene
That else had utter darkness been:
I love the beautiful—and thou
Hath beauty, Greece; it lingers still
At sunset on each glorious hill,
It looks when rosy morning smiles
Across thy seas and hundred isles,
But most of all where laurel bowers
Grow by Athena's fallen towers;
City of temples! on whose hill
The Parthenon looks proudly still,
Spite of the marring touch of time,
And fiercer grasp of war and crime.
Enough is left to tell how great
She was,—enough to tell her fate!
Land of the myrtle and the rose,
Memory a beauty round thee throws;
The sage's tomb, the patriot's grave,
The purple seas, thy rocks that lave,
The past hath clothed with beauty, caught
From daring deed and noble thought;

And one charm more, the last, the best.
On which the christian heart can rest
Without a sigh; through thee first came
To Europe's shores a Saviour's name.[21]

III.

Breathe softly, 'tis the choral hymn
Sung while the evening shadows dim
Fall on the sleeping city—low
And soft as dew its numbers flow;
Binding all the listener's soul
With mystic but with strong control;
The past, with all its smiles and tears,
The future, with its shrouded years,
Are with us, and alone forgot
Are present scenes and present lot.
There may be mirth when music brings
Light hearts, young steps, around its strings,
In gilded hall or courtly bower,
But not when heard at evening's hour
And heard alone;—ah! then along
It floats like Peri's sorrowing song,[22]
Mourning, as eastern fables tell,
The paradise from which she fell.

It was a Grecian hymn that stole
   O'er sleeping Athens—years have gone
   Since the soft music of its tone
Died on the winds—the voice is hushed
And the lyre broken whence it gushed.
Ages of darkness and of gloom
Of Greece have made a living tomb,
Since that sweet music floated o'er
The city of the sunlit shore.

---

21 [Poet's Note: The first account we have of the preaching of the gospel in Europe is in the Acts XVI. chap., [sic] where St. Paul is said to have passed over from Troas, on the Asian shore, to Philippi, in Greece.] Acts 16:9–10: 'And a vision appeared to Paul in the night; there stood a man of Macedonia, and prayed him, saying, "Come over into Macedonia, and help us." And after he had seen the vision, immediately we endeavoured to go into Macedonia, assuredly gathering that the Lord had called us for to preach the gospel unto them.' Macedonia here refers to the region of north-eastern Greece.

22 Peri: from Persian and Iranian mythology, the Peri is descended from fallen angels who have been denied paradise until they have done penance. A possible source for Hawkshaw is Thomas Moore (1779–1852), who refers to the sad song of the Peri in his Oriental romance, *Lalla Rookh* (1817). 'The Story of Paradise and the Peri' is the second section of the work, which is made up of four narrative poems interconnected by prose.

Whence came that strain? 'twas from a shrine
That polished Athens called divine,
But on the unwilling ear it fell
Of one who bowed not to its spell,
Though he alone was kneeling there,
And in the attitude of prayer.
He yielded not to its control,
Yet felt that all its sweetness stole
Upon him; for his lofty mind
The gentle and the stern combined.
He had not learned with cynic's scorn
To view the arts which life adorn;
But yet one master feeling kept
Strong watch and ward and never slept.
It was no dream of earthly fame,
But pure the source from whence it came:
A spirit in him urging still
To combat with each form of ill,
Whether in pleasure's guise it came,
Or in the whirlwind or the flame.

Where the cool Cydnus rolls its stream[23]
From where the peaks of Taurus gleam,
Beneath Cilician skies that glow
Upon its towering heights of snow,
He drew his earliest breath, and gave
His memory to that crystal wave:
'Tis more than Greece's classic earth
To me, since, Paul, it gave thee birth.

He prayed that to the moral night
The Power that said, "Let there be light,"—
And light, like a transparent robe,
Was wrapped around the new made globe,—

---

23 [Poet's Note: The waters of the Cydnus, now called the Tersoors river, are extremely cold, caused by their combination with the melted snows from the ridges of mount Taurus. Alexander the Great nearly lost his life by injudiciously bathing in them. Tarsus, the birth-place of St. Paul, stands in a plain on the banks of the Cydnus; it is still a town of some importance, and was, anciently, one of the most important cities of Asia Minor; it had a school for the study of philosophy and the arts, according to Strabo, superior to those of Athens and Alexandria. St. Paul, speaking of his native place, says he was a "citizen of no mean city." The lofty tomb of Julian, the apostate, stood on the banks of the Cydnus.—(*See Penny Cyclopaedia, Art, Cilicia, and Gibbon,* Vol. IV. page 224.)] Hawkshaw's source is the entry for 'St Paul' in *The Penny Cyclopaedia of the Society for the Diffusion of Useful Knowledge*, vol. 17 (1840), 320–22. Hawkshaw uses St Paul's words from Acts 21:39: 'But Paul said, I am a man which am a Jew of Tarsus, a city in Cilicia, a citizen of no mean city: and, I beseech thee, suffer me to speak unto the people.' Edward Gibbon is also cited as a source.

Again might speak: around him rose
Sleeping in moonlight's soft repose
Temple, and portico, and shrine,
And columns in their stately line.
Like an Aeolian harp the breeze[24]
Played softly through the acacia trees
Its fitful music, and that tone
The midnight silence broke alone.
"God of my fathers! has thy hand
"Thus poured thy blessings o'er this land,
"And yet not one to bend the knee,
"Or breathe one earnest prayer to thee,"[25]
Burst from Paul's lips.—"Around me rise
"Art's wonders e'en beneath these skies,
"Where all is wonderful and bright,
"Save man; with him 'tis night, 'tis night;
"He slumbers in the moral tomb:
"Daystar of nations, pierce its gloom.
"Alone I am, like him of old
"Who stood on Carmel, calm yet bold
"Among the priests of Baal—alone
"God's champion 'mid his shrines o'erthrown![26]
"I stand amid a mingled crowd
"Of men and Gods, but solitude[27]
"With its still voices tells me more
"Of God, than doth this peopled shore.
"Man knows him not, and hath defaced
"Even the land his bounty graced,
"With idol altars! grot, and tree,[28]
"And river, have their deity;
"But what, my God, is given to thee?"

He ceased, yet sought no couch of rest—
Too deep the thoughts that filled his breast;
There, through the silent night, he stayed,
And by that altar mused and prayed,

---

24 Aeolian harp: a stringed instrument sounded by the wind. The name derives from Aeolus, Greek god of the winds.

25 Having cited St Paul's words in the footnote to this section, Hawkshaw now imaginatively recreates a narrative for St Paul, based on his arrival in Athens (Acts 17).

26 Reference to biblical account of the prophet Elijah's defeat of the priests of Baal at Mount Carmel (1 Kings 18).

27 [Poet's Note: It has been said that it was easier to find a god than a man in Athens.] This satirical saying is attributed to Roman writer Petronius (c. AD 27–66).

28 From Acts 17:16: 'Now while Paul waited for them at Athens, his spirit was stirred in him, when he saw the city wholly given to idolatry.'

Till o'er Hymettus' heights the sun[29]
Rose, and another day begun.

IV.

Morning broke, with its wonted smile,
O'er burnished fane and marble pile,
Gilding the Parthenon till shone
Its pillars of pentelic stone,[30]
Like glaciers on an alpine height;
While glittering in the morning light,
The helmet of the goddess queen,
As far as Sunium's cape was seen,[31]
A beacon to the mariner,
Guiding his home-bound bark from far:[32]
While bearing perfume on its wing
The breeze came o'er those bowers of spring;
Those scented bowers that voice and lute[33]
So seldom suffered to be mute:
For though beneath the Roman's sway,
Athens was still the vain, the gay.
The spirit that on Marathon
Looked o'er the field of freedom won,
Or pointed, with a sorrowing pride,
To where the Spartan patriots died,
Then slumbered: she hath woke again,
For Greece hath snapped the Turkish chain;
It could not be that she should sleep
For ever, by that blood-stained steep:
It could not be that never more
Her voice should wake that silent shore:
And while the clouds of slavery hung
Above her favourite land, she kept
Long vigils where her heroes slept;

---

29 Hymettus: Mount Hymettus, mountain range in Athens.
30 pentelic stone: of or relating to Mount Pentelicus, near Athens; designating the famous white marble quarried there (adj. 'Pentelic' *OED*).
31 Sunium's cape: the southernmost promontory of the Athenian area of Attica.
32 [Poet's Note: A bronze colossal statue of Minerva, the defender, the work of Phidias, stood near the Parthenon on the rock of the Acropolis. The spear and helmet of this figure were seen towering above the surrounding heights in approaching Athens by sea, as soon as Cape Sunium was rounded.—(*See* Pausanias, book I. 28.)] The source here is Pausanias (c. AD 110–180), Greek geographer and traveller from the second century. *The Description of Greece* is a ten-book work which begins with a volume on Attica, from which Hawkshaw draws. *The Description of Greece* was available in translation from the late 1700s: it is not clear which edition Hawkshaw is using.
33 [Poet's Note: Attica was famous for its aromatic plants.]

Sharing the eagles rocky height,
She mocked from thence the tyrant's might;
Albania's mountain children fired,
And Suli's softer sons inspired:[34]
Altars of liberty are ye
Dark mountains! last homes of the free!
And there, till brighter days returned,
The sacred lamp of freedom burned.

That morning woke to care and strife,
The pleasures, and the ills of life,
The crowds of Athens: some to weep
O'er languid hopes, or anguish deep;
And some, like insect o'er the flower,
To flutter through life's little hour;
Sons of to-day, mere passers by,
Light as the clouds on summer's sky,
That leave upon the trackless space
Of the wide heavens, nor sign, nor trace.
From the Italian shore there came,
Full many a youth of noble name,
To learn that tongue, whose gentle flow
Was like the sound of music borne
O'er waters when the winds are low.
And others came to gaze and learn,
From chiselled bust and sculptured urn;
Some loiter in the laurel bowers,
To braid their shining locks with flowers;
Or by Illissus' crystal stream,[35]
Wander to read the poet's dream;
Or wake the lute; while from the fanes
Soft voices answered back the strains.
From many climes were gathered there,
The gay, the gifted, and the fair;
But like the cistus flowers they wreathed,
They past; or like the songs they breathed,
Their very language is no more;
The songs that Grecian breezes bear,
Startle the echoes of her shore:
'Tis not the speech of Plato's tongue,[36]
Nor that which gifted Sappho sung.[37]

---

34 Suli: Suli, or Souli: area in Epris, the north-west region of Greece, bordering Albania.
35 Illissus: a river in Athens.
36 Plato: Greek philosopher (c. 429–347 BC).
37 Sappho: poetess of Lesbos (c. 610–570 BC).

Within the forum's spacious square
Gather all ranks, all ages there;
Beneath yon plane trees' sheltered walk
The sons of Epicurus talk;[38]
While with cold brow and scornful eye
The stoic views the passer by.[39]
Discussing questions wrapped in shade,
And by their doubts still darker made,
A group assembled: "Why" said one,
Who from his fellows lived alone,
"Why will ye smile when all around
"Is but one vast sepulchral mound;
"All that we have is for the grave,
"Nor love, nor hope, nor prayer, can save.
"And when a few short years are past
"Death carries all with murky blast
"To darker shores:" "Nay, rather say,"
Another answered, "that the day
"That hides the body from the light
"Quenches the soul in starless night;
"'Tis but a transient spark that dies
"With the last look on these bright skies;
"And they are bright, despite the men
   "Who in the sun can darkness find,
"Or say the shining stars are dim,
   "When 'tis themselves are blind;
"Men die, and unto native clay
"Nations and kindreds pass away;
"But there arise to fill their place
"Another, and as joyful, race:
"Weep'st thou because the winter's blast
   "Hath stripped the forest? Wait awhile,
"And the returning spring shall wake
   "Its blossoms with her smile:
"I pluck them smiling while I may,
"And think not of the coming day:
"I wreathe them while in beauty's bloom,—
"For thee, they only deck a tomb;
"Live for the present hour, and leave

---

38 Epicurus: Greek philosopher (c. 341–270 BC). Founder of the school of philosophy called Epicureanism, which advocated the living of a simple life and the avoidance of physical pain (*aponia*). Epicureans considered pleasure as the highest good, and worked to achieve a state of tranquillity (*ataraxia*) and freedom from fear.

39 The stoic: one of the stoic school of Greek philosophy characterised by the austerity of its ethical doctrines. One who practises repression of emotion, indifference to pleasure or pain, and patient endurance (n. 'stoic' OED).

"The future for itself to grieve."
But mingling with that crowd was one,
In thought, in feeling, all alone;
Young, yet upon his youthful face[40]
Deep thought had left its earnest trace:
He leaned beside a funeral urn;
"And will," said he, "no spring return
"To wake my spirit from its sleep?
"Will death his watch for ever keep?
"Plato, were all thy dreams in vain?
"Bound in his adamantine chain,
"Slumbers thy spirit? which so high
"Soared even while mortality
"Fettered its wing. Oh for a voice
　"To break the silence of the tomb!
"Or for one ray of light to break
　"The shrouded future's gloom!"
"'Tis broken!" said a stranger's voice,
　"Triumphant shall the spirit rise

---

40 [Poet's Note: In introducing Dionysius here, as young, I would observe that I have not confined myself to his traditional history, but simply to the scriptural account that he was converted to Christianity by hearing St. Paul at Athens.] Hawkshaw makes a distinction here between the 'traditional history' of Dionysius, and the 'scriptural account' of his conversion to Christianity in Acts 17:34: 'Howbeit certain men clave unto him and believed: among the which was Dionysius the Areopagite, and a woman named Damaris, and others with them.'

Although this is the only mention of Dionysius the Areopagite in the New Testament, his name had been part of Christian theology since the Middle Ages. Over time, the name 'Dionysius the Areopagite' had become associated with separate but not entirely unconnected identities. Early in the sixth century, the scriptural account of the conversion of Dionysius by St Paul became connected with the *Corpus Areopagiticum*: a collection of writing that had a profound influence on Christian theology. Later tradition developed the history of Dionysius by claiming him as not only the first Bishop of Athens, but as apostle to the Gauls, the first Bishop of Paris later canonised as the Patron Saint of France. Such claims for Dionysius had their early dissenters, as doubts were raised as to the date of the *Corpus Areopagiticum* and therefore the validity of claiming the Dionysius the Areopagite of the scriptures as their author. The complex tradition of Dionysius only began to be unravelled in the twelfth century by the French philosopher and theologian, Pierre Abélard (1079–1142). His suggestion that, far from dating from the first century, the *Corpus Areopagiticum* was written at the end of the fifth or beginning of the sixth century threw into doubt theories which cited the scriptural Dionysius as the originator of the work. Despite evidence to suggest that the ten letters and four treatises of the *Corpus Areopagiticum* were written according to the rhetorical practice known as *declamatio* (in which a pseudonymous name from the scriptures is adopted in order to suggest a context or perspective), a complex history of Dionysius had been established that was subject to conjecture well into the nineteenth century. In selecting Dionysius as the subject of her poem, Hawkshaw enters into dialogue with historical and theological narratives of Dionysius the Areopagite, using the scriptural account as the basis for her own imaginative reconstruction of his spiritual journey towards the Christian faith.

"Beyond these perishable skies,
"For ever to rejoice!
"The dying struggle, parting sigh,
"Its heralds to eternity!
"Nor shall the body in her cold
"Embrace, the earth for ever hold.
"Ages may pass, yet it shall wake,
 "Conqueror o'er death, the grave, and hell!
"Laid down in weakness, raised in power,
 "Amid celestial light to dwell
 "In bliss ineffable!"
So spake the Apostle: round him stand
The learned of that learned land;
But armed by truth, he sees, nor hears,
The idler's laugh, the cynic's sneers:
Wrapt by his lofty theme on high,
He reasons for eternity.
No faltering told of inward doubt;
 But deep, and passionate, and strong,
Flowed on the tide of eloquence
 In rapid words along.

V.

There is no ruin old and grey,
Telling of glories passed away;
A few rude moss-clad stones, decay
And warfare's rage have left; yet there
Though lone, and desolate, and bare,
The rugged hill uprears its head,
The historic muse its light hath shed;
And in its loneliness sublime
That rock still towers 'mid wrecks of time:
For oft in Athens' early days,
 Her purest court assembled there,
Nor did the oppressed breathe in vain
 For justice an unheeded prayer.
Beneath a rustic roof they sate,
In moral dignity, not state;
Art was not summoned to adorn
Their lowly seats of simple stone.
Yet with no flattery on their tongue
Their presence awed a rabble throng;
And made the guarded despot feel
Power needed not his bars of steel.
And there, too, in degenerate times,
 When the high spirit of the past

A parting shadow only cast
On the bright land that gave her birth,
Paul stood, before that ancient court
By those who lately heard him brought,
And thus he spoke:—

                "Athenians, hear;
"I know the unknown God ye fear.
"Ye might have spelt his wonderous name
"From earth and ocean's mighty frame.
"Ye might have learned his skill and power
"From sun, from sky, from plant, from flower:
"The meanest thing which crawls, doth grace
"Well its befitting time and place.

"I know from chance ye say they came;
"But see ye now from chance the same?
"See ye from random atoms whirled
"In giddy dances, rise a world;
"As some of those among your wise,
"Thought that this earth we tread might rise?
"Could chaos bid from out its breast
"This flower arise, in beauty dressed?
"Ah! see ye not ye need a God,
"Each spring to deck the verdant sod;
"A never ceasing energy,
"To people earth, and sky, and sea,
"Renewing what disease and death,
"Have blighted with their withering breath?

"Ye might have learned that matter lives
"And moves, when mind the bidding gives,
"And then alone; for when the soul
"Escapes at death from its control,
"Inert and hastening to decay
"The body lies a lump of clay.
"This much from nature ye might learn,—
    "That, through her mighty frame, a power
    "Is working ceaseless every hour!
"But answer none can she return
"From tuneful earth, or sounding wave;
"Is there a land beyond the grave?
"And will offended justice save?
"Ask this! and through the silent sky,
"Breaks no glad message of reply.
"The sages, on whose dust ye tread,

"Who held high converse with the dead,
"Died doubting, whether they should find
"That brightest vision of their mind—
"That far beyond the darkening west
"There lay some island of the blest,
"Where they, immortal, good, and pure,
"In bliss and glory should endure.
"It was a thought of heavenly birth
"That crossed their minds, not born of earth;
"A lingering record of that truth
"Revealed when time was in his youth,
"And but a single being trod
"This earth, fresh from the hands of God!

"I hear ye say, 'Why idly tell
"The truth our sages knew too well,
"That darkness dwells upon the tomb,
"And faint the light that gilds the gloom?'
"Because at length have rolled away
"The shadowing clouds that o'er it lay:
"Time shall not ever run his round;
"A trumpet through the heavens shall sound;
"Like a burnt scroll shall pass the skies!
"And then the slumbering dead shall rise!
"Mock ye the truth? He were no God
"If every footstep that he trod,
"And every portion of his plan
"Your mind could grasp, your eye could scan.
"Look round, it is a mystery all,
"From ocean's ceaseless rise and fall
"To this poor blade of grass. What powers
"Reside in sunbeams and in showers
"From a mean seed to waken flowers?
"No greater wonder in the truth,
"That, wakening with immortal youth,
"My mortal body shall arise,
"Than in me, or around me, lies.

"Thou liv'st, thine active limbs obey
"Thy will, and at its bidding play.
"But how the secret influence works,
   "And how on matter acts the mind,
"Thou know'st as little, as of light
   "Can know the blind.
"Only believe what thou canst see,—
"That only truth that's clear to thee.

"Why then, thy truth must be a lie
"To him who cannot soar so high.

"Is God thus great? It is not, then,
"In temples built by mortal men,
"He dwells, whom eye hath never seen
"Without a shadowing cloud between.
"Think not the uncreated One
"Who dwells in light, unseen, alone,
"Your hands can shape in gold or stone!
"The times of pagan night are past,
"Celestial day hath dawned at last:
"And Time, at length, shall fold his wings;
   "Yon ocean's restless waves be still;
"Like blasted figs the stars shall fall;
   "The burning sun grow pale and chill.
"Then! the dark slumbers of the dead
"Shall wake at Time's retreating tread!
"And all before their judge shall come,
"To hear their doom! their righteous doom!"

VI.

The voice hath ceased; the crowd is gone;
But he still lingers there alone,
Who asked for one celestial ray
To light the tomb. Around him lay
City and island, rock and flood.
Beneath, that Doric temple stood,[41]
Which Time, relenting of his rage,
Bequeathed to many a distant age:—
Temple of Theseus! not a bone[42]
Remains of those who hewed thy stone;
Yet fresh as from the sculptor's hand
Thy stately line of pillars stand.
The young Athenian bent his gaze
Down on that shrine of other days,—
"Yes!" he exclaimed, "if all of man
"Earth bounds, he hath a meaner span
"Than his own works;—the marble bust
"Lives when the sculptor's hand is dust."
Silent he stood absorbed in thought.
Long had his spirit vainly sought

---

41 Doric: the name of one of the three Grecian orders (Doric, Ionic, Corinthian), of which it is the oldest, strongest and simplest (adj. 'Doric' *OED*).
42 Temple of Theseus: temple erected for Theseus, mythical founder king of Athens.

For peace; peace with itself and heaven.
From sages' and from nature's voice
He asked reply, yet none was given.
But the new faith the apostle taught
Contained each truth his mind had sought.
Yet can he own such truth, proclaimed
By one whom only scorn had named?
Thoughts too of her he loved found way,
Mid the mixed musings of that day.[43]

"It cannot be," at length he said,
As down he went with hasty tread;
"Perish the creed that would divide
"Thy fate and mine, my destined bride.
"And yet, these thoughts of coming doom,
"Hang on my spirit like the gloom
"Of Erebus: if truth he told[44]
"'Twas glorious, for away it rolled
"The shadows of eternity,
"And lighted up its shoreless sea!"

Onward he went, nor paused, till where,
Embowered amid its gardens fair,
A stoic's mansion stood: the home
   Of his betrothed: a mingled sound
Of a sweet voice and silver lyre,
   Was floating round.
Sad was the song: 'tis ever so
   With those who love: a shadow lies
On the young spirit—not of woe,
   But made of gentlest sympathies:
The heart with all things deep allying,
And far from scenes of pleasure flying.
But there were two within those bowers,
Both beautiful as different flowers:
Myra, the loved one, light and gay,
Lovely as sunbeam's prismed ray;
O'er her fair neck her black hair spread
In ringlets from her graceful head;

---

43 Up to this point the poem has been based on the scriptural account of St Paul's ministry in Athens (Acts 17:16–34); Hawkshaw recreates St Paul's meditations on the idolatry of the city and charts the challenge to Christian faith presented by Stoic and Epicurean philosophers. The poem's focus now shifts to Hawkshaw's own story of Dionysius's conversion to Christianity.

44 Erebus: the proper name of a dark region between Earth and Hades, and as such a place of blackness and gloom.

Pale pearls of ocean lent their aid
And bound her arms with costly braid,
While glittered round her head a band
Of jewels sought in many a land.

A thoughtful brow, Corinna, thine,
On which no glittering circlets shine.
Thine was such loveliness as lies
In the mild light of evening skies;
Such beauty as awakens thought,
A beauty from expression caught.
Left orphan in her early years,
Before the loss could wake her tears,
To share the lovely Myra's home,
The fair and gentle child had come;
And years of happiness had flown,
And loved and loving they had grown.

Dionysius came—Corinna gone,
With Myra he is left alone;
Young as she was, unused to scan
The deeper workings of the man,
She saw some secret filled his breast
Or hidden care his heart oppressed.
Oh love! a look, a word, a sigh
Can wake thy fears unconciously.[45]
Both sunk in silent reverie,
So deep, that from a distant bower,
   They heard Corinna's voice—her song
Seemed to have syllabled in words
   The thoughts which he had buried long:
He listened, and once more the strain
In soft clear numbers rose again.

"Oh! beautiful art thou, luxuriant earth,
   "With thy o'er-arching heavens and circling seas,
"And yet no gladsome dreams, no thoughts of mirth,
   "Wake in my heart thy many melodies;
"For as we gaze in sadness on a face
"We love, but have to leave, 'tis thus thy charms I trace.

---

45 unconsciously: transcribed from original.

For peace; peace with itself and heaven.
From sages' and from nature's voice
He asked reply, yet none was given.
But the new faith the apostle taught
Contained each truth his mind had sought.
Yet can he own such truth, proclaimed
By one whom only scorn had named?
Thoughts too of her he loved found way,
Mid the mixed musings of that day.[43]

"It cannot be," at length he said,
As down he went with hasty tread;
"Perish the creed that would divide
"Thy fate and mine, my destined bride.
"And yet, these thoughts of coming doom,
"Hang on my spirit like the gloom
"Of Erebus: if truth he told[44]
"'Twas glorious, for away it rolled
"The shadows of eternity,
"And lighted up its shoreless sea!"

Onward he went, nor paused, till where,
Embowered amid its gardens fair,
A stoic's mansion stood: the home
   Of his betrothed: a mingled sound
Of a sweet voice and silver lyre,
   Was floating round.
Sad was the song: 'tis ever so
   With those who love: a shadow lies
On the young spirit—not of woe,
   But made of gentlest sympathies:
The heart with all things deep allying,
And far from scenes of pleasure flying.
But there were two within those bowers,
Both beautiful as different flowers:
Myra, the loved one, light and gay,
Lovely as sunbeam's prismed ray;
O'er her fair neck her black hair spread
In ringlets from her graceful head;

---

43 Up to this point the poem has been based on the scriptural account of St Paul's ministry in Athens (Acts 17:16–34); Hawkshaw recreates St Paul's meditations on the idolatry of the city and charts the challenge to Christian faith presented by Stoic and Epicurean philosophers. The poem's focus now shifts to Hawkshaw's own story of Dionysius's conversion to Christianity.

44 Erebus: the proper name of a dark region between Earth and Hades, and as such a place of blackness and gloom.

Pale pearls of ocean lent their aid
And bound her arms with costly braid,
While glittered round her head a band
Of jewels sought in many a land.

A thoughtful brow, Corinna, thine,
On which no glittering circlets shine.
Thine was such loveliness as lies
In the mild light of evening skies;
Such beauty as awakens thought,
A beauty from expression caught.
Left orphan in her early years,
Before the loss could wake her tears,
To share the lovely Myra's home,
The fair and gentle child had come;
And years of happiness had flown,
And loved and loving they had grown.

Dionysius came—Corinna gone,
With Myra he is left alone;
Young as she was, unused to scan
The deeper workings of the man,
She saw some secret filled his breast
Or hidden care his heart oppressed.
Oh love! a look, a word, a sigh
Can wake thy fears unconciously.[45]
Both sunk in silent reverie,
So deep, that from a distant bower,
    They heard Corinna's voice—her song
Seemed to have syllabled in words
    The thoughts which he had buried long:
He listened, and once more the strain
In soft clear numbers rose again.

"Oh! beautiful art thou, luxuriant earth,
    "With thy o'er-arching heavens and circling seas,
"And yet no gladsome dreams, no thoughts of mirth,
    "Wake in my heart thy many melodies;
"For as we gaze in sadness on a face
"We love, but have to leave, 'tis thus thy charms I trace.

---

45 unconsciously: transcribed from original.

"Shall I then perish and in silence lie
    "Forgetting and forgotten. Will no sound
"Of childhood's merry laugh, nor friendship's sigh,
    "Nor music's tones break through the grave's profound?
"Why has the wish for immortality,
"E'er crossed the heart if we no more must be?"

Slowly to silence died the strain,
But not the thoughts it woke:—a chain
Is life made up of things too small
To notice as they pass, yet all
Are linked: perhaps in happier hours
Those words, like perfume from the flowers,
Had passed unheeded; now they broke
The spell which bound him, and he spoke:
"'Tis so; we do not fear to die,
"But in forgetfulness to lie.
"Who, who but shrinks from that? The sire
"Hopes to live in his son—the lyre,
"The minstrel thinks, shall breathe his name
"To distant ages—for this fame
"Our heroes died upon yon plains,—
"Our fathers reared those marble fanes.
    "I have but just begun to live,
"If it is life to know, and feel,
    "The powers within me; yet how soon
"Death on my steps will steal.
    "If there be life beyond the tomb
"The mystery of my being's solved;
    "The manhood of the soul is there,
"And good from evil is evolved,
    "And from confusion order fair.
"But let us seek Corinna now."
    They found her bending o'er her lyre,
More gloom than wont was on her brow,—
    Her fingers trembling on the wire;
And there, while round them closed the flowers,
He told what never Grecian bowers
    Had heard before—in silence both
The lovely listeners heard—but one
    Listened to truth, the other's ear
Heard but that voice she loved alone,
Nor record, more than music's tone,
When she and Dionysius part,
Left those high themes on Myra's heart.

VII.

Time passed. A still and starry night
Looked with its countless eyes of light
Upon the world: beneath that sky
Dionysius wandered silently.
Upon his couch he could not rest,
For many cares his heart opprest.
He felt the Christian faith was true;
To own that faith was to undo
The strongest ties that bind to life,
And his heart quivered with the strife.
For Myra's father was of those
Who were the Christian's bitterest foes;
A stoic cold, and proud, and stern,
Whom neither prayers nor fears could turn.
Amid the dwellings of the dead
The Athenian's silent footsteps tread;
A spirit of repose profound
Seemed to have shed its influence round,
Where, pale beneath the moonlight, shone
The funeral urns of Parian stone,[46]
Round which affection's hand had spread
Sweet flowers, to wither o'er the dead.
Around, above, the midnight breeze
Sighed through the darkening cypress trees;—
Ah! on the heart, in sorrow's hour,
All nature hath a saddening power;
Her sweetest harp hath jarring strings
From which the heart no music brings,
But only discord.—
     On his ear
There came a voice, soft, low, but clear.
He started at the well known tone;
And there, beside a funeral stone,
Like willow bending to the gale,
Corinna knelt, with forehead pale.
Back from her face her veil was flung,
And round her slender form it hung.
If from each narrow resting place,
Had looked a dim and shadowy face,
Not Dionysius more amazed
Upon the solemn scene had gazed.
Before her, with his hands outspread

---

46 Parian stone: of or relating to Paros; designating the fine white marble, prized in antiquity by sculptors, for which the island was renowned (adj. 'Parian' *OED*).

Above Corinna's bended head
The apostle stood: he saw him last
As from the hill of Mars he past;
But there was something sweeter now
Upon his careworn furrowed brow;
For in that maiden kneeling there
He saw an answer to his prayer.
"In the Almighty Father's name,
"In his who as a Saviour came,
"In his the Spirit's, one in three!
"The all pervading Deity!
"I do baptize thee:" then was shed
The water on her youthful head.
He prayed; and with low solemn tone
Spake thus, as at the Eternal's throne:
"It seems as if from off my heart,
"Like shadows that in life depart
"Fade now the things of earth; forgot
"Like trifles that concern it not;
"And all the joys and charms of life
"And death, with its appointed strife,
"Vanish into a brighter sky
"That reaches to eternity.
"Yet daughter, know to die is gain,
"But not to live on earth is vain.
"Wait calmly till the summons given
"Shall bid thee rise to God, to heaven.
"Use, not dispise, the gifts of life,[47]
"Faint not amid its toils and strife.

"Peace rest upon thee! Now I go
"To labour 'midst this world of woe.
"Thou, like a lamb upon the wild,
"Must still be left, poor orphan child;—
"But then if storms shall here assail thee,
"The help of God will never fail thee.
"Time is a shadow, fast 'tis fleeting!
"Eternal dawn, thee, me, is greeting."
She rose in silence; meekly clasped
His aged hand in hers, and passed.

VIII.

'Tis evening—that still quiet hour
Which falls with soft but mystic power

---

47 despise: transcribed from original.

On human hearts—when passions cease
Their tumult and subside to peace;
When from the deep and strong control
Of sense escapes the wearied soul,
And looks within herself; and none
For converse asks, but fain alone
To talk unto herself would be,
And muse in thought unchecked and free.
Then with a slow and solemn pace
We walk to look on nature's face,
While on the lagging breezes come
The evening insects' drowsy hum;
And if, by chance, the sound of horn,
Or sprightlier strain be on it borne,
The listener starts disturbed, and fain
Would shrink into himself again.
Then not so much we strive to pry
Into a dim futurity,
Or turn with sad and wistful gaze
Back on the scenes of other days;
Nor in the things around doth find
Aught that she loves, the pensive mind;
But chiefly to herself she turns
And with herself communes and learns.

Musing alone, at that still hour,
Corinna sate within her bower,
When Dionysius entered. "Start
"Not maiden at what I impart;—
"With courage far beyond thy years,
"Conferring not with woman's fears;—
"At midnight, by the lonely dead,
"I heard thee with no voice of dread
"Confess the Christian faith. I, too,
"Believe the Christian creed is true.
"Nor sceptic doubts, nor coward fears,
"Have made me shrink, but Myra's tears.
"Were mine alone the destiny
"Of suffering, it would lighter be;
"Or had she but that purer faith
"That triumphs over griefs and death,
"I could have kissed her brow in peace—
    "Peace when compared to what I feel—
"'Twould be but parting, till should cease
"These throbbing pulses; and the tomb
"Should re-unite our severed doom;—

"As two fair barks together starting,
"But on life's stormy ocean parting,
   "Yet anchoring side by side at last;
"Sailing apart on life's dark sea,
"But meeting in eternity.

"Hard hath the struggle been—for days
"Have seemed as years—but now delays
"Are criminal; and ere yon sun
"Shall have his morrow's course begun,
"I am a Christian. Now, farewell!
"I sought thee that thou mightest tell
"To Myra that I come not—say
"Not where I go; the coming day
"I will myself reveal the cause,
"But now, I cannot. Fare thee well;
"I go to where the Christians dwell."

IX.

How sweetly wakes the earth from rest,
As if it held no aching breast;
Bright clouds are on the mountain's crest,
And trembling shadows on the plain,
And whispering winds upon the main.
A voice of hope, a sound of mirth,
Go forth upon the peopled earth,
Arousing man to toil again,
Yet kindly, with a joyous strain.
For every feeling hath its hour,
Wherein, with deep unwonted power,
It presses on the heart—each one,
Too, hath its place—amid the aisles
In the dim light of Gothic piles,
Or in the homes of races gone
Where the sad night wind sighs and swells,
That sister of the past, pale memory, dwells.
Hope hath the field of waving grain,
The cottage home, the cultured plain;
And on the lofty mountain's breast,
With shadowy sides and sunny crest,
Wake feelings deep, though scarce defined,
Feelings that elevate the mind.
Although there may an awe o'erspread
The stranger's heart, when o'er his head
Hang the dark beetling rocks,—'tis not

Such awe as haunts the lonely spot,
Where thick and tall the forest trees
Bow not their heads to passing breeze;
Where all below, 'mid grass and weed,
The toad and stealthy serpent breed,
And where the gladdening light of day
Ne'er reaches to the lonely way,
Nor sunbeams pierce, nor branches play.
E'en common minds, that seldom look
In nature's vast and varied book,
Can feel the different influence made
By alpine steeps, or forest shade.
And thus the Druids' altar stood,
Deep in some unfrequented wood,
Or on the wild and dreary plain;
Fear bound them in her slavish chain,
And fear alone the scene inspired:
But loftier thoughts the Persian fired,—
On high his shrine of flame he piled,
Dark superstition's purest child.
Fair Greece! not bloody rites were thine,
No human victim to thy shrine
Was bound in sad despair,—thy fanes
Arose in beauty on thy plains,
Or mid the light and graceful grove
Where shades and sunbeams were inwove.
In symbolled forms the Egyptian shrined
The workings of a deeper mind;—
Greece had the beautiful—the dim
And mystic thou, oh! Mizraim.

There is such lone, but lovely spot,
That busy man hath now forgot:—
But morning, when she wakes in smiles,
O'er Grecian seas and Ægean isles,
Forgets it not, but gives a beam
To light its unremembered stream,
And sends her winds with gentle tones
Throughout its cavern's fretted stones.
Save here and there a sculptured stone,
With moss and ivy overgrown,
Nature again hath claimed her own
From man—for once these silent bowers
He made the scene of mystic powers—
And near them shrine and altar stood
Embowered within an ancient wood;
Where anxious Myra sought to know

"As two fair barks together starting,
"But on life's stormy ocean parting,
    "Yet anchoring side by side at last;
"Sailing apart on life's dark sea,
"But meeting in eternity.

"Hard hath the struggle been—for days
"Have seemed as years—but now delays
"Are criminal; and ere yon sun
"Shall have his morrow's course begun,
"I am a Christian. Now, farewell!
"I sought thee that thou mightest tell
"To Myra that I come not—say
"Not where I go; the coming day
"I will myself reveal the cause,
"But now, I cannot. Fare thee well;
"I go to where the Christians dwell."

IX.

How sweetly wakes the earth from rest,
As if it held no aching breast;
Bright clouds are on the mountain's crest,
And trembling shadows on the plain,
And whispering winds upon the main.
A voice of hope, a sound of mirth,
Go forth upon the peopled earth,
Arousing man to toil again,
Yet kindly, with a joyous strain.
For every feeling hath its hour,
Wherein, with deep unwonted power,
It presses on the heart—each one,
Too, hath its place—amid the aisles
In the dim light of Gothic piles,
Or in the homes of races gone
Where the sad night wind sighs and swells,
That sister of the past, pale memory, dwells.
Hope hath the field of waving grain,
The cottage home, the cultured plain;
And on the lofty mountain's breast,
With shadowy sides and sunny crest,
Wake feelings deep, though scarce defined,
Feelings that elevate the mind.
Although there may an awe o'erspread
The stranger's heart, when o'er his head
Hang the dark beetling rocks,—'tis not

Such awe as haunts the lonely spot,
Where thick and tall the forest trees
Bow not their heads to passing breeze;
Where all below, 'mid grass and weed,
The toad and stealthy serpent breed,
And where the gladdening light of day
Ne'er reaches to the lonely way,
Nor sunbeams pierce, nor branches play.
E'en common minds, that seldom look
In nature's vast and varied book,
Can feel the different influence made
By alpine steeps, or forest shade.
And thus the Druids' altar stood,
Deep in some unfrequented wood,
Or on the wild and dreary plain;
Fear bound them in her slavish chain,
And fear alone the scene inspired:
But loftier thoughts the Persian fired,—
On high his shrine of flame he piled,
Dark superstition's purest child.
Fair Greece! not bloody rites were thine,
No human victim to thy shrine
Was bound in sad despair,—thy fanes
Arose in beauty on thy plains,
Or mid the light and graceful grove
Where shades and sunbeams were inwove.
In symbolled forms the Egyptian shrined
The workings of a deeper mind;—
Greece had the beautiful—the dim
And mystic thou, oh! Mizraim.

There is such lone, but lovely spot,
That busy man hath now forgot:—
But morning, when she wakes in smiles,
O'er Grecian seas and Ægean isles,
Forgets it not, but gives a beam
To light its unremembered stream,
And sends her winds with gentle tones
Throughout its cavern's fretted stones.
Save here and there a sculptured stone,
With moss and ivy overgrown,
Nature again hath claimed her own
From man—for once these silent bowers
He made the scene of mystic powers—
And near them shrine and altar stood
Embowered within an ancient wood;
Where anxious Myra sought to know

What coming years had to bestow.
A veil concealed her lovely face,
On which sad tears had left their trace;
While she upon the altar placed
A crystal vase with gems enchased.
"I come," she said, "to seek your aid,
"Ye Dryads of this sacred shade;
"And thou, dread power, whate'er thou art,[48]
"That canst to winds and streams impart
"The voices of futurity,
"Tell what my coming fate may be.
"Olympian gods, and ye who dwell
"With him who rules the world of hell;
"And ye who tread with silver feet
"On ocean's breast, whose deep retreat
"Beneath the ever sounding wave
"No mortal eye hath seen,—Oh! save,
"Nor blast with all consuming fire,
"Him who denies you, in your ire.
"Accept this vase, as from his hand,
"Enriched with gems from many a land;
"And I, on each returning year,
"Will duly at this shrine appear,
"With costlier gifts, if o'er his head
"Ye still the sacred Ægis spread.[49]

"But other griefs oppress my heart
"Than that in which he bears a part.
"The snake beneath the rose may bask;
"And if, beneath fair friendship's mask,
"Seeming the loving and the true,
"There lurks deceit—in her who grew
"In the same home—avenging powers,
"To punish, and to judge, be yours."

'Neath a small cavern, overhung
With climbing flowers, a fountain sprung;
And by it, seated on a stone,

---

48 [Poet's Note: The answers of some of the oracles were obtained by listening to the sound of the wind as it passed through the sacred groves, or from the murmuring of running waters.—(*Travels of Anacharsis, the younger. Abbé Barthélemy.*)] Hawkshaw's source is *The Travels of Anacharsis the Younger in Greece* (1788), a fictional travel journal written by the French classical scholar Jean-Jacques Barthélemy (1716–95). Printed in translation over several editions. It is not certain which edition Hawkshaw uses as her source.

49 Aegis: from classical mythology, a shield, piece of defensive armour, or garment carried or worn by Zeus (Jupiter) or Athene (Minerva) (n. 'Aegis' *OED*).

A fair young priestess sate alone;
Pale was her brow, the lines of thought,
Or passion, there had traces wrought.
Her eye was bright with wandering fire,
Wild as the music from her lyre,
Amongst whose strings her fingers strayed,
And sad uncertain measures played.
With mind half wrecked, deceived, betrayed,
By one she loved, that hapless maid
Came wandering to the sacred shade;
From wily priests a home receiving,
Living deceived and deceiving.
The tool of more designing minds,
She, in the streams and sighing winds,
Fancied she heard sweet voices speak,
And words of mystic import break.
Beside her Myra knelt and told
   Her griefs and questions—while the tears
Stole from her downcast eyes—the tale
   Wakened the memory of past years
In the young Sybil's heart, who raised
Her eyes, and long on Myra gazed:
But soon, like wandering lights that gleam
A moment o'er a turbid stream,
That transient ray of mind departed,
And from her seat she wildly started;
And with her lyre uplifted, strung,
With rapid hand, its chords, and sung:—

"Back from my sight the present hold;
"Scenes of futurity unfold;
"Voices that never yet have spoken,
"Words that upon no ear have broken,
"Come, come,"—then o'er the fountain bent
She sadly chanted as she leant—
"I see, upon thy crystal face,
"The sunbeam hath not left a trace
"That glittered there at dawn of day;
"Thus, hopes of mortals pass away.

"Spirit of the wind, though near thee,
"Mortal maiden need not fear thee,
"Ever changing as thou art;
"For she trusts a fickler heart.
"Thou hast stolen the sweets away,
"In the rose's bud that lay;

"Thou hast swept across the lyre,
"Hushed its music, snapt its wire;
"Canst thou carry back again
"Those sweets or that forgotten strain?
"Then the heart, once more, may cherish
"Hopes that love hath made to perish.

"Young and beautiful is she,
"Fountain Nymph, who asks of thee
"What her future fate may be:
"I hear thee in these tones replying,
"Sad as Sappho's song when dying;
"And her scenes of coming life,
"With their hopes, and fears, and strife,
"One by one arise before me;
"Dim and shadowy they restore me
"By-gone years: through yon blue sky
"I've seen our twin stars wander by;
"I watched them rise without a cloud;
"I saw them set behind a shroud
"Of cold dark vapours: is her fate,
"Then, like to one so desolate?

"The past and future are our all
"Of life—as leaves unnoticed fall,
"So drop the present hours—the past
"Had hopes and joys that did not last;
"The future, too, shall have its dream,
"But fainter, darker, it shall seem.
"Once, with a mortal race I moved,
"And, as a mortal, thought and loved;
"But now, 'mid coming years, I tread,
"As 'mid the living stand the dead.
"But listen! think ye 'twas the wind?
"A deeper voice it left behind.
"Look! see ye but the fountain play?
"I see the deeds of many a day
"Pictured upon its dancing spray;
"I heard that voice say, 'Trust not thou
"To friendship's faith, to lover's vow;
"Both soon will fail thee, as that spray
"Upon the water dies away.'

"I see a low unhonoured tomb
"Appear through clouds of coming doom,
"That gather round their paths who scorn

"The altars of our gods—forlorn,
"From Jove's immortal wrath, they tread[50]
"The dreary regions of the dead.

"The dark sea hath its wrecks—how deep
"The gold and gems of navies sleep.
"Man, with long years of care and toil,
"Uproots them from their native soil;
"But, in an hour, its wrathful waves
"Give them to strew its silent caves.
"Earth hath her wrecks—in lonely halls
"The lizard creeps; on mouldering walls
"The ivy twines; the wild wind sings
"Its requiem o'er the place of kings.

"But time hath sadder wrecks; the truth,
"The hope, the trust, the love of youth;
"Weep for them as they fade; yet tears
"Bring not again departed years.
"But when, upon thy youthful brow,
"The cloud is gathering, when the glow
"Is fading from thy rosy cheek,
"These sacred shades and fountains seek,
"And read the sealed book of fate
"For others, though it be too late
"To change thine own. Away! away!
"'Tis now but the soft wind at play
"Amongst the leaves—the pictures fade
"Upon the fount. Go, Grecian maid!"
The skies with sunset splendour burned
As Myra to her home returned.

Sunset,—that radiant hour which lies
Upon the verge of darkening skies
Like hope by disappointment; life
Upon death's threshold. 'Tis an hour
Of potent, but of varied power;
Not joyous, as the wakening light;
Not solemn, as the starry night;
Not calm as twilight; but of these
Made up, as are our destinies:
Then hope and memory draw, by turn,
Their records from the heart's deep urn.

---

50 Jove: poetical equivalent of Jupiter, name of the highest deity of the ancient Romans (n.'Jove' *OED*).

And thus did Myra's heart that night
With sadness sink, with hope grow bright;
Drawing from the sighing air
Motives for a deep despair;
Building up fairy bowers of ease
On sunbeams trembling o'er the seas;
Ah long! ah long! such hearts will cling,
With hope, to the most hopeless thing.

X.

The wave still laves the Ægean shore,
But the lyre echoes back no more
The music that its waters make;
And still, o'er Grecian mountains break
As bright a sun as ever shone
When freedom called the land her own.
And live there none to hail those beams
As omen of their better dreams;
None who, while seeing sky and sun,
Remember what their sires have done.
Snapt is the chord, and souls of fire
Live not, when dust bestrews the lyre:
Thy shores are silent, tuneful Greece:
Who, who, shall bid the silence cease?

'Twas noontide; on the gorgeous room
A cloud was settled, of perfume;
For not a breath of wind was there,
The rich and balmy scents to bear;—
When a luxurious indolence
Steeps every thought and every sense,
And the mind loves alone to brood
In the voluptuous solitude
Of half closed rooms, with not a sound,
Save water falling to the ground
From marble fountain, whose dull tone
Lulls as the ceaseless shower is thrown.
Then half awake, and half asleep,
The drowsy senses pastime keep.
Visions, like eastern fables, rise
And float before the charmed eyes—
Of streams whose crystal waters run
O'er golden sands to meet the sun;
Or, sailing on a shoreless sea,
Lulled by the drowsy melody,
Far, far, away we seem to be.

Upon a couch, from Persian loom,
Sate the fair Myra in that room,
So full of beauty and perfume.
But she, its mistress, bent in tears
Above the hopes of early years;
And Dionysius knelt beside
Her, destined not to be his bride:—
"Call me not false," at length he said,
"My first, last love is on thee staid;
"Call me not false, my heart remains
"Still bound to thine by stronger chains
"Than bind to life; death's dreaded dart
"May pierce the frame, but this, the heart."

"Then wherefore," said the weeping girl,
Her dark eyes lifted to his face,
"This stranger's mystic creed embrace?
"Thou might'st have known my sire would scorn
"A doctrine all so basely born.
"Or, why not build a secret shrine,
"And worship there this god of thine?"

"Oh! tempt me not;—eternity
"And the soul's endless destiny
"Hang on a breath, and not the tears
"Of anguish, shed in after years;
"Not tears of blood might have the power
"To wash the guilt from such an hour.
"I dare not hide my faith: this name
"Must be my glory, not my shame."

"Then we must part; oh! that my tears
"Could bring me back my childhood's years;
"For all that I shall have of thee,
"In past, not future years will be.
"Or for the power to be again
"A careless child, to break the chain
"That binds me to thee. Wherefore give,
"Ye gods, the wretched boon, to live
"And yet to suffer? Ye who know
"No sorrow, still might pity woe."

Tearless and motionless she stood,
With lip and brow so sadly pale,
As Ariadne o'er the flood

Had watched her Theseus' darkening sail,[51]
When he had risen to depart,
And once more clasped her to his heart,
Saying, in accents low and broken,
In words expressed, though scarcely spoken,
"I love thee, with a love beyond
"All things beside, save that I give
"To him, in whom I move and live,
"The power who, though unseen, yet nigh,
"Hath watched our steps from infancy.
"And still his sheltering wing shall spread
"Above the severed path we tread;
"And when the stream of life shall be
"Fast ebbing to eternity,
"My dying prayers shall be for thee."

Night came, and the fair moon arose
In its still beauty, from repose,
Full, clear, and cloudless; and the wave
Back her reflected image gave.
Night came, with soft and gentle hand
Closing the flowers of that fair land,
And scattering from her urn the dew,
Their drooping blossoms to renew;
Or whispering in the sleeper's ear
Tones that he never more shall hear.

But other light is on the stream
Than the moon's soft and silvery beam;
A thousand flickering torches gleam,
Half seen, half hidden, as the gale
Waved to and fro the feathery veil
That the tall palm trees' foliage made,
Screening the temples in their shade,
As the procession moved along
With festive dance, and choral song.
For 'twas a festival that night,
And Athens sent her fair, and bright,
And young, and gifted, to entwine
With songs and flowers Diana's shrine.[52]

---

51 In Greek mythology, Ariadne was the daughter of King Minos and Queen Pasiphae of Crete. She fell in love with Theseus and against her father's wishes helped him to escape the Minotaur's labyrinth. In return for her assistance, Theseus had promised marriage, but later deserted her on the island of Naxos.
52 Diana: goddess of the moon and hunting.

Children in snowy tunic dressed,
With hands crossed on each happy breast;
Youths crowned with laurel; these are past,
But come the loveliest and the last,
The maids of Athens; soft they tread,—
A basket on each graceful head,
Of choicest flowers, on which was flung
A veil which o'er the maiden hung.
And, Myra, must thy heavy heart
Take, 'mid this pageantry, a part?
Yes, she is in the festive band,
The loveliest daughter of the land.

Onward they passed. There is a power
Indwelling in the moonlit hour,
Not like the sun's; the rays it throws
Lull the deep passions to repose.
Dreams, that 'mid noonday splendours sleep,
Thoughts, linked with feelings loved and deep,
Which hearts, 'mid noise and toil, will keep,
Gush forth as its long shadows fall
O'er the still lake or lonely hall.
'Tis memory's hour, for back it brings
Thoughts of our lost and loveliest things;
Hopes, loves, and friendships buried long,
The lute-like sound of childhood's song;
The mirth, the music, and the flowers
Of mountain homes or woodland bowers.
For 'tis not rudely then the chord
Of memory's touched; there wakes a note
Softened and mournful as the tones
That round the Egyptian statue float,
When the last beam of parting day
Is passing in the west away.

But listen, 'tis the voice of song
And music's tones that float along—
Music o'er moonlit waters stealing—
Dead is the heart to love, to feeling,
That hears unmoved, nor breathes a sigh
For what was loved in days gone by.

Now from the grove emerge the band,
And round the sylvan altar stand,
And then again the voice of song,
Breezes and waters bear along.

"Goddess of the sylvan bow,
"Youths and maidens hail thee now,
"While softly fall thine own pure beams
"Like silver arrows on the streams:
   "Latona's daughter, hail![53]

"Hear us from the forest glades,
"Hear us from the grotto's shades,
"Where thy tall majestic mein
"In the fountain's wave is seen:
   "Latona's daughter, hail!

"Spare, oh! spare, the youthful band,
"That around thine altar stand;
"Let no matron desolate
"Share in the sad mother's fate;[54]
"But send thy vengeful shafts afar
"In the sports of sylvan war:
   "Latona's daughter, hail!"

Who stands in silence by that stream
On which the torch and moonlight gleam?
'Tis he, who now an exile seems,
Even by his native streams.
Parted from her he loved, he sought
Some lonely spot where burdened thought
Might be unchecked, when music's strain
Roused him to consciousness again.
There was a music sad and wild
In the lyre's tones when wafted o'er
The still clear waters, and he stood
Listening them die upon the shore.
Bright shone the temple's gilded pile,
Young faces beamed with many a smile,
But Dionysius' softened eye
Gazed but on one impassionedly:
Back from her face her veil was thrown,
And pale as monumental stone
Were cheek and brow; the drooping lid,
With its long fringe, the dark eye hid;

---

53 Latona's daughter: in Roman mythology, Latona's daughter was Diana, goddess of the moon and hunting. The Greek equivalent is Artemis. The reference to Roman mythology anticipates the move to Rome in part 2 of the poem.

54 [Poet's Note: Niobe.] In Greek mythology, Niobe's children were murdered by Apollo and Artemis (Diana), who were enraged when Niobe claimed to be superior to their mother Leto (in Roman mythology, Latona).

One fair, but fading, cistus flower
Her hand had gathered from her bower,
And placed amid her shining hair;
And as it drooped and withered there,
It seemed an emblem of her fate,
Blighted by one who did not hate.
Oh never, never, did she seem
So like the being of his dream
As when, with bending head, she stood
That night beside the crystal flood.

She saw him not, but turned again
To join the home-returning train.
He gazed on her retiring tread
Like one who looks upon the dead,
And when each sound and form were past
Still gazed where he had seen her last,
Nor moved, nor spoke: for common grief
May find in tears, in words, relief;
But there are woes we cannot speak,
And greater than bedew the cheek.

XI.

Morn came, but with a lurid light
That followed on the steps of night,
Not darkness and not light,—but gloom
That seemed to speak of hastening doom.
Hushed nature, listening, seemed to wait
The signs or woes of coming fate.
The sea, with deep and sullen roar,
Without a wind swept on the shore,
And sounds of revelry were o'er.

At last arose a general cry,
First, faint and low, then swelling high,
And on it passed, still gathering strength
Throughout that crowded city's length.
Each one was hurrying to and fro,
As if to shun some dreaded foe.
Some turned them to their homes to die;
Some prayed for pity from the sky;
Some cursed the gods who would not save
Their votaries from a loathsome grave.

The plague had come! its wings were spread[55]
As o'er a city of the dead—
Come, like a spirit from the deep,
The carnival of death to keep—
Its drink a nation's tears; and sighs
Of dying men the melodies
That charm its ears: on, on, it came,
First-born of death, with fearful name.
    It passed with noiseless footstep by,
Numbering the living with the dead;
    Unseen its form of mystery,
As on it sped!
It spared not beauty in its pride;
It snatched the bridegroom from the bride;
It breathed upon the sleeping child,
While in its mother's arms it smiled;
And as the mother o'er it wept,
Throughout her veins the poison crept;
And while she caught its dying sigh,
Death darkened o'er her tearful eye.[56]

There was no glitter, naught to hide;
'Twas death unmasked, and in its pride:
Treading alike o'er prince and slave;
Not giving e'en a costlier grave,
The last poor boon the great can claim
Above the man of meaner name:
No, in that hour of fear and doom,
All shared alike a common tomb!

Days passed; and silence reigned around—
Silence unbroken by a sound
Of choral hymn, or harp, or lute,
Or gladsome foot; all these were mute—
Yes, it was silence, though 'twas broken,
For words were whispered and not spoken.

Weeks passed; and grass and wild flowers grew
In silent homes, and wild birds flew
Down temple aisles, and empty streets,
Unscathed as in their own retreats.

---

55 Although anachronistic, this is a likely reference to the plague of Athens (AD 430), which killed more than a quarter of the city's population.
56 This section (from 'Unseen its form of mystery') is included in John Evans's review of *'Dionysius the Areopagite', with Other Poems* in *Lancashire Authors and Orators* (1850); see Appendix A.

The boats lay rotting on the shore,
With starting plank and splitting oar;
The galleys drifted to and fro,
Where'er the breeze might chance to blow,
With colours drooping o'er their side,
And cordage dragging in the tide.
While masts, and spars, and useless sails,
Rich spices, gums, and precious bales
From Persian looms, unheeded lay,
To the fierce sun and waves, a prey.
Treasures untold were on that strand
Untouched by human spoiler's hand!
Who thought of treasures, cared for gems?
Death bargained not for diadems.
Died in all breasts, love, hope, and pride;
And last of all, e'en avarice died!

Some drifted on, with canvass spread,
Dark charnel houses of the dead;
For breathed there none of mortal mould
Within the lone and loathsome hold,
None left to tell the dismal tale,
None left his fellow to bewail!

But worst of all, the fate of him,
 Who, watching by his shipmate's clay,
Saw the last rays of light grow dim,
 And then to darkening shades give way,
Leaving him there, 'mid death and gloom,
Like the last lamp within a tomb,
'Mid noxious vapours faintly gleaming,
And none of its existence dreaming.

Foe thought no more of foe, nor friend
Thought of his friend; 'twas passion's end:
A hideous quiet brooded o'er
The city and the silent shore.
Priests, by the shrines they watched, were lying,
The sacred lamps around them dying;
The bard beside his lyre was laid,
And the wild wind his requiem played
Among its silver chords; in dust,
The sculptor left the unfinished bust;
Men crept along the empty street,
With fearful look and lagging feet.
And were there none to nobly dare

Death, 'mid this pestilential air,
To aid their fellows? none to cheer
The lonely orphan's bitter fear?
None, with kind hand, to dry its tear?
Yes, there were some, a little band,
The Christians of that classic land.
And first, 'mid danger in that form,
More fearful than of field or storm,
Wert thou, Athenian: friend or foe
Alike to thee, if common woe
Made them alike—thy footsteps fall,
At midnight, through the silent hall;
And by the dim forsaken shrine,
When the first rays of morning shine,
By the deserted sick wert thou,
Though with pale lip and mournful brow.
Oft, when with toil and watching worn,
The weary body was o'erborne,
He sought, in one forsaken home,
    An hour of quiet, not of rest;
The echoes of its silent halls
Woke other feelings in his breast.
The fountain threw its ceaseless shower
O'er choking weed and withering flower;
The wind its dirge-like music played
Through empty hall and colonnade;
Still, ranged around the lonely room,
The vases stood, but no perfume
Breathed from the flowers, which, pale and dead,
Their withered blossoms round had shed.
One sound, one footstep only broke
The silence, and the echoes woke;
The watch-dog still his station kept,
And by the threshold altar slept,[57]
Guarding the lonely spot with care
As if still Myra's home were there.
'Tis vain, thy faithful care, 'tis vain;
Her hand, from off thy neck, the chain,
Poor dog, shall never loose again:
Far from her own bright land is she,
In the soft clime of Italy.

---

57 [Poet's Note: An altar dedicated to Mercury, and a Watch dog, were generally placed by the Athenians at the door of their houses; *both* were intended to guard against thieves.] Mercury: messenger of the gods; god of thieves, trade and travel (Roman mythology).

When first arose the general cry
That told the common foe was nigh,
All fled who had the power to fly,
Save those whom love restrained: and he,
Votary of stern necessity—
The stoic—he too fled, and bore
His daughter to the Italian shore.
With her Corinna went; the tie,
By friendship twined from infancy,
She would not break, although her heart
Sunk, from her native land to part.
And now, beneath a palace dome,
They dwelt within imperial Rome.

'Twas evening when the vessel bore
Those exiles from the Grecian shore;
And the pine woods on mountains high
Stood out against a glowing sky.
With earnest eye Corinna stood
Gazing across the Ægean flood
To the receding shore—with hands
Clasped on her breast pale Myra stands,
While down her cheeks the ceaseless tears
Flow o'er the faded hopes of years—
All centred in that land, whose shrines
Are sinking fast to shadowy lines;
E'en as she looks—in tears alone
Her grief can make its sorrows known;
But calm Corinna's found a tone,[58]
In song that softly floated by,
Borne by the wind upon those shores to die.

Corinna's Parting Song

"There is a voice comes o'er the deep blue sea,
"In solemn tone it speaketh thus to me—
"'Daughter, this land thine eyes no more shall see;'
"And then the caverns of the silent shore
"Take up the words, and echo back, 'No more.'

"That voice speaks not unto the outward ear;
"But still its tones my lonely heart can hear,

---

58 [Poet's Note: The modern Greeks frequently give expression to their feelings in song when about to leave their country; it is not unnatural, therefore, to suppose that their more poetical ancestors did the same.]

"Chilling it with a sickly sense of fear—
"A dark foreboding of a coming doom,
"I know not what, perchance an exile's tomb!

"Farewell, my glorious land! Thy hills and streams,
"In yon far land, will flit across my dreams,
"As through thy laurel bowers glance summer's
            golden beams,—
"Making a transient sunshine 'mid the shade
"That on my young but troubled heart is laid.

"There is a brighter land than thine, fair clime,
"Beyond the bounds of earth, the shores of time,
"Beyond the reach of sorrow, and of crime;
"Eternity's vast ocean round it rolls,
"It is the spirit's home! the home of ransomed souls!"

Part II.

I.

The dust of ages is upon thee, Rome;
Dark were thy deeds, and dark hath been thy doom.
The blood of martyred saints bedewed thy sod,—
Its voice ascended from thy hills to God;
The winds took up their dying groans—the wave
Back to the earth its answering echo gave.
And o'er thy vine-clad shores, thy sunny sea,
It brooded like the voice of prophecy.
And vengeance heard its tones, and woke at last,—
At the still midnight pealed the Gothic blast,
And through thy streets the hosts of Alaric passed![59]

All vices thine, the savage and refined,
That waste the body, enervate the mind.
What were thy pastimes? Let the arena tell;
Where, for thy sport, the gladiator fell.
Far from the stormy lands that gave him birth,
He sank unpitied in thy crimson earth;
But died not unavenged: that stormy north
Sent its dark hordes of fierce barbarians forth.

---

59 Alaric: king of the Visigoths (c. AD 370–410) who captured Rome in AD 410. This opening section of part 2 is included in the review of *'Dionysius the Areopagite', with Other Poems* in *North of England Magazine*; see Appendix A.

Shorn of thy might, abused like him who trod
In Gaza's prison when forsook of God,[60]
Beneath their footsteps thou didst sink—to rise
A blasting meteor in malignant skies—
To shine o'er slumbering Europe's mental night,
With blinding flashes of uncertain light.
Mother of crimes and errors thou hast been,
In every age, except thine earliest scene.
Then thou hadst savage virtues, such as grace
The desert Arab, or the red man's race.
Canadian woods, Zahara's wastes, can tell[61]
Where freedom conquered and where valour fell:
Then boast not thou. Thine empire passed away
I cannot mourn. But temples in decay,
The crumbling arches, and the ruined fanes,
That strew with wrecks thy solitary plains,
I do regret; for they should keep alive
The flame of art, and empire's fall survive.

Listen! what sounds are on the breeze?
The whisper of the olive trees,
And Tiber's deep and solemn tide,
The fall of fountains.—Naught beside?
Yes, songs and music, and the beat,
On marble floors, of dancers' feet,
And childhood's laugh so glad and clear,
And charger's tramp, and clanging spear,
And chariot's rattle, and the throng
Of myriads as they sweep along:
Yes, these are there, but on the breeze
My spirit hears more sounds than these.
The sigh of misery borne along
By the same wind that bears the song;
Oppression's scarcely uttered plaint;
The dying groan of martyred saint;
The captive's voice, that from the gloom
Breaks of the dungeon's living tomb,
With dull sepulchral tone; the glee
And laugh of wild insanity;
Revenge's slowly uttered vow;—
These through the city's murmurs flow.

---

60 An allusion to the Old Testament judge Samson, whose great physical strength lay in his long hair. When he revealed the secret of his strength to his mistress, Delilah, she betrayed him to the Philistines who imprisoned him in Gaza, cut off his hair and blinded him (Judges 16).
61 Zahara: form of Sahara, relating to the desert of that name.

What see'st thou? Rome! imperial Rome!
Untouched by age, unmarred by doom:
Though centuries since its birth have gone,
And the fourth Cæsar fills the throne.
I see its capitol, that shrines
The ancient Sybil's mystic lines:
The invader's hand, the tempest's shock,
Have left it on its native rock,
To look in proud defiance o'er
Campagnia's plain and Ostia's shore.[62]
I see amid its gardens rise,
With all that luxury can devise,
The Cæsars' "golden palace," gems
That might have glowed in diadems,
With rich mosaic stud its walls,
And glitter in its marble halls.

Spoils from the east, spoils from the west,[63]
Are poured into that city's breast.
The pearls in Persia's gulf that gleam,
The diamond that hath caught its beam
Of splendour from an orient sun,
She hath desired, and she hath won.
Amber the Roman bought of thee,
Dark Danube, and thou tideless sea;
And Babylonian looms supplied
Carpets of hundred colours dyed;
While Grecian vases in her rooms
Were filled with far Ceylon's perfumes.

---

62 Campagnia: Campania; a region in southern Italy; Ostia: the first colony founded by ancient Rome. The city lies on the western coast of Italy.

63 [Poet's Note: The most remote countries of the ancient world were ransacked to supply the pomp of Rome. The forests of Scythia afforded valuable furs. Amber was brought overland from the shores of the Baltic to the Danube. There was a considerable demand for Babylonian carpets and other manufactures of the east; but the most important foreign trade was carried on with Arabia and India. Every year, about the summer solstice, a fleet of one hundred and twenty vessels sailed from Myos-hormos, a port of Egypt on the Red Sea. The coast of Malabar or the island of Ceylon was the usual end of their navigation, and it was in these markets that the merchants from the more remote parts of Asia expected their arrival. The return of the fleet was in December or January, and as soon as their cargo had been transported on the backs of camels from the Red Sea to the Nile, and had descended that river as far as Alexandria, it was poured into the capital of the empire. The objects of oriental traffic were splendid and trifling: silk, a pound of which was esteemed not inferior in value to a pound of gold; precious stones, and a variety of aromatics that were used in religious worship and in funerals.—(Vide Gibbon's *Decline and Fall of the Roman Empire*, vol. I. chap. II. page 88.)] Much of the wording here is taken from vol. 1, ch. 2 of Edward Gibbon's *The History of the Decline and Fall of the Roman Empire*.

Bring the Falernian wine! bring flowers![64]
And watch not as the tempest lowers.
Patrician! tread thy halls to night,
Forgetting, ere the morrow's light,
Secret and swift from yonder hall,
The tyrant's axe may on thee fall.
They live not for the coming day
Who live beneath a Nero's sway.
The mariner on ocean's wave
Forgets that from a stormy grave
A plank divides: the mountain child
Sports where the avalanche is piled
And poised upon a breath: then sound
The lyre, and bid the bowl go round!
Hushed be the voice of weeping—shed
No tear above the murdered dead;
Tell not the winds thy grief; forbear
To tell the waters thy despair,—
Breathe it not in the city's crowd,—
Whisper it not in solitude,—
Trust not thy fellows,—live apart,—
Though 'midst them with suspecting heart.

II.

The city sleeps. At dead of night
There shoots to heaven a spire of light;
'Tis but a meteor's flash, it dies,
And darker seem the starless skies.
Again it glows—it is the light
Kindled upon the Alban height,[65]
The watch-fire of the guards—'tis gone,
And all again is dark and lone.
It burst again—one sheet of flame,
As if from Ætna's breast it came![66]
Reddening along the midnight sky,
And with it rose the troubled cry
Of frighted thousands rushing by;
Rushing they knew not whither—still
On rolled its fiery waves, until

---

64 Falernian wine: celebrated wine originating from the *ager Falernus* in Campania (adj. 'Falernian' *OED*).
65 Alban: of Alba Longa, a city of ancient Latium (n. and adj. 'Alban' *OED*).
66 Ætna: Europe's highest active volcano, in Sicily.

The city looked one funeral pile,
Seen o'er the plains for many a mile.[67]

It sunk at last, and pitchy smoke
From out the smouldering ashes broke.
Where is the splendid city now,
That stood upon the seven hills' brow
But yesterday? The roofless halls,
And gaping cracks, and blackening walls,
Columns still standing, but o'erthrown
The sculptured pediment of stone
Which rested on them; these proclaim
That well hath done its task that flame.
Time, in his slow and solemn march,
Twines the bright ivy round the arch
He crumbles with his touch; but fire,
Like human conqueror in his ire,
Spares naught, gives naught, but leaves a waste,
Blackened, and lonely, and defaced.

Days past—but days may do the work
Of years, and in a moment's space
May crowd the fate of centuries,
Or nations' weal embrace.
Days past—and Rome in ruin lies;
The winds her starving peoples' cries
Bear to the guilty monarch's ears,[68]
And for his throne the tyrant fears.
He gives the Christians to their ire,
And blood, *their* blood, to quench the fire.
Oh! shroud the picture—pass it o'er;
The pains those suffering Christians bore
Are mystery now,—we shrink to read
More than the martyr shrank to bleed.

---

67 [Poet's Note: This dreadful conflagration lasted for nine days, and destroyed the greater part of the city. Upon its ruins Nero erected his celebrated "Golden Palace," which seems to have been more remarkable for its vast extent, and the richness of its materials, than for the beauty of its architectural design. I have been guilty of an anachronism in the preceding page, in representing this palace as existing before the fire. Although the Christians had suffered insult and cruelty from outbreaks of popular fury, as in the case of Stephen, at Jerusalem, and of Paul, at Lyconia, they did not experience a general persecution until the one under Nero, which took place in consequence of the fire in Rome.] Hawkshaw refers here to the fire which destroyed half of Rome in AD 64. Emperor Nero (AD 37–68), ruler of Rome from AD 54–68 rebuilt the city after the fire and constructed the 'Golden House', a vast palace in the centre of Rome.

68 Suspected by his people of starting the great fire which destroyed much of Rome, the Emperor Nero sought to blame the Christians and began to persecute them.

III.

Those few brief days thy faith revealed,
Corinna, and thy fate was sealed.
Her heathen friend, and foreign birth,
 Had screened her from the oppressor's hand,
If no betrayer had been found
 Within their household band.
Mycale, Myra's favourite slave,
The needful information gave.
Born 'mid Thessalian rocks—her mind,[69]
Though with no common strength combined
Was superstition's own; no ray
Of mental culture cheered her way;
But in her dark untutored breast,
One feeling stronger than the rest,
Fidelity—no change could change,
No distance and no time estrange—
Burnt quenchless to the last: her love
For her she served, arose above
E'en reverence for a pagan creed.
That love had prompted her to hate
Corinna, whom she falsely thought
Had brought a cloud o'er Myra's fate.
Beside Corinna she had been
Amid that sad and gloomy scene,
When she received the Christian's rite,
Beneath the silent vault of night.
Some fearful and mysterious power,
She thought, was given by that hour.
And when she saw on Myra's cheek
The colour fade—and week by week
Her once bright eyes grow sad and dim
With many tears, and all for him
Who, like Corinna, now despised
The gods and rites for ages prized;
She thought Corinna's spells had changed
The heart, that thus appeared estranged;
And hatred deep as blind, possessed
The dark recesses of her breast.

Hints of her doubts and fears, the slave
Oft to her sorrowing mistress gave;
And though, at first, they seemed to glide

---

69 [Poet's Note: Thessaly was famous for its oracles. Its inhabitants were much addicted to witchcraft and other superstitions.]

From off her mind, they did divide
Hearts once in friendship joined—no word
Of anger told it, but the tone,
And looks, and actions, nameless all,
That tell us we are loved, were gone;
And intercourse grew cold and strange,
Though words could not express the change.
'Twas felt, not seen—a poisonous wind
Known by the waste it left behind.

Aroused, at midnight, from repose,
Corinna yielded to her foes.
Borne to a neighbouring court, she stood
'Mid those prepared to shed her blood,
Alone, unaided. "Hail the god
"Who rules Olympus with his nod;"
Said the proconsul, "in yon flame
"The incense cast, invoke his name,
"And bow before his dreaded shrine,
"And life and liberty are thine.
"Speak'st thou not? Wilt thou throw away,
"In the bright morning of thy day,
"The life that others hoard with care?
"How wilt thou death's fierce torture bear?
"Whence art thou?" "From the Grecian shore
"I am." She could not utter more.
Through the fast falling tears, her eyes
Seemed to look on her native skies,
With starlight on the Athenian plain,
Where she must never tread again.

Perhaps some touch of pity stole
E'en through that Roman judge's soul.
In tones less harsh he spoke,—"And thou,
"Ere care hath wrinkled o'er thy brow,
"What canst thou know of creeds? thy sires
"Adored these gods—your poets' lyres
"Were tuned to praise them—all that's great
"And noble in your past estate,
"And all you still have in those piles
"That rise upon your plains and isles,
"Your statues, wanting breath alone,
"Humanity transferred to stone
"As by Medusa's touch—all sprung[70]

---

70 Medusa's touch: in Greek mythology, anyone who looked at Medusa would be turned to stone. Medusa was a mythical female with snakes for hair, who took mortal form.

"While to your ancient gods ye clung.
"Is there no charm in life?—no pain
"In death?—bethink thee yet again."

Low, but distinct, her answer rose,
Amid the silence of her foes.
"Is there no charm in life," she said,
And slowly raised her drooping head,
While from the brow they late had shaded,
Her long bright ringlets fell unbraided—
"Is there no charm in life? Does earth,
"Then utter forth her sounds of mirth,
"And spread her scenes of beauty o'er
"The azure sea and peopled shore
"In vain?—and can the human heart,
"From all it loves and loved, depart
"Without a sigh?—hath death no pain?
"Ask those who choose the cankering chain
"For years, and bless the dungeon's gloom
"That saves them from the darker tomb.
"I fear expiring nature's strife,
"I shrink from suffering, cling to life;
"Yet I, e'en I, am here to die,
"Rather than him—my Lord—deny.
"Men for their native land expire;
"Friend dies for friend, and child for sire;
"And may not I this life resign
"For him who gave his life for mine?"

"Enough," replied the judge, "away!—
"Lead her, ye guards."—The guards obey.

'Twas not to instant death—but doom
As fearful—'mid the damp and gloom
Of a small prison—day by day
To feel life's pulses ebb away;
To watch the morning sunbeams creep
Across the floor—to bend and weep
Alone—then hear the moaning breeze
At midnight through the arches sigh;
To dream of the far sounding seas
And isles that on their bosom lie,
In sunlight bathed,—and then to wake
And hear the chain and fetter shake,
With darkness like the graves around.

But where's the history?—who may tell
The story of that captive's cell?
Ask the dark walls, who on them traced
The lines that damp and time effaced?
Or ask the moonbeam how its gleam
Woke the pale inmate from her dream
Of other days? or ask the ray
That found its lone and devious way
Through the small lattice—ask how long
The feeble frame endured the gloom,
The damp, the chain, the living tomb?
And ask how long the immortal mind,
The spark within that frame enshrined,
Burnt brightly, ere it winged its flight
From dungeon gloom to rayless light,—
Scorning the fetter and the chain
That would have bound it, but in vain?
Yet, judge not happiness by things
That make it not; 'tis not enshrined
In palaces; its home is mind!
Go not to woods nor wilds; they keep
No secret charms, nor can the deep
Soft tones of nature lull to sleep
Passion's wild tumults. Can the voice
Of fame the wearied heart rejoice?
Turn to that heart, it holds within
Its little space a depth of woe
Or happiness that all may know.
The lowliest couch of pain may be
A place of rest and peace to thee,
If, in calm confidence resigned,
On heaven and God repose thy mind.

Weeks sped their flight; they left no trace
On many a young and happy face:
Nor tinged they with a richer dye
The foliage of that southern sky,
Nor gave its winds a deeper sigh.
But measure not by days and hours
Man's life; ye may the life of flowers
Or insects—one dark day may call
Forth energies, the silent fall
Of years had left unknown, to sleep
Within the soul's recesses deep.

Weeks sped their flight, and left a trace,
A withering touch on one young face,
That paler grew from day to day,
A snow-wreath passing fast away.
Corinna, did thy spirit rise
In triumph to thy native skies?
Or did it calmly pass away
Like stars that fade at dawn of day?
Who, who, may tell; there was not one
To watch beside thy couch of stone;
But there were those who heard thy hymn,
When evening threw its shadows dim
Across thy cell—it ceased at last,
And silence told that all was past.

IV.

There was a footstep in that cell,
'Twas not the jailor's, for it fell
Soft as the snow flake: and a form
Of female beauty glided through
The open door; her feet with dew
Were wet, for she had left her bower
In secret at that early hour.
'Tis Myra—but beyond the hate
Of foes or love of friends art thou,
Corinna: she hath come too late!

What will not even woman dare,
Prompted by sorrow or despair?
Mycale had the truth concealed,
That she Corinna's faith revealed,
Until the previous day: the thought
That thus for her the crime was wrought
Was agony to Myra's heart,
That whispered, too, the foolish part
That she had acted, and each word
Of hasty anger, long interred,
Seemed sounded in her ears again,
Mixed with the clanking of the chain
That bound her friend: and bitter tears
Flowed as she thought of other years.

She bribed the guards, and stood alone
Beside Corinna's couch of stone.
Calm as in sleep the martyr lay;
On her pale brow the morning's ray

Shone as in mockery. Myra crept
Beside her, thinking that she slept,
And bent to kiss her cheek—'twas death!
Though death as beautiful as sleep,
That met her gaze of anguish deep:
She did not move, she did not weep,
But bent above the martyred dead,
Till sight, and sound, and reason fled.
How long she lay unconscious there
None knew: she said 'twas months, 'twas years,
An age of agony and fears,
That storms laid desolate and bare:
For reason, though it gleamed again,
No more burnt calmly in her brain.
They found her seated by the dead—
She turned not at their heavy tread—
She neither seemed to hear nor know
A sight or sound but *that one woe*.
But when she saw them rudely take
   That form, and bear it from the cell,
She seemed as from a dream to wake,
   And burning tear drops fell:—
A burst of wild and passionate grief,
Yielding the heart no kind relief.

They led her home, and calmer hours
Stole o'er her, but her mind its powers
No more regained: 'twas like the flowers
The tempest shakes, that may live on,
Though all their sweets and bloom be gone.
Still beautiful she looked—her hair,
Shading a brow so deathly fair,
   Yet circled with its jewelled band;
For still her maids arrayed with care
Her form, as if to hide the truth
That canker gnawed the bud of youth.
There was a tinge upon her cheek
That more of death than life might speak;
As fading colours on the sky,
When night or storm, are gathering nigh;
A parting beam of beauty past—
Most beautiful, because the last.
She named no wish, no joy, no pain;
But if she heard a Grecian strain
She hid her face—yet never wept:
   Save that first burst of tears—her eye

Was like a desert fountain, dry,
O'er which the burning wind hath swept.

She twined a wreath of fading flowers
    Around Corinna's silent lyre;
Flowers that one day of beauty see
    And then expire.
Each morn her hands the wreath renewed
From buds with midnight dews embued;[71]
But if her fingers touched its string,
    She seemed like one whose hand profanes
A relic or a sacred thing.
She never spoke of him, by name,
Whose memory like slow burning flame
Was in her heart—but when alone
They heard her oft in gentle tone,
With voice so sad, and yet so sweet,
The story of their love repeat.
No angry thoughts her bosom crossed;
Not false she called him now, but lost.
Oft raising to the evening skies
Her beautiful but mournful eyes,
It seemed as if o'er memory came
Some vague and dream-like thought of hours
Passed with him in their Grecian bowers:
And she would slowly murmuring say,
As on her gilded couch she lay,
"I loved him, oh! how well!" She died
When spring gave earth again its flowers—
She died, her father's last, sole pride.

Not long before her spirit passed,
Like lamps that brightest burn at last,
Reason returned:—"I am," she said,
    "Like one awaking from a sleep,
"Disturbed by wild and fearful dreams,
    "And who but wakes to weep.
"I feel that this is death—and death,
"What is it but the feeble breath
"Passing away? Is there no more
"Of life than I have journeyed o'er?
"Is there not yet another shore?
"Or am I foundering on a sea
"Immeasureless, no more to be?

---

71 imbued: transcribed from original.

"Tell me, nor leave me thus to die
"Trembling in sad uncertainty—
"Is it a dream? or am I past
"The stream of death, and look, at last,
"On those whom I have loved!—I see
"My Dionysius—yes, 'tis he!"

A moment, and his arms were thrown
Around that fair but wasted form,
That soon the grave would call its own.
One long embrace, and then the tears
Of joys, of sorrows, and of fears,
Like drops from many fountains sprang,[72]
Mixed in one stream as on they ran:
Still to her lover's arm she clung,
But o'er her face a deeper shade
Than ever earthly passion made
Soon stole—she fixed a troubled eye
On the tints fading from the sky,
Saying, "Ere night perchance I die.
"I deemed all earthly thoughts were lost
"In the wild sea on which I tost;
"But sight of thee has joined again
"The links of many a broken chain.
"But no, it must not be—no bride
"But death's can Myra be; my guide
"To brighter shores, if such there be,
"Not what thou wert in thee I'll see.
"I feel the time is brief—nor tears
"Must choke thy voice—nor doubting fears
"Must fill thy heart:—I scorned these themes
"When filled with pride and passion's dreams—
"Yes, dreams they were, from which I woke
"To die."
                    Like one a sudden stroke
Has stunned, yet rouses by the fear
Of danger or of suffering near,
Dionysius nerved himself to speak,
Though grief had blanched his lip and cheek,
And his deep voice was low and weak.
Calmly she lay upon his arm—
As if there were some sacred charm
In the high themes of which he told,
That soothed her heart to hope and peace—

---

72 Original publisher's errata note: 'for "sprang" read "sprung"'.

Yet did not speak; but if he paused,
She motioned him still not to cease.
Raising her eyes to his—one sigh,
So soft, 'twas scarcely heard—the tie
Of nature broke—the spirit fled—
The loved, the beautiful, was dead.

A tinge still on her cheek reposed,
But the dark eyes no more unclosed.
Too beautiful to yield to death
Seemed the fair form; and long he kept
His station by her couch and wept.

Years with their changes, swept away
The scenes of many an after day,
But on his memory fresh they left
That scene—the high white forehead bare,
In cold and unchanged beauty there:
It seemed as if relenting death
Had only gently stopped the breath,
Not marred with ruthless hand one trace
Of loveliness in form or face:
A statue from her own bright clime
She looked; and not a thing for time
So soon to give to dust: and thus
   Her image on his memory rose
In after years, calm, cold, but fair,
   In the still beauty of repose:
Not her the beautiful and gay,
   But Myra as in death she lay.

V.

A day—'tis but a day, brief hours,
Marked by the closed and opening flowers,
By golden light upon the skies
At morn, and by the roseate dyes
On evening's stilly cloud that lies:
Yet who, when those few hours are run,
Is the same being who began
His course with the uprising sun?
I speak not of the mortal frame,
It is not, yet may look the same;
But who, when evening shades are creeping
Across the vale, and flowers are sleeping,
Feels as he did when morning broke
In splendour, and to life he woke:

The heart, as if the body's rest
It too had shared, within the breast
Beats lightly, thought upon the wing
Is soaring, hope imagining,
And fortitude with steadfast eye,
Calmly awaiting destiny.
But evening comes, and weary hearted,
Back to the goal from which we started
We look again; upon it lie,
Like mists, the dreams of vanity;
And 'mid the gathering glooms arise,
As phantoms to the sleeper's eyes,
Dark guilty thoughts, lost hopes, lost time,
Youth's follies, or fierce manhood's crime!

How was he changed who sat that night
By Myra's couch of dreamless sleep?
Thoughts cherished at the wakening light,
Like it, had faded from the sky,
Like her, had been but loved, to die:
At morn he sought the Italian shore,
With hopes that now exist no more.

There stood beside that couch of death
　　Her sire: he had not watched her die,
　　But now with fixed and tearless eye,
He gazed upon the dead—his breath
Deeply he drew, but not a word
Told how his inmost heart was stirred.
The past, the future, o'er him came—
Slowly at length he named her name,
And said, "She was my only one,
"And now I tread the world alone!
"Well, be it so, the hand of fate
"Hath made a father desolate;
"But 'tis beyond its power to shake
"His steady soul;—the reed will break
"Before the storm, and such a reed
"Art thou, and such thy Christian creed."

Upon him Dionysius turned:
Once at such scorn his cheek had burned;
But he had learned a lesson, taught
Not in the schools of men, and wrought
A conquest o'er himself.
　　　　　　　　　"A reed

"Thou think'st me, and my Christian creed,
"Because I weep in anguish o'er
"The form I soon shall see no more:
"Oh! less than human should I be,
"To shed no tear o'er thee, o'er thee!"
And on her chilly brow, again
Fell the warm tears like summer rain.
"Speak not of her, unless thy voice
   "Can wake the dead."
              "And is that all
"Your sages teach?" Dionysius said—
   "To let oblivion's curtain fall
"Upon the past, and not regret
"The loved one gone, but to forget.
"Forgetfulness I will not learn,
"But carry to the silent urn
"The memory of the sleeper there,
"Yet learn the grief to calmly bear;
"And from this sad, this midnight hour,
"I give to God my all of power,
"My all of time. Ye stars above,
"That seem to look with eyes of love
"Upon a guilty world, and thou,
"Foe though thou art, attest my vow.
"This is no time for secret faith,
"When the fierce persecutor's scath
"Hath swept so many down: I go
"Bearing within my heart a woe,
"That neither distance, time, nor change
"Can cure. No country now, no friend
"I have, and lonely to the end
"Must be my journey, and my grave
"Unknown as if in ocean's wave.
"In years and feelings young, but old
"In loneliness; with griefs untold,
"With joys unshared, 'mid solitudes
"Alone; and in the city's crowds
"Yet lonelier still—the funeral pall
"Upon the corpse, the prison wall
"Around the captive, severing not
"More surely than my faith, my lot!
"But then, when life is o'er, the chain
"Broken on earth will link again;
"And brightly o'er my path of gloom
"Breaks light immortal through the tomb."

"Vain dreams fond youth, poetic dreams;
"Scattered and faint are all the beams
"That gleam upon the shades below,
"Whither departed spirits go.
"The wisest live in doubt, and die
"In gloomy dark uncertainty.
"One hopes to reach the isles of bliss
"Whose shores the stormless waters kiss,
"Where flowerets spring as soon as culled,
"Where, by meandering rivers lulled,
"All passions die, and o'er the breast
"Settles a calm ethereal rest.
"A second thinks to wander back,
"And in a different form to track
"A bright or darker path of life.
"Another hopes eternal sleep
"Shall soul and body ever keep
"Fast in its cold and lasting chains.
"And wilt thou, hades' dark domains
"Talk of, rash youth, as if to thee
"They were no land of mystery?
"Or, like Ulysses, thou hadst trod,
"The kingdom of the gloomy god.[73]
"Thy fancy, by thy passions fanned,
"Hath a strange scene of phantoms planned,—
"A union in the spirit's land!
"And if beyond the grasp of time
"There be indeed such shadowy clime,
"What right hast thou to enter there,
"Or *she*, though once as Hebe fair?[74]
"'Tis for the brave, the wise, the great,[75]
"Sages who smiled contempt at fate;
"And heroes who have died to save
"The land that could but give a grave;

---

73 In Greek mythology, the king of Ithaca, Odysseus (Roman name Ulysses), descended to the underworld during his journey home after the Trojan War.
74 Hebe: in Greek mythology, the daughter of Hera and Zeus.
75 [Poet's Note: In the Elysium of the ancients we find none but heroes and persons who had either been fortunate or distinguished on earth. The children, and apparently the slaves, and lower classes, that is to say, poverty, misfortune, and innocence, were banished to the infernal regions.—(*Chateaubriand*, "*Génie du Christianisme.*")] From *La Génie du christianisme* (1802) by François-René de Chateaubriand (1768–1848). This precise quotation and reference is used by Felicia Hemans as a headnote to her poem 'Elysium', first published in *The Siege of Valencia: A Dramatick Poem; The Last Constantine: with Other Poems* (1823). This, rather than Chateaubriand, would seem to be Hawkshaw's source.

"Or those who touched the lyre and shrined
"In song the fantasies of mind;
"But ye, unknown to fame, must die
"A common death, like wild flowers lie
"Cut by the mower."

       "Purer far,
"Stoic, than thou hast imaged, are
"My hopes of bliss beyond the tomb;
"It hath to me no cloud, no gloom.
"Elysium not to thee is given[76]
"By man, aught like the Christians' heaven.
"And what does fancy give to thee?
"Fair land of ideality;
"All that can charm the ear and eye
"But not the soul; bright lakes that lie
"In the clear sunlight; waves that die
"On golden sands, whose melody
"Mingles its murmurs with the tone
"Of music that from earth hath gone.
"These too may be in heaven; but bliss,
"Pure and unchanging, is not this.
"But 'tis to feel for ever free
"From mortal taint; it is to be
"Made liker unto Deity;
"It is, as endless years go round,
"To search the depths of love profound
"Hid in redemption's glorious plan,
"Or vast creation's works to scan;
"And with unbaffled mind explore
"The universe from shore to shore;
"It is to feel immortal love
"To all below, to all above;
"And with thyself to be at peace,
"Knowing the calm shall never cease.
"Ask'st thou what thought can cheer the gloom
"That darkens now the Christian's doom,
"What light yet lingers in his sky?—
"*This Hope of Immortality!*"

---

76 Elysium: the supposed state or abode of the blessed after death in Greek mythology (n. 'Elysium' *OED*).

Part III.

I.

A generation died—the sun,
In the bright heavens alone the same,
Looked as when first our tale begun.
Empires had passed, and kings gone down
To chambers where the only crown
Is worn by death; and solitudes
Had started at new cities' crowds;
The sapling had become a tree;
The child upon its mother's knee
A man; temples and creeds had changed;
Hearths had grown silent, friends estranged.
Nature, it is but change; a power
Remodelling slowly, hour by hour,
All things around; nor man, nor time,
Can alter that decree sublime
That naught shall waste—earth shall not be
Less worthy of its deity,
Less fit for man when in the skies,
For the last time yon sun shall rise,
Than now; although the mountain range
With ocean's bed its place may change;
Still on the shores the waves shall sweep,
Until they utter wild and deep,
To earth and time their last farewell,
Sounding expiring nature's knell.
No atom of primeval dust
Hath perished, though its form and place
Have changed a million times: in vain
Would fancy all its changes trace:
The towers of ancient Babylon
Have crumbled, but no grain is gone;
The hand of change, but not decay,
Hath given them back to native clay:
The dew that fell on Eden's flowers,
May mingle with these seas of ours.

Those thirty years! how like a dream
To many a heart their flight would seem;
The same in length, in change, in strife;
The dreams of night and those of life,
How like each other—good and ill,
Shadows and lights, commingling still.

Back on the past with pensive pain
We look, yet not to tread again
The path of life desire: ah! no;
The happiest hearts too much of woe,
The best, too much of error know.
And yet this space of dream-like date
Had been the minister of fate
To kingdoms. To his righteous doom
Nero had gone, but over Rome
A deeper tyrant ruled; not slave
Of headlong passions, not the brave
But hasty foe; but dark and cold,
Cast in humanity's worst mould,—
Domitian reigned. And Britain's isle,[77]
On which the Romans deemed the smile
Of day departed; thou, my land,
Then bowed beneath a conqueror's hand:
But he was mild in peace as brave[78]
In war, and to the conquered gave
The arts of life, nor taught in vain
The arm he bound to loose its chain.

But wherefore pause on history's page?
The same dark story every age
Writes down in blood: first the rude home
Of savage life, with power to roam
Through unclaimed wilds; and then the strife
For lands, for liberty, for life,
With polished men, armed with the might
Which arts confer, but not with right:
That is the savage's, who sees
The hut he built beneath those trees,—
Whose boughs so long had o'er him grown,
He thought they were indeed his own,—
Fall by the stranger's axe—a race
Of aliens fill his dwelling place:
    Like leaves swept by the autumn wind,
The remnant of his race pass on,

---

77 Domitian: Titus Flavius Domitian (AD 51–96), Roman Emperor from AD 81–96, persecutor of Christians.

78 [Poet's Note: Cnæus Julius Agricola. At the close of the campaign in which Agricola defeated the Britons under Galgacus on the Grampian hills, a Roman fleet, for the first time, sailed round Britain, as if to mark the extended boundary of the Roman empire.—(*See Penny Cyclopaedia, Art., Agricola.*)] Hawkshaw's source is the entry for 'Agricola' in *The Penny Cyclopaedia of the Society for the Diffusion of Useful Knowledge*, vol. 1 (1833), 217–18. Gnaeus Julius Agricola (AD 40–93): Roman general and governor of Britain AD 78–84.

Casting a wistful glance behind
To scenes where all they loved is gone,
And old familiar sounds have ceased.
Say not the sum of bliss increased
To others, compensates for all
The ills the savage may befall;
Even were it so, eternal right
Is outraged; and for that alone
There is no good that can atone.
But 'tis not so, a withering blight,
A curse from heaven pursues the deed:—
Doubt it, the Spaniards' history read.
And yet earth shrines their names who came
O'er her fair scenes with sword and flame,
Making her Edens desolate—
The spoilers whom mankind calls great—
But finds no voice to tell of those
Who strove to heal her deepest woes,
The woes of mind. A poet sung
E'en a Domitian's praise! What tongue[79]
Of bard, what tuneful lyre was strung,
To tell of those who toiled to win
A pagan world from woe and sin?
They had no poet, had no page
Of earthly history, yet each age
Must be their debtor; for all time
They laboured, and for every clime;
They wrought a change no conqueror wrought;
They taught what sages never taught:
Mind feels the impulse still they gave,
For they propelled its deepest wave.

Sublime the themes they gave to mind,
And pure the lessons taught mankind.
The themes—a life beyond the tomb—
A day of audit and of doom,
When earth, from all her thousand coasts,
Shall call her sons, and death his hosts
Shall render back to life—all time
Centring in that one point—each clime

---

79 [Poet's Note: The poet Statius dedicated to Domitian his *Thebais* and *Achilleis* and commemorated the events of his reign in his *Silvae*.] Hawkshaw's source is the entry for 'Domitianus' in *The Penny Cyclopaedia of the Society for the Diffusion of Useful Knowledge*, vol. 9 (1833), 75. Publius Papinius Statius (c. AD 45–c. 96): Roman poet whose work includes the Latin epics *Thebais* and *Achilleis* (unfinished), and *Silvae*, a collection of shorter poems published in five books.

And race they knew alike to him
Who looks not at the hue or limb;
And these immortal truths they told
To bond, to free, to young, to old.

As shores seen o'er a misty sea,
Glimpses of immortality
Had sages in their musings caught;
But there were minds too mean they thought,
And eyes too vulgar to be taught
To lift their glance so high,—revealed
In academic shades—concealed
In mystic forms, was all they knew;
'Twas little, and 'twas known to few.
They scorned the man who sought the shrine
And deemed its deity divine:
They bowed with look as grave as he,
Yet thought it a nonentity:
The temple had no god; the rite
No meaning in the sages' sight;
The altar was a pile of stone;
They hailed an empty name alone.

Look at the apostles—turn to those
Who made almost a world their foes
Rather than hide one truth they knew;
Oh! dauntless hearts, the firm and true;
Theirs was a courage uninspired
By praise—by doubt and scorn untired.

Earth has its mysteries, and time
Its lengthened ages—both sublime—
And the wide pathless sea—and men
Who've searched these beyond the ken
Of others, seeking nature's stores
Buried upon untrodden shores
Millions of years ago; or swept,
As with an angel's wing, through space,
And marked what suns and systems kept
Their vast and changeless round; all these
Come out from dull mortalities
Sublime and noble. But to stand
Alone amid a heathen land,
Careless of scorn, of chains, of death;
To be unspotted when each breath
Lures with a syren's song to sin;

To stand those stately piles within,
Where Greece adored her gods, and feel
Their beauty and their music steal
Upon the heart, yet burst the spell,
And the stern solemn fact to tell,
That they were vanity and dust,
A broken reed on which to trust;
And not one humbling truth to hide
In prejudice to human pride—
This is sublime beyond what earth
Can shew; 'tis not of earthly birth.

Earth has its histories; so hath heaven,
   Wherein are writ the deeds of men,
And actions up to motives traced
   By an impartial pen;
Stripped of the tinsel and the gloss
With which man strives to gild the dross.
There those who take a brother's life,
By slavery's woes or murder's knife,
Are ranked together; they who hold
Their fellows bound, with those whose gold
Fits the fleet vessel to convey
From Afric's shores its human prey.
There to be good is great, and not
The accident of birth or lot:
Genius is valued by its use;
Wealth by the good it can induce;
The conqueror, he who conquers self.
Could but the history of one age
Be copied from that heavenly page,
How would it look by one of earth?
How each declare from whence its birth?
Oh! world so lovely, yet so vile,
So beautiful with nature's smile,
So marred by man, hast thou no spot
That crime and sorrow visit not?
Some little "island of the blest,"[80]
Some Eden of the untrodden west?
No, none, where man hath been, he reigns
The savage o'er uncultured plains;
The oppressor or the oppressed, he treads
Where art in vain its lustre sheds:

---

80 'island of the blest': the Islands of the Blest were the mythical winterless home of the happy dead, far west.

Oh! when shall war's dark flag be furled,
And love walk through a peaceful world;
When shall the murmurs of the sea,
The mountain wind, the forest tree,
Echo one sound—"All, all are free:"
And earth become one hallowed sod,
One mighty temple of her God!

II.

There was a cypress, and a stone
O'er which had moss and ivy grown;
A single lily of the vale,
With its small blossoms pure and pale,
Quivered beside it in the gale:
And near it columns overthrown,
And fountain with wild flowers o'ergrown,
Told that amid its gardens fair
A stately mansion once stood there;
Within whose halls had Myra wept;—
Beneath that mossy stone she slept.
Far from the land that gave them birth,
Corinna lay in foreign earth:
Where is her grave? it is with things
Forgotten, with the dust of kings,
The swords of heroes and their tombs,
Beneath a city's silent domes.
None wept above it—'tis a spot
Unknown, unthought of, and forgot.
O'er it hath pealed the invader's blast,
O'er it have venging armies past;
And ages in their silent tread
Have scattered o'er her lowly bed
The dust of Rome;—but Myra laid
Where first in infancy she played;
Her ashes from the Italian shore
Her faithful slave to Athens bore;
But she too died—then all were gone
Who once had Myra loved, but one.

For thirty years the flowers had grown
Around that monumental stone;
Each year they sprung, and bloomed, and faded,
Emblems of her whose tomb they shaded.
All sounds that told of life were gone—
The sudden fall of mouldering stone

From ledge to ledge when winds were high,
The night-birds' wild and doleful cry,
These were the only sounds that woke
The echoes there, the silence broke.
Lonely are Afric's voiceless sands,
Silent the arctic's frozen strands,
But earth has drearier scenes—the spot
Once filled by man, by man forgot:
Awe-struck, the invaders paused, when first[81]
Egypt's vast city on them burst,
With temples silent as its dead,—
Home of a hundred ages fled!

It was a night of soft repose,
Such as those southern climes disclose,
When the wind scarcely shakes the rose,
That closed o'er Myra's silent bowers,
And shut that lily's spotless flowers:
Its lengthened shadow o'er the grass
   The urn of Parian marble threw,
And the night's melancholy flowers
   Were glistening in the midnight dew:—
When to that urn an old man came.
Age had not bent his manly frame,
But toil or grief had left their trace,
In the deep furrows on his face,
And marked his brow with lines of care:
Awhile he stood in silence there,
And then, with trembling hand, withdrew
The weeds that round the marble grew,
As if to read what name it kept,
Then knelt beside the stone and wept.
I've seen an aged father weep
   Beside his dying daughter's bed,
And bitterer seemed to me his tears
   Than those our younger eye-lids shed:
Though age we think should feel less pain

---

81 [Poet's Note: It is said the whole French army, when in Egypt, made an involuntary halt when they came in sight of the ruins of Thebes.] Several sources cite Dominique-Vivant Denon (1747–1825) as recording this episode in *Travels in Upper and Lower Egypt*, which was published in translation in 1802 and 1803. Denon had travelled with the Napoleon to Egypt in 1798 and his account of the expedition was highly influential in the rise of early nineteenth-century Egyptology. Hawkshaw's wording is close to that used in an article on 'Thebes' published in *The Penny Magazine of the Society for the Diffusion of Useful Knowledge*, vol. 14 (23 June 1832), 113; also referred to in *The British Museum: Egyptian Antiquities*, vol. 1 (1832), 62–3.

Parting, to meet so soon again.
Yet Dionysius wept above
The ashes of his first, last love:
But how unlike those passionate tears
Shed on her brow in long past years,
When dying, on his arm she lay,
Fading in loveliness away.
They were but such as fill the eye
When mournful music passes by,
Or some fair scene, or spoken words,
Touch softly one of memory's chords,
And tears of tenderness will start
Fresh from the fountains of the heart.
He seemed to hear the very tones
   Of the last words she said—the strain
Of the last song he heard her sing
   Seemed to come on the air again;
And memory pictured, one by one,
Words, looks, and scenes, for ever gone;
Calling up beauty from the dust,
And the lyre's music from its rust,
But softening every tone and shade,
As scenes in distance softly fade.

He thought of her, a happy child,
Whose merry laugh, so clear and wild,
Rang through her father's halls, whose feet
Went bounding through each green retreat;
A butterfly of Cashmere's spring,
Mounting upon an untried wing;
   He saw her bending o'er her lyre
In the first bloom of early youth,
   With eye all soul and heart all fire,
Dreaming that its romance was truth.
Too soon, too soon, those dreams were broken,
When once love's passionate words were spoken;
Then the heart was itself no more,
That shadow of a cloud came o'er
Her brow, and the long fringes hid
The eye which drooped beneath its lid;—
   In thought he saw her thus—to him
More lovely than the laughing girl
   Standing beside the fountain's wave.
To braid with flowers her brow of pearl.

Quickly those scenes of memory past,
Then came the tenderest and the last,
   When, passing from the heart away,
All it had loved or hoped or dreamed,
   In silence on her couch she lay;
Her eyes, where no more lustre burned,
To his in dying sadness turned.
At length he spoke, "The loved, the dead,
"Alone are here," he calmly said.
"How are we changed! The marble's trust
"Is only now a little dust,
"And I with time have nearly done;
"'Mid darkening clouds, as setting sun,
"My lamp of life shall pass away,—
"Thine darkened when it yet was day.
"Like visions former scenes have past
"And fleeted by, except the last.
"I did not think to find it thus;
   "Dark ivy creeping round the stone,
"'Mid ruined halls and silent bowers,—
   "I am then in the world alone,
"The only one who thinks of thee,
   "I breathe an unremembered name,—
"Oh! time, without eternity!
"Oh! life, without the life above!
"What is there for the heart to love?"

The Past

I.

Where is the record of the past inscribed,
   And where the chronicle of ages gone?
What is the gift with which grey time was bribed
   To spare the tablets it is writ upon?
Hold the dark pyramids the mystic scroll?
   Do the pale genii of departed years,
In sunless caverns as the centuries roll,
   Record the sum of human hopes and fears?

II.

No! the past writes its history everywhere,
   On the dark mountain, in the savage glen;
Man treads no spot, however lone, but there
   He finds memorials of his fellow men,

Or nature's history of an elder time:
    The past—'tis written on the human heart,
Told by tradition's tongue from clime to clime,
    Heard in the speech of many a busy mart.

III.

What gave the Grecian his immortal theme?
    What gave to Tasso his undying lay?[82]
The past—whose dim rememberings, like a dream,
    Were fading in obscurity away;
They heard the voices of departed time
    And gave them to the future—pausing oft,
As many a vision rose of blood and crime,
    Or woman's gentle tones in pleading accents soft.

IV.

The present age shall be the theme of song
    To future ages—when the mists of time
Have softened down the outline now too strong,
    Making the dim and shadowy seem sublime:
And as the walls of many a ruined pile
    Outlast the lovelier but the frailer part,
The daring deed survives, though dark and vile,
    The gentler feelings of the human heart.

V.

The nations of the past, where are they now?
    Some, with the cities which they built, decayed,
Some died away we know not why or how;
    Their fated hour arrived though long delayed;
One only hath it given us still unchanged,—
    The dweller of the desert is the same:
Kingdoms have changed around him since he ranged
    Across Arabia's sands, and bore the robber's name.

VI.

Cities sprung round him, but he turned away,
    Armies enclosed him, but he mocked their might,
Empires arose, he bowed not to their sway,
    Art spread her works, he heeded not the sight:

---

82 Tasso: Torquato Tasso (1544–95), Italian poet and prose writer.

His vices and his virtues all his own,
   He gives not, borrows not from polished men;
His home the desert, and a tent his throne,
   His grave, the cavern or the mountain glen!

VII.

The cities of the past, they stand alone
   Vast and majestic in their slow decay;
Year after year but crumbles down a stone,
   And ages watch them as they pass away;
Some have outlived their name, and some their date,
   Like tombs recording not whose dust they shrined;
While unto others, Time a different fate
   Hath given—their name alone remains behind.

VIII.

A heap of ruins only marks the spot
   Where once the Ephesian's splendid city stood,[83]
The very sea hath now its shores forgot,
   And dread malaria broods, where once the flood
Brought Asia's riches to those marble streets:
   One pillar, in its solitude sublime,
Alone upon the plain of Sardis meets[84]
   The stranger's gaze—a beacon left by time!

IX.

Oh! let those silent cities still remain
   Untouched, unmarred, by things of present date,
Let the old temple on its native plain
   There meet the slow arrival of its fate;
Drag not the shattered capital away,
   The shaftless base, to mingle in our halls
With things that speak but of the present day,
   No! let them moulder by their ancient walls.[85]

---

83 A reference to the ancient Greek city of Ephesus, a prosperous port and site of the temple of Artemis, which was considered to be one of the Seven Wonders of the World.

84 Sardis: ancient city, capital of Lydia in Asia Minor.

85 A reference to the Elgin Marbles, the collection of classical Greek architectural fragments brought to Britain by the 7th Earl of Elgin, Thomas Bruce (1766–1841). Taken mainly from the Parthenon in Athens, the marble sculptures were transported to Britain between 1803 and 1812, ostensibly to protect them from destruction in situ during the conflict between Turkey and Greece. The British government purchased the marbles from Elgin in 1816 for display in the British Museum in London, where they remain. The removal of the sculptures divided opinion in Britain, and poets such as Byron (George Gordon, Lord Byron, 1788–1824) responded to

X.

The cities of the past—some stand apart
    In solitudes, unbroken by the sound
Of even the beating of a human heart,
    A silence as the very grave's profound;
Some hath the earth entombed and some the sea;
    Deep in her forests some hath nature hid;
And, in the western world, the tropic tree
    Waves beside many a nameless pyramid.

XI.

Like spell-bound giants of an earlier day,
    Enchanted in their vast and silent halls,
The Egyptian statues watch their shrines decay,
    Where not a flower smiles on the sun-scorched walls;
The burning wind that sweeps the desert's sand,
    And strews it round until it heaps their tomb,
Sighs like a dirge around them, as they stand
    Waiting the slow approaches of their doom.

XII.

It is not so with thee, immortal Greece,
    Thy statues hail not in their native land
The olive, springing by the shrine of peace,
    And freedom's lamp relighted on thy strand;
They fled thy coasts when anarchy and crime
    And long oppression bowed thee to the dust,
To waken genius in our colder clime;
    Be what thou wert again, and we resign our trust.

XIII.

Beyond the past in science we have gone,
    But not in art—those antique statues stand
Like beings of another race, alone,
    Amid the grand around them yet more grand,
Amid the beautiful, the loveliest still;
    We gaze and fancy that the god will speak,
The nymph step from her marble pedestal—
Oh! move not, breathe not, or the spell will break!

---

denounce their removal: 'Dull is the eye that will not weep to see / Thy walls defaced, thy mouldering shrines removed / By British hands, which it had best behoved / To guard those relics ne'er to be restored:— / Curst be the hour when from their isle they roved, / And once again thy hapless bosom gored, / And snatch'd thy shrinking Gods to Northern climes abhorred!' (*Childe Harold's Pilgrimage: A Romaunt* (1812), canto 2, stanza 15, ll. 3–9).

XIV.

We have not learned to love the beautiful
    As Grecians loved it; as a childish play,
(Though still the earth of loveliness is full,)
    We deem such feeling in our wiser day:
Is it an idle play! when He who spread
    The vault of heaven gave it a thousand hues,
And strewed the very ground on which we tread
    With tinted cups, to hold the evening dews.

XV.

The pencil and the lyre—both live and die
    With the deep earnest love of what is fair;
They give the past an immortality,
    But of that glory shall the present share?
Or must we link their names with days gone by?
    Oh! never let it be—the poet's lyre
Hath mourned his country with a patriot's sigh,
    Hath roused to energy a nation's fire.

XVI.

What first shook Europe from her death-like trance,
    Her long dark night of ignorance and crime?
Dante's stern thought, and Petrarch's eloquence,[86]
    Breathed in the music of Italian rhyme;
They woke the memory of departed things,
    Pointing to relics of the ages gone,
And long as freedom loves the lyre's deep strings
    Will she remember him of Avignon.[87]

XVII.

Harp of my country, left in silence now,
    Thy tones have roused thy sons in other days,
When Cambria gathered on the mountain's brow[88]
    Freedom's last hosts, who answered to thy lays:
The voice of freedom ceased not till the tone
    Of thy last harp was silenced;—would the strain
That roused thy children in the ages gone
    Might echo through their island home again.

---

86 Dante's stern thought, and Petrarch's eloquence: referring to Dante Alighieri (1265–1321) and Francesco Petrarca (Petrarch; 1304–74), Italian poets who used themes from classical antiquity in their work.
87 A further reference to Petrarch, who spent much of his early life in Avignon.
88 Cambria: classical name for Wales.

XVIII.

Though not to bid them quell a foreign foe,
  But wake the love of country in their breast;
For in the crowded street, the voice of woe,
  The low faint cry of poverty opprest,
Sounds like the requiem of my country's peace,
  The dirge for her long day of glory fled;
Harp of my country, waken ere it cease,
  And the last spirit of the land be dead!

XIX.

The songs of other days—they linger still
  In ancient legends and in antique rhymes;
Nor has the heart which loves yet ceased to thrill
  At thy sad songs, thou bard of troubled times;[89]
Who breathed thy numbers o'er the lost one's urn
  E'en from the loneliness of our dark towers;
How oft in those long years would'st thou return
  In hope, and memory, to thy southern bowers!

XX.

Those sweet but mournful songs thy country shrines
  Amid her choicest treasures of the past,
And round thy princely brow the laurel twines,
  Son of Orleans, while his is withering fast
Who gave thee in this land an exile's doom.
  For thee the child of song shall breathe the strain,
While history gives, to decorate his tomb,
  The conqueror's bloody wreath, the persecutor's chain.

XXI.

Where sleep the bards? Go ask tradition's tale:
  The historic page records not how they lie;
The crested helm, the lance, the coat of mail,
  On stately cenotaphs attract the eye
Beneath the arches of the gothic pile;
  But lowly are the tombs which bear the lyre;

---

89 [Poet's Note: The Duke of Orleans, who was taken prisoner at the battle of Agincourt by Henry the Fifth, and kept a prisoner in this country twenty three years, chiefly in the Tower, where he composed some of his most beautiful poems.] Charles, duke of Orléans (1394–1465): prince and poet, author of a large body of lyric and narrative poetry in French and English, much of which was written during his time in captivity.

In the old temple of our native isle
    His name has perished, of our song the sire.[90]

XXII.

The past! it is a thing on which to pause,
    A name breathed softly as that word, "farewell,"
A theme to muse on at the evening's close,
    When best on solemn thoughts the heart will dwell.
'Tis like a land of which we oft have heard,
    Yet seen of its far stretching shores but part,
Yet on that little portion are interred
    How many hopes and loves, alas! how many a heart.

XXIII.

Still in that land each one an interest hath,
    An atom of the whole—yet more to him,
In thought to tread some old familiar path,
    Than the long tracts with shadowy distance dim:
'Tis more to him, that tangled briers creep
    Upon those walls where rose and jessamine grew,
Where a kind mother watched his infant sleep,
    Than that the hand of time, Palmyra's halls o'erthrew.[91]

XXIV.

The flight of years change not our hearths alone,
    Far more they change ourselves—we never meet
As last we parted—voices lose their tone,
    Bright eyes grow dim, and hearts less lightly beat.

---

90 [Poet's Note: A few years since I saw the tomb of Chaucer, in Westminster Abbey, with no inscription except "Chaucer," written with chalk.] Several contemporary sources comment on the neglected memorial to Chaucer. In *The Monuments and Genii of St. Paul's and of Westminster Abbey* (London: John Williams, 1826), George Lewis Smyth observes: 'A little to the right of the entrance into the Poets' Corner of Westminster Abbey, are the relics of a Gothic tomb, in black stone, which is now greatly mutilated, and destitute of any inscription or symbol by which the object of its erection may be known. Yet this ruin was once a handsome memorial of the fame of Geoffrey Chaucer, the venerable father of English poetry; whose earthly remains, as well as can be conjectured from the description of the spot given by Caxton, the printer, were deposited somewhere near the front of the contiguous monument to Dryden. There are few readers who can contemplate the modern neglect of such a grave without a feeling of honest sorrow; nor can any friend to literature learn without indignation, that a name which was justly honoured by former ages with the most signal tributes of regard, should be thus abandoned to utter decay by the present generation' (250).

91 Palmyra: ancient city and oasis in the Syria desert on the site of present-day Tadmur; an important cultural and trading centre from the first to the second centuries AD.

The smile of childhood, and the hopeful brow
   Of youthful beauty, change to pensive grace
And quiet thought—as sunny beams endow
   The skies with softened tints before they leave their place.

XXV.

In form, in heart, in mind, the past hath brought
   A change to all we love, to all we know;
For good, or evil only hath it wrought?
   A blessing or a curse it must bestow.
Have all the sorrows, all the griefs, the tears
   That we have seen, but made us feel the less
For human woe; or has the lapse of years
   Softened the heart to tenfold tenderness?

XXVI.

And have the wonders of creation woke
   Of adoration not a loftier strain,
As one by one upon the mind they've broke,
   And yet are moving on, an endless train?
If, when a child, thine eye was raised above,
   In wonder, to the God who spread the sky
With sparkling gems, how deep thine awe and love
   Who know'st them now, as worlds, and suns on high.

XXVII.

Let not the simple homage of the child
   Condemn the heartless worship of the man;
Nature, to it, was mystic, strange, and wild;
   To thee 'tis full of wonders, yet of plan:
It looked above, around, and sky and earth
   Alike were beautiful—it knew no more,
But hushed the throbbings of its infant mirth
   To bless its God—oh! how should'st thou adore!

XXVIII.

Men count the past by years, or months, or days,
   While history notes it by the ages sped;
But science far beyond extends her gaze,
   And reckons by her mighty cycles fled:
The deeds which history calls of ancient date,
   She numbers with the things of yesterday:
One stops to mark the ruined city's fate,
   The other tells of systems passed away!

XXIX.

The historic muse points to the roofless hall,
    The lonely pillar, or the sculptured shrine,
Where silently the feet of centuries fall,
    And the green branches of the ivy twine;
Where, in the midnight hour, the owlet moans,
    And autumn gales strew round the withered flowers,
And winter sighs with deeper, sadder tones,
    And the pale blossom, spring plants on the mossy towers.

XXX.

These are the chronicles of empires past,
    The work of hands now mouldered to decay,
Strewing the earth—but things more strange and vast
    Nature entombed, long ere these passed away—
With skill beyond the sculptor's graved their forms
    Upon the enduring rock and left them there;
Nor did the beating of ten thousand storms
    Those records of an elder world impair.

XXXI.

But pause not there; still further backward turn;
    Before that time perchance bright suns had set,
No more in their far distant skies to burn,
    Whose scattered light hath never reached us yet!
Think of the hour when they began their course,
    And rose in silent grandeur to the sky;
Then pause—and of the past be that the source—
    Time stretches not beyond—there is Eternity!

The Future

I.

Who shall unveil the future—who unfold
    The fate of systems, empires, and of man?
Ceased is the voice of prophecy of old,
    And dim the eyes which once its glooms could scan:
The prophet's harp is silent as his tongue,—
    Both rest together by Judea's streams;
Land of the loftiest and the holiest song,
    Land of a scattered people's hopes and dreams!

II.

Who shall unfold the future? Man hath sought
    To pierce its mystic shade in every age:
For this, with ceaseless toil and patient thought,
    Watched on Chaldea's plains the hoary sage;
His book of destiny the midnight sky,[92]
    And each bright planet in its ceaseless course
The silent messenger of fate on high,
    Alike unbribed by gifts, unawed by force.

III.

For this, in Lybian deserts rose the shrine,[93]
    And in the Delphian shade the Pythia stood,[94]
For this, the Sybil breathed the mystic line,
    And the pale priestess in the Grecian wood
Listened the murmurings of the southern wind
    Through the dim pine grove, by the sacred streams;
Nor strange if in their tones such heart could find
    The voice of coming years, like music heard in dreams.

IV.

Each one is his own prophet, and each heart
    A shrine where many a warning voice is spoken,
And visions glide which make the gazer start;
    And vows are uttered which too soon are broken.
To some, the voice of hope, so glad and wild,
    Alone gives answers at that secret shrine;
While others by her tones are ne'er beguiled,
    They hear but melancholy's mournful line.

V.

We read the future's history in the past—
    Cities have perished, empires died away,
And human schools and systems found at last
    They held the seeds of premature decay:
Whate'er of truth each system had endures,
    The rest is gone—and in a coming age
False shall our falsehoods seem, for time ensures
    The life of truth alone, not dogmas of the sage.

---

92 Chaldea: ancient country in present-day southern Iraq. The Chaldeans ruled Babylonia between 625 and 539 BC and were renowned astrologers and astronomers.
93 [Poet's Note: The Temple of Jupiter Ammon.]
94 Pythia: the priestess of Apollo at Delphi, by whom the oracular pronouncements were delivered (n. 'Pythia' *OED*).

VI.

This cheered Galileo in his dungeon's cell;[95]
    And the great bard when blind, despised, and old;[96]
Gleams from the future o'er his harp-strings fell,
    Voices of distant ages round them rolled.
The future renders justice to the past,
    And in her hands they calmly left their fame;
On coming years a glance prophetic cast,
    To live in them, their lofty hope and aim.

VII.

The cities of the future, shall they rise
    'Mid the untrodden forests of the west?
Or where the coral isle in beauty lies
    Upon the southern ocean's azure breast?
Or far away on undiscovered shores,
    By unknown oceans washed, and nameless streams,
Where nature watches by her unseen stores
    Of bird, and flower, and tree? who, who shall read such dreams?

VIII.

And who shall tell thy fate, my native land?
    Who could have guessed it, when on Thanet's shore
He saw the stranger Hengist's faithless band,[97]
    And the rude barks our circling ocean bore?
Not even thou, immortal Alfred,—thou,[98]
    The king at once in heart, and mind, and face;
Would that the diadem had decked thy brow
    In England's brighter day, pride of thy Saxon race.

---

95 Galileo: Galileo Galilei (1564–1642), Italian physicist and astronomer, whose belief in the Copernican system saw him tried by the Inquisition in 1633. He was placed under house arrest for the remainder of his life.

96 And the great bard when blind, despised, and old: a likely reference to the English poet, John Milton (1608–74). Milton had visited Galileo in Florence in 1638.

97 Hengist and Horsa: Germanic brothers and leaders of the Anglo-Saxon invasion of Britain in the fifth century. They are associated with the creation of the kingdom of Kent and were said to have been given the Isle of Thanet by the warlord Vortigern, against who the brothers later rebelled.

98 Alfred: Alfred the Great (849–99), king of Wessex and of the Anglo-Saxons (871–99). Alfred withstood Viking attempts to invade the southern kingdoms and in doing so laid the foundations of a united England. During the nineteenth century, 'Alfred the Great' was associated with a growing sense of England's national identity in light of the expanding British Empire. He was venerated as a warrior and a scholar, with 'King Alfred' becoming synonymous with all that was seen as good and noble about England past and present. Hawkshaw engages directly with Alfred as national myth in *Sonnets on Anglo-Saxon History* (1854), in which she responds to the eulogising of Alfred by prominent historians.

IX.

Through every state, my country, thou hast past,
    Conquered, oppressed, and then in freedom risen,
And arts and power—and must this be thy last?
    Art thou, too, doomed to fall? Forbid it heaven!
For thee how many a noble heart has bled,
    How many a patriot voice hath wished thee well:
"Be thou perpetual," the Venetian said,[99]
    When on his dying couch—yet Venice fell!

X.

But thou shalt be perpetual if thy guide
    Be sacred virtue, and if justice sway
The counsels of thy land; and power and pride
    Crush not the millions who thy rule obey.
Let ocean whelm thee in her deepest caves,
    Let the white billow sweep the cultured plain,
Rather than freedom's children sink to slaves,
    Or bind round others the oppressor's chain.

XI.

The day-star of earth's freedom has arisen
    Amid the islands of the western main;
A glimmering ray hath reached the captive's prison,
    And slavery trembles while he locks the chain:
Brightly it gilds the palm groves of the west;
    Slowly yet surely shall it mount the sky,
Till every clime its noontide beams hath blessed,
    And one glad sound be heard—the song of liberty!

XII.

Nor shalt thou be forgotten, captive land,
    Whose silent plains the kingly minstrel trod;
Upon those shores again thy sons shall stand,
    Where bard and prophet swept their harps to God.
Where are Judea's children? Ask the wind
    That sighs a requiem o'er Siberia's snow,
Question the city, 'mid the Oasis shrined,
    Or ask the billows round the world that flow.

---

99 'Be thou perpetual': or 'Esto perpetua', said to be the final words of Venetian theologian and scholar Paolo Sarpi (1552–1623), who had defended the interests of the Venetian Republic. The republic lost independence in 1797, having been conquered by Napoleon Bonaparte during the First Coalition.

XIII.

All, all shall answer, "Here the lonely child
    Of wasted Judea finds an outcast's home:"
There is no race, the polished or the wild,
    Earth has no shore, that's washed by ocean's foam,
But there he dwells, yet ever dwells alone;
    Nor is that land a father-land to him;
Judea's lonely wastes, and piles of stone,
    He calls his native clime;—captive in heart and limb!

XIV.

Still, in the portico of wisdom's hall,
    Stand the high spirits of the present day;
The distant sounds of truths around them fall,
    And from the interior comes a glimmering ray,
Revealing, yet half hiding, glorious scenes
    For coming ages, and for other minds;
And they shall tread the part which intervenes;
    It with the future thus the present binds.

XV.

Much hath been done—yet little hath been done.
    What know we even of the earth we tread?
What spicy vales beneath a tropic sun,
    In unseen loveliness their beauties spread?
What unknown forms of life may rove the wood,
    Or skim the waters of that distant land,
Round which the vast Pacific rolls its flood,
    Where England's sons as exiled outcasts stand?

XVI.

Around, above, beneath us, there are themes
    We know not of, for science and for art,
And wild imagination's wildest dreams;
    Pine not for these, for we have had our part;
We give the coming years what may remain,—
    A gift more glorious than the past bequeaths,
We leave them untouched wonders, nature's reign;
    It left us ruins twined with laurel wreaths.

XVII.

Greatest of all, we leave the fate of man;
   The destiny of mind, what shall it be?
For it was woven nature's mighty plan:
   Spirit that breathes of immortality,
Shall it advance, as future years advance,
   Deeper, and broader, loftier be its range?
Or shall it sink again in death-like trance,
   From gloom to darker gloom, its only change?

XVIII.

No! the great nations of the present day
   May cease to be the learned and the wise,
But not for that shall knowledge quench its ray,
   Its light on other climes and realms shall rise:
Its home may change, and science build a shrine,
   In lonely islands of the distant sea,
Or where round Grecian fanes the ivy twines,
   But stop it cannot, 'tis for ever free.

XIX.

How can it pause? It was not made to rest
   In a dull quietude which is not bliss—
Like forest circled lake, whose sunless breast
   No tempests sweep, no summer breezes kiss—
For ever, and for ever journeying on,
   Regretting not what it hath left behind;
For higher themes still may it dwell upon—
   This is the lofty destiny of mind!

XX.

Through the long circle of six thousand years
   It hath been busy, for in Eden's bowers
It woke, ere yet the first sad human tears
   Fell withering on their amaranthine flowers.
Enough it had e'en then to fill its range
   In the fair universe,—itself and God;
Yet for a new made world would we not change
   This earth, by many generations trod?

XXI.

More themes for thought each century will give,
    And future ages of our own will learn:
Long as the heaven enkindled flame shall live,
    And spirits with immortal fire shall burn,
These themes shall never fail: for He who made
    This restless, busy mind, before its gaze
Can spread new wonders not to us displayed,
    In evening dew-drops, or in morning rays.

XXII.

Naught is exhausted—like a history read
    From the torn fragments of an ancient scroll,
We learn earth's history in the epochs fled;
    The future may the mighty whole unroll.
Nations have left, in hieroglyphic forms,
    Their archives, graven on the sculptured walls;
But coming men shall tread those silent homes,
    And pierce the mystery which around them falls.

XXIII.

Like him, who by the founts of Nilus stood,[100]
    In Afric's solitudes unknown to men,
And felt, while gazing on that infant flood,
    All his long toil was compensated then:
Yet as to him, amid his pride there came
    Visions of home, by distant Scotia's streams—
The love of country, with the thought of fame,
    Shall mingle still in many a wanderer's dreams.

XXIV.

Oh! there are earnest longings in the heart
    To pierce yet further through the mystic shades
Which hide the works of God in every part:
    For silent mystery all around pervades.
Divide the mass to atoms—trace the cause
    Still backward through an ever lengthening chain,
There is a point at which at length we pause,
    And where the loftiest spirits still remain.

---

100 [Poet's Note: Bruce.] James Bruce (1730–94), Scottish explorer and author of *Travels to Discover the Source of the Nile in the Years 1768–73* (1790).

XXV.

Had he who plucked the lightening's fiery wing,[101]
    And stayed the thunder on its cloudy throne,
Some high yet undefined imagining
    Of the strange wonders that of it are known?
Scarce deem we spirit is a mystery now,
    When there is something which pervades all space,
And yet unseen, and noiselessly doth flow,
    But once unchained would overwhelm our race.

XXVI.

That mystery of life, may it be solved?
    Shall future ages know the force, the power,
Hidden in human frames? whence it's evolved?
    From what mysterious cause? And shall an hour,
The triumph of long years of anxious thought,
    Dawn on some lonely sage in coming time
And prove the long sought truth? One glance thus caught
    Were worth those years of toil—that moment were sublime!

XXVII.

For 'tis not by the length of years alone
    That we should value life. Are there not those
Whose minds have moved to one unvarying tone,
    A long, dull cadence, without change or pause?
While there are spirits who in one short hour
    Will live such sleepers' mental life of years:
Better sometimes to feel excitement's power,
    Although its smiles are not unmixed with tears!

XXVIII.

Science hath much to teach to future time,
    But other lessons still it hath to learn;
Lessons, than hers, more solemn and sublime,
    To which the spirit would do well to turn.
The good may be forgotten in the great;
    The moral, in the mental; and the hand
Who built and furnished all the fair estate,[102]
    Be unremembered 'mid the works He planned.

---

101 [Poet's Note: Franklin.] Benjamin Franklin (1706–90), American revolutionary politician, writer and natural philosopher. Franklin formulated a theory of electricity which suggested positive and negative elements; by 1750 he had devised experiments to prove that clouds became electrified and that lightning was a discharge of electrical energy.

102 Original publisher's errata note: 'for "the" read "this"'.

XXIX.

Let memory take the past; we give to hope
    The future, with its store of radiant things;
Bright as the tints of heaven's ethereal cope,
    She stretches to it her immortal wings;
And yet some think she should survey its shore,
    So dimly seen, but with an anxious glance;
For vain alike is wisdom's treasured store,
    Or her gay dreams, to pierce its vast expanse.

XXX.

We stand like those who on the new world's shore,
    Watched for the mists of night to pass away;
Behind them rolled wild oceans voyaged o'er,
    Before, an unknown land in darkness lay;
While as they gazed upon that summer isle,
    The morning broke; o'er palm groves rose the sun:
And thus, we greet the future with a smile,
    We see its dawn, and then our task is done!

Wild Flowers

Wild flowers, wild flowers, ye are sweeter far
Than the garden's prouder beauties are;
Kissed by the sun, fanned by the wind,
Blooming and blushing all unconfined;
Wet with the shower of the early spring,
Brushed by the butterfly's wandering wing,
Lulled by the bee in the noontide hours,
Are ye, in your lonely retreats, wild flowers.

Ye are born in the depths of the mountain glen,
Far from the noisy haunts of men;
Bathed with the spray of the wild cascade,
Deep 'mid the gloom of the forest shade;
Nursed, with Alpine steeps of snow
Above, and the Leman lake below,[103]
Where the chamois bounds untamed and free,
And the winds are the breath of liberty.

---

103 Leman lake: Lac Léman, French name for Lake Geneva, large lake in south-west Switzerland and eastern France.

Like banners ye wave on the ruined tower;
Like gems ye are scattered round beauty's bower;
Ye are decking the martyr's lowly grave;
Ye bend o'er the desert fountain's wave;
Where the foot of man hath never trod,
On the secret altars of nature's God;
By the mighty Jumna's hidden springs;[104]
Ye sleep in beauty, ye fair wild things.

Oh! that I had a home like yours,
As once I had, ye sweet wild flowers;
For the wild-birds' song, and the breezes' sigh,
And the lulling sound of waters nigh,
And autumn's tones so deep and wild,
Are music and song to nature's child;
And far away I long to be,
From crowded cities, alone with ye!

The Welsh Bard's Last Song

My hand is on my harp,
    I'll wake it once again,
Wake it, and pour one last wild song,
    Then snap its chords in twain.

Harp, thou hast roused the brave,
    Hast nerved the coward's hand,
And never shall thy numbers sound
    But in a freeman's land.

Spirit of other days!
    Let visions of the past,
Float o'er yon dusky mountain's brow;
    Let voices on the blast,

Tell me of other times,
    And ages that are fled;
Let me hold converse with the shades
    Of bards and warriors dead.

Let me forget I live
    Degenerate and a slave;
Or let me find, 'mid yonder rocks,
    A free, unconquered grave.

---

104 Jumna: river in northern India, rising in the Himalayas.

My spirit could not rest,
    If o'er the minstrel's head,
The foeman's hostile bands should pass,
    The tyrant's footsteps tread.

But let the mountain goat,
    The tameless and the wild,
Bound o'er the last and narrow home
    Of freedom's child!

Spring to the Flowers

TO THE PRIMROSE.

Primrose bud, be thou the child
Of the woodland thicket and dingle wild;
Spring by the fountain's dashing wave,
Smile on the infant's lowly grave,
Peep by the peasant's cottage gate,
Be the violet's friend, and the cowslip's mate.

TO THE DAISY.

Daisy, not of my train art thou,
I see thee on summer's burning brow,
In the glowing wreath that autumn wears,
In the withered crown that winter bears:
Go wander, unconstrained and free,
In every place thy home shall be;
On mount and moorland, rock and tower,
In woodland lone, and cultured bower.

TO THE LILY OF THE VALLEY.

Far from the homes of men away,
Far from the summer's scorching ray;
By the lonely stream, and the forest tree,
Lily of beauty, thy home must be;
Emblem of purity, shroud thee well
In the glossy leaves of thine emerald cell:
Thy head shall bend with the breath of spring,
And quiver and shake at the wild bird's wing:
Lonely thy home, but the young and fair,
Led by thy perfume, shall seek thee there.

TO THE WATER LILY.

Where the crystal wave, 'neath sunny skies,
Calm as a glassy mirror lies;
Or far 'mid the mountain solitudes,
Where the kingly eagle proudly broods,
And the lakes in their secret hollows lie,
Unseen by all save the king-bird's eye;
Floating upon that wave at rest,
Stirred as the water-bird leaves its nest,
There is the home I give to thee,
Queen of the lonely lake to be.

Sonnet—To America[105]

Queen of the western world, upon thy brow
    There is a spot of blood, a crimson stain
    That dims thy greatness,—and it is in vain
Thy snowy sail on every sea to show;
Or through thy streets that streams of commerce flow,
    Or that thy cities rise on every plain:
Though thou art loud when freedom is the strain,
    Yet thou to heaven prefer'st a faithless vow;
Think not thy brightest deeds will weave a veil
    To hide from God or man thy *one great crime*;
Wrongs that will turn the cheek of pity pale.
    History shall write of thee in after time;
And future ages on one page shall see
The slave's unheeded prayer,—the song of liberty!

---

105 This sonnet can be usefully considered as a companion poem to 'Land of my Fathers'; its anti-American sentiment is illustrative of Britain's perspective of moral supremacy in the years following the Slavery Abolition Act of 1833 (see note 108). The final couplet is quoted by John Hawkshaw in his memoir *Reminiscences of South America: From Two and a Half Years' Residence in Venezuela*, which was published in London by Jackson and Walford in 1838 – four years before the publication of Ann's *Dionysius* volume. In concluding his critique of the United States' continued reliance on compulsory labour, John Hawkshaw asserts: 'and hence it will be affirmed of this country, as it has been written,— 'Future ages on one page shall see / The Slave's unheeded prayer—*the song of Liberty*' (*Reminiscences*, 52).

Palestine

Is this Judea? this the promised land
Where conquering Joshua led his Hebrew band?
Is this the clime that flowed with oil and wine,
This lonely waste,—can this be Palestine?

Yes even so—for he who cannot lie,
Whose word must stand though suns and systems die,
To prophet bards and holy seers of old,
The scroll of dark prophetic lore unrolled;
Their lips foretold, and firm the word remains,
And silent horror broods o'er all her plains.

The heathen Gentiles in her cities tread,
The thistle waves above her kingly dead;
No olive springs upon its favourite hill,
Nor lily bends by "cool Siloam's rill:"[106]

On Carmel's mount, on Tabor's sacred height,
No beams of glory strike the astonished sight—
As wont of old—when seraphs wandered there,
And angel harpings floated on the air—
The prostrate pillar, and the moss-grown stone,
Where lizards creep and birds unholy moan;
Where roofless halls are filled with drifting sand,
These are the cities of that sinful land!

Yes, for her sins, and for her sins alone,
The locks of glory from her head were shorn;
For this, the rose from Sharon's field is gone,[107]
Nor cedar forests wave o'er Lebanon;
For this, in Judea's vales, the harp, and lute,
And minstrel's song, and voice of mirth, are mute;
For this, in every clime, in every land,
From Russia's snows to Afric's burning sand,

---

[106] 'cool Siloam's rill': from the popular Sunday School hymn 'By Cool Siloam's Shady Rill', written by Reginald Heber (1783–1826). The allusion here, and in the reference to 'the rose from Sharon's field' later in the stanza, is to the hymn's opening and third verse: 'By cool Siloam's shady rill / How fair the lily grows! / How sweet the breath, beneath the hill, / Of Sharon's dewy rose!'; 'By cool Siloam's shady rill / The lily must decay; / The rose that blooms beneath the hill / Must shortly fade away.'

[107] Sharon's field: a fertile plain in the north of Palestine. In addition to Heber's hymn, there is direct reference to the rose of Sharon in the Old Testament: 'I am the rose of Sharon, and the lily of the valleys' (Songs of Solomon 2:1).

A weary, worn, and persecuted race,
Her children seek in vain a resting place:
Ages have passed, yet still their heart remains
Dark and unfruitful as their native plains.

Land of my Fathers[108]

Land of my fathers, isle of the free!
Go look ye abroad o'er land and sea,
On the glowing east, on the distant west,
On the islands that lie on ocean's breast,
Basking in sunlight, and gemmed with flowers;
They are not fair like this isle of ours.

Homes of beauty it has, that sleep
In quiet peace in its valleys deep;
Wealth it has, and the sunbeams fall
On many a palace and gilded hall;
And its vessels float on every tide,
But it is not these that make its pride.

No! land of my fathers! but 'tis thou art free;
Free as the wave that encircles thee;
Free as the winds that rock to rest
The eagle upon his mountain nest;
Thou hast broken the fetter, and burst the chain;
A slave cannot breathe in thy wide domain!

To Fountain's Abbey[109]

It is a common record
   Thy hoary ruins bear,
And yet thy vaults are eloquent,
   Though silence' self be there!

---

108 This nationalistic and celebratory poem reflects Britain's redefining of its world role in line with abolitionist politics following the Slavery Abolition Act (1833) which gave slaves in the British Empire the opportunity of freedom. The poem supports Linda Colley's observation that 'successful abolitionism became one of the vital underpinnings of British supremacy in the Victorian era, offering – as it seemed to do – irrefutable proof that British power was founded on religion, on freedom and on moral caliber, not just on a superior stock of armaments and capital'; see *Britons: Forging the Nation, 1707–1837* (New Haven and London: Yale University Press, 2005), 359.

109 Fountain's Abbey: the well-persevered ruins of a twelfth-century Cistercian monastery near Ripon, North Yorkshire.

A tale of glory gone—
    Of splendour passed away—
Of pomp; like youthful hopes and loves,
    Changed for decay!

Where are the hands that reared thee,
    Thou ivy-mantled pile?
Where are the tongues that breathed the hymn
    Down thy long pillared aisle?
Ask not the now deserted shrines
    Who bent the suppliant knee—
Ask not tradition's thousand tales—
    But ask Eternity!

Not one, of all, who in thy courts,
    From age to age have trod,
Can rest, as thou ere long shalt rest,
    For ever 'neath the sod.
In all the proudest works of man,
    The seeds of death are shrined;
But immortality has stamped
    The seal of life on mind.

I sigh to think thy walls shall live
    Soon, but in history's page;
Though child of superstition thou,
    Reared in a darksome age.
More beautiful in slow decay,
    Thy mouldering halls to me,
Than when a hundred torches gleamed
    On monkish pageantry.

To a Bereaved Father[110]

Weep,—for the silent grave
    Hath closed above thy son;
Weep,—yet rejoice; for hath not he
    The crown of conquest won?
Borne from the treacherous river's breast
On heaven's unchanging shore to rest.

---

110 This is one of five poems to deal with the death of children. See also: 'To―― on the Death of Three of her Children', 'To―― after the Death of her Daughter' (*Dionysius the Areopagite', with Other Poems*), 'Ada' (*Poems for My Children*), 'In Memoriam' (*Cecil's Own Book*).

Plant on his youthful grave
    The blossoms of the spring;
The bending lily, pale and pure,
    Bring from the valleys, bring;
And on his ashes let them be
The types of immortality.

For as returning spring
    Shall wake their flowers again,
So shall his slumbering body break
    Mortality's cold chain;
When the last beams of yonder sun
Shall dimly tell his work is done.

And ere that glorious day,
    Safe from the storms of time,
With rapture shall his spirit greet
    Thee to the blessed clime;
He is but gone a while before
To hail thy coming to that shore!

The Exile Song

I live upon the memory of the past;
    Of the clear fountains and the woodland streams:
Oh! that their pleasant harmonies would last
    That murmur still like music through my dreams;
For 'mid the crowded city, and its throng
Of busy men, what hath the child of song?

There is a voice, a deep and meaning tone,
    When through the pine wood sweeps the winter's blast;
And there are visions in the clouds that throne
    Themselves on rocks, when storms are gathering fast,
And the white avalanche prepares to leap
Down to the valley from its Alpine steep.

Give me for home, the mountain and the wild,
    There's health and freedom in its roughest gale;
This is no home for inspiration's child,
    Amid the crowd with toil and commerce pale,
And these dark heavy piles which their coarse dreams
Embody forth—give me my own bright streams;

Give me the works of God; or if of men,
    Let it be those who inspiration drew
From the deep solemn gloom of wood and glen,
    And copied nature to their model true,
And loved to turn from their own works to trace
The purer forms from whence they caught their grace;

And give me nature's sounds;—can music's tones,
    Fashioned by art, such thrilling feelings bring,
As when, throughout the cavern's fretted stones,
    The low, deep waters, and the breezes sing;
Or when, across the wild and sullen sky
And leafless wastes, the autumnal gale sweeps by.

Mysterious ocean, in thy ceaseless roar
    There is a strange music of unearthly power,
As one long billow chases to the shore
    Its dying fellow, in the midnight hour;—
Thine is a deeper voice than Gothic pile
From solemn organ sends down its long pillared aisle.

Keep, keep my heart, the treasures which thou hast
    Of sounds and scenes that now have passed away,
Things far too beautiful on earth to last,
    Earth that but holds her treasures for decay!
And let soft voices of the woods and streams
Come floating round me, though but in my dreams.

The Mother to her Starving Child[111]

Oh! sleep; I dread to see those eyes
    To mine in silent grief appealing;
Sleep, and I will not breathe a sigh,

---

111 Pagination from the original has been replicated here with spacing after lines 6 and 24. The change of tone and emphasis in each of the three sections is significant to Hawkshaw's engagement with idealised notions of childhood death and the reality of a child dying from starvation. The poem engages directly with the Poor Law Amendment Act (1834) in which outdoor relief for the able-bodied poor was abolished in favour of the workhouse. As with the mother and child in Hawkshaw's poem, people starved to death on the streets, rather than apply for the poor relief that would send them to the workhouse. The poem is one of a number written during the 1830s and 1840s to depict the hardship of the impoverished. Prominent social protest poets include Caroline Norton ('A Voice from the Factories', 1836), Thomas Hood ('The Song of the Shirt', 1843), John Critchley Prince ('The Death of the Factory Child', 1841) and Elizabeth Barrett Browning ('The Cry of the Children', 1843).

Though down my cheeks the tears are stealing;
My breaking heart be still awhile,
He sleeps, and I may almost smile.

I might have born it if disease
   Had changed thee thus, and only wept,
As others oft have wept before,
   And in my heart thy memory kept,
And treasured there, like parting token,
Each lisped word that thou had'st spoken;
I should have dreamed of thee by night,
A blessed thing with wings of light;
I should have thought of thee by day,
And all that thou wouldst do or say;
I should have heard the very tone
   Of thy soft voice in every sound,
Then wept to know myself alone,
   And thou beneath the church yard ground:
But they had only been such tears
As memory keeps for by-gone years,
Softening the heart like summer's showers,
That bend, but do not break its flowers.

But now, my tears for thee will fall
   Like burning drops to scorch my heart;
Fancy nor memory e'er recall,
   My child, why, how, we part.
There was a sound, long years ago,
   By Rachael's grave,—a voice was heard[112]
In Ramah,—'twas a cry of woe
   From mothers' hearts to madness stirred;
A sorrow that refused relief,
And such, ay such, will be my grief![113]

---

112 Rachael: the biblical mother of Joseph whose lamentations for her lost children are prophesied in the Old Testament book of Jeremiah and then realised in the New Testament gospel of St Matthew: 'A voice was heard in Ramah, lamentation, *and* bitter weeping; Rachel weeping for her children refused to be comforted for her children, because they *were* not' (Jeremiah 31:15); 'Then Herod, when he saw that he was mocked of the wise men was exceeding wroth, and sent forth, and slew all the children that were in Bethlehem, and in all the coasts thereof, from two years old and under, according to the time which he had diligently enquired of the wise men. Then was fulfilled that which was spoken by Jeremy the prophet, saying, "In Rama was there a voice heard, lamentation, and weeping, and great mourning, Rachel weeping *for* her children, and would not be comforted, because they are not"' (Matthew 2:16–18).

113 In the second edition of *English Poetry of the Victorian Period 1830–1890* (Harlow: Longman: 2001) Bernard Richards includes a chapter on women poets, which although dominated by Richards's discussion of Barrett Browning's *Aurora Leigh*, is extended to include women poets who had

To—— on the Death of Three of her Children[114]

I do not know thee, but one kindred tie
   Binds us together,—though my name may wake
No gentle memories of the days gone by,
   Yet, if the bard and soldier for the sake
Of lyre and sword are brothers, I may dew
Thy children's grave with tears;—I am a mother too.

Oh! name, most sainted of the names of earth;
   None but a mother knows what mothers feel,
When the clear voice is hushed of childhood's mirth;
   And on the laughing eyes death puts his seal:
A sound of music from the earth is gone.
Nor art, nor nature, can give back the tone.

But the heart hears it in the sleepless night;
   And dreams give back the soft familiar tread;
Oh! cease, deceiving phantasies; the light
   Must wake the weeping mother to her dead,
Or bring them with angelic pinions by,
Painting them as they are, where they can never die.

Through the dim shadowy land of death they've past,
   To homes of brightness, and to bowers of rest;
But we on earth have still to look our last;
   The dying pillow still hath to be prest;
Oh! weep not for the dead, but weep for those
Whose eyes have yet in death's dark sleep to close.

'an interest in writing poetry about repressed and humiliated members of society', because they themselves were 'subjugated and silenced in the ordinary social circumstances' and so used poetry as 'an opportunity to vent their feelings' (216). Ann Hawkshaw is cited by Richards as a 'typical protest poet', even though Richards gives no critical evaluation of Hawkshaw's work beyond the listing of poem titles that include repressed or humiliated members of society, namely 'Why am I a Slave?' and 'The Mother to her Starving Child'. Richards's choice of poems suggests that he was familiar with Hawkshaw's work primarily through the entry in *Nineteenth-Century Women Poets: An Oxford Anthology* (Oxford: Clarendon Press, 1996). In her discussion of the poem in *Victorian Poetry: Poetry, Poetics and Politics* (1993), Isobel Armstrong suggests that Hawkshaw's 'pun on the "relief" of madness is sombre, with the ironic social meaning of "poor relief" shadowing the psychological term' (323). Debbie Bark discusses the political and aesthetic implications of the poem in 'Poetry of Social Conscience, Poetry of Transition: Ann Hawkshaw's "Introductory Stanzas" and "The Mother to her Starving Child"', in *Poetry, Politics and Pictures: Culture and Identity in Europe, 1840–1914*, eds Ingrid Hanson, Jack Rhoden and Erin Snyder (Oxford: Peter Lang, 2013) 45–65.

114 This is one of five poems to deal with the death of children. See also: 'To a Bereaved Father', 'To—— after the Death of her Daughter' (*'Dionysius the Areopagite', with Other Poems*), 'Ada' (*Poems for My Children*), 'In Memoriam' (*Cecil's Own Book*).

To—— after the Death of her Daughter[115]

Oh! tell me not the loved and lost forget
   That heavenly hearts no earthly love can hold;
Hath dark oblivion there its signet set,
   And can the feelings as the grave be cold?
Pure and allied to heaven they are by birth,
Shrined first in forms that trod a sinless earth.

Say thou, who weeping o'er a daughter's dust,
   Liftest from thence the eye of faith above,
How sweet the confidence, how firm the trust,
   That still she treasures thoughts of thee with love,
And through the azure of the upper skies
Looks down on those she loved with calm and happy eyes.

We have our loved ones in those brighter skies,
   Nor can they seem a stranger's clime to be:
Religion, time, and death, unloose the ties
   Of earth, to link them to eternity:
The heart's affections, with unbroken chain,
Bind those whom earth hath lost with those who yet remain.

Lines on a Friend lost at Sea

Art thou too gone? the loved, the kind, the young;
   And do the breezes o'er thy place of death
Sigh with their wild and melancholy song,
   As if thy voice still mingled with their breath;
Art thou, too, gone? and does the ocean wave
Roll with its dirge-like music o'er thy grave?

It seems but yesterday since last we met;
   When youth's bright hopes and generous thoughts were thine;
And more than these—thy youthful heart had beat
   In pure devotion at religion's shrine.
Those hopes and thoughts thou hast engulphed, dark sea,
They rest among thy treasures; but in thee
Are no wrecked hopes of immortality!

---

115 This is one of five poems to deal with the death of children. See also: 'To a Bereaved Father', 'To—— on the Death of Three of her Children' (*'Dionysius the Areopagite', with Other Poems*), 'Ada' (*Poems for My Children*), 'In Memoriam' (*Cecil's Own Book*).

No!—from the stormy wave the spirit bore
    Its holy breathings and its lofty trust,
And only left amid the billow's roar
    The sullied things of earthliness and dust,
Rising immortal from the ocean's foam
To amaranthine bowers—an everlasting home.

Lost did they say thou wert? Yes, lost to earth,
    That hath such need of holy ones like thee;
Lost to the lovely spot that gave thee birth;
    Its ancient woods, with solemn melody,
Waving around its Gothic towers, retain
No echo of thy voice,—'tis now a by-gone strain.

But not to memory lost;—kind hearts will hold
    Thine image 'midst the treasures which they keep
Of scenes beloved they shall no more behold—
    Of voices hushed in silence—eyes that sleep
In death's dark slumber—bright hopes passed away—
And all they loved, now yielded to decay.

Nor lost to heaven;—endowed with angel powers,
    Thy mind creation's glorious works shall scan,
And watch till time shall close his finished hours,
    The ways of God, the destinies of man:
What is earth's boasted wisdom now to thee,
Amid the wonders of Eternity!

The Prophet's Lament

"And Jeremiah lamented for Josiah."

II CHRONICLES 35:25

Weep, lonely daughter of Judea, weep,
    Bow, widowed queen, thy faint and crownless head;
Among the tombs thy midnight vigils keep,
    Wail 'mid the chambers of thy mighty dead;
Raise not thine eyes, they shall but view afar
Chaldea's eagles gathering to the war.

I hear a voice upon the tempest's blast,
    My spirit trembles at the dreary sound;
Bow to the dust thy cedars, Lebanon;
    Great ocean, hide thee in thy depths profound;
Earth, cast away thy gorgeous robes, and sigh,
And be thou clothed in sackcloth, orient sky.

I hear that sound for ever—in the wind,
    And in the dashing water's troubled roar—
In the deep thunder—in the desert's blast—
    In the wild billows on the lonely shore—
It is a spirit's voice that speaks in all
Storms, winds, and waters, of my country's fall.

And by my couch, at midnight, visions pass
    Of coming years—and shadowy figures creep
In dim uncertain gloom, yet with a sound
    That gathers as they come;—then onward sweep
Chaldea's hosts, and pomp and pride are there,[116]
And Judah's captives in their mute despair.

I see the temple on Moriah's brow,[117]
    Our holy house, by heathen conquerors' trod;
I see their ensigns waving in the wind,
    E'en on the altars of Judea's God;
Our fathers' sepulchres in ruins laid,
And night-birds gathering where our prophets prayed.

Let clouds and darkness on Megiddo's plain[118]
    Rest now for ever—let not there the sound
Of pleasant music, or the voice of song,
    Or hum of busy men, henceforth resound;
For there Josiah, 'mid the heathen, died,
There sunk in dust, our buckler and our pride!

Song

Though a smile is on my lip,
    And my words are light and free,
Yet my heart unchanging still,
    Thinks, ever thinks of thee.

---

116 Chaldea: ancient country in present-day southern Iraq.
117 Moriah's brow: biblical reference to the temple at Mount Moriah (2 Chronicles 3:1), Old Testament site of Abraham's offering of his son Isaac as sacrifice (Genesis 22:2).
118 Megiddo: ancient city of north-west Palestine.

Between us ocean rolls;
    And years must intervene
Ere thou canst tread with me again
    Each loved familiar scene.

But time, with chilly hand,
    Can never sweep away
The records traced on memory's page,
    Of many a happier day.

This throbbing, anxious heart,
    Cold in the tomb must be,
E'er I can tear thine image thence,
    And cease to think of thee.

The Greek Girl's Song

Fling on oblivion's wave,
    My own, my sunny clime,
The records of thy history
    That tell of bonds and crime.

Dark was the night of slavery;—
    At length awoke
The spirit that had slumbered long,
    And all thy fetters broke.

That spirit which had nerved
    The bosoms of our sires,
Had edged the patriot warrior's sword,
    Or tuned the minstrel's lyres—

The fields where those who fell
    For Greece in other days,
The songs of those who told their deeds
    In wild poetic lays,—

Kept living (though for centuries
    It vain and dimly burned)
The flame of sacred liberty,
    Till brighter days returned.

> For who, of thy degenerate sons,
> > Could look on Marathon,[119]
> > Or tread thy pass, Thermopylæ,[120]
> > Nor think of glory gone.
>
> But now, around the hero's brow,
> > Let Grecian maidens twine
> > The laurel, that for ages past
> > But decked the ruined shrine.
>
> And let the voice of song be heard
> > O'er the blue Ægean sea;
> > Waken again the Doric lute,
> > For Greece is free!'[121]

The Captive King

II KINGS, CHAP.25.[122]

> Long years, long years ago,
> > Upon this furrowed brow
> > Glittered the circlet of a realm;
> > Where is it now?
> > Where is it? On the head,
> > Of him who bound this chain
> > Around these limbs, and slew my sons
> > On Riblah's fatal plain.
>
> My sons;—I saw them die;
> > And then they steeped in night
> > These eyes, that pity might have closed
> > Before the horrid sight.

---

119 Marathon: township on the north-east coast of Attica in Greece, site of the Battle of Marathon in which the Athenian's defeated an invading Persian army in 490 BC.

120 Thermopylae: site of the second Persian invasion of Greece in 480 BC. During the Battle of Thermopylae an outnumbered Grecian army sought to defend their land against the Persian invasion led by Xerxes I.

121 A reference to the Greek War of Independence (1821–32) which secured Greece's liberation from Turkish rule under the Ottoman Empire.

122 The reference to II Kings 25 indicates that the speaker here is Zedekiah, last king of Judah before the destruction of the kingdom by Babylon. Zedekiah was brought before King Nebuchadnezzar at Riblah, where his sons were slain before him and his eyes gouged out, before being taken in chains to Babylon where he was imprisoned until his death.

And now in darkness laid,
   Shut in this living tomb,
By day, by night, I picture still
   My children's bloody doom.

Long years, long years have passed,
   I'll number up the sum;
Yet no, to darkness let them pass,
   As darkly they have come.
Long years,—yet still I live
   Within my prison wall;
Ah! would that this might be the last,
   To break the captive's thrall.

The strong, in manhood's eager strife,
   Have paused, and passed away;
And beauty in the grave has found
   The chambers of decay;
Yet still I live, though bowed with age,
   Blind, wretched and alone;
Death, hast thou too forgotten me,
   Here on this dungeon's stone?

Why am I a Slave?[123]

"One poor wretch died here (Isle of France) broken hearted, constantly exclaiming, 'Why am I a Slave?'"

BENNET AND TYERMAN'S VOYAGE ROUND THE WORLD[124]

Why do I bear that cursed name?
   Why, why am I a slave?
Why doomed to drag a wretched life
   In sorrow to the grave?
Born 'mid the mountain solitudes,
   And as the lion free,
Who had a right to bind these limbs
   And make a slave of me?

I looked—there stood the white man's home,
   'Mid pleasant founts and flowers,
'Mid waving woods and waters clear,
   Green vines and rosy bowers;
It had an air of loveliness
   That suited not despair—
I turned away, for well I knew
   That happy hearts were there.

I knew that happy hearts were there,
   For voices full of glee

---

123 In the chapter 'Msrepresentation [sic]: Codes of Affect and Politics in Nineteenth-Century Women's Poetry', in *Women's Poetry, Late Romantic to Late Victorian: Gender and Genre, 1830–1900* (Basingstoke: Palgrave Macmillan, 1999), Isobel Armstrong argues that from the 1790s to the 1830s, slave and factory poems moved 'from the sphere of politics to that of affect' at the hands of female poets (7). At one end of the spectrum, Armstrong places Anna Laetitia Barbauld's blatantly political 'An Epistle to William Wilberforce Esq. on the Rejection of the Bill for Abolishing the Slave Trade' (first published in 1791); at the other, Ann Hawkshaw's 'Why am I a Slave?' – 'a lyrical cry of anguish, as the slave's question is dramatized by a feeling narrator' (7). The intimate first-person narration of the slave speaker draws comparisons with the archetypical Victorian poetic representation of slavery: Elizabeth Barrett Browning's 'The Runaway Slave at Pilgrim's Point' (1848). Debbie Bark discusses the connections between these works and Frederick Douglass's autobiographical slave narrative *My Bondage and My Freedom* (1855) in 'Sight, Sound, and Silence: Representations of the Slave Body in Barrett Browning, Hawkshaw, and Douglass', in *The Victorian Newsletter* 114 (Fall 2008): 51–68. The reviewer of '*Dionysius the Areopagite', with Other Poems* in *Court Magazine and Monthly Critic* (June 1843) reprints 'Why am I a Slave?' to preface a politically charged antislavery declaration; see Appendix A.
124 As the epigraph suggests, this is a poetic reworking of a Mauritian plantation slave's lament, as recorded in the travel log of missionaries George Bennet and the Reverend Daniel Tyerman: *Journal of Voyages and Travels*, 2 vols (London: Frederick Westley and A. H. Davis, 1831). Of their observations of slavery on the island of Mauritius (Isle of France) they write: 'One poor wretch lately died at this place, heart-broken, continually exclaiming, till voice and breath failed, "Why am I a slave?"' (vol. 2, 494).

Came on the air, and from their tone
    I knew that they were free;
Unlike the low faint murmuring sound,
    That marks the wretched slave,
Words wrung from misery's quivering lips,
    That sound as from the grave.

I turned—there stood my lonely hut,
    I call it not my home,
For no beloved face is there,
    And no familiar form,
No voice to break its solitude,
    And none to soothe the woe
Of him who was but born to sigh,
    Whose tears must ever flow.

Why does the rose bestrew his path,
    And mine the pricking thorn?
Why was the white man born to smile,
    And I to sigh and mourn?
I know not, only this I know,
    Till in the silent grave
There is no hope, no joy for me,
    I am a slave—a slave!

Sonnet to———[125]

I love my country, for I love my kind—
    Man is my brother wheresoe'er he roam—
    I love my father's hearth, my childhood's home,
And all the hopes and memories round it twined:
I love the deep thoughts and the cares which bind
    The mother to her children—in my heart
    These, and the love of song have each their part:
But not a part for thee alone, I find,
    For 'tis all thine—as light that fills no space
And yet pervades all nature, and which gives
    All forms their beauty, loveliness, and grace,
And energy and hope to all that lives;
So unto me hath been thy love—then take
This song of mine, and keep it for my sake.

---

125 The sonnet is included in the review of *'Dionysius the Areopagite', with Other Poems* in *North of England Magazine* and in John Evans' review in *Lancashire Authors and Orators* (1850); see Appendix A.

1843

'LIFE'S DULL REALITY'

This poem is not included in Hawkshaw's published collections. It was published in a volume of original poems entitled the *Athenæum Souvenir; original Poems, &c., contributed by various Authors, in aid of the Funds of the Athenæum Bazaar, held in the Town Hall, MANCHESTER, October 1843*: a compilation of poetry by Manchester poets on sale at the Manchester Athenæum Bazaar on 2 October 1843. This fundraising event was held to raise funds for the Manchester Athenæum, an institution founded in 1835 for the 'advancement and diffusion of knowledge'. The *Manchester Guardian* review of the bazaar highlights 'Life's Dull Reality' as one of the outstanding poems in the volume. The poem was printed in full in the *Manchester Guardian* on 11 October 1843, with the following introduction:

'We copy the following beautiful little poem from the *Athenæum Souvenir*,—the volume containing the collected poetic contributions of a number of gifted writers in aid of the Bazaar funds:—'

"Life's dull reality!"—ah! say not so;
   Speak rather of its solemn mystery.
What there is in it hidden, none shall know,
   Until they read it in eternity.
It is not life, nor earth, but *we* are dull.
   There is a meaning in all things around:
The lowliest life of poetry is full:
   Each home, a shrine,—each grave, a sacred ground.

Is not our dwelling in the universe,
   Whose course we see? But whither doth it tend?
Look not upon it as mankind's vast hearse:
   It hath yet *other* destiny and end.
Are not the starry skies above thy head?
   Are their far-gleaming lights no mystery?
Is not the wild flower trembling to thy tread—
   The dew-drop glittering on the path by thee?

Where is thy home?—amid the haunts of men?
   Sigh not to have it otherwise than there.
Or is it nestled in the mountain-glen,
   Wash'd by clear waters, fann'd by purer air?
Each of the busy crowd can hope and fear,
   And know and live, and silently must go
Through Death's lone portal, nor shall disappear,
   Leaving no trace to work for weal or woe.

And who is there that ever felt the power
    Of nature, 'mid her solitudes, could deem
The all of life is but the little hour
    Of earthly being, passing as a dream?
For then the heart, with earnest longing, yearns
    For something holier, purer, deeper far:
And to the spirit-land instinctive turns,
    Seen dimly through the veil of things that are.

How thin the veil, how near the spirit-land,
    Those many strivings of the heart declare!
Look trustingly, and from this mortal strand
    Its shores shall stretch before thee, faint, yet fair;
And when a whisper to thy spirit comes,
    Borne on no breezes, let not earthly strife,
And the world's cares, or honour's noisy dreams,
    Drown the still voice: it speaks to thee of life!

1847

POEMS FOR MY CHILDREN

Poems for My Children was published in July 1847 in London (Simpkin & Marshall) and Manchester (Simms & Dinham) under the name 'Mrs Hawkshaw'. A review of the collection appears in the *Athenæum* on 15 January 1848, in which Thomas Kibble Hervey commends Hawkshaw's melodious tone in the delivery of the prerequisite moral instruction required of poetry written for children. 'The absence of cant is a charming feature in the seriousness of these little songs', notes Hervey, who highlights Hawkshaw's combination of didacticism with an aesthetic appeal designed to enchant rather than harangue her child readers.[1] Several poems from the collection are reprinted in anthologies of children's poetry and educational readers in England, Ireland and the United States from 1847 until at least 1913: 'Common Things' and 'The Wind' are the most frequently anthologised, and reprinted in a variety of regional newspapers: Appendix B gives full details of republications.

The final stanza of 'Common Things' ('There are as many lovely things, / As many pleasant tones, / For those who sit by cottage hearths, / As those who sit on thrones!') seems to have been adopted as a mantra for egalitarian thought. In March 1853, the *Essex Standard* report on 'The Bawdsey Lectures' uses a barely amended version of Hawkshaw's words. The object of the lectures was 'to afford (especially to the labouring classes) amusement and improvement combined', and to teach that:

> There are as many precious things,
>   As many pleasant tones
> For those who sit by cottage hearths
>   As those who sit on thrones.
> (*Essex Standard*, 25 March 1853)

In March 1862 the *Bury Times* reports on a lecture attended by thirteen hundred people in the hall of the Bury Athenæum, where the vicar of Deane spoke on the theme of 'Happy Homes, and How to Make Them':

There were in his opinion four things requisite to make a happy home—health, competence, temperance and godliness. Health was very important, for though a good man might be happy under all circumstances, still ill health affected happiness, and chilled the genial warmth of his spirits. If the master was healthy, the family partook of the benefits arising from it. In England at least home

---

1 Also reviewed in the *Manchester Times* (20 July 1847) and the *Manchester Courier and Lancashire General Advertiser* (21 July 1847). John Evans reviews *Poems for My Children* and *'Dionysius the Areopagite', with Other Poems* in his survey of regional writers, *Lancashire Authors and Orators* (1850). See Appendix A for details of these contemporary reviews.

implied a house, and it was therefore a matter of the first consideration to have a healthy house:

> There are as many precious things,
>   As many pleasant tones
> For those who sit by cottage hearths
>   As those who sit on thrones.

A handsome house was not requisite for a happy home. If the house was not healthy, those who lived in it could not be. (*Bury Times*, 15 March 1862)

A later use of the final stanza of 'Common Things' appears under the heading 'Conservative Opinion of Working Men' in a letter to the editor in the *Portsmouth Evening News* (22 June 1892). Here, an agitated respondent takes on an earlier contributor who 'quotes these lines and would make out that the so-called Gladstonian policy will provide the elixir of content all round, whether for peasant or prince'. The respondent urges an outright rejection of 'the dissemination of false sentimentality' and declares that 'the great untaught must wash themselves, teach themselves, suit themselves' and 'work by the candle and the dawn' to achieve place or prosperity by their own means rather than through parliamentary policy. A rather more light-hearted citation of Hawkshaw's poem appears in an advertisement for 'Fairweather Fairlie', the cash-price tailor covering Tisbury, Fordingbridge and Ringwood, 'where you get such good value that you can save money every week. There should be as many happy hours, and as many pleasant tones, for those who sit round cottage hearths, as for those who sit on thrones' (*Western Gazette*, 1 July 1898).

When *Poems for My Children* was published there were five young Hawkshaw children: Mary Jane Jackson (b. 1838), John Clarke (b. 1841), Henry Paul (b. 1843), Editha (b. 1845) and Oliver (b. 1846). Of the collection's 27 poems, 6 are addressed to these children by name, whilst others include dialogue between a mother and her child. The poignant elegy 'Ada', which draws the collection to a close, suggests that despite her death in 1845, aged just five, Ada was still very much part of the Hawkshaw family. In this way, Hawkshaw's first collection of poetry for children is positioned as a personal poetic offering that found its way to print, rather than a collection written with an external audience in mind. That said, unlike *Cecil's Own Book*, printed for private circulation in 1871, *Poems for My Children* was published to be sold and includes several poems conveying obligatory lessons in mid-nineteenth-century middle-class morality and devotion.[2]

The collection's series of five poems on British history anticipates Hawkshaw's ambitious survey of pre-conquest history, *Sonnets on Anglo-Saxon History*, published seven years later in 1854. Like the discrete yet interconnected snapshots of history conveyed through the sonnets in her later sequence, Hawkshaw presents history to her children as individual 'scenes' – moving chronologically from the 'Scene in the Time of the Druids' through 'Scene in the Time of the Romans', 'A Scene in the Time of the Saxons', 'Scene in the Time of the Normans', to 'A Scene in the Time of the Crusades'. Rather than being printed consecutively, the history poems are the 3rd, 7th, 15th, 23rd and 26th of the collection's 27 poems.

---

2 Hawkshaw's use of informal dialogue between parent and child as a means of teaching and entertaining her children mirrors the pioneering work of essayist and poet Anna Letitia Barbauld (1743–1825), whose *Lessons for Children* (4 vols, 1778–79) was influential in the development of children's educational literature.

In this way, Hawkshaw conveys a sense of distance and distinction between these periods in history, rather than blocking the poems together thematically as 'the history poems'. The effect of this infusion of history punctuating the personal interactions between mother and child that make up many of the poems in between is that history and the past are positioned as part of the present, with a relevance to day-to-day concerns.

Alongside several poems celebrating the natural world are others set firmly in Manchester's urban landscape. Poems such as 'Mary's Wish' and 'The City Child's Complaint' suggest Ann's growing confidence in, and optimism towards, the city. Many poetic representations of industrial cities at this time uphold an antithesis between the nostalgic rural idyll and the spirit-sapping urban landscape, yet Hawkshaw's poems reconfigure the city entirely in terms of what it offers, rather than what it takes away; maybe reflecting the Hawkshaws' position as beneficiaries of the city's expansion. In looking for evidence of God in man's work as well as in nature, Hawkshaw conceptualises the physicality of Manchester's cityscape in terms of a manifestation of human intelligence, and this intelligence as a product of a good and loving God.[3]

Each of the collection's pages is bordered by a line-drawn vine curling around the framed page, merging into a stylised figure of a bird in each corner. There are a number of woodcut illustrations in the volume, some attributed to engraver and publisher Henry Vizetelly (1820–94). The illustration to the opening poem brings Hawkshaw's children, nature and poetry together in a drawing titled 'Gathering Spring flowers'. With three children in the foreground, and the figure of a mother in the background, this is a likely representation of the eldest of the Hawkshaw children, Mary, John and Henry, gathering flowers with Ann. This opening illustration includes the book's title, 'Poems for My Children', set out in a stylised font with letters resembling twigs and tree bark, which merge with the trees under which the children sit. The accompanying poem, 'Spring is Coming', resonates with images of hope and regeneration, prompted by the anticipation and certainty of the coming season.

---

3 Debbie Bark discusses Hawkshaw's confidence in Manchester's industrial landscape in 'Reconfiguring the Urban Child: Ann Hawkshaw's *Poems for My Children* (1847)' in 'Victorian Childhoods', *Leeds Working Papers in Victorian Studies* 11 (2010): 19–29.

Spring is Coming

There is a whisper in the woods,
 The breath of soft winds passing through,
And rustling 'mid the dry brown leaves,
 Where last year's primrose grew;
And high upon the leafless boughs
 Blithe Robin cheerily is singing,
And to and fro the anemones
 Like fairy bells are swinging!

The rivulet is murmuring
 Within its pebbly bed,
For the ice bands which held it fast
 With the last sunshine fled;
And many-coloured lichens creep
 O'er the old trees and stones,—
There are a thousand pleasant sights,
 A thousand gladsome tones:

For Spring is coming—and the flowers
 Will waken as from sleep;
The birds will warble in the bowers,
 In streams the fishes leap;
The butterflies will flutter past,
 The bees begin their humming;
Cold winter does not ever last,
 Spring, pleasant Spring, is coming!

Mary's Wish[4]

I often wish that I could see,
This country as it used to be;
For where now busy cities stand,
There once was moor and forest land,
And the tall elk and freedom bounded,
Ere hunter's bugle had been sounded!

How quiet must those shores have been,
Where now a thousand ships are seen!
There was no sound of steam, or oar,
Scarcely a foot-print on the shore,
And the sea-eagle from the cliff,
Soared, startled at the passing skiff.

Where quay and warehouse crowd the edge
Of rivers,—once, 'mid reeds and sedge,
The otter watched his fishy prey,
With none to frighten him away,
Unless a tall grey heron came,
Its share of booty, too, to claim.

Where now the wavy cornfields spread,
Once stood the Briton's mud-built shed;
And round it savage children played,
While stretched beneath the oak-tree's shade,
Their father strung his bow afresh,
Or in his fish-net wove a mesh.

Where now such peaceful dwellings are,
Were heard the sounds of barbarous war;
And mothers with their children fled
At midnight from the burning shed;
The smoke from engines now is seen,
Where blazing hamlets once had been.

I do not think that time was good,
For then men shed each other's blood,
Without a thought that it was wrong,
And the weak fell beneath the strong;
But still, I often wish to see
This country as it used to be!

---

4 Spoken through the perspective of Hawkshaw's eldest daughter, Mary Jane Jackson, born on 1 March 1838. The review of *Poems for My Children* in the *Manchester Times* (20 July 1847) cites this poem (see Appendix A). Appendix B gives details of the poem's republication.

The Festival of the Last of October—Scene in the Time of the Druids[5]

The Druids in Britain had three great festivals; one on the eve of the first of May, the second at Midsummer, and the third on the last of October, which was kept as a thanksgiving for the harvest. Before this festival, all fire used in private dwellings, or for common uses, was put out, but sacred fire was kept burning with great care on the altar. At the festival no excommunicated person was allowed to take fire from the altar; and all were forbidden to give the outcast food, fire, or shelter.

> Upon a wide and lonely moor
>   There is a circle of old stones;[6]
> The summer sunshine warms them yet,
>   The winter wind among them moans.
>
> Sometimes a passing stranger comes,
>   And sits him down beside that spot,
> And muses there on times gone by,
>   And things by busier men forgot.
>
> Why there do strangers sit and think?
>   What are the scenes they muse upon?
> Who placed with so much labour there,
>   Those huge grey stones in ages gone?
>
> Come listen—'t was an autumn eve,
>   Misty and cold,—and all around
> Was cheerless,—but amid yon stones
>   A single fire gleamed near the ground.
>
> Awhile it glimmered faint and dim,
>   Then burst at last a ruddy flame;
> Showing to those across the wild
>   It from a Druid's altar came.
>
> Beside it stood a white-robed priest
>   With oak-leaves twined around his head;
> While near him, bound with leathern thongs,
>   Upon the ground a savage bled.

---

5 This is the first in the collection's series of five poems on British history, which move chronologically from the Druids through the Romans, Saxons, Normans and the Crusades. Hawkshaw's epigraph provides historical context which is reworked in the poem through the perspective of an individual's experience.

6 a circle of old stones: this is a likely reference to Stonehenge, the prehistoric stone circle on Salisbury Plain, Wiltshire.

We call him savage—for he knew
    Nothing of all these arts of ours;
Yet by his mud-hut far away
    There grew a root of primrose flowers,

Which he had brought for many a mile,
    And planted there to please his child;
For well he loved his little one,
    Although he was both rude and wild.

But vainly now that boy may call,
    He never, never can come back;
And vainly all through wood and heath
    His faithful hound his way may track.

They did not kill him in revenge,
    He did not fall in angry strife;
The man who slew him, till that day,
    Had never seen him in his life.

They offered him in sacrifice,
    A victim for a nation's crimes;
Believing thus their gods to please:
    This was religion in those times.

At last the sacrifice was o'er;
    Then each of the vast crowd drew near,
And stood around the altar-fire,
    With looks of reverence, but of fear.

Each at the flame then lit a torch,
    And quickly to his home returned;
For, till that festival was o'er,
    No fire on any hearth-stone burned.

That morning, watched with ceaseless care,
    Fire burned upon the altar-stone;
But none besides throughout the land
    From temple or from cottage shone.

The priest, the worshippers are gone—
    But one remains—a lonely man,
Seated beside a blasted tree,
    To death doomed by the Druid's ban.

No cheerful fire for him must blaze,
    No food, no home, to him be given;

For he had dared to disobey
    The priest,—the messenger of heaven.

Awhile he sat—then fierce despair
    Possessed him, and he wildly ran
To the dark forest;—and no more
    Was heard or seen that doomèd man!

Common Things[7]

The sunshine is a glorious thing,
    That comes alike to all,
Lighting the peasant's lowly cot,
    The noble's painted hall.

The moonlight is a gentle thing,
    It through the window gleams,
Upon the snowy pillow, where
    The happy infant dreams.

It shines upon the fisher's boat,
    Out on the lonely sea;
Or where the little lambkins lie,
    Beneath the old oak-tree.

The dew-drops on the summer morn,
    Sparkle upon the grass;

---

7 The review of *Poems for My Children* in the *Athenæum* (15 January 1848) cites this poem, as does John Evans' review of *Poems for My Children* in *Lancashire Authors and Orators* (1850); see Appendix A. The poem was republished in various anthologies and newspapers; see Appendix B for details.

The village children brush them off,
    That through the meadows pass.

There are no gems in monarchs' crowns,
    More beautiful than they;
And yet we scarcely notice them,
    But tread them off in play.

Poor Robin on the pear-tree sings,
    Beside the cottage-door;
The heath-flower fills the air with sweets,
    Upon the pathless moor.

There are as many lovely things,
    As many pleasant tones,
For those who sit by cottage hearths,
    As those who sit on thrones!

The Little Wanderers

Part I.—The Resolve

'T was morning—and the valleys lay,
    Still in the mountain's shade,
While near a Switzer's cottage-door
    Two little children played.

One was a gentle girl, whose face
    Was bright with health and joy,
Though birds and streams were all her books,
    A flower her only joy.

She sat upon a log of wood,
    Pleased with her rustic seat,
A little basket full of flowers,
    Was placed beside her feet.

The other was a noble boy,
    With forehead broad and high,
And eyes, that looked from their clear depths,
    Like stars from out the sky.

He was a brave and fearless child,
    Yet modest, kind, and meek;
But how a tale of wrong would flush
    With crimson his young cheek!

Their father, on the mountain heights,
    Hunted the chamois wild;
And often told of daring feats,
    Before his listening child.

And Pierre's young eyes would sparkle then,
    "I'll be a hunter, too,"
He shook his curly locks and said,
    "Father, and do like you."

Pierre climbed the cliffs, and brought the flowers
    To Ella where she sat;

While she with slender fingers twined
   Them round his rustic hat.

She lifted up her mild blue eyes
   To where the mountains lay,
All glittering in the thousand lights
   Of a bright summer's day.

"All beautiful that land must be,
   All glittering and all fair,"
She softly whispered to herself,
   "I wish that we were there."

"I wonder if 't is fairies' land,
   And if they light it so,
That little ones, like Pierre and I,
   May see the way to go.

"They love good children, and I'm sure
   That Pierre is *very* good;
He walked with me last night an hour
   To seek flowers in the wood;—

"Although he likes to climb the cliffs
   Better than gather flowers,
Or seek the falcon's nest—than walk,
   Like me, through woodland bowers."

Whilst thus she whispered to herself
   The flowers dropped from her hand,
And earnestly her eyes were bent
   On that far-off fairy-land.

"Ella, you have not wreathed my hat,
   The flowers are all around;
What makes you look so wonderingly
   Up to yon mountain ground?"

"Oh, Pierre," the little one replied,
   "It is so bright and grand,
The rocks must all be made of gems,
   It must be fairy-land!"

Pierre looked and saw the morning sun
   Gleaming on peaks of snow;
And lower down the crystal streams
   From hidden fountains flow.

He almost heard the torrents gush,
    And the proud eagle's cry,
As with a slow, majestic flight,
    It sought its nest on high.

And his heart bounded at the sight,
    And he, too, longed to climb;
Not to seek Ella's fairy-land,
    But mountain cliffs sublime.

Pierre seized his hat, bedecked with flowers,
    "I'll go, I'm sure we can;"
And with his sister's hand in his
    Away they swiftly ran.

Part II.—The Avalanche

Down the green slope they swiftly ran,
    On which their cottage stood:
Crossed at the foot a little brook,
    Then passed into a wood.

They lingered not to gather flowers,
    Or watch the squirrel leap;
For now they heard the torrent fall
    Into its basin deep.

From age to age, from rock to rock,
    It fell with thundering sound,
And balls like snow, of shining foam,
    Were scattered all around.

They gazed awhile with trembling awe,
    Up to the rocky ledge
O'er which it fell, and then began
    To clamber by its edge.

From bush to bush, and stone to stone,
    O'ergrown with moss, they went;
And sometimes o'er the dangerous cliff
    The fearless children bent.

An eagle, screaming, left its nest,
    And rose into the sky;
A wild goat o'er the torrent leaped,
    And passed them swiftly by.

All was so new, and strange, and wild,
   They gazed delighted round;
Till suddenly their ears were stunned
   By a terrific sound.

It was not thunder, yet it seemed
   To shake the very earth,
And high amid the mountain peaks
   It had its sudden birth.

Clasped in each other's arms they stood,
   Their rosy cheeks turned white;
And as the sound yet louder grew,
   They held each other tight.

Poor Ella closed her fearful eyes,
   But Pierre still dared to look
Up to the mountain's snowy heights,
   Though all around him shook.

"Noise will not hurt us, sister, dear,"
   The daring brother cried:
"I hear it still—I hear it now,
   Come down the mountain's side."

"I *see* it too—an avalanche!
   Look Ella! look and see!
'T has broken now a piece of rock,
   Now it has crushed a tree."

"Look how it bears the stones along,
   And tears up tree and bush,
Now from yon overhanging cliff
   'T will like a torrent rush."

"It has! and it has reached the plain,
   And plunged into the lake."
"Then we are safe!" "Ah, Ella, no,
   The lake its bounds may break."

The avalanche had fallen where
   The lake and river met;
And fiercely now against its base
   The chafèd waters beat,

And swiftly spread across the plain,
   And all before them swept;

The shepherd left his sheep and fled,
   Or in some cavern crept.

Onward it spread, till all the vale
   Became one watery plain,
Which rolled between them and the home
   They longed to now regain.

They saw it on its sunny slope,
   Their parents were not there;
And not a creature was in sight,
   To witness their despair.

A distant sound of dying cries
   Was borne upon the breeze,
Mixed with the roar of waves, and noise
   Of crashing rocks and trees.

Poor Ella wept in wild despair,
   Then sunk upon the ground;
When Pierre, by danger calmer made,
   Looked earnestly around.

"Sister," he said, "come, dry your tears,
   They will not help us now."

There was a something in his tone,
    A something on his brow,

That made her feel she must be calm;
    She had a spirit, too,
Though meek, yet full of fortitude,
    To *bear*, if not to *do*.

"We cannot now return," he said,
    "But we must try to find
Our way behind that mountain cliff
    To which the sun inclined,

"When yesternight we watched him set;
    And should we lose our way,
Then we must creep into some cave,
    And wait till coming day.

"Have you not heard our father tell
    How in the olden time,
When cruel tyrants ruled the land,
    And there was war and crime,

"How many good and holy men,
    Women, and children too,
Were forced to fly, and hide in caves?
    What they *did*, we can *do*."

He took his sister's hand in his,
    And down they bent their way;
Quickly they went, there was no time
    For lingering or delay.

The sun, already in mid-heaven,
    Betokened it was noon;
And the deep valleys they must pass,
    They knew would darken soon.

They wandered on from hour to hour,
    And hope the time beguiled;
But stranger all the mountains grew,
    And wilder still, and wild.

They from each other kept their fears,
    Impelled by love or pride,

Till Ella, without cry or tear,
   Sank lifeless at his side.

Part III.—The Cave in the Mountains

A little distant from the spot
   Where Ella fainting lay,
There was a cavern, which had oft,
   In persecution's day,

Hidden from the oppressor's power,
   Till brighter days returned,
The brave and good, within whose hearts
   Pure, noble thoughts had burned.

'T was known to many a peasant child,
   For round the winter's fire
They talked of those whose memories
   With time would not expire.

"The cave of liberty" 't was called,
   By those who lived around;
And many a hunter trod the spot
   As if 't were holy ground.

And so it was,—more sacred far
   Than aught beneath the sun,
Should ever be to us the place
   Where noble deeds were done.

Bright crystals, pendent from the roof,
   Like glittering diamonds gleamed;
When on them, at the evening's hour,
   A ray of sunlight streamed.

The sound of hidden waters came
   Upon the ear all times;
Low, soft, and musical, it came
   Like distant tinkling chimes.

Dry moss and withered leaves were driven
    In autumn by the wind,
In sheltered corners of the cave
    A resting-place to find.

A heap of these, which might have been
    A lonely hermit's bed,
Upon a low, flat shelf of rock,
    Last autumn's wind had spread.

Upon them Pierre his sister laid,
    For he had seen the place,
And in his hand pure water brought,
    And sprinkled on her face.

He watched beside her, till at length
    She opened her blue eyes,
And gazed upon the sparry vault
    With innocent surprise.

But she was faint, and closed them soon;
    And the low, lulling sound
Of winds and waters, once again
    Her eyes in slumber bound.

Unconscious of approaching night,
    O'erwearied thus she slept,
Whilst watching the fast-fading light,
    Pierre his sad station kept.

He sat, till on the cavern's roof
    The sunbeams died away;
He sat, till in the western sky
    There lingered not a ray.

He watched—still darker it became,
    Long shades the mountains threw,
The night wind made its mournful tone,
    And bats and owlets flew.

"O God," he said, and bent his knees
    Upon the rock and prayed,
"O God preserve thy children safe,
    And make us not afraid.

"The dark and light are one to thee,
    And thou canst see us here,

Amongst these rocks, as when we rest
    At home without a fear.

"Elijah was by ravens fed,[8]
    When by the brook he sat;
And God can feed us even here,
    Oh, I am sure of that!"

Just then, before the cavern's mouth,
    He saw a creature pass;
With noiseless step it quickly ran
    Across the dewy grass.

What was it, wolf or bear? Ah! now
    What could the brave boy do?
'T was vain alike to fight or fly;
    To Ella's side he flew.

Resolved its victim first to be,
    He took his station there;
While she, in happy slumbers wrapt,
    Knew nought of his despair.

Nearer it came,—then with a bound
    Leaped wildly on his breast;—
The scream of agony he gave
    Roused Ella from her rest.

---

8 Elijah was by ravens fed: a reference to the biblical account of the Hebrew prophet Elijah being fed by ravens whilst hiding in Cherith (1 Kings 17)

She started up, but wolf nor bear
    Met her awakening sight:
But springing from her couch she gave
    A cry of wild delight.

It was her father's faithful dog,
    And in a moment more,
Their weeping parents knelt beside
    Their children on the floor.

The father bore his little girl
    Safe down the mountain-side;
But Pierre walked manfully along,
    At his glad mother's side.

The Wind[9]

The wind it is a mystic thing,
    Wandering o'er ocean wide,
And fanning all the thousand sails
    That o'er its billows glide.

It curls the blue waves into foam,
    It snaps the strongest mast,
Then like a sorrowing thing it sighs,
    When the wild storm is past.

And yet how gently does it come
    At evening through the bowers,
As if it said a kind "good-night"
    To all the closing flowers.

It bears the perfume of the rose,
    It fans the insect's wing;
'T is round me, with me everywhere,
    Yet 't is an unseen thing.

How many sounds it bears along,
    As o'er the earth it goes;
The songs of many joyous hearts,
    The sounds of many woes!

---

9 The review of *Poems for My Children* in the *Athenæum* (15 January 1848) cites this poem (see Appendix A). The poem was republished in various anthologies and newspapers; see Appendix B for details.

It enters into palace halls,
   And carries thence the sound
Of mirth and music;—but it creeps
   The narrow prison round,

And bears away the captive's sigh,
   Who sits in sorrow there;
Or from the martyr's lonely cell
   Conveys his evening prayer.

It fans the reaper's heated brow;
   It through the window creeps,
And lifts the fair child's golden curls,
   As on her couch she sleeps.

'T is like the light, a gift to all,
   To prince, to peasant given;
Awake, asleep, around us still,
   There is this gift of heaven:

This strange, mysterious thing we call
   The breeze, the air, the wind;
We call it so, but know no more,—
   'T is mystery, like our mind.

Think not the things most wonderful
   Are those beyond our ken,
For wonders are around the paths,
   The daily paths of men!

Scene in the Time of the Romans

The Druid's time had passed away,
And moored a Roman galley lay
   'Neath England's chalky cliffs;
And barks of firmer texture skim
Gaily upon the ocean's brim,
   Than Briton's wicker skiffs.

For many years did Britons fight,
For hearth and home, and freeman's right,
   But 't was in vain they bled;
The Romans in that conquering hour
Had met with none to check their power,
   They were the wide earth's dread.

Yet from their conquerors much of good,
For all this loss of human blood,
   The hardy Britons learned:
The mud-walled town had disappeared,
And in its place were mansions reared,
   And peaceful days returned.

Now from that galley to the shore
There came a boat, with dashing oar;
   At length it touched the strand;
From it a stately warrior stept,
Upon the shore his followers lept,
   With sword and spear in hand.

To meet him was a motley crowd,
And from it rose a shout so loud,
   'T was heard for miles at sea.
He was a ruler come from Rome,
Many from him shall hear their doom,
   For life and death bore he.

Upon the cliff a temple stood,
Raised to the monarch of the flood;
   To this the Roman went,
And offered there, at Neptune's shrine,
A cup which British pearls intwine,
   And there his knee he bent.

Next he his high tribunal kept;
Many that fatal council wept,
   Led from his bar to die;
Some from their native isle were sent,
In sad and lonely banishment;
   Some to the forests fly.

Now marching past his seat appears
A band of British youths. Fond tears
   From mothers' eyes had wept their fate;
For they were bound to distant climes,
Destined to fight for Roman crimes,
   With men they did not hate.

At last the sunset of that day
Died in the western sky away.
   Then to his splendid tent,
Where silken cushions for his bed
Were on a floor of mosaic spread,
   The Roman general went.

The City Child's Complaint[10]

"The trees and flowers are beautiful,
    The sky is blue and high,
And the small streams make pleasant sounds,
    As they run swiftly by.

"But all these things are not for me,
    I live amid dark walls;
And scarcely through these dusty panes
    A single sunbeam falls.

"I never hear the wild bird's song,
    Or see the graceful deer
Go trooping through the forest glades:
    What can I learn from here?

"They say *God's works* are wonderful,
    In sea, and sky, and land;
I never see them for *men's works*
    Are here on every hand."

Oh murmur not, thou little one,
    That *here* thy home must be,
And not amid the pleasant fields,
    Or by the greenwood tree.

There is a voice can speak to thee,
    Amid the works of men;
Speak, with a sound as loud and clear
    As in the lonely glen.

Do not the works thou seest around
    Spring from man's thoughtful mind,
And in *that*, is there nought of God,
    For thee, for all, to find?

The earth, with all its varied blooms,
    Will have to pass away;
But man's immortal mind will live
    Through everlasting day:

And without mind these sheltering walls
    Around thee had not been,

---

10 The review of *Poems for My Children* in the *Athenæum* (15 January 1848) cites this poem (see Appendix A). The poem was republished in various anthologies and newspapers; see Appendix B for details.

These busy engines had not moved,
   Nor whirling wheels been seen!

The First Spring Flowers

Bring me a nosegay? Where shall I go,
For short is the time since melted the snow?
Go to the garden's warmest bed,
There the bright crocus-flowers are spread,
Yellow, and purple, and white—while between
Shoot up their lance-like leaves of green.

Go to the sunniest bank you can find,
Where the hedge-row keeps off the frosty wind,
Where a faint, sweet perfume fills the air:
Search, you will find the violet there,
Of stainless white,—or of a hue
Deeper than Italy's sky of blue.

Go look beneath the forest trees
For those fairy bells the anemones,
Gracefully bending to every gale
Their feathery leaves, and blossoms pale;
And pass not on the unsheltered height
The flowers of the winter aconite.

And forget not the laurestinas gay,
With blossoms for March like those of May.
Gather a sprig of ivy, too,
Though flowerless now, yet I love its bright hue,
That does not fade like the summer flowers,
But looks like a friend through wintery hours;
A kindly friend, who seems to say,

"I have come on this frosty winter's day,
When I thought all others would stay away."

To Editha[11]

The dew is on the grass,
    And the bird is in its nest;
Come Editha, my little one,
    And lie thee down to rest.

Sleep: thou mayest calmly sleep,
    No dreams of coming ill,
No thought of misspent hours—no fears
    Thy happy bosom fill.

Yet thou wilt dream, but not
    Of joys forever fled,
No envy at another's lot,
    No sorrow for the dead!

But of the flowers, and bees,
    And butterflies of spring,
And pleasant voices that have made
    Thy nursery walls to ring.

---

11 This and the following poem are addressed to Hawkshaw's daughter Editha, born 5 January 1845.

The dew is on the grass,
    And the bird is in its nest;
Come Editha, my *blessed gift*,[12]
    And lie thee down to rest.

Editha[13]

One evening little Editha
    Sat by a forest well,
And she heard a low and pleasant tone,
    Like the chime of a silver bell;
And she looked around, but nought could she see,
Yet it was not the wind through the forest tree.

She did not say, like a foolish child,
    I'll listen no more, but she bent her head,
And she heard the same soft, silvery sound,
    Floating around beneath her tread:
If she ceased to listen, it went away,
Or if she forgot it, and thought of play.

Then meekly little Editha
    Knelt down upon the ground,
And a root of blue forget-me-not
    Close by the water found;
And waving to and fro it said,
"Think of the absent and the dead."

Marvelled much the little maid,
    But she bent again her ear,
And she heard a happy voice

---

12 [Poet's Note: Editha is a Saxon name, and means the "blessed gift."]

13 The poem is addressed to Hawkshaw's daughter Editha. This is one of four Hawkshaw poems to be included in the anthology *The Children's Casket: Favourite Poems for Recitation*, compiled by Annie M. Hone (London: Griffith, Farran, Okeden and Welsh, 1891). Appendix B gives details of the poem's republication.

From a yellow primrose near;
And it said, "Be cheerful still,
Hope, and wait, and do God's will."

From its home amid dry leaves,
    Fallen there from many a tree,
"I can ring a fairy chime,"
    Said the wood anemone;
"And so can I," the snow-drop said,
Waving to and fro her head.

Then the flowers began to sing,
And the bells in concert ring;
"Happy little Editha,
    She can hear our voiceless singing,
We no more are mute to her,
    Music ever round her ringing;

Many on this wondrous earth
    Never hear its harmony;
Blessed little Editha
    It no more is dumb to thee."

The Oak Tree[14]

The oak it is a noble tree,
    The monarch of the wood;
Through winter's storms a thousand years,
    Its hardy trunk hath stood.

It is not stately, like the beech;
    The elm more tall may be;
And gracefuller the lovely lime;
    Yet 't is a noble tree.

An acorn, by a squirrel dropped
    Amid a tuft of grass,
May be an oak, on which we look
    With wonder as we pass.

But then it years, long years, must grow,
    And this may teach to all,

---

14 The review of *Poems for My Children* in the *Athenæum* (15 January 1848) cites this poem (see Appendix A).

What mighty things in after times
   May come from means now small.

How little did they think who saw
   A green oak sapling spring
In some old forest long ago,
   That it would float a king!

Perhaps some ancient Druid came
   To pluck from it a bough;
'T is now a gallant ship—but *he*,
   Where is that Druid now?

Perhaps an acorn from that tree
   Dropped on his nameless grave,
And o'er it now in summer green,
   Dark, tangled branches wave.

How beautiful the oak's young leaves,
   In the bright days of Spring;
Or, when a richer tint the skies
   Of early autumn bring:

And all upon the dewy ground
   The acorn-cups are laid,
Like richly chasèd spoons are they,
   For fairy banquets made.

So, monarch of all forest trees,
   On every English plain;
We crown thee still, thou brave old oak,
   And long, long be thy reign!

I do not love the Night

"I do not love the night, mamma,
    The long, dark, dreary night;
The day is far more beautiful,
    With its beams of sunny light.

I know the darkness on the sky,
    Like a thick curtain spreads;
That we may all more calmly sleep,
    Like flowers upon their beds.

For you say the young flowers fold their buds,
    When the night comes o'er the sky;
I often think they grieve, mamma,
    To bid the sun good-by.

There is no sound of song or wing
    From bird—no insect's hum;
All pleasant voices, too, are hushed,
    And all the world seems dumb.

The night-wind, as it goes along,
    Like mournful music seems;
I often think I hear it still
    Go past me in my dreams.

I do not love the night, mamma,
    The chilly, darksome night,
How beautiful would be a world
    Where it was always light."

"And such a world there is, my boy!
    No sun, no moon, are there;
Yet 't is a land that hath no night,"—
    "Where is it? tell me where."

"It is the land of blessedness,
    The home of *all the good*,
We cannot travel to its shores
    By land, or o'er the flood.

To reach it we must die, my boy,
    Yet tremble not for this,
Kind angels wait to show the way
    To that bright land of bliss."

Thinking and Dreaming

"You tell me I must think—I thought
   Last night a long, long time,
As I sat listening on the hill
   To the church bell's pleasant chime.

The sun shone on the old church clock,
   Upon the ivy tower,—
Seven when I went, eight when I left—
   So I sat there an hour.

And I was thinking all the time,
   How pleasant it would be,
To live upon a little isle,
   Far in the southern sea;

With waters like a mirror clear
   All round my island spread,
And branching trees, and sun-bright flowers,
   And blue skies overhead.

And I would have a cottage there,
   Beside the sounding sea,
Rich vines should cluster o'er its roof,
   And on its sheltering tree.

And pretty pictures I would have,
   And books, and music too,
And I would play, or read, or sing,
   Or roam the forest through.

And sometimes I would have a friend
    To come and see me there;
Oh! should not I be happy then,
    With all around so fair?"

"No, Mary, not more happy there[15]
    Than in thy present lot;
For the chief source of happiness,
    My child, thou hast forgot.

A life of selfish indolence
    For us was not designed,
It is not places make our bliss,
    'T is fashioned by the mind.

Think, in that path of life thou tread'st,
    Thy duty well to do;
'T is dreaming to imagine flowers,
    Thus on that path to strew.

I told thee thou must think—not thought,
    But only idle dreams
Are all these fairy, cloud-built homes,
    And visionary schemes.

They will not nerve thy heart to bear
    The many storms of life,
Nor arm thy heart with cheerfulness
    To smile amid its strife.

Leave in His hands thy destiny,
    Who guides the swallow's flight;
A God of love will surely do
    To all his creatures right!"

---

15 The reference to Mary suggests that this is dialogue between Hawkshaw and her eldest child, Mary Jane Jackson, who would have been aged nine at the time of publication.

King Alfred and His Mother—a Scene in the Time of the Saxons[16]

The Saxons, or Northmen, began to invade Britain before the departure of the Romans, and after much fighting obtained possession of it; this was not a misfortune, but a happiness, as they were better fitted to rule the land than the Britons, who had become idle. Although Alfred could not read until he was twelve years of age, he afterwards became a learned man, and wrote many books to improve his people. He was called "*The Truth-teller.*" Was it not a noble title, my child? And now we will take a peep into the old palace, where he lived so many ages ago.

> It was a winter's evening,
>   And fast the snow was falling,
> The shepherd on the mountain side
>   His wandering sheep was calling;
> The weary ox had left the field,
>   And to its shed was wending;
> Each man and beast that had a home,
>   Back to that home was tending.

> There sat a lady in rich attire
> That evening by a blazing fire,
> That burnt within an antique hall;
> Rude tapestry hung upon its wall,
> Which oft the night-wind swayed and shook,
> Entering by many an unseen nook.
> She sat and played upon her harp,
>   And pleasantly its music rung;
> While the blazing faggots cast a glow
>   On the gifted lady as she sung,

---

16 Hawkshaw dedicates several sonnets to King Alfred in *Sonnets on Anglo-Saxon History* (1854). This is one of four Hawkshaw poems to be included in the anthology *The Children's Casket: Favourite Poems for Recitation*, compiled by Annie M. Hone (London: Griffith, Farran, Okeden and Welsh, 1891). Appendix B gives details of the poem's republication.

And glanced and sparkled here and there,
On spear and buckler round her hung.

It was a wild Norse song she sung,
    Of the old Valhalla's mystic hall;[17]
Where the souls of valiant heroes go
    At Odin's call;[18]
And she sung of the rugged Jotuns, too[19]
    The giants of frost, and fire, and flame,
And many a tale of ice-bound *Thule*,
    That now we Iceland name.[20]
She told how the daring sea kings roved
    In their frail vessels o'er the sea,
Until they reached the English shore,
    Its future kings to be.

Then the lady ceased her song,
    And she put her harp away,
When she heard a voice say, "Would those tones
    Ever upon the air would stay!
Would that music ne'er would die,
Or deep words into silence fly!"

"Alfred, is it thou," she said,
    "Sighest that my song is done;
True, the harp chords now are hushed,
    But the song still lives, my son."
"Yes, it lives, but not for me,"
    Said the boy; "when words are hid
In books, they are like precious gems
    Locked down beneath a casket's lid
To him who cannot read the line,
    And, lady, such a lot is mine."
"My son," she said, "this book shall be
Thine own when thou can'st read to me
Its songs of ancient melody."[21]

---

17 Valhalla's mystic hall: in Old Northern mythology, the hall assigned to those who have died in battle, in which they feast with Odin (n. 'Valhalla' *OED*).
18 Odin: in Scandinavian mythology, supreme god and creator.
19 Jotuns: in Scandinavian mythology, the Jotuns are a supernatural race of giants.
20 Thule: the ancient Greek and Latin name for a land six days' sail north of Britain, which was considered to be the most northerly region in the world (n. 'Thule' *OED*). In modern usage, Thule is most often identified with Norway, although at the time of Hawkshaw's writing the connection to Iceland was commonplace.
21 Here Hawkshaw recreates the story of the book of Saxon songs (*carmina Saxonica*) recounted by Asser in *Life of King Alfred* (893). Having recited the poems and songs to Alfred and his brothers,

"It shall be mine, and soon;" how well
  He kept his word, let history tell.

But you must tell me, who were Odin and the Jotuns, and what was the Valhalla that the Queen sung of to little Alfred? Odin was a famous leader and king that the Northmen once had; he governed them wisely and well, and when he died they thought he could still protect them, and do them good, and they worshipped him as a god; and the Valhalla was the hall where he dwelt, and where he feasted those who, during their lifetime, had been brave and good. The Jotuns were giants; perhaps they meant frost, and fire, and flame by these giants, because they are powerful and mysterious things, about whose nature we know little.[22]

The Angel Friend

Mother, do angels ever come
  From their starry home on high;
Do they ever wander down to earth,
  Those dwellers in the sky?

How sweet to have an angel friend,
  Who would come to the mortal's land,
And tell us what they do in heaven,
  That bright and holy band:

To tell of the crystal streams which flow
  By the fadeless trees of life;
And the fresh, and fragrant, winds which blow,
  Without the tempest's strife:

And to tell me, if those indeed are worlds
  That in the midnight sky
Seem but like shining specks of light,
  When seen by mortal eye.

For angels know a thousand things
  We do not know on earth,
For they have lived through countless years,
  And watched creation's birth.

Osburga showed the book to her sons and promised to give it to whoever could memorise it the fastest: Alfred learned and recited the book first.

22 Here Hawkshaw's voice as mother and educator can be heard. The 'question and answer' style of the notes suggests that these are poems to be read aloud to children, to prompt conversation and stimulate curiosity.

They saw the lovely Eden bowers,
    Which our first parents trod;—
The Hebrews o'er Arabia's sands,
    Led by the cloud of God.

They've seen great cities turn to dust,
    And people pass away;
Chaldea's stately palaces[23]
    All trodden into clay.

They saw where Jesus bowed in prayer,
    On mount—in lonely glen—
They know where many a martyr died,
    Far from the homes of men.

Oh! sweet to have an angel friend,
    With a heart all full of love;
To bring down to this lower world
    The bliss from that above.

The Stream

Oh! is there ought more beautiful
    Than the clear stream in its bed;
With the willows whispering on its banks,
    And the blue sky o'er it spread.

It cometh from its mountain home,
    Like the snow so pure, so cold;
Its home but passed by the mountain goat,
    Or the chamois hunter bold.

Like a slender line of silver sheen,
    When the sun-beams on it play,

---

23 Chaldea: ancient country in present-day southern Iraq.

It looks as down the mountain side
    It taketh its lonely way.

'Tis one of the strings of nature's harp,
    And it seems to bear along
The tones of many a silent voice,
    And many an olden song.

For its gentle music hath been heard
    Sounding by night and day;
Long years ere up that rocky path
    The peasant took his way.

And the merry trout shall find a home
    Within its waters clear,
As on its course it still shall flow,
    For many a coming year.

The Poor Fly—for my little Harry[24]

Once there was a little fly,
    Dancing on a window pane,
And naughty Harry made it die,
    And it will *never* dance again.

Poor little fly with gauzy wings,
    It liked to flutter in the sun;
And sleep within the curtain folds,
    When its merry game was done.

---

24 Addressed to Hawkshaw's son Henry Paul. Born 17 January 1843, Henry ('Harry') would have been four at the time of publication. The gently didactic tone advocating kindness to all creatures pre-empts the most well-known of this style of poem written for children, Christina Rossetti's 'Hurt No Living Thing', published in *Sing-Song* (1872).

It had its pleasures and its pains,
    Though but an insect of a day;
It had a right to *live*, and you
    No right to take its *life* away.

The Land of my Dreams

"I know there are sunny lands that lie
Beneath the blue of a southern sky;
Where the sea and the earth alike are fair,
And the fragrant citron scents the air,
And the vine twines o'er the trellised bowers,
And the jessamine spreads its starry flowers—
But there is a fairer land to me,
Than even the clime of Italy.

"There are beautiful islands which seem to sleep
In the 'midst of the great Pacific deep;
Where the cocoa-nut grows to the ocean's brink,
And its roots the wave's salt waters drink:
Where, from sandy shore to mountain height,
There is one mass of verdure bright—
But I know more lovely isles than those,
That on the Southern Sea repose.

"There are strange temples, built of yore,
On sultry Egypt's wondrous shore,
Where, buried in the desert's sand,
Are idols of that ancient land—
Where Hebrew slaves in sorrow past
Long years—all there is old and vast;
Strange things are those, but yet to me
Is a land of deeper mystery!

"'Tis the land to which I go in dreams;
More lovely far than earth it seems:
In a boat of cloud I seem to glide,
In a boundless space so new and wide;
And all I have loved on earth are there,
And all I have seen, but far more fair;
As a lovely place in the sunshine seems
It ever looks, that land of dreams.

"Mother, how can it be, when sleep
Closes my eyelids in slumber deep,
And the soft pillow rests my head,
And darkness o'er the world is spread,
That I can see these glorious things?
Is it my spirit that hath wings?
And can it leave this mortal frame,
And go to God, from whence it came?"

"I cannot tell thee, child; to me,
As to thyself, 't is mystery;
For 't is but little we can know
While in this life we stay below;
The wonders of our souls are known
To God—and but to Him alone:
I cannot tell thee where may fly
The soul in dreams, to know it we must die!"

The History of a Coral Islet

Ages ago, beneath the deep,
    The coral insects reared
Their stony homes upon the rocks,
    Nor storms nor billows feared.

They laboured with unceasing toil,
    Those million tiny things,
And they have built more lasting homes
    Than palaces of kings.

Long as the waters o'er them rolled,
    Their labours did not cease;
But when they reached the ocean's brim
    They sunk to death in peace.

The sea-weed and the floating plank,
    From some bark washed away,
The bamboo, and uprooted palm,
    Soon on the islet lay.

Borne by the winds, or on the waves,
    Seeds, fruits, and insects came,
Until a fairy spot it beamed,
    That isle without a name.

Each year more lovely than the last
    Its solitudes appeared,
Sweet flowers were there, and cocoa-trees
    Their lofty heads upreared.

The pelican upon the shore
    Watched for his fishy prey,
While lurking in the tangled grass
    The glittering serpent lay.

The waves a ceaseless murmur made
    Upon the pebbly shore,
But not a sound of human life
    The wandering breezes bore.

Thus ages passed—at length a sigh,
    A human sigh, was heard;
And the wind caught the passing tone
    Of many a sorrowing word.

He was a shipwrecked mariner,
    Borne by the winds and waves,
From where his comrades slept in death
    Deep in the ocean caves.

He thought of home—he thought of all
    Who once had loved him there;
He thought how at their mother's knee
    His children knelt in prayer.

He thought perhaps they prayed for him,
    And then he bowed his knee
Upon that little coral isle,
    Beneath a cocoa-tree.

God heard his prayer!—from east, from west,
    Lone isle, or hidden grot,
If there the voice of prayer ascends,
    By God 't is unforgot!

A vessel bore him from that spot
    To his far home once more,
His the first foot, and his the last,
    That trod that coral shore.

The Hermit, the Chieftain, and the Child—a Tale about Happiness[25]

It was a summer's evening,
    And the long shadows fell
From tree and overhanging rock
    On old St. Ronan's well.[26]

All round upon the old grey stones
    Green ferns and mosses grew,
And when the wind the branches moved,
    Came gleams of sunshine through.

There was a little cell hard by,
    And there a hermit dwelt,
Who now beside St. Ronan's well,
    Upon the edge-stones knelt;

And in a scallop shell he took
    A draught of water there:
His hair was white, and on his brow
    Were lines of grief or care.

"For thirty years," said he, "I've drunk
    Each evening from this well,
But I am feeble now, and soon
    The grave will be my cell.

---

25 This is one of four Hawkshaw poems to be included in the anthology *The Children's Casket: Favourite Poems for Recitation*, compiled by Annie M. Hone (London: Griffith, Farran, Okeden and Welsh, 1891). Appendix B gives details of the poem's republication.

26 St. Ronan's well: a spa in the village of Innerleithen in southern Scotland, renowned for its healing properties; the setting for Sir Walter Scott's novel *St Ronan's Well* (1824).

"I've listened to the water's fall,
   I've heard the breezes sigh,
And through the creaking boughs at night
   The winter wind sweep by.

"I know each pathway through the woods,
   I've watched yon willows grow
From saplings into agèd trees,
   Down by the stream below.

"I thought that I should happy be
   Far from the haunts of men,
With none to care for, none to fear,
   Within this lonely glen.

"But ah! with me this hath not been—
   For, with myself at strife,
Sixty long, useless years I've passed,
   None better for my life."

While thus he spoke, a footstep came,
   He started at the sound,
For it was seldom other feet
   Than his had trod that ground.

There stood a steel-clad warrior by,
   Leaning upon his lance,
And from beneath his plumèd helm
   He looked with earnest glance.

"I've lived in courts and camps," he said,
   "I've travelled east and west,
And yet I have not happy been—
   I've sought, but found no rest!

"I heard of thee, thou hermit old,
   And I had come to ask
If thou wert happy—but thy words
   Have spared me now the task."

Just then they heard a gentle voice
   Say, "Is this Ronan's well?"
And on a maiden's golden curls
   A ray of sunshine fell.

She was a simple village child,
    Meanly, but cleanly clad;
A pitcher of the rudest kind
    Within her hands she had.

"I've come," she said, "for many a mile,
    To seek St. Ronan's well,
Because it hath a healing power,
    The country people tell.

"My mother hath been ill long time,
    But if she drink, they say,
Of this good water it will take
    Her sickness quite away."

She filled her pitcher at the well,
    Then at the old man's knee
She knelt, and said, "A blessing grant,
    Good father, unto me."

"And art thou happy, little maid?"
    The aged hermit said,
As on her curling locks his hands
    To bless her forth he spread.

"Happy," she said, "what does it mean?
    I labour all the day,
But when the old tree's shadow falls,
    I run abroad to play.

"I work for mother, when I'm good
    At night she gives a kiss;
I know not what the 'happy' means,
    Unless that it be this."

The old man sighed; "Sir Knight," said he,
    "We've sought in different ways,
I in this forest solitude,
    Thou 'midst the great world's praise,

"For happiness, but found it not;
    But, without search or thought,
This little child hath found her bliss
    In doing what she ought!"

God is Love[27]

Oh, that I know, indeed, is true,
For He has made the sky of blue,
And spread the earth with quiet green,
While azure waters flow between,
Because those colours are the best
On which the wearied eye can rest.

Oh yes, all tells us God is love,
Around, beneath us, or above:
Round us are flowers, that without care
Grow wildly, blooming everywhere,
And noble trees, beneath whose shade
The pale Spring flowrets bloom and fade.

Beneath us, deep within their bed,
The precious gems and ores are spread,
Diamonds and rosy rubies shine,
And metals fill the secret mine,
And that dark mass which we require[28]
At eve, to light our cheerful fire.

Above us is the glorious sun;
And when his brighter course is run,
The silvery moon looks forth, and makes

---

27 The source of the title is likely to be the New Testament verse, 'He that loveth not knoweth not God; for God is love' (1 John 4:8).
28 [Poet's Note: coal].

A path of light o'er seas and lakes;
And in the hushed and solemn night
Wander the starry worlds of light.

Within us, as around, above,
Something still whispers God is Love;
For He hath given us hearts to feel
A gladness tongue cannot reveal—
Vainly had beauty round us been,
Had we no minds to love the scene!

The Monk of Chester—a Scene in the Time of the Normans

Britons, Saxons, and Normans have all contributed to form the English nation; for many good and brave men must die before a people can become great and wise. As no really good or great thing is ever done on this earth without trouble, you may be sure that if we have now wise laws and good institutions, many have toiled and suffered before we could enjoy them. Our rude Saxon chiefs, our old Norman kings, let them be honoured for whatever good thing they have given us. The Saxon Harold and the Norman William have long since passed away, but whatever good they did while living has left some trace on the earth: great deeds do not die.

It is generally said, Harold died at Hastings; but there is a tradition that he was not killed, but died in the time of Henry I, a monk, at Chester.[29]

In Chester's ancient convent dim,
Slowly awoke the vesper hymn,
And borne o'er many a verdant dale,
It softly told its peaceful tale.
Mildly the autumn sunshine fell
On tomb, on effigy, and shrine;
While many a knight and abbot slept,
    With epitaph of uncouth line
Their rudely-chiselled tombs upon,
In the old chapel of Saint John.

---

29 Harold: Harold Godwineson, or Harold II (c. 1022–1066), reigned 1066; last Anglo-Saxon king of England, defeated at the Battle of Hastings by William the Conqueror. By the twelfth century a number of legends claimed that King Harold had survived Hastings, fleeing to Germany where he wandered as a pilgrim for many years. According to legend, he returned to England as an old man, first living as a hermit in a cave in Dover before travelling to Chester where he lived as a monk until his death; confessing on his deathbed that he had been born Harold Godwineson.

That evening came a lonely man,
    His pilgrim-dress was travel-worn;
His brow was scarred, his look like one
    Who had much toil and sorrow borne.
He sat him down beside the shrine;
    They asked him not from whence he came,
He spoke not of his history,
    Nor told his name;
But said, "I come, a wearied man,
    To seek a home—a grave with you;
Ask me not who, or whence I am,
    With that you have not aught to do."
And o'er his faded features pass'd
A look of pride—it was the last;
For meekly dwelt he from that day
A monk within their cloister grey,
With heavy sighs oft shook his breast,
Strange dreams, too, oft disturbed his rest,

And unconnected words would fall
   From his pale lips, as if in sleep
His memory would the deeds recall
   He strove to hide so deep.

Years passed, and he was bent with age,
   His glossy hair had turned to grey:
When the first Henry o'er the land
   Held regal sway,
   Upon his dying couch he lay.
The good monks stood around his bed,
And watched and prayed: "I die," he said,
"Last branch of a far-spreading tree,
Doomed by the Norman axe to be
Hewn to the earth." "It matters not,
My dying brother, what thy lot
Hath been in other years, to thee,
Just entering on eternity;
But we, who through long years have seen
What days of sorrow thine have been,
Would fain thy name and history know."
Thus spake a monk, in accents low,
And bending o'er the dying man,
   In silence and in night they stood;
For the curfew-bell had sounded far
   O'er land and flood.
'T was sad in darkness thus to stand,
A mournful, solitary band,
Around the bed of death. "Thy name,
   Tell us, at least, thy name," they said;
"*Harold*"—They bent to hear again,
   But he was dead!

A Talk in Furness Abbey.—to J.C.H[30]

"Mamma, my sister's gone,
   And I am left alone."
"Then come, my boy, and sit by me
   Upon this mossy stone;
And let us talk of those
   Who long since passed away;
'Tis well to think on other days,
   'Mid ruins old and grey.

"For though now o'er the grass
   Scarcely a footstep steals,
Once men dwelt here, and lived, and moved,
   Feeling what man now feels:
They were our brothers, though they lived
   In ages long ago;
For they could joy like us, and weep,
   Like us, for human woe.

---

30 The poem is dedicated to Hawkshaw's eldest son John Clarke, born 17 August 1841. The line drawn illustration accompanying the poem depicts a seated young woman speaking to a small boy standing at her side, set against a backdrop of abbey ruins. It is likely that Ann had taken her children to visit the ruins of Furness Abbey, the twelfth-century Cistercian monastery at Barrow-in-Furness, Cumbria, as she had an interest in historical sites which she shared with her children. In his (unpublished) diary, complied in 1913, John Clarke recalls a family holiday to Tunbridge Wells in 1857: 'My mother took us children to many interesting old buildings in the neighbourhood of Tunbridge Wells, Hurst Monceaux, Hever Castle, Bayham Abbey, and Battle Abbey.'

Here round the wide stone hearth,
    With blazing fagots piled,
They say, while many a wondrous tale
    The wintry hours beguiled.
Yonder the trout-stream flows,
    Still in its ancient bed;
From it how many a savoury dish
    Upon their board was spread.

"Beneath yon ruined arch,
    On which bright mosses creep,
They bore the dead—in that green spot
    Priest and crusader sleep;
But now their very names are gone,
    We know they lived—they died;
See there the nameless warrior lies,
    With his lady at his side.

"*Their* age hath passed away,
    Passed even as the chimes
That filled this vale with pleasant tones,
    We live in other times—
In other, and in happier times:
    Yet much of good was hid
Oft in these lonely halls—like gems
    Beneath a coffin lid.

"How many a lone, benighted guest
    Hath passed beneath this door,
How many a kindly hand hath fed,
    Upon yon step, the poor.
We ought not *now*, like those old monks,
    In Abbey walls to dwell,
But in all time there is the power
    To *think*, and to *do* well.

A Little Girl's Wish

I wish I had wings to fly away,
    Away, away, o'er the deep blue sea!
I would go to each old and famous shore,
Where busy cities stood of yore,
    Though silent now they be.

I would go where Tadmor's ruins lie,[31]
    Amid the desert's drifting sand;
And the lizards creep, and the night-winds moan,
Amid its temples overthrown
    By stern Aurelian's hand.[32]

I would go where the stately palm-trees rise,
    And the Campanero's voice is heard,[33]
Like the solemn sound of a convent bell,
Of the quiet hour of prayer to tell,
    When the leaves by the evening breeze are stirred:

And where the bright flowers of the cactus spring,
    From the clefts of the bare and sunburnt rocks,
And where for miles, from bough to bough,
The troops of chattering monkeys go,
    And the parrots fly in flocks.

I would go, too, where in northern skies,
    Upon their long and frosty nights,
When through the pine-wood howls the blast,
And the rivers in ice are all bound fast,
    Shoot bright and high the northern lights:

And where, upon the icy seas,
    Around the north and southern pole,
The stately icebergs, to and fro,
Like rocks of glittering diamonds go,
    Where the dark waves chance to roll.

I would go when the birds of passage go,
    When the flowers are dead, and the skies look grey;
I would follow the swallow's unknown track,
And like it in the Spring again come back;
    Oh, I wish I had wings to fly away!

---

31 Tadmor: another name for Palmyra, ancient oasis city in Syria.
32 Aurelian: Lucius Domitius Aurelianus (c. AD 215–75), Roman Emperor from AD 270–275; led the conquest of Palmyra in AD 272.
33 [Poet's Note: The Spanish name for the Bell-bird, a kind of Tucon, whose note exactly resembles the sound of a bell: it is often heard, on quiet nights, in the forests of South America.] The bell-like sound of the campanero is described by John Hawkshaw in his travel memoir *Reminiscences of South America: From Two and a Half Years' Residence in Venezuela* (1838), 85, 117.

Sir Oswald's Return—a Scene in the Time of the Crusades

Part I.

'T was winter, and the snow fell fast;
   The setting sun looked dull and red;
For shelter to the leafless boughs,
   Or old grey walls, the birds had fled;
When o'er a wild and trackless moor
   A solitary horseman past;
And on he urged his gallant steed
   To face the snowy blast.
He wore a falcon for his crest,
A red-cross on his shield and breast:
A knight was he, and that the sign
That he had been to Palestine.

Long years before, across that plain,
   A hundred followers with him past:
Some on Judea's hills were slain,
   Some perished by the simoon's blast,[34]
   And he alone was left—the last.
And now he bent his lonely way
To where he lived in childhood's day:
A lonely castle, old and grey,
Built on a high projecting cliff
   That overlooked the Northern Sea,
That foamed and thundered at its base.
   For miles there was no shrub or tree:
It was a bleak and lonely spot;
   And yet he loved it better far
Than all the perfumed palmy vales
   In Eastern lands that are.
And oft beneath the starry skies
   Of Syria's clime, so clear and bright,
When sleep pressed down his wearied eyes,
   In dreams he stood upon that height,
Watching the sea-gull skimming o'er
The crested wave or sandy shore.
And when he woke, and heard no sound
   But soft winds whispering through the palm
That waved above his sleeping head,
   He would have given those airs of balm
For one rude gale like that which now
Beat fiercely on his sun-burnt brow.

---

34 simoon's blast: a simoon is a hot, dry, suffocating sand-wind which sweeps across the African and Asiatic deserts at intervals during the spring and summer (n. form of 'simoom' *OED*).

Onward he rode: more wildly blew
The storm, and fast the snow-flakes flew;
But not of that Sir Oswald thought,
   For now his castle was in sight,
And as if meant to guide him home,
   From many a window gleamed a light.
"How will my lady Edith look,
   And my young son? She scarce will know
   Her husband with his furrowed brow;
And my brave cousin, good Sir Childe,
   I doubt not he hath faithful been,
And guarded well my Edith fair,
   As if she had been England's queen.
And my old henchman, Ethelstan,
   Who served me when I was a boy,
I wonder if he lives; how great
   Will be the old man's joy
To see his master home once more,
   Never to leave his native shore."
Thus to himself Sir Oswald spoke;
   And by that time he gained the beach:
Wildly the waves upon it broke,
   And far as eye could reach,
All whitened with the glittering spray
Were the high rocks around the bay.
There, for a moment, paused the knight
Before he climbed the dangerous height
   On which his castle stood: his steed
The sound of coming footsteps heard,
   And pricked his ears; for he good heed
Had learned to take when danger stirred.
Nearer and nearer came the sound—
   Behind a rock Sir Oswald drew,
And soon before him on the shore,
   What sight of horror met his view!
Seen in the dim uncertain light;
For day was changing into night:—

Two men in armour dragged along
    An old and venerable man,
And a young child, whose lip and cheek
    With fear were pale and wan,
And placed them in a crazy boat,
    And pushed it forward to the sea;
"Now seek thy father, boy," they said;
    "Thy path is wide and free."
The child bent down his head and wept
    Upon the old man's knee;
And he looked up to heaven and said,
"For this dark deed upon thy head,
    Sir Childe, will curses be!"

Rude laughed Sir Childe, and turned away,
    Thinking he left them for a prey
To the sea-wolves—the chilling spray[35]
Dashed o'er the child, and, in despair,
The old man tore his thin grey hair.
But for one moment paused the knight,
Till dark Sir Childe was out of sight,
Then dashed into the waves and brought
    The fair and slender boy to shore:—
"Now once again, my steed," he said,
    "And then thy toils are o'er."
The good horse reached the boat again,
    And safe the old man bore—
"Know'st thou the falcon-crest, old man,"
    Sir Oswald said; "I do not ask
If thou would'st know thy master now,
    For that would be a different task;

---

35 sea-wolves: seals or sea-lions, or a fabulous amphibious beast of prey (n. 'sea-wolf' *OED*).

For war and toil have left their trace,
In many a line, upon his face."

The old man dropped upon his knee,—
"My eyes are dim; I cannot see,
Amid this gloom, thy noble brow;
But 't is thy voice—that voice I trow
Has never left me year by year,
Though never thought again to hear.
Come, child, and kiss thy father's hand,
Whom we deemed slain in Holy Land."
The boy drew back, as if in fear;
But in the knight's dark eyes a tear
Stood trembling, as he clasped his child,
Who, re-assured, looked up and smiled,
And said, "Now mother will not weep,
    Nor I and my good Ethelstan
Be left to die upon the deep."
    "Where is my lady?" said the knight;
The old man to the castle looked,
    And pointed where a single light
Gleamed faintly from a distant tower:
"There sits your lady, at this hour,
Weeping her weary life away,
While in your halls Sir Childe hath sway."
"False kinsman, vengeance on thy head
Will surely rest," Sir Oswald said;
"But seek some shelter for the child,
Good henchman, for the night is wild.
I and my steed will now away:
My errand will not bear delay."
    So saying, up the rocky height
He sprung, and soon was out of sight.

Part II.

Sir Oswald reached the castle-gate:
"Who knocks?" the warder said; "'t is late
For guest; and if no guest thou art,
From hence 't were better to depart.
We do not suffer strangers here:
This castle hath some shapes of fear
As well unseen by stranger's sight—
I give thee warning, and good night."
"I thank thee for thy warning, friend,
But further onward cannot wend:
For food and shelter much have need

Both rider and his jaded steed,"
The knight replied. "Not thus of yore
Did stranger parley at this door;
Not closed to either friend or foe
It was, on such a night, I trow."
"Know'st thou my lord?" the warder said,
"My own good lord, in Syria dead?"
"Ay, know him as I know myself,"
Sir Oswald said: "Then thou shalt be
Tended as meets his friend by me,
Though on the morrow I be thrown
    For it into the sea."
And open wide the gate he swung;
Upon the court-yard pavement rung
The good knight's armour, as he sprung
From off his horse, and once again
Trod in his own and old domain.
He from his face undid his casque—
    "Now, Randolph, dost thou know thy lord?"
The warder gazed in fright, and said,
    "What! hath the grave its dead restored,
And sent thee, messenger of wrath,
To haunt thy guilty kinsman's path?
But oh! if spirits can be kind,
    And thou canst visit yon grey tower,
Be gentle there as summer rain,
    When falling on a broken flower:
For there a broken flower is dying"—
    "Randolph," the knight replied, "be still,
And listen, for the time is flying:
I am no spirit but a man,
    Sir Oswald, lord of this domain,
A red-cross knight from Palestine,
    Resolved to have his own again,
Or perish: till the mid of night
I'll keep me from my kinsman's sight,
While thou shalt tell to those who still
Are ready to obey my will,
That I am here, and at that hour
Will meet them by the western tower.
Meanwhile thy fire and evening meal
I'll share; for the night-wind, like steel,
Cuts through my frame, unused to bear
The rough kiss of your northern air.
God help my child, who hath to share

This night, perhaps, the sea-calf's den;[36]
But better *there* than in the home
   Of wicked men."
Randolph a pile of faggots threw
Upon the fire, and then withdrew
To spread among the vassal-train
News of their lord returned again;
While the knight, full of anxious thought,
   Sat listening for the midnight chime:
Whoever sat in solitude,
   Waiting for coming time,
And did not feel the solemn power
There is in such a watching hour?

'T is midnight—the rude festival
Hath ceased, and silent is the hall.
Sir Childe in heavy slumber lies
   Before the failing fire—around
His guests and followers, wrapped in sleep,
   Lie stretched upon the ground;
For wine and weariness combined
In slumber deep to steep each mind.
Trusty Randolph cautiously
   Mustered by the western tower
All the followers of his lord
   At the appointed hour.
One and all had joyfully
   Responded to the call;
And silently they follow now
   Their chieftain to the hall.
The porter at a signal given
   Did the bolts undo;
The oaken door fell back, and all
   Passed quickly through.
"Bind you traitor," said the knight,
   Pointing to Sir Childe, "but shed
No blood of his; for he hath shared,
   In boyish days, my home and bread."
They bound, and to a darksome vault,
   Reached by a secret stair,
Conveyed, and left him on the floor
   To waken in despair.

---

36 sea-calf: a seal (n. 'sea-calf' *OED*).

And now loud shouts of warfare ring
   Throughout the bloody hall,
As man to man, and foe to foe,
   They fight and fall.
Once on the floor Sir Oswald sunk,
   O'erpowered by many foes,
And, but for noble Randolph's aid,
   Had died beneath their blows.
He sprang before his honoured lord,
   Received the blow of death—and fell!
How many a faithful follower then
   Thus died, of whom no records tell!
That matters not; for if the deed
Be good, it hath but little need
Of earthly records for its meed.
Ere morning dawned the fight was done;
Sir Oswald had his castle won.
And when the evening fire again
   Gleamed brightly in the ancient hall,
Where now the red-cross banner waved
   In triumph from the wall,
Old Ethelstan led in the child,
   And placed him on his mother's knee,
Who clasped him with a long embrace,
   And tears fell fast and free.

"Bring forth Sir Childe," Sir Oswald said:
   They led the traitor to his lord.
Each brow frowned darkly, and each hand
   Was ready on his sword;
And hate and scorn each face revealed,
For now they thought his doom was sealed.
"Go," said Sir Oswald, "go, and seek
   Forgiveness of thy crimes from Heaven;
I do forgive thee, as I hope
   By God to be forgiven;
But in this realm thou must not stay:
Seek distant lands; begone—away!"
They all fell back as out he passed
   With hurried footsteps from the hall:
None spoke or moved until no more
   They heard that footstep's fall.

Years passed—Sir Oswald's hair was grey,
   Yet strong of heart and limb was he,
And often, with his youthful son,

Went to the chace right merrily.
It chanced one day the good knight rode
   Alone upon that silent shore
Where he had found old Ethelstan,
   And his young son, of yore:
And he rode thinking of that time,
Or listening to the sea-waves' chime.
   He reached a cavern in the cliff,
And there he saw an aged man,
   Kneeling beside a crucifix.
His cheek was pale and wan;
A palmer's dress he wore, and oft
   The tears stole down his aged face,
On which an Eastern sun had left
   Its burning trace.
"Give me thy blessing, holy man,"
   Sir Oswald said, and bent his knee;
"I am a sad and sinful man,"
   Replied he.
"Though once a brave and gallant knight,
   Of high degree,
For years I've wandered o'er the earth,
   With pilgrim-scrip and scallop shell;
I've knelt by many a famous shrine,
   I've drunk from many a holy well;
I've sat upon Mount Olivet,[37]
   On mournful Calvary I've wept,
And by the Jordan's sacred banks
   Have laid me down and slept.
But still no peace I've found—no rest;
Still dark and guilty is my breast.
No strength have I to wander now,
   Nor hope that penances will save;
Now I will pray to God alone,
   And here will find a grave.
Here, by the side of this wild sea,
That tales of other years to me
Tells with its ceaseless melody."
And then for years he lived alone,
   Nor sought for converse with mankind;
Yet the benighted wanderer oft
   With him would food and shelter find.
More tranquil and more mild he grew
   As in his solitude he dwelt;

---

37 Mount Olivet: Mount of Olives, east of Jerusalem.

And ever, at the midnight hour,
   Upon the shore to pray he knelt.

At length, Sir Oswald died—in state
   They laid him in a chapel near;
Wax-tapers gleamed and banners waved
   Around the warrior's bier.
That night the hermit left his cell,
   And slowly sought that burial-place;
More feeble than was wont his step,
   Yet tranquil was his face:
It seemed as if the gloom had passed
From off his furrowed brow at last.
"I come to watch beside this bier,"
   He said, and as he passed along,
A murmuring sound of blessings came
   From the assembled throng:
A faint smile passed across his face,
As at the bier he took his place.

Next morn they found him cold and dead—
   His hands were folded on his breast;
And calm and happy now he looked,
   Like tired wanderer sunk to rest.
Between his folded hands they found
   A ring—his name and crest!
They laid him in their chieftain's tomb,
   That aged hermit of the wild;
And on that tomb two names were graved—
   Sir Oswald and *Sir Childe*!

Ada[38]

Ada, the flowers of spring are blooming now;
    The flowers we talked of in the wintry hours,
When at my feet thou sat'st, thy thoughtful brow
    And fair face turned to mine; we talked of flowers,
Spring's sunny days, and birds amid the trees,
Themes that thy gentle heart could ever please.

And they are here; but thou art gone my child;
    And even the sunshine seems a mournful thing
To my sad heart, that flattering hope beguiled,
    To look with gladness to the coming spring:
For in those hours I had no secret dread;
Gazing on *thee*, I thought not of the dead.

The snow was on the ground, the biting blast
    Swept the bare earth when in the ground we laid
Thee, our first smitten flower: but they have past,[39]
    And earth again in beauty is arrayed:
Oh that the sunbeam could awake the flower
That withered by me in that bitter hour!

It cannot be!—ah me, how much of woe
    In the few words are hidden, "I shall see
Thee here no more," till now I did not know:
    Yet doth one thought bring comfort e'en to me,—
Thou art my child, my Ada still; not death
Can wither love e'en with his blighting breath:

---

38 Ada, the Hawkshaws' second child, was born at Islington House, Salford, on 22 April 1840. She died of hydrocephalus on 11 March 1845, six weeks before her fifth birthday. This is one of five poems to deal with the death of children. See also: 'To a Bereaved Father', 'To—— on the Death of Three of her Children', 'To—— after the Death of her Daughter' (*'Dionysius the Areopagite', with Other Poems*) and 'In Memoriam' (*Cecil's Own Book*). 'Ada' is one of four Hawkshaw poems to be included in the anthology *The Children's Casket: Favourite Poems for Recitation*, compiled by Annie M. Hone (London: Griffith, Farran, Okeden and Welsh, 1891). Appendix B gives details of the poem's republication. The review of *Poems for My Children* in the *Manchester Courier and Lancashire General Advertiser* (21 July 1847) cites the poem in full (see Appendix A).

39 our first smitten flower: there is a prescience here in Hawkshaw's use of 'first' that anticipates the deaths of more children, as two further children did die. The Hawkshaws' youngest child Oliver died of typhoid fever on 15 September 1856 whilst the family were holidaying in Pitlochry, Scotland. He was 11 years old. Then on 7 April 1863 the Hawkshaws' eldest child Mary died of puerperal mania, 11 days after giving birth to a son, Cecil. She was 25. Further details of these deaths and their impact on Hawkshaw can be found in the biographical introduction and in the notes accompanying *Cecil's Own Book*.

No, he but purifies it—'t is no more
    Of earth or time but of eternity.
Time cannot now my hopes or joys restore,
    And earth can offer nought, dear one, to thee,
'T is love unmingled with all meaner dreams
Of pride, or selfishness, or earthly schemes.

Therefore I will not say to thee farewell:
    No, none shall fill thy place within my heart.
There love for thee, and thoughts of thee shall dwell
    Until we meet again to never part:
A spirit dwelling in a home above
It is a sweet and solemn thing to love!

1854

SONNETS ON ANGLO-SAXON HISTORY

Sonnets on Anglo-Saxon History was published in November 1854 by the London publisher John Chapman and attracted largely favourable reviews.[1] Hawkshaw's sequence of one hundred sonnets retells the history of Britain from the advent of its earliest inhabitants through to the Norman Conquest. In both form and broad subject matter, *Sonnets on Anglo-Saxon History* responds to William Wordsworth's poetic survey of Church history, *Ecclesiastical Sketches*. First published in 1822, then revised, expanded and renamed *Ecclesiastical Sonnets* in 1845, Wordsworth's sequence of 132 sonnets is divided into 3 parts covering church history from its introduction to Britain through to the early nineteenth century. Hawkshaw is responding specifically to the 39 sonnets that make up part 1 of *Ecclesiastical Sketches* ('From the Introduction of Christianity into Britain, to the Consummation of the Papal Dominion'), which begins with paganism in prehistoric Britain, moves chronologically through to the Norman Conquest and the Crusades, and ends with the reign of King John (1199–1216). Hawkshaw's sequence ends at the Norman Conquest (1066). Technically challenging to execute and requiring extensive depth of research, Hawkshaw's accomplishment is remarkable, particularly as Wordsworth's use of the sonnet sequence to capture an historical narrative is often considered to be unique.[2]

Of the 100 sonnets in *Sonnets on Anglo-Saxon History*, 98 are faced on the page by a short prose extract from the work of prominent contemporary historians of the Anglo-Saxon period, or from early nineteenth-century translations of Anglo-Saxon texts. Hawkshaw's sources include Sharon Turner's landmark study, *The History of the Anglo-Saxons: From the Earliest Period to the Norman Conquest*, published in four volumes between 1799 and 1805, and reprinted in eight editions up to 1852; Francis Palgrave's *History of the Anglo-Saxons* (1831); and John Mitchell Kemble's *The Saxons in England* (1849). The complete list of her sources reflects the availability of Anglo-Saxon texts in translation by the mid-nineteenth century: Hawkshaw draws on Asser's *Life of Alfred*, King Alfred's translation of Bede, the English Historical Society's translation of Bede's *Ecclesiastical History* and the Bohn's Antiquarian library translation of Bede's *Ecclesiastical History* and the *Anglo-Saxon Chronicle*. The incorporation of historical sources into her sonnet sequence sees Hawkshaw interacting with historians rather than simply citing them as a source. Instead she responds to, and challenges the prominent Anglo-Saxon scholars of her day through her reflective and suggestive response to history and through the idiosyncratic formatting of the sequence. In quoting her prose sources, sometimes verbatim, otherwise in précis,

---

1 See Appendix A for the following reviews: *Westminster Review* (July–October 1854); *Manchester Guardian* (8 November 1854); *Living Age* (6 January 1855); *Athenæum* (20 January 1855); *Monthly Christian Spectator* (January–December 1855); *Eclectic Review* (July–December 1855).

2 In the introduction to his study of Wordsworth's sonnet sequence, John Delli Carpini makes the following observation: 'The *Ecclesiastical Sonnets* are innovative. Although the sonnet sequence [...] became popular again after Wordsworth in the nineteenth century, no one before or after him has written a public history of any kind in sonnet form.' *History, Religion and Politics in William Wordsworth's 'Ecclesiastical Sonnets'* (Lewiston: The Edwin Mellen Press, 2004), xvi.

on the left-hand page facing each sonnet, Hawkshaw presents an implicit critique of traditional historiography. Different sources are often quoted together on the same page, and occasionally the reader is directed back to the historical text itself, with an instruction to 'See Sharon Turner's *History of the Anglo-Saxons*'. By reworking the conventional historical narrative through a more intimate and personalised perspective in the facing sonnets, Hawkshaw makes a sustained challenge to traditions of historiography by noting its limitations and filling in the gaps.

In using the sonnet sequence for her historical project, Hawkshaw places her work within a poetic tradition defined by exacting expectations of structure and form. Not surprisingly therefore, reviewers of *Sonnets on Anglo-Saxon History* tended to evaluate Hawkshaw's skill as a sonneteer over and above the historical scope of her work. It is fair to say that Hawkshaw's efforts elicited a mixed response. Where one reviewer finds that 'Miss Hawkshaw's pen glides gracefully round the stiff settings of this very artificial form of poetical composition',[3] another concludes that although the collection exhibits 'industry and considerable vigour, […] the authoress possesses no adequate power for rendering the soul of history "rhythmically visible"'.[4] Although acknowledging that *Sonnets on Anglo-Saxon History* has 'an artistic shape', with subjects that are 'well selected, and chosen, with poetical taste, rather for their suggestiveness than for the pictures they present', George Thornbury, writing in the *Athenæum*, considers Hawkshaw's deployment of the sonnet to fall well short of expectations: 'As sonnets they do not rank very high, for, though metrical and not wanting in vigour, they require the full diapason that should consummate the fourteen lines,—and instead of one thought fully worked out they often contain two or three thoughts crowded and unelaborated.'[5]

In approaching the sonnet sequence with precise expectations of form and purpose, Thornbury not only finds Hawkshaw lacking in skill, but also difficult to classify: 'We can scarcely class Miss Hawkshaw as an addition to our female writers, for though tender, polished, pious, and sincere, she aims more at the manly excellencies of Wordsworth than the plaintive cadence of Mrs. Hemans or the Byronism of L.E.L.' (77). So although too ambitious to be judged alongside the more conventional female poetic output of Hemans and Landon, *Sonnets on Anglo-Saxon History* does not reach the 'manly excellencies' of Wordsworth and the male-gendered sonnet tradition that he had sought to reclaim from the female-authored elegiac sonnet revival of the late eighteenth century. It seems that for Thornbury, the combination of sonnet sequence, austere subject matter and female author placed *Sonnets on Anglo-Saxon History* outside of ideological expectations of gender and form.

Whilst this may have rendered Hawkshaw's sonnet sequence problematic for her reviewers, it is because of this subversion of expectation that *Sonnets on Anglo-Saxon History* is particularly striking, both as a historical project and for Hawkshaw's use of the sonnet to articulate her distinct perspective on history. In producing what the *Manchester Guardian* terms a 'charming little gallery of poetic historiettes',[6] Hawkshaw is able to

---

3 'Literary Notices', *Monthly Christian Spectator* (January–December), 55; see Appendix A.
4 *Eclectic Review* (July–December 1855), 376; see Appendix A.
5 *Athenæum* (20 January 1855), 76–7; see Appendix A.
6 *Manchester Guardian*, 8 November 1854, 10. The phrase 'charming little gallery of poetic historiettes' looks to emphasise the female authorship of the collection, but in doing so underestimates the subversive scope of Hawkshaw's sonnet sequence.

switch between moments, subjects and perspectives to produce a multi-layered history of the Anglo-Saxon period narrated from a variety of viewpoints. Without preamble or explanation, Hawkshaw can narrate one sonnet in her own voice, another through the thoughts of an Anglo-Saxon king or layman, and another through the imagined speech of one of her sonnet subjects, who are often female.[7] She can write her sonnet in the past tense, immersing her narrator in the imagined moment, or in the present tense to energise the historical narrative and draw the past and the present together, inviting her readers to experience the past as if it were their present – as Hawkshaw suggests it is. As the intervening narrator, Hawkshaw can speak as herself or from the representative position of 'we', 'our' and 'us', as she views the past in relation to her immediate present.

In transcribing the prose notes, the original formatting of titles and authors of sources has been standardised, but Hawkshaw's wording has been retained.

---

7 Debbie Bark discusses Hawkshaw's repositioning of the female voice in the national historical narrative in 'Mothers, Wives and Daughters Speak: The Recovery of Anglo-Saxon Women in Ann Hawkshaw's *Sonnets on Anglo-Saxon History*', in *Women's Writing* 19, no. 4 (December 2012): 404–16.

Introductory.[8]

'T is a hard thing to judge the past aright,
    Harder to judge the present, though it be
    Before our eyes in stern reality:
Nought of the beautiful, the ideal, the bright,
Haloes the things that meet the common sight:
    To find the lovely in the walks of life,
    The music of humanity in strife,
Kindness in sternness, gentleness in might,
May try the mind as much as to unfold
    The mouldering records of departed times,
And more shall try the heart; too warm, too cold,
    To judge of present hopes, and schemes, and crimes;
How changed will they appear throughout the gloom
Of coming years—our life seen from our tomb!

---

[8] This is one of the thirteen sonnets included in the *Manchester Guardian* review of *Sonnets on Anglo-Saxon History* (8 November 1854); see Appendix A.

I.

TACITUS says that the Gauls peopled Britain;[9] and the venerable Bede asserts that the first inhabitants came from Amorica [sic].[10] There are Danish traditions of expeditions from Jutland and the neighbouring coasts. The Welsh Triads say that before the race of Cymry came to Britain it had no people, but was occupied by "bears, wolves, beavers, and the oxen with the high prominence;" elks and wild boars were also numerous.[11] Amid the solitudes of the Grampians, or the heights of Snowden and Cadir Idris, the eagle still remains, the last of Britain's primeval denizens.

---

9 Tacitus: Tacitus (AD c. 56–c. 118), Roman historian, author of *Agricola* (AD 97–8).
10 Bede: the Venerable Bede (c. 673–735), theologian, monk and historian.
11 The wording of this section is a précis of extracts and footnotes from Sharon Turner's *The History of the Anglo-Saxons: From the Earliest Period to the Norman Conquest*, published in four volumes between 1799 and 1805, and reprinted in eight editions up to 1852. References throughout will be to the sixth edition, published in three volumes by Baudry's European Library, Paris (1840). It is not certain which edition Hawkshaw used, but as Baudry's sixth edition has been digitised in its entirety it is easily available for further reference if required. Here Turner refers to Tacitus and Bede in his discussion of Britain's earliest occupants, with footnotes citing Tacitus's *Agricola* and Bede's *Ecclesiastical History of the English People*; an ecclesiastical and political history of England in Latin (*Historia ecclesiastica*), completed in 731 (see *History of the Anglo-Saxons* (1840), vol. 1, 20–21). Welsh Triads: medieval manuscripts which organise fragments of Welsh folklore, mythology and history in a triadic form. The quotation from the Welsh Triad is cited by Turner as 'Triad 1' from a series of triads printed in *Archaiology* [sic] *of Wales*, vol. 2, 57–75 (*History of the Anglo-Saxons*, vol. 1 (1840), 21).

I.

The beginning.[12]

MAN to our island came; but from what land
    Were the first wanderers? Driven by adverse wind,
    And mourning for the homes they left behind,
Perchance they came; and on the silent strand
They stood a lonely and deserted band:
    The startled eagle, screaming, left the shore,
    From the thick forest looked the tusky boar,
While in the vale the stately elk reclined.
Oblivion's stream hath swept all deeper trace,
    They lived, toiled, died, and on the fertile plain
The rude descendent took his father's place,
    And felt his wants, and lived his life again:
Saplings chance rooted in the mountain cleft,
Seeds that the winds of time bore there and left.

---

[12] This is one of the thirteen sonnets included in the *Manchester Guardian* review of *Sonnets on Anglo-Saxon History* (8 November 1854); see Appendix A.

II.

THE Phenicians, in their commercial voyages, colonised many of the islands, and some of the coasts, of the Ægean and Mediterranean seas. Inscriptions in their language have been found in Malta. They occupied Spain, and founded Cadiz,[13] and procured tin and lead from the British isles, a trade which they endeavoured studiously to conceal from the rest of the world.[14] Some suppose that the religious system of the Druids was in part derived from the Phenicians, and that they introduced some of the arts of civilised life into Britain cannot be doubted.[15]

---

13 The wording to this point is from Turner in *History of the Anglo-Saxons*, vol. 1 (1840), 30.
14 This is a précis of an account given by Turner in *History of the Anglo-Saxons*, vol. 1 (1840), 30; he cites the Greek historian and geographer Strabo (c. 63 BC–c. AD 23) as his source.
15 Turner gives an account of the origins of the Druids in relation to the Phenicians in *History of the Anglo-Saxons*, vol. 1 (1840), 45.

II.

Progress.[16]

PROGRESS is nature's stamp on man; the mark
    Of his divine and his humanity;
    And dimly through the night of years we see
Britain's first impulse onward: that strange bark
Making its way across the billows dark
    Of unknown seas, from far Phenicia's shore,
    Another treasure bears than eastern store;
Thoughts that the heart shall feel, words that the ear shall hark.
E'en as the tropic stream bears through the tide
    Of icy seas the seed-grains of its home,
Man hath his conscious schemes of wealth and pride,
    But his unconscious ones, where'er he roam,
Work through the outer; o'er all life there lies
The soft, deep colouring of the heavenly skies.

---

16 This is one of the thirteen sonnets included in the *Manchester Guardian* review of *Sonnets on Anglo-Saxon History* (8 November 1854); see Appendix A.

III.

THE system of the Druids began in Britain, and passed from thence into Gaul. None of their sacred mysteries were committed to writing, although they used the Greek character for common purposes: they believed in the immortality of the soul, and Cæsar says they taught many things concerning the stars and their motions; the size of the world and its countries; the nature of things; and the force and power of the immortal gods.[17]

They were divided into three classes—Druids, Bards, and Vates.[18]

---

17 This is a précis of Turner's account of the Druids. In places the wording is taken directly from Turner, who cites Julius Caesar (100–44 BC) as a source (*History of the Anglo-Saxons*, vol. 1 (1840), 43–4).

18 Turner gives a more detailed account of these classes, citing Strabo as a source: 'The Druidical order consisted of three sorts of men; Druids, Bards and Ouates. The Bards were the poets and musicians, of whom some were satirists and some encomiasts. The Ouates sacrificed, divined, and contemplated the nature of things. The Druids cultivated physiology and moral philosophy' (*History of the Anglo-Saxons*, vol. 1 (1840), 44).

III.

The Druids.

Man's heart could listen then, as now, and hear
   The voice of God that speaketh evermore;
   And he that hears must listen and adore;
The softer tones might perish, those of fear
Alone would strike upon the inward ear.
   The child in heart, rude sounds his bosom stirred,
   The harmonious under-tones passed by unheard,
He bent his knee, but could not give a tear.
These different tones go sweeping by us now,
   And stern and gentle hearts hear each a part;
One veils his face before the awful brow
   Of a dread sovereign; one, with loving heart,
Looks to a father; what the soul can stir
Changes the creed, but makes the worshipper.

IV.

TACITUS says that Cæsar did not conquer Britain, but only showed it to the Romans; it was Agricola who completed its conquest, and who brought into extensive use the arts and luxury of Rome.

That the Britons at the time of Cæsar's invasion were not the barbarians they are sometimes represented, is evident; Cassivellaum [sic] had war-chariots when he opposed the Romans; and coined money was used by his successor Cunobelin, whose coins, with his name on them, have been found, and also one with a bard and harp upon it.[19]

---

19 Turner refers to Gnaeus Julius Agricola, Roman general and governor of Britain from AD 78–84; Cassivellaun (or Cassivellaunus), British chief at the time of Caesar's invasion in 54 BC; Cunobelin, King of the Catuvellauni in south-east England during the late first century BC and renowned for his prolific minting of coins (*History of the Anglo-Saxons*, vol. 1 (1840), 45–50).

IV.

The Romans.

DEAR to the Briton was his island home
    And the rude freedom that his fathers gave,
    But Cæsar's galleys float upon the wave,
And Greek and Gaul have bowed their necks to Rome.
Yet on the beach all crimsoned rolls the foam,
    Ere on that shore the Roman dares to leap,
    Or the fell eagle broods o'er Dover's steep.
But no rude valour then could Britain save.
Years passed to ages, and the conqueror brought
    Luxurious arts—the forest disappeared
Where Vates sacrificed, and Druids taught,
    And stately shrines to stranger gods were reared;
While for her slaughtered sons on Syria's plain,
Or Danube's banks, the mother wept in vain.[20]

---

20 With the River Danube forming a natural border for the northern territories of the Roman Empire its banks would have been the site of many battles. Turner makes several such references to the Danube in *History of the Anglo-Saxons*.

V.

LITTLE did the Roman philosopher, who contemptuously called Christianity the religion of an obscure sect, think, that in a few ages its churches should occupy the place of all the idol temples of Europe; as little did its humble and suffering followers suppose how changed its peaceful and loving doctrines would become in the hands of priests and monarchs.[21]

---

21 It is not clear which Roman philosopher is alluded to here, or whether Hawkshaw is referring more generally to accounts of early Christianity by Roman historians such as Suetonius and Tacitus.

V.

Christianity.

ROME's clarion-blast had thundered through the air,
    And died with scarce an echo, when there rose
    A tone so soft, that 'mid the din of foes
It was unheeded; with the voice of prayer,
The sighs that agony of woe declare,
    With lofty hymns of triumph and of trust,
    Proclaiming spirit sovereign over dust,
It came, earth's melodies to mingle with and share.
All the pure utterance of ages past,
    The words of sages, and the poet's song,
It blended into music, best and last
    Of all God's voices; as it floats along,
Stirring the listening heart to deeds of love,
To hope for man, to higher life above.

VI.

IN 525, St. Deiniol founded a college at Bangor, which was raised to a bishopric about 550;[22] it was destroyed by the pagan Saxons, 1071, and the monks cruelly murdered, but, in 1102, it was rebuilt by funds collected by a Synod held at Westminster for reforming the church. King John, in 1212, took the then bishop prisoner, whilst officiating at the altar, but released him on receiving a large ransom.[23]

The remains of several Welsh princes lie in this cathedral. The tomb of Prince Owen Gryffrydd is still in a perfect state beneath an arched recess.[24]

---

22 St. Deiniol: St Deiniol, sixth-century Welsh saint; founder of the monastery of Bangor Iscoed in Wrexham.
23 King John: king of England from 1199–1216.
24 Owen Gryffrydd: Owain Gwynedd (c. 1100–1170), king of Gwynedd from 1137–70. The wording of this section is taken from the entry for 'Bangor' in *The Penny Cyclopaedia of the Society for the Diffusion of Useful Knowledge*, vol. 3 (1825), 372–3.

VI.

Christianity in Britain.[25]

OH! beautiful as light when down it streams
    Through cloudless ether, was the truth when taught
    By the Great Master; but how soon it caught
A tinge of earthly colouring; Grecian dreams,
The Eastern's slavish fear, the mystic gleams
    Of light through darkness struggling in the soul
    That could not break an earlier creed's control,
Obscured, though never quenched, its heavenly beams.
But purer far was that beclouded light
    Than aught before e'er seen in Britain's isle:
Oft the lone wanderer in the wintry night
    Sought shelter in old Bangor's monkish pile,
And by the wood-heaped fire then waning dim,
Heard from the low-roofed church the Christian's hymn.

---

[25] This is one of the thirteen sonnets included in the *Manchester Guardian* review of *Sonnets on Anglo-Saxon History* (8 November 1854); see Appendix A.

VII.

BRITAIN, after its final abandonment by the Romans, about the year 410, appears to have become divided into a number of small republics, answering to the Roman districts into which it had been divided. These engaging in contests with each other, a number of petty tyrants arose, for we find Kings of Cornwall, Devonshire, Kent, Glastonbury, &c. Amid this incessant warfare, and the incursions of the Picts, Scots, and Saxons, many of the buildings erected by the Romans must have been destroyed. The corrupted civilisation of Rome, grafted on the barbarism of Britain, was not likely to produce good or lasting results.

VII.

Change.

At length they leave, those masters of the world,
   The northern island they so long have held;
   The forest rose again their axes felled,
Past the weed-covered fount the streamlet purled
In its old bed; and giant winter hurled
   As toys to his frost sons, the stones that spanned
   The vale or river, and spring's fairy wand
Gave flowers to wave where banners had unfurled.
They left the slave's dull heart and toiling hand,
   But not the mind to prompt, the will to do;
A hideous stupor brooded o'er the land,
   And storms alone, perchance, could health renew;
Dark truth, that fixes but a deeper blot
On those who duty, nature, God forgot.

VIII.

It is probable that the Saxons had for centuries visited and settled in Britain before the date fixed as the time of the arrival of Hengist, about 449. The Romans had an officer called the Count of the Saxon Coast, whose Government extended from near the present site of Portsmouth to Wells in Norfolk. The coming of Hengist and his brother seems to have been accidental, as they had but three small vessels with them.[26] Nennius says they were exiles.[27]

---

26 Hengist and Horsa: Germanic brothers and leaders of the Anglo-Saxon invasion of Britain in the fifth century. They are associated with the creation of the kingdom of Kent, and were said to have been given the Isle of Thanet by the warlord Vortigern, against who the brothers later rebelled.

27 Nennius: ninth-century Welsh scholar. This is a précis of Turner's account in *History of the Anglo-Saxons*, vol. 1 (1840), 151.

VIII.

The Saxons.—I.

THE polished Roman left how slight a trace,
    Compared to those wild rovers of the deep
    Whose language still, whose very thought we keep;
Rude thought, with nothing of Italian grace,
But wild and wonderous as its native place,
The fiords and the forests of the north,
Where Winter's steeds the fierce winds hurry forth,
    And whirlpools boil, and mountain torrents leap.
All men are brothers; but as in one home
    Features and minds may differ, so one race
Another does excel; like ocean foam
    Nations have melted, and their vacant place
Been filled by stronger minds, or hardier frames,
While others blend like drops, and do but change their names.

IX.

"THE Saxons were an agricultural and pastoral people; they required land for their alods— forests, marshes, and commons for their cattle ... Nor can we reasonably imagine that such spoils as could yet be wrested from the degenerate inhabitants were despised by conquerors whose principle it was that wealth was to be won at the spear's point."—See Kemble's *Saxons in England*.[28]

---

[28] Extracted from Kemble's *The Saxons in England: A History of the English Commonwealth till the Period of the Norman Conquest*, vol. 2 (1849), 293–4.

IX.

The Saxons.—II.

AND soon the polish and the splendour fled
    That Rome had brought; 't was of a southern birth,
    And would not root itself in northern earth;
And from the Druid's uncouth cromlech spread[29]
The ivy to the Roman shrine, and wed
    Both to oblivion with its clasping rings;
    Another race, another sort of kings
Than those in Cæsar's golden palace bred,
Are on the shore; the sea-king's ocean-steed
    Bounds o'er the stormy wave; the Saxons come.
In their own souls their destiny they read,
    And see in British vales their future home:
By manly toil, by thought, by peace and strife,
They made us England—theirs was inborn life.

---

29 cromlech: a prehistoric structure made up of a large flat unhewn stone which rests horizontally on three or more stones set upright (n. 'cromlech' *OED*).

X.

THERE are passages of great beauty and of mysterious import in the Edda, as that which describes the "Twilight of the Gods," or the final conflict between the gods and the giants, when destruction shall overwhelm the universe, but from which a new creation shall emerge;[30] so also that in the beginning of all things—"At the beginning of time there was nothing; neither land nor sea, nor foundations below; the earth was nowhere to be found: nor the heaven above: There was an infinite abyss, and grass nowhere."[31]

---

30 Edda: referring to the Old Norse texts: *Poetic Edda*, a thirteenth-century collection of Old Norse poems on traditional and mythical subjects; *Prose Edda*, a handbook to Icelandic poetry, thought to have been written by the Icelandic historian Snorri Sturluson in c. 1220. *Ragnarokkr*, or 'Twilight of the Gods', is referred to in both.
31 From 'Völuspá', the first poem of the *Poetic Edda*. The likely source for these lines is Turner, who cites them in an appendix (*History of the Anglo-Saxons*, vol. 1 (1840), 135).

X.

Saxon Mythology.

In the soft melody of winds and streams
    The voice of Deity the Grecian heard,
    And all the love of beauty in him stirred;
But the snow-girdled Hecla, with its gleams[32]
Of lurid flame, wake sterner, wilder dreams
Within the Northman's heart, and, clothed with form,
Became the polar frost, and fire, and storm,
    Things, living things to him, not as to us a word.
He looked around, and saw that mystery veiled
    All nature, and behind that veil, to him,
There sat a Deity, and it he hailed,
    And bowed his rugged head and sinewy limb;
Not to luxurious gods could he resign
His faith; to him the strong was the divine.

---

32 Hecla: a volcano in southern Iceland.

XI.

Many indications exist of a spreading disbelief in their old faith, which prepared the northern nations for the reception of the nobler truths of Christianity. Bartholin has collected some instances of this kind.[33] One warrior says that he trusted more to his strength and his arms than to Odin;[34] another, "I do not wish to revile the gods, but Freya seems to me of no importance: neither she nor Odin are anything to us."[35]

---

33 Bartholin: Thomas Bartholin (1659–90), Danish scholar, author of *Antiquitatum Danicarum* (3 vols, 1689).
34 Odin: from Scandinavian mythology, supreme god and creator.
35 Freya: in Scandinavian mythology, goddess of love and the night. This section is a précis of Turner who refers to the work of Bartholin and cites this quotation in an appendix (*History of the Anglo-Saxons*, vol. 1 (1840), 137).

XI.

Christianity received by the Saxons.—I.

THE time for change had come! what once had might
    To sway the spirit and to bless the heart
    In that old faith had now fulfilled its part,
And silently it passes into night;
The horologe of time proclaimed the light
    Of Christian day was dawning; silently
    It rose above the heaving restless sea
Of Saxon mind, and made its billows bright.
Thus passed for ever Scandinavia's gods,
    As passed before the Greek's, and ere these died
Egypt's had vanished from their rock-abodes,
    And the Assyrian's from the Tigris' side.[36]
Forms change, creeds alter, but the truth still lives,
And to them all their power and beauty gives.

---

36 Assyrian: of the ancient empire of Assyria in the Middle East, in what is now northern Iraq; named after the city of Ashur on the River Tigris.

XII.

"When he (Edwin, King of Northumbria)[37] inquired of the high priest (Coifi) who should first profane the altars and temples of their idols, with the enclosures that were about them, he answered, 'I; for who can more properly than myself destroy those things which I worshipped through ignorance?'[38] ... As soon as he drew near the temple he profaned the same, casting into it the spear which he held; ... the place where the idols were is still shown, not far from York, to the eastward, beyond the River Derwent, and is now called Godmundingham."*—See Bede's *Ecclesiastical History*.[39]

* Or, "The home of the protection of the gods." Its modern name is Goodmanham, East Riding of York.[40]

---

37 Edwin: Eadwine (c. 586–633), king of Northumbria (616–33).
38 Coifi: pagan high priest of the temple of Goodmanham, Northumbria. He abandoned his old religion and in doing so contributed to Edwin's own conversion to Christianity, an action that was followed throughout Yorkshire and Lincolnshire by noblemen and thanes.
39 This section is extracted from J. A. Giles's *The Venerable Bede's Ecclesiastical History of England, also The Anglo-Saxon Chronicle* (1847), 96. The *Anglo-Saxon Chronicle* was established during the reign of King Alfred (871–99). Written as annals in Old English, the chronicle was updated by ecclesiastical clerks in monasteries across England, recording events from the departure of the Romans up to the decades following the Norman Conquest. The *Anglo-Saxon Chronicle* is a term used to describe the composite set of annals which includes material from multiple sources.
40 The footnote is not from Bede, but appears verbatim in J.A. Giles's *The Venerable Bede's Ecclesiastical History of England, also The Anglo-Saxon Chronicle* (1847), 96. Of the nineteenth-century editions of Bede, edited by Stevenson (1841), Giles (1842), Hussey (1846), and the translation included in *Monumenta Historica Britannica* (1848), Giles is Hawkshaw's likely source.

XII.

Christianity received by the Saxons.—II.[41]

'T is easy on the accustomed path to tread,
   Worn by the feet of generations past;
   But he who treads it first, or treads it last,
Venturing where all is silent as the dead—
Or lingering there when all besides are fled—
   These are the lofty spirits who unfold
   New views of greatness, or preserve the old.
Both noble, but by different natures led.
The Saxon story tells of one who flung
   His fateful arrow at the idol's shrine,
While others round the mouldering ruins hung,
   Whose desolation was to them divine:
Types of two classes who must ever be
Within a land that would be strong, yet free.

---

41 This is one of two sonnets included in the review of *Sonnets on Anglo-Saxon History* in the *Living Age* (6 January 1855); see Appendix A.

XIII.

MERLIN, or more properly Merdhin, is supposed to have lived about the middle of the fifth century.[42] Sharon Turner says, in his "Vindication of the Ancient British Poems,"[43] "I think I cannot more decisively prove that these were extant in the time of Giraldus' poems of the sixth century,[44] and of Merlin, than by translating some passages from him on the subject,"[45] and adds from Giraldus, "The memory of Merlin's prophecies had been retained among the British bards, whom they call poets, verbally by many—in writing by very few."[46] Merlin wrote a little poem, entitled "Avallenau; or, the Orchard," which contains many personal allusions, and a wild and touching account of a madness from which he suffered.[47]

---

42 Merlin: a probable antecedent of the Scottish and Irish legend of Myrddin (Merddin) the mad prophet, Merlin's position as a bard and wizard in Arthurian legend was established by Geoffrey of Monmouth's twelfth-century text, *Historia regum Britanniae* (*History of the Kings of Britain*).
43 Reference to Sharon Turner's *A Vindication of the Genuineness of the Ancient British Poems of Aneurin, Taliesin, Llywarch Hen and Merdhin with Specimens of their Poems* (London, 1803).
44 Giraldus: Giraldus Cambrensis, or Gerald of Wales (c. 1146–1223), medieval clergyman and chronicler who wrote extensively about Ireland and Wales.
45 From Turner's *A Vindication of the Genuineness of the Ancient British Poems* (1803), 145–6.
46 From Turner's *A Vindication of the Genuineness of the Ancient British Poems* (1803), 147.
47 Avallenau: a series of prophetic stanzas written in the first person and ascribed to Myrddin (Merlin); each stanza beginning with the phrase 'Afallen beren', or 'Sweet apple tree'. Turner's account of the Avallenau includes the following quotation, to which Hawkshaw seems to refer: 'I am a wild, terrible screamer, affliction wounds me—raiment covers me not' (*A Vindication of the Genuineness of the Ancient British Poems* (1803), 122).

XIII.

Merlin.

AND what art thou?—an ideal of the great;
   The personation of a nation's thought;
   A giant figure by the ages wrought?
Rather a man for whom time would not wait,
But with rough hand consigned thee to the fate
   Of a rude people and untutored age,
   To bear the name of wizard, not of sage,
To be a thing of fear, and doubt, and hate.
Yet, wert thou not of nature's worshippers,
   And knelt beside her mountain altars—lone
And silent—where the ocean-sounding firs
   Bent (like thy soul) upon their rocky throne,
As the storm with its phantom-wings swept by,
Bearing the voices of Eternity?

XIV.

"When he (Augustine) had sat down,[48] pursuant to the king's commands, and preached to him and his attendants then present the word of life, Ethelbert answered thus:[49]—'Your words and promises are very fair, but they are new to us, and of uncertain import; I cannot approve of them so far as to forsake that which I have so long followed with the whole English nation ... We will not molest you, but give you favourable entertainment; ... nor do we forbid you to preach and gain as many as you can to your religion.'"—Bede's *Ecclesiastical History*.[50]

---

48 Augustine: St Augustine (d. 604), appointed first archbishop of Canterbury in 597 having arrived on the Isle of Thanet in Kent from Rome, sent as a missionary by Pope Gregory the Great to convert the pagan English to Christianity.
49 Ethelbert: Aethelberht I, king of Kent until c. 616.
50 From Bede in J. A. Giles's *The Venerable Bede's Ecclesiastical History of England, also The Anglo-Saxon Chronicle* (1847), 38.

XIV.

Ethelbert examining the Christian Doctrines.

NATURE hath mighty things, and what are they?
   The avalanche, the earthquake, and the storm?
   These for a while, but for a while deform;
The mightiest things are those of every day,
That like great Time pass noiseless on their way:
The forest grows unheard, the mountain chain
Cycles in silence build, and then again
   Crumble and mould it in another form.
'T is thus with mind, the greatest change it knows
   From error unto truth, by patient thought,
Not noisy speech, within the spirit grows;
   Nor doth that earnest struggle lead to naught,
He who hath felt that truth is hard to reach,
Will for another's faults find gentle speech.

XV.

ETHELBERT was king of Kent in 597; he had extended his dominions as far as the river Humber, by which the Southern Saxons were divided from the Northern. Before the arrival of Augustine, he had heard of the Christian religion from his queen, Bertha, who was a Frank.[51] Bede says, "he compelled none to embrace Christianity ... For he had learned from his instructors and leaders to salvation that the service of Christ ought to be voluntary, not by compulsion."[52]

---

51 Bertha: queen of Kent (c. 565–c. 603), daughter of Charibert, the Merovingian king at Paris (561–7), and of Queen Ingeborg; she was given dispensation to continue to practise her Christian religion after her marriage to then pagan King Ethelbert.
52 From Bede in J.A. Giles's *The Venerable Bede's Ecclesiastical History of England*, also *The Anglo-Saxon Chronicle* (1847), 39.

XV.

Ethelbert embraces Christianity.

NOT from indifference, not with hasty tread,
   From Odin's altars turned that king away,[53]
   The first beside the Christian shrine to pray;
Pure was the light his moral influence shed.
Calmly he waited till the mists had fled
   From the dark minds who still in faith could cling
   To their old altar as a sacred thing;
And not from bigot zeal one victim bled.
Colours must blend to form one stainless ray,
   And sounds, to make one perfect harmony,
And many minds, each in a different way,
   The dark enigma of our being see,
And from the strivings of the whole evolves
An answer that sufficeth, though not solves.

---

53 Odin: see note 34.

XVI.

EDWIN, at the age of three years,[54] was driven from his paternal dominions of Deira[55] by Ethelfrith, king of Northumbria;[56] he was generously brought up by Cadvan in North Wales.[57] On arriving at manhood he was compelled to leave Wales, and wandered many years in secret to escape Ethelfrith's pursuit. Being at length sheltered and assisted by Redwold,[58] king of East Anglia, he obtained the throne of his unrelenting foe. Edwin fell in battle in his forty-eighth year, A.D. 633.[59]

---

54 Edwin: Eadwine (c. 586–633), king of Northumbria (616–33).
55 Deira: early Anglo-Saxon kingdom in northern England.
56 Ethelfrith: Aethelfrith, king of Northumbria (d. c. 616). Became king of Bernicia in 592 and in 604 added the neighbouring kingdom of Deira, forming Northumbria.
57 Cadvan: Cadfan, king of Gwynedd.
58 Redwold: Raedwald, king of the East Angles (d. c. 625).
59 The wording of this section is a précis of Turner's account of Edwin in *History of the Anglo-Saxons*, vol. 1 (1840), 205–15.

XVI.

The great Edwin of Northumbria.—I.

I CALL thee great—as such, would honour thee,
   Though history hath not titled thus thy name
   (Oft to be 'mid her great ones is but shame);
True man thou wert, and no nobility
Could add a prouder title to the tree
   Of thy ancestral lineage; king and sage
   A brief memorial on a monkish page
Is all that fate hath given thy memory:
Yet 't is enough if we but look; the shell
   Tells the rock's history, and the crumbling arch
The temple's date; and so it needs no swell
   Of pompous words to trace through Time's rough march
The great and good—dim shapes, but as we gaze,
Each form the human and the race displays.

XVII.

THE vicissitudes of Edwin's early life had made him thoughtful and contemplative;[60] he was more intellectual than any of the Anglo-Saxon kings who had preceded him. His history, related by the Venerable Bede, though brief, is full of interest. Having solicited the hand of the daughter of the Christian King of Kent,[61] her brother objected to her marriage with a worshipper of Odin. Edwin promised not to interfere with her religion or that of her friends; and added, if he found on examination that Christianity was a religion more worthy of God than his old faith, he would himself adopt it.[62]

---

60 Edwin: Eadwine (c. 586–633), king of Northumbria (616–33).
61 daughter of the Christian King of Kent: Aethelburh (d. 647), married Eadwine of Northumbria in c. 624.
62 This section is a précis of Turner's account of Edwin which draws on Bede's *Ecclesiastical History* as a source (*History of the Anglo-Saxons*, vol. 1 (1840), 208).

XVII.

Edwin of Northumbria.—II.

He sat beside an antique shrine and thought
   Upon the past, as ever think the wise;
   From it the shapes of the dim future rise,
And out of it the present must be wrought:
A true response to many doubts he sought
   From God, from nature, from his heart, and ne'er
   Did these leave earnest questioner in despair;
In thousand ways an answer may be brought.
Not upon nullities do nations live,
   It is belief alone can give them power;
He felt the present had but forms to give,
   And the past taught him they but live their hour;
"The twilight of the gods" hath come, he said,[63]
And o'er us glooms Hel's* empire of the dead.[64]

---

63 "The twilight of the gods": see note 30.
64 [Poet's Note: *Hel, or Hela, was the Scandinavian death-goddess.] Hel: goddess of the underworld and of the dead (n. 'Hel' *OED*).

XVIII.

The life of Edwin[65] was attempted by an assassin commissioned by Cwichhelm, the pagan King of Wessex.[66] Pretending to be a messenger from his king, he was admitted to Edwin's presence, and attacked him with a poisoned dagger. The king was unarmed, but a thane, to whom he was much attached,[67] was near him; he saw the king's danger, and, having no shield, threw himself before his master, and received in his own body the blow which it was impossible to arrest.[68]

---

65 Edwin: Eadwine (c. 586–633), king of Northumbria (616–33).
66 Cwichhelm: Cwichelm, the West Saxon king (d. 636).
67 thane: a servant, minister, attendant (n. 'thane' *OED*). Bede and Turner name this thane as Lilla.
68 This section is a précis of Turner's account of Edwin in *History of the Anglo-Saxons*, vol. 1 (1840), 208.

XVIII.

The Thane Lilla saving Edwin.—III.

Hadst thou been Greek, thy name had been enshrined
   In living song, and altars had been raised
     To thee,—loud history would have blazed
Thy deed hadst thou been Roman; but I find
Few who know e'en thy name and how entwined
   It is with nobleness; we turn away
     From records of our country's early day
As if it naught had held of heart or mind.
Thou mad'st thy heart a buckler for thy king;
   Saxon, 't was nobly done! and I am fain
This slow, late-blooming flower of song to bring
   Unto thy grave; tribute to thee, how vain,
But not for us; one worthy deed well read
Thoughts can revive that common life keeps dead.

XIX.

CAEDMON[69] appears to have had the care of the cattle of the Abbey of Whitby during the time of Hilda.[70] So far from appearing when young to possess the gift of song, when the harp was passed to him at convivial meetings, he would shrink away and withdraw in tears. One night having thus withdrawn, he laid down and slept; during his sleep a voice said to him "Caedmon, sing me something;" "I cannot sing," said he; "Yet thou must sing to me," said the voice; "What shall I sing?" "The origin of things." His short ode on the Creation is in Alfred's translation of Bede.[71] He was admitted by Hilda among the company she had gathered round her, and died at Whitby, A.D. 680.

69　Caedmon: seventh-century Anglo-Saxon monk and poet; often regarded as the first of the English poets. As an illiterate herdsman, Caedmon is said to have been inspired in a dream to compose poetry along Christian themes.
70　Hilda: St Hilda (614–80), English abbess; founded the monastery in Whitby in 657.
71　The first translation of Bede's *Ecclesiastical History* was completed in the ninth century during King Alfred's reign, under his programme of translation. The 'ode on Creation' referred to by Hawkshaw appears as follows in Giles's *The Venerable Bede's Ecclesiastical History of England, also The Anglo-Saxon Chronicle* (1847): "'We are now to praise the Maker of the heavenly kingdom, the power of the Creator and his counsel, the deeds of the Father of glory. How he, being the eternal God, became the author of all miracles, who first, as almighty preserver of the human race, created heaven for the sons of men as the roof of the house, and next the earth", to which Bede adds: "This is the sense, but not the words in order as he sang them in his sleep; for verses, though never so well composed, cannot be literally translated out of one language into another, without losing much of their beauty and loftiness"' (218).

XIX.

Caedmon the Anglo-Saxon Poet.

The ocean billows, and the rock-bound shore,
   The still, wide moorland, or the northern sky
   Of changing beauty, on his infancy
Pressed with their silent influence evermore;
Childhood went by, then evening breezes bore
   From Hilda's gothic pile the chanted hymn,
   And in the cloister or the chapel dim
Knelt the lone youth in silence to adore.
Thus Nature trained him for his work through years
   With a wise sternness,—oft the starry night,
On which he gazed with longing and wild tears,
   Seemed opening for him to the infinite,
And thoughts and dreams his heart had kept, awoke,
And the closed lips at last in music spoke.

XX.

"Almost every monastery had its own historiographer or historian, whose business, or, at least, whose general practice, it was to copy the history of preceding times from those who were already known to have written them with success, and to continue the narrative during his own times, in his own words, to the best of his ability."—Preface to the *Saxon Chronicle*, Bohn's Antiquarian Library.[72]

---

72 From J.A. Giles's *The Venerable Bede's Ecclesiastical History of England, also The Anglo-Saxon Chronicle* (1847), xxxvi. Published by Henry Bohn, London, as part of the 'Bohn's Antiquarian Library' series.

XX.

The Chronicler.

In massive chair of oak-wood, rudely made,
   Sits a grey-headed monk, whose placid face
   Of time or passion shows but little trace;
Safe in that old secluded convent's shade,
The world's rough conflict to his mind displayed
   Seems more a shifting picture, than a thing
   Of life reality; its voices ring,
But as an echo by the breezes stayed.
Yet hath that still old man a kindly heart,
   Loving all gentle things, from bird and child
To tree and flower; and now he sits apart
   From monkish tattle in the sunshine mild,
Noting the records of his times: aside
He puts his vellum page with conscious pride.

XXI.

THE place of Bede's birth is said by himself to have been in the territory afterwards given by King Egfred[73] to Benedict Biscop,[74] abbot of the united monasteries of Wearmouth and Jarrow; this abbot, who had formerly been a thane, was unwearied in the pursuit of knowledge and in ameliorating the condition of his country. He travelled four or five times to Rome, and brought to England not only literature but arts till then unknown: he was the first who brought masons and glaziers home with him, having need of them for the noble buildings which he erected. With this great and good man Bede was placed when he was seven years old, and at Wearmouth and at Jarrow he passed the rest of his life.[75]

---

73 Egfred: Ecgfrith (c. 645–85), king of Northumbria (670–85).
74 Benedict Biscop: St Benedict Biscop (628–c. 89), founder and first abbot of the Benedictine abbey at Wearmouth (674) and founder of the monastery at Jarrow (682).
75 The wording of this section follows closely that of the preface to Giles's *The Venerable Bede's Ecclesiastical History of England, also The Anglo-Saxon Chronicle* (1847). In the final chapter of his *Ecclesiastical History*, Bede gives a short autobiographical sketch, providing the foundation for all that has been written of his life since.

XXI.

The Venerable Bede.—I.[76]

ONCE by thy ruined but time-honoured cell
    In years gone by I stood; I thought not then,[77]
    For I was but a child, that ever pen
Of mine should write thy name, or mine eyes dwell
In interest on thy antique page,—yet well
    Hath memory kept that picture; the mossed stones
    In the dull churchyard—e'en the north wind's tones,
As from the distant past, seem round me still to swell.
A book like thine is a most precious thing
    By mind bequeathed to mind; it hath outlived
Thousands that much of fame and wealth could bring
    For a brief space; for he who wrote, believed,
Aye, and believing words, whate'er they be,
Have on them stamped an immortality.

---

76 This is one of the thirteen sonnets included in the *Manchester Guardian* review of *Sonnets on Anglo-Saxon History* (8 November 1854); see Appendix A.
77 This moment of personal reflection suggests that Hawkshaw had visited Bede's cell at Jarrow.

XXII.

"On almost every occasion Bede gives the name and designation of his informant, being anxious, apparently, to show that nothing is inserted for which he had not the testimony of some respectable witness. The author received secondary evidence with caution: statements received through a succession of informants are always pointed out with scrupulous exactness, whatever opinion he may entertain, as in the case of some visions and miracles, of the credibility of the facts themselves."—Preface to *Bede's History*, published by the English Historical Society, 1838.[78]

---

78 This section is extracted from Giles's analysis of Bede's *Ecclesiastical History* in the preface to *The Venerable Bede's Ecclesiastical History of England, also The Anglo-Saxon Chronicle* (1847), xxviii–xxix. Giles quotes at length from the preface to an earlier translation of Bede by Stevenson, which was published by the English Historical Society in 1838.

XXII.

The Venerable Bede.—II.

WE call them childish fables that he tells;
   They are to us, they were not so to him.
   The howl of demons, or the angel's hymn
Heard in the lonely vigil; and the hells
Of fire and frost, where the dark spirit dwells,
   Were things at which men shuddered and grew pale—
   For they believed—untutored hearts must quail,
Though they against the thraldom still rebel,
Forgetting 'mid life's duties their dark creed:
   And softly Nature's voices still are heard
In that old history, and the heroic deed,
   The patient suffering, or the truthful word,
Thy hand did write, old monk, thy heart did feel,
And it is these that do thyself reveal.

XXIII.

"… HE passed the day joyfully until the evening; and the boy above mentioned" (a youth to whom he was dictating his translation of the Gospel of John) "said to him, 'Dear master, there is one sentence not written.' He answered, 'Write quickly.' Soon after the boy said, 'The sentence is now written.' He replied, 'It is well, you have said the truth. It is ended; receive my head into your hands, for it is a great satisfaction to me to sit facing my holy place, where I was wont to pray, that I may also sitting call upon my Father.' And thus, on the pavement of his little cell, he breathed his last."—Cuthbert's Letter on the Death of Bede.[79]

He died on the 26th May 735.

---

[79] The letter written by Bede's disciple Cuthbert, to Cuthwin (of which little is known), details the circumstances of Bede's death. Cuthbert's letter on the death of the Venerable Bede is included by Giles in the preface to *The Venerable Bede's Ecclesiastical History of England, also The Anglo-Saxon Chronicle* (1847), xx–xxi; extracts are quoted here by Hawkshaw.

XXIII.

The death of Bede.—III.

SIMPLE and saintly as the histories told
   In holy writ, is one upon the page
   Of Saxon story in a darksome age;
It cometh like a whisper from that old
And distant world, of what it did enfold,
   Of pure and gentle things, and cheers the heart
   Apt to grow sad when looking on one part
Of that stern age, and men of Titan mould.
I would not add one line to that old tale
   Fresh from a loving heart, it hath a power
All foreign words would render poor and stale,
   A portion of the Past's unreckoned dower
Bequeath it to the Future, for this age
Writes few such stories on her tinsel page.

XXIV.

THE Emperor Charlemagne cruelly persecuted the pagan Saxons in Germany to compel them to adopt the Christian faith; many of them fled to Jutland and became pirates, harassing for many years the coasts of France and Britain.[80] They ever manifested a peculiar animosity against the priests, and destroyed the churches and monasteries. They first landed in England in 787.[81]

---

80 Emperor Charlemagne: Charles the Great (742–814), king of the Franks (768–814), emperor of the Holy Roman Empire (800–814).
81 The first landings of the Northmen are dated at 787. The plundering of St Cuthbert's monastery at Lindisfarne, Northumberland in 793 marked the beginning of the Viking raids.

XXIV.

The Northmen.

SPRUNG from a Saxon stock, by bigot zeal
    Forced from their homes they sought the Baltic shore,
    Where they might still their ancient gods adore;
Strange error! to convert with fire and steel,
And by the body's death the soul to heal;
    The Anglo-Saxon heard Augustine's voice,[82]
    Death or religion was the German's choice,
They chose the first; or saw their homes no more.
Fierce and revengeful o'er the waves they sweep,
    The wild sea-kings of many a northern tale,
And in their hearts a deadly hatred keep
    To Christian priests and creeds where'er they sail;
And thus for ever it will be through time:
Truth is too holy to be helped by crime.

---

82 Augustine: St Augustine (d. 604), appointed first archbishop of Canterbury in 597.

XXV.

"A.D. 870 … the same winter King Edmund fought against them,[83] and the Danes got the victory and slew the king, and subdued all the land, and destroyed all the minsters they came to … At that same time they came to Medeshamstede (Peterborough), and burned and beat it down, slew abbot and monks, and all that they found there. And that place, which before was full rich, they reduced to nothing."—*The Anglo-Saxon Chronicle*.[84]

---

83   King Edmund: St Edmund the Martyr (841–869), king of the East Angles.
84   From the *Anglo-Saxon Chronicle* entry for the year 870, as recorded by J. A. Giles in *The Venerable Bede's Ecclesiastical History of England, also The Anglo-Saxon Chronicle* (1847), 352.

XXV.

Destruction of the Abbey of Peterborough by the Northmen.

<blockquote>
The music of the vesper hymn had died
   In the hushed woodlands; and o'er vale and hill
   The evening mist-clouds rested cold and still;
The wood-fire blazed within the chimney wide,
Shedding its light afar; a welcome guide
   It oft had been to weary serf, when day
   Closed o'er his steps; to-night upon its way
It leads a host that tears and force defied.
The sun arose to shine on blackened walls,
   And echo answered back his steps who trod
(The one survivor) through those silent halls,
   Seeking beside the altar of their God
His slaughtered brethren, who had perished there,
Unarmed and patient, by their shrine of prayer.
</blockquote>

XXVI.

"ONE of the greatest boons that Christianity gave to the poor Saxon serf was the enjoyment of the Sabbath.[85] The master who compelled his serf to work for him on that day could be obliged to give him his freedom."—Palgrave's *History of the Anglo-Saxons*.[86]

---

85 serf: a person in a condition of servitude or modified slavery (n.'serf' *OED*). The *OED* definition distinguishes between serfdom and slavery in the following way: 'In most of the typical examples of serfdom, the serf was "attached to the soil" (*adscriptus gleboe*), i.e. he could not be removed (except by manumission) from the lord's land, and was transferred with it when it passed to another owner.'
86 Rather than a direct quotation, this is a précis of extracts from Francis Palgrave's *History of the Anglo-Saxons* (1831), 68.

XXVI.

Under-Currents.[87]

But silently beneath this noise and strife,
   Worked countless energies of heart and head,
   And men, the glooms of time have overspread,
Nor left a single annal of their life;
Who tells what savage shaped from ore the knife?
   Toil for the good of man, but ask not fame,
   Ages may bless thy work, not know thy name,
No good once done time in the dust can tread.
The marsh is drained, the yellow harvest waves
   Where the lone heron watched the lazy stream,
Wood-lighted hearths were there, flower-sprinkled graves,
   And love and hope; 't was life, and not a dream,
And that blest gift to wearied man from heaven
Came to the toil-worn serf—one day of rest in seven.

---

87 This is one of the thirteen sonnets included in the *Manchester Guardian* review of *Sonnets on Anglo-Saxon History* (8 November 1854); see Appendix A.

XXVII.

A LARGE portion of the Anglo-Saxon population was in slavery during their pagan state, but, after the diffusion of Christianity, a regard for its benevolent precepts, affection for those who had formed part of their households, and sometimes superstition (as in the case where two slaves are freed for the good of an abbot's soul), caused emancipation to proceed rapidly. As serfs were allowed to accumulate property, they often redeemed themselves and their families.[88]

---

88 This is a précis of Turner's discussion of the emancipation of serfs in *History of the Anglo-Saxons*, vol. 3 (1840), 55–6.

XXVII.

The Serf.[89]

MASTER and slave! strange words are those to hear
    Among a family of brethren named,
    Within a world a father's goodness framed,
Harsh 'mid its harmonies upon the ear
They fall; conjuring up every shape of fear
    That haunts the oppressor or the oppressed's path,
    Pride, avarice, cruelty, revenge, and wrath;
All that from misery wrings the bitterest tear;
All that brings into human hearts the blight
    Of selfishness, before whose poisonous breath
Love's flowers droop withering, and day fades to night,
    And the great gift of life turns to a death;
War's hurricane sweeps past, but while we sleep
Slavery's dark vapours poison as they creep.

---

89 This is one of the thirteen sonnets included in the *Manchester Guardian* review of *Sonnets on Anglo-Saxon History* (8 November 1854); see Appendix A.

XXVIII.

The form used in liberating a serf was simple and striking; giving him a shield and spear, they placed him on the highway, and bid him go wherever he pleased, to the right hand or to the left.

A law passed by the great Alfred,[90] and Witenagemot,[91] contributed much to lessen the number of the servile class; it was enacted that no one could buy a Christian slave for more than six years,—on the seventh he should depart free, without payment, and with the wife and clothes he had at first.[92]

---

90 Alfred: Alfred the Great (849–99), king of Wessex and of the Anglo-Saxons (871–99).

91 Witenagemot: the assembly of the witan, the national council of Anglo-Saxon times (n. 'witenagemot' *OED*).

92 This is a précis of Turner's discussion of the emancipation of serfs in *History of the Anglo-Saxons*, vol. 3 (1840), 55–6.

XXVIII.

The Serf Freed.

"Be free," they said, and placed within his hand
    The shield and spear, and bid him choose his way,
    And the serf stood a freeman from that day,
With right to feel an interest in the land,
With right to call his own that household band
    His wife and children; and to feel he trod
    With brothers the great universe of God:
A slave, he did but there an atom stand.
Proud souls there were that chafed beneath the yoke,
    Mild hearts that pined in hopelessness away,
Fierce spirits that the galling thraldom broke,
    And minds that meanest passions made their sway:
Yet one dark circle fettered all; one doom;
Life without progress; death without the tomb.

XXIX.

IN 721 Ina, after a prosperous reign of thirty-seven years, resigned the crown, and with his queen went to live in Rome.[93] He there founded a Saxon school for the instruction of his countrymen. Ina and his queen after their retirement lived in humble seclusion: he often laboured with his own hands for their support. He published a collection of laws in the early part of his reign, which still exist;[94] Ina died at Rome.[95]

---

93 Ina: Ine (d. 726), king of the West Saxons (688–726).
94 Ina developed an extensive legal code which Alfred the Great appended to his own code of laws in the ninth century.
95 This is a précis of Turner's account of Ina in *History of the Anglo-Saxons*, vol. 1 (1840), 236–7.

XXIX.

Ina resigning his Crown.

Did he do well and wisely, who resigned
    For a monk's cowl the monarch's jewelled crown,
    And from a throne to humblest life came down?
If to avoid the thorns within it twined
Is the best motive for the deed we find,
    Not saint but coward, is the name to give,
    He who for others' good refused to live;
But yet no fear of toil could daunt the mind,
Methinks, of that old chief—no, deep within
    The darkened mind there is a want of God,
A longing for the pure, a sense of sin,
    A loathing of the guilty path once trod,
Then to some unknown goal it wildly springs,
Thinking sin mixed with all familiar things.

XXX.

In 688, Ceadwalla travelled to Rome on pilgrimage;[96] some years after two other Anglo-Saxon kings, Cenred of Mercia,[97] and Offa of Essex,[98] resigned their crowns, pilgrimaged to Rome, and became monks: Offa is described as a most amiable youth.

"A.D. 883. And that same year Sighelm and Athelstan went to India on pilgrimage to St. Thomas and St. Bartholomew."—See *Anglo-Saxon Chronicle*.[99]

---

96 Ceadwalla: Caedwalla (c. 659–89), king of Wessex (685–7).
97 Cenred: Coenred (d. 709), king of Mercia (704–709).
98 Offa: Offa (d. c. 709), king of Essex (c. 707–709).
99 This section is a précis of Turner's account of Coenred and Offa's pilgrimage to Rome in *History of the Anglo-Saxons*, vol. 1 (1840), 232–3.

XXX.

The Pilgrim.—I.

PEACE, peace, is what I crave, the last, best gift
   Man seeks on earth, for joy I ask not now,
   It sitteth ill upon a furrowed brow:
As o'er life's ebbing sea away I drift,
Oft to the spirit-land mine eyes I lift,
   And ask if there be peace, if there at last
   To calm shall sink fierce passion's howling blast;
It now from point to point doth only shift.
I have done all that I was told to do:
   Barefooted, lonely, I have gone my way,
My fearful pilgrimage is travelled through,
   Yet I remember but one peaceful day,
It was when in my face a little child
Whose lamb I saved, looked into it and smiled.

XXXI.

SVEIN, the eldest son of Godwin,[100] and brother to Harold the Saxon,[101] to obtain peace to his guilty conscience, walked with naked feet from Flanders to Jerusalem.[102] Six years before he had murdered his cousin Beorn;[103] but it is not to any particular person I refer in the three sonnets entitled "The Pilgrim,"—they are but an endeavour to give utterance to thoughts that may have passed through many minds.

---

100 Godwin: Godwine (1001–53), earl of Wessex.
101 Harold: Harold Godwineson (c. 1022–66), reigned as Harold II, king of England (1066), last Anglo-Saxon king of England.
102 Svein: Sweyn Godwineson (d. 1052).
103 This section is a précis of Turner's account of Svein's pilgrimage in *History of the Anglo-Saxons*, vol. 2 (1840), 225.

XXXI.

The Pilgrim.—II.

Have I done well the priest alone to hear,
    Are there no teachers but the tongues of men,
    No voices on the mountains, in the glen,
No tones but enter by the outward ear?
My heart ne'er conjured up such shapes of fear
    As men have pictured to me, nature tells
    Another story in her silent dells,
There, to mine eye hath come the unbidden tear.
They told me of my immortality:
    I felt it on the mountains; He who reared
Their giant frame-work, He, too, moulded me,
    And the enduring to my soul endeared,
And voices sound, as from the deeps of space,
"Still ever onward, upward, is thy race."

XXXII.

"It must be admitted that nowhere did Christianity make a deeper or more lasting impression than in England. Not only do we see the high nobles, and the near relatives of kings among the bishops and archbishops, but kings themselves—warlike and fortunate kings—suddenly and voluntarily renouncing their temporal advantages, retiring into monasteries, and abdicating their crowns, that they may wander as pilgrims to the shrines of the apostles in Rome.[104] Well-descended men cannot rest until they have carried the tidings of redemption into barbarous lands,[105] a spectacle which compels us to believe in the deep, earnest, conscientious spirit of self-sacrifice and love of truth which characterised the nation."—Kemble's *Saxons in England*.[106]

---

104 Hawkshaw omits the following: 'We find princesses and other high-born ladies devoting themselves to a life of celibacy, or separating from their husbands to preside over congregations of nuns.'

105 Hawkshaw omits the following: 'A life of abstinence and hardship, to be crowned by a martyr's death, seems to have been hungered and thirsted after by the wealthy and the noble,—assuredly an extraordinary and an edifying spectacle among a race not at all adverse to the pomps and pleasures of worldly life.'

106 From Kemble's *The Saxons in England*, vol. 2 (1849), 363–4, with the omissions as detailed above.

XXXII.

The Pilgrim.—III.

I will resign thee to the earth again,
    Thou mouldering skull, to ever muse on thee
    Fits not a soul for its high destiny;
Changed by the sunbeam and the gentle rain,
I shall perchance behold thee on the plain
    A many-coloured flower, and thou shalt tell
    Thy tale of change, not death, and in my cell
By the deep-meaning cross thy place regain.
I mused on death until the world appeared
    One mighty charnel-house, I read decay
On rock and flower alike, all nature weird
    Of doom, but now through life I take my way,
Changed amid changing things; another fate
Would leave the heart lone, seared, and desolate.

XXXIII.

Alfred of Northumbria,[107] whom Eddius[108] calls "the most wise," was educated by Wilfred.[109] His youngest brother being raised to the throne by the Northumbrian Witena,[110] he retired into Ireland that he might there pursue his studies in religion and philosophy. After fifteen years of retirement he was called to the throne on the death of his brother Egfred[111] in 684.[112]

---

107 Alfred of Northumbria: Aldfrith (d. 705), king of Northumbria (685–705).
108 Eddius: a reference to Eddius Stephanus, or Stephen of Ripon, author of *Life of Saint Wilfrid* (c. 709).
109 Wilfred: St Wilfrid (c. 634–709), bishop of Hexham and Northumbria.
110 Witena: the assembly of the witan, the national council of Anglo-Saxon times (n. 'witenagemot' OED).
111 Egfred: Ecgfrith (c. 645–85), king of Northumbria (670–85).
112 This section is a précis of Turner's account of Alfred of Northumbria in *History of the Anglo-Saxons*, vol. 1 (1840), 229.

XXXIII.

Alfred of Northumbria.—I. Retirement.

First of the Saxon kings whom learning led
    From courts and camps unto her sacred cell,
    And bid him there in studious quiet dwell.
The crown that almost glittered on his head,
The power for which men toil and sin, all fled,
    Like shadows of unreal things, before
    The prophet's song, the sage's thoughtful lore,
And high communings with the mighty dead.
Thus years passed by, and not in vain they past;
    Stronger his mind and purer grew his heart,
And when to life's stern work he comes at last,
    Not back from duty doth he idly start:
He who hath learnt obedience in his youth
Is fit to rule, and judge himself of truth.

XXXIV.

"Though Alfred was attached to the studies of the clergy,[113] he was not their undiscriminating instrument. He had made his early instructor, Wilfred, a bishop;[114] but when, in his opinion, that prelate was unduly pressing points which he disapproved, he remained immovable in what he thought right;[115] nor could the urgencies of Pope John VII shake his determination. He reigned over the province which his knowledge enlightened, and his virtues cherished, for nineteen years."— See Sharon Turner's *History of the Anglo-Saxons*.[116]

---

113 Alfred: Aldfrith (d. 705), king of Northumbria (685–705).
114 Wilfred: St Wilfrid (c. 634–709), bishop of Hexham and Northumbria.
115 Hawkshaw omits a section detailing correspondence between Alfred and Pope John VII.
116 Extracted from Turner's account in *History of the Anglo-Saxons*, vol. 1 (1840), 230–31.

XXXIV.

Alfred of Northumbria.—II. Self-Reliance.

AND so he did, nor weakly bowed his mind
   To priest or prelate; he has earned the right
   To think and act alone by inner might:
The pleasant memories of the past were twined
With Wilfred's name, but not e'en that could bind
   The self-reliant one, or make him yield
   His mental freedom; and if that but shield,
The soul an onward, upward, way will find.
Freedom of mind! it is a thing unknown;
   Chains strong as adamant, unseen as air,
Are round our spirits, and they least will own
   The bondage, who have learnt the chain to wear,
Till of themselves it hath become a part,
Gnawing and rusting to the inmost heart.

XXXV.

In 627 Paulinus built the first Christian church in Northumbria;[117] it was of wood, and also another of stone at Lincoln; in 676 Benedict erected the monasteries of Wearmouth and Jarrow.[118] Wilfred, who had travelled to Rome, built in 709 the church of Ripon, and one at Hexham, which was superior to any building on this side the Alps.[119] The Abbey of Croyland[120] was erected on a vast number of piles of oak and alder, on account of the marshy nature of the ground, and earth was brought in boats, nine miles, to be mixed with the timber and marsh to complete the foundation: it was built in 716.[121]

---

117 Paulinus: St Paulinus (d. 644), bishop of York and of Rochester.
118 Wearmouth and Jarrow: Benedictine abbeys at Wearmouth (founded 674) and Jarrow (founded 682).
119 Turner cites Eddius's *Life of Saint Wilfrid* as his source (see note 108).
120 Abbey of Croyland: Croyland (or Crowland) Abbey, Lincolnshire.
121 This section is a précis of sections of Turner's account of Anglo-Saxon buildings in *History of the Anglo-Saxons*, vol. 3 (1840), 280–82.

XXXV.

The Monastery.

Not useless, in that age of war and strife,
   Rose in the sheltered vale the sacred pile;
   There might the homeless stranger rest awhile,
Or peaceful merchant scape the robber's knife;
There the crushed heart might seek again for life;
   For there are crimes and woes the heart and God
   Alone should know, and cloisters might be trod
By feet that slid on paths with pleasure rife.
The man of action, and the man of thought
   Alike are needful for a nation's weal;
In softer times may other cells be sought
   Than could be found in days of Saxon steel,
But when the northern vi-king rode the wave,
The cloister was a home, and not a grave.

XXXVI.

The betrothed husband of Ethelberga[122] had been treacherously murdered by her father, Offa of Mercia;[123] she fled from her home to the Abbey of Croyland. Many years after, she saved the life of Wiglaf,[124] king of Mercia, by concealing him in her cell from the search of Egbert,[125] until the negotiations of the venerable Abbot of Croyland effected a reconciliation between them, A.D. 777.[126]

---

122 Ethelberga: Ethelburga, daughter of Offa of Mercia.
123 Offa of Mercia: Offa (d. 796), king of the Mercians (757–96).
124 Wiglaf: Wiglaf (c. 827–c. 840), king of the Mercians (827–29, 830–40).
125 Egbert: Ecgberht (d. 839), king of the West Saxons (802–39).
126 This section is a précis of Turner's account of Ethelburga in *History of the Anglo-Saxons*, vol. I (1840), 253–4. Turner cites Ingulf as a source: Ingulf (c. 1045–1109), Benedictine Abbot of Crowland (Croyland) Abbey and for centuries credited with the authorship of a history of the abbey. The dating of the document has since been disputed and the chronicle is now referred to as the Pseudo-Ingulf.

XXXVI.

Ethelberga.

Home, love, and faith in God and man were gone,
    She neither hoped nor feared to live or die;
    Around her pressed a chilling vacancy,
And through it ever sounded but one tone,
The knell of the young heart, "thou art alone;"
    She fled, and He who guides the swallow's wing
    O'er pathless oceans to the climes of spring
To the one goal still left, guided the wanderer on.
And there the storm-uprooted flower revived,
    And blossomed in pale beauty, and the heart
Learned that its holiest treasures yet survived,
    And earthly things still claimed of it a part;
Till in her narrowed sphere of life at rest,
She made of earth a spot, more bright and blest.

XXXVII.

The Anglo-Saxon freemen were often servants, but their rights and liberties were protected by law. Whoever put a freeman into bonds was to forfeit twenty shillings: he might lose his freedom by crime; one thus reduced to slavery was called a "*wite theow*," a penal slave.[127]

---

[127] This is a précis of sections of Turner's account of servitude in *History of the Anglo-Saxons*, vol. 3 (1840), 51.

XXXVII.

The benighted Ceorl.[128]

Through the bare forest rushes past the wind,
   Autumn's last leaves are trampled into clay,
   And the night closes o'er a gloomy day:
Woe to yon ceorl, who o'er the moors must find
His way alone! he hears, though far behind,
   Amid the hurried pauses of the blast,
   The wolf's long howl;—Speed on, thy strength may last,
And the limbs prove as faithful as the mind.
Inured to danger, strong from active toil,
   This was no thing to daunt his hardy soul;
Yet had it fears that in a viewless coil
   Bound it within a dread and stern control.
He stops; though speed is life, before his sight
A phantom rises from the realm of night!

---

128 Ceorl: an Old English freeman of the lowest class (n. 'ceorl' *OED*).

XXXVIII.

THE principal duties of the Saxon Witena-gemot were, to determine the succession to the throne, to make laws conjointly with the king, and assist him in making military preparations. Impeachments of great men were made before the Witena, and examinations made by it into the state of the churches, monasteries, and their possessions: grants of lands were made and confirmed; and inquiries made respecting the morals of the clergy. In 903, an ealdorman stated that his title-deeds had been destroyed by fire, and applied to the Witena to have new ones, which were ordered to be made out to him, as nearly similar to the former as memory could make them.[129]

---

129 Extracted from Turner's extended account of the witenagemot in *History of the Anglo-Saxons*, vol. 3 (1840), 125–7.

XXXVIII.

The Witena meeting at Easter.

'T was early spring, the yellow catkins waved
   Upon the willows by the Thames' clear stream,
   For then untainted in the sunny beam,
Deep, still, and full it flowed; then shy birds laved
In its pure waters, and the lilies paved
   Its surface with broad leaves and golden flowers;
   For time to Nature gives his different dowers,
What she had once, she never more must crave.
Slow winding by those silent banks appeared
   High-born ealdorman, thane, and uncouth knight,
Grave citizens for wisdom, too, revered,
   Chosen to plead before the great for right,
And guard alike with care their country's weal
From hidden treason, or from Danish steel.

XXXIX.

"Among the Anglo-Saxons, land held in common was designated by the names of Mark, and Gâ, or Shire. The smallest of these common divisions is the mark or march (*mearc*); the next in order to the private estates or alods of the markmen, as its name denotes, it is something marked out or defined, having settled boundaries. It is the plot of land on which a greater or lesser number of free men have settled for the purposes of cultivation, and for the sake of mutual profit and protection; and it comprises a portion both of arable land and pasture, in proportion to the numbers that enjoy its produce."—Kemble's *Saxons in England*.[130]

---

130 From Kemble's *The Saxons in England*, vol. 1 (1849), 36–7.

XXXIX.

The Markman's Cottage.—I.

MENDING his hunting-spear before the fire
   The markman sits, while at her graceful task
   His young wife plies the wheel; before them bask,
On the warm hearth, the stag-hounds, stained with mire
From the day's chase, for none then dared inquire
   Of the free Saxon why he roamed the woods,
   And tracked the wild deer to its solitudes,—
It was a right bequeathed him by his sire.
"I hear a voice," she says, and bends her head,
   Yet listening as she whispered; "hearken thou,
Is it the demon calling up the dead
   To walk the earth awhile?" upon her brow
Cold drops were gathering, when before them stood
A form as wild as goblin of the wood.

XL.

It was about the year 981 that the Icelanders discovered Greenland. Eric the Red,[131] being condemned to banishment on account of a murder he had committed, fitted out a vessel and told his friends he would go and seek the land which one Gunbian said he had seen.[132] His son Leiss afterwards discovered Vinland or America.[133] The account of the discovery of Vinland was committed to writing eighty years before Columbus visited Iceland to obtain nautical information.

---

131 Eric the Red: Erik the Red (c. 950–c. 1003), Norse explorer.
132 Gunbian: Gunnbjørn Ulfsson, tenth-century Norwegian explorer who tradition credits as the first European to sight North America.
133 Leiss: Leif Ericson (c. 970–c. 1020), Norse explorer and son of Erik the Red; regarded as the first European to land in North America.

XL.

The Markman's Cottage.—II.

It was a wearied man, and that gave claim
   To ask for human sympathy and aid;
   Fresh faggots on the smouldering fire were laid;
The board was spread; and by the mounting flame
The stranger's face is scanned; and then his name,
   Country, and errand asked: he tells the tale
   Of the Red Eric, whom the stormy gale
Of northern regions could not daunt or tame.
The tasks are put aside, the busy wheel
   Ceases its humming, and the unfinished spear
Rests on the floor, and closer to him steal
   His listeners, as he tells the wild career
Of the old northmen, whom the ocean bore
First on its icy waves to Greenland's shore.

XLI.

As early as 692, missionaries left England to teach the Pagan nations of the Continent; in that year Willebrad,[134] and eleven companions with him, went to Heligoland[135] and Friesland.[136] In 715 Boniface[137] preached to the Thuringians[138] and Hessians.[139] And, besides others, Adalbert,[140] son of a king of the Northumbrian kingdom of Deira, in 790, went to Germany for the same purpose.[141]

---

134 Willebrad: St Willibrord (658–739), Northumbrian monk, archbishop and missionary. Turner cites as 'Willebrod'.
135 Heligoland: one of the North Frisian Islands located in the North Sea off the coast of Germany.
136 Friesland: the western part of the ancient region of Frisia, north-west Europe.
137 Boniface: St Boniface (c. 675–754), archbishop, missionary and martyr.
138 Thuringians: inhabitants of Thuringia, Central Germany.
139 Hessians: inhabitants of Hessia, Germany.
140 Adalbert: St Adalbert of Egmont (d. c. 710), Northumbrian missionary and contemporary of St Willibrord (658–739), Northumbrian monk, archbishop and missionary.
141 Extracted from Turner's account in *History of the Anglo-Saxons*, vol. 3 (1840), 291.

XLI.

True Workers.[142]

FORTH from their homes they went, a simple band,
   To toil in heathendom; no cumbrous plan
   Fettered the movements of the earnest man;
Faith had he in his soul, and in his hand,
And needed not to work what others planned:
   It is a living soul, and not a thing
   Of mechanism, to which hearts will cling,
Or that to life can rouse a dying land.
There is more power in one deep truthful word,
   One honest, noble deed, than in all schemes
That men have planned, whose hearts no faith hath stirred,—
   More power in one great poet's glorious dreams
Than in a thousand systems hard and cold,
That but the mortal, not the man unfold.

---

142 This is one of the thirteen sonnets included in the *Manchester Guardian* review of *Sonnets on Anglo-Saxon History* (8 November 1854); see Appendix A.

XLII.

EGBERT was left early to the care of his mother, his father being dead.[143] His talents excited the fears of the reigning King of Wessex, and Egbert was obliged to seek refuge in exile: he went to Charlemagne,[144] with whom he remained some years, diligently improving the advantages that a residence at the Frankish Court afforded. His sisters were sent to the Continent to be educated, and there they became nuns.[145]

---

143 Egbert: Ecgberht (d. 839), king of the West Saxons (802–39).
144 Charlemagne: Charles the Great (742–814), king of the Franks (768–814), emperor of the Holy Roman Empire (800–814).
145 This section draws on Turner's account of Egbert in *History of the Anglo-Saxons*, vol. 1 (1840), 249–51.

XLII.

The Mother of Egbert.

'T was a rude pile, although a noble dame
   Called it her home; upon the Kentish shore,
   Sheltered by hills that ever hear the roar
Of ocean waves, it stood; they are the same,
Those hills and waters, changed alone in name
   Since that sad mother, in her silent hall,
   Watched on the rush-spread floor the shadows fall,
And murmured low her absent children's name:
"My hearth is dreary as my heart is lone,
   For all are gone that made my pleasant cheer—
Some convent cells, and one the churchyard stone
   Have covered up from life; and thou, so dear
Because the last, art now an exile gone,
And my eyes ne'er shall look thy face again upon."

XLIII.

WHEN Egbert, after three years of exile, was called to fill the throne of Wessex, he governed with great ability and moderation, and it was more by the influence of his mind than the force of arms that he ultimately became sole king of the West-Saxons:[146] he was the most distinguished of all their monarchs before Alfred the Great,[147] but there does not seem any proof that he was ever denominated King of all England, as sometimes asserted: he began to reign in 800, and died 836.[148]

---

146 Egbert: Ecgberht (d. 839), king of the West Saxons (802–39).
147 Alfred the Great: (849–99), king of Wessex and of the Anglo-Saxons (871–99).
148 This section draws on Turner's account of Ecgberht in *History of the Anglo-Saxons*, vol. 1 (1840), 255–6. Note that the dates cited by Turner, and replicated by Hawkshaw, differ from the current dating of Ecgberht's reign (802–39).

XLIII.

Egbert.

BEFORE his powerful genius had bowed down
   The Saxon princes; and he reigned alone,
   Gathering around the yet unsettled throne
The wisest of the land; years ere the crown
Begirt his thoughtful brow, Fate's adverse frown
   Had driven him forth an exile; but the strong
   Can wring a good from suffering—e'en from wrong;
And Egbert, wanderer through each land and town
Of ancient story or of rising power,
   Learned lessons that, within his native isle,
No books had ever taught him, and no hour
   Of silent study in the cloistered pile.
By years of toil, as well as days of thought,
Must the perfection of the soul be wrought.

XLIV.

ETHELWULPH succeeded his father Egbert in 836:[149] he had been a monk, and left the cloister to ascend the throne; he had a mild disposition, but was of inferior abilities; he possessed, however, in Alstan, Bishop of Sherborne,[150] a great and wise minister, who had been the friend of his father Egbert, and who had the rare fortune to enjoy his preferments for fifty years. Ethelwulph, while a monk, appears to have lived in the monastery at Winchester.[151]

---

149 Ethelwulph: Aethelwulf (d. 858), king of the West Saxons (839–58), father of Alfred the Great (849–99), king of Wessex and of the Anglo-Saxons (871–99).
150 Alstan: Eahlstan (d. 867), bishop of Sherborne (c. 820–67).
151 This section is a précis of Turner's account of Aethelwulf in *History of the Anglo-Saxons*, vol. 1 (1840), 286–7. Turner records that Aethelwulf was educated in his early life by Helmstan, bishop of Winchester.

XLIV.

Ethelwulph leaving the Cloister.—I.

'T was an old chapel, and a sunny ray
   Gleamed through the window's tracery of stone,
   And fell upon a monk who sat alone
Upon the altar-steps; from evening grey
He there had watched till night had passed away;
   But now he rises, and the cowl and gown,
   All but the cross, with reverence slow lays down;
Then with a freer step goes forth his way.—
Egbert's last son—he must not tarry there;
   Once more in life again he takes his place,
But the heart's conflict hath been long and drear,
   And marked with deeper lines his pallid face;
For Nature's voice, that whispered he did right,
Oft he had thought a demon's in that night.

XLV.

ETHELWULPH'S[152] first wife was Osberga, the daughter of Oslac, his cupbearer;[153] she was the mother of Alfred the Great, and a woman of intellect and virtue; but she died when her celebrated son was a child. The northmen, though often repulsed, continued to make frequent incursions.[154] "853 ... King Ethelwulph sent his son Alfred to Rome, 855. This year the heathen men, for the first time, remained one winter in Sheppey. And the same year he (Ethelwulph) went to Rome in great state, and dwelt there twelve months, and then returned homewards, and Charles, King of the Franks, gave him his daughter to wife"[155]—*Anglo-Saxon Chronicle*.[156]

---

152 Ethelwulph: Aethelwulf (d. 858), king of the West Saxons (839–58).
153 Osberga: Osburga, or Osburh, mother of Alfred the Great (849–99), king of Wessex and of the Anglo-Saxons (871–99). Hawkshaw's earlier poem 'King Alfred and his Mother' (*Poems for My Children*), recreates dialogue between Osburga and her young son.
154 This section is a précis of Turner's account of Osburga in *History of the Anglo-Saxons*, vol. 1 (1840), 288–9.
155 Aethelwulf's second wife, Judith (c. 843–c. 70).
156 The wording follows closely these sections of the *Anglo-Saxon Chronicle* as recorded in J. A. Giles's *The Venerable Bede's Ecclesiastical History of England, also The Anglo-Saxon Chronicle* (1847), 49–50, although Hawkshaw does not quote directly.

XLV.

Ethelwulph.—II.

Arouse thee, Ethelwulph, it is no time
    For monkish dreams; not thus thy father dreamed
    Irresolute, when o'er the ocean streamed
The northmen's banners: want, distrust, and crime,
Are hovering o'er thy land, and in their prime
    Fate dooms thy sons to die—all, save that one,
    Who, calmly mounting on the shattered throne,
Shall make it like himself, time-honoured and sublime.
I see beside thee kneel a princely child,
    Thy youngest, best-beloved, and o'er his head
Thy hands are stretched to bless, loving and mild
    He bends before thee, then there comes the tread
Of armed attendants, and to wondrous Rome
They bear the young chief from his island home.

XLVI.

When Wiglaf,[157] who had been allowed to retain Mercia as a tributary vassal of Egbert,[158] heard of the death of the noble-minded but unfortunate Ethelberga,[159] who had sheltered him in her cell at Croyland, he was so overcome by grief that it brought on sickness that confined him to his bed, and it was with difficulty that he could be withdrawn from her grave. In her tomb he buried his wife and son.[160]

---

157 Wiglaf: (c. 827–c. 840), king of the Mercians (827–29, 830–40).
158 Egbert: Ecgberht (d. 839), king of the West Saxons (802–39).
159 Ethelberga: Ethelburga, daughter of Offa of Mercia.
160 This section is a précis of Turner's account of Wiglaf's response to Ethelberga's death in *History of the Anglo-Saxons*, vol. 1 (1840), 253–4, 289.

XLVI.

The Tomb of Ethelberga.

THY story conjures up a thousand things
   Of mournful gentleness; true woman, thou
   Of the brave heart, the sad but thoughtful brow:
How to the human all the human clings,
For while the echo of past warfare rings
   Upon the ear as discord, sweetly steals
   The tone that aught of mortal love reveals,
Or grateful sorrow's soft rememberings.
A truest shrine was thy low tomb, for there
   Love buried its best treasures, and such tears
As men alone can weep, bedewed it; rare
   Were such pure drops amid the strifes and fears
Of that dark age,—aye, they are rare e'en now,
Though fashion frames soft words and smooths the brow.

XLVII.

"A.D. 837. And the same year Ethelhelm the Ealdorman fought against the Danish army at Portland-isle with the men of Dorset, and for a good while he put the enemy to flight; but the Danish-men had possession of the field, and slew the Ealdorman."—*Saxon Chronicle*.[161]

In A.D. 868, Algar and five other chiefs, with a few followers, had by their valour and skill nearly defeated the Danes, when the rash bravery of their men involved them all in destruction. They had devoted themselves by a religious ceremony to die for their country, and all perished.

---

161 Taken from J. A. Giles's *The Venerable Bede's Ecclesiastical History of England, also The Anglo-Saxon Chronicle* (1847), 348.

XLVII.

Anglo-Saxon Patriots.

Who sleep beneath thy earth, my native land?
    The wise, the brave, who gladly died for thee—
    How many perished ere thou couldst be free!
In the far distant past I see a band
Of Saxon patriots like a bulwark stand
Against the Danish hordes, till, one by one
Hewed down but unsubdued, they all are gone:
    That place is holy as Thermopylae.[162]
There waves the yellow corn, and a clear rill
    Goes singing on beneath the summer skies,
And children wander at their own wild will,
    Free as the wind that fans them as it flies;
But if no suffering there had ever been,
Far other sights than these our eyes had seen.

---

162 Thermopylae: site of the second Persian invasion of Greece in 480 BC.

XLVIII.

ALFRED was sent by his father to Rome when he was four years old;[163] he travelled by land through France, across the Alps, with a large retinue. In his seventh year he attended his father again a second time to Italy, and remained a year in Rome. He is said by some chroniclers to have had delicate health, and to have been sent into Ireland when a child, and placed there under the care of a religious lady called Modwenna.[164]

---

163 Alfred: Alfred the Great (849–99), king of Wessex and of the Anglo-Saxons (871–99).
164 Modwenna: English nun and saint associated through legend with Alfred the Great. This section is a précis of Turner's account of Alfred's childhood in *History of the Anglo-Saxons*, vol. 1 (1840), 297–8.

XLVIII.

Alfred the Great.—I. The Child.

TRUE, he was but a child, but a child's heart
   Is a strange mystery, clear but fathomless,
   Knowing but little of itself, we less;
Bright things it holds, but then it hath no art
To bring them forth into the world's great mart,
   So like the pearls of ocean there they dwell,
   Glistening in beauty in a closed shell:
And painted there and never to depart
Are nature's scenes, that daily, silently,
   She places deeper in the inmost heart;
And like sun-pictures, that we never see
   Till shaded from the light that bade them start
Into strange beauty, 't is amid the strife
Of manhood, that we view our scenes of early life.

XLIX.

"HE (Alfred) was loved by his father and mother, and even by all the people, above all his brothers ...."[165] As he advanced through the years of infancy and youth, his form appeared more comely than that of his brothers; in look, in speech, in manners, he was more graceful than they .... He was a zealous practiser of hunting in all its branches, and hunted with great assiduity and success."—Asser's *Life of Alfred*.[166]

---

165 Alfred: Alfred the Great (849–99), king of Wessex and of the Anglo-Saxons (871–99).
166 Asser: Asser (d. 909), Welsh monk, later Bishop of Sherborne, a contemporary of Alfred; his *The Life of King Alfred* (893) informed several nineteenth-century histories of Alfred the Great, such as J. A. Giles's *The Life and Times of Alfred the Great* (1848), from which this extract is taken (81–2).

XLIX.

Alfred the Great.—II. Remembrances.

It could not be that he had trod in vain,
   A thoughtful child, beneath the cloudless sky,
   That overhangs with deep blue canopy,
Rome's glorious temples; they would rise again
'Mid the dark forest, or the marshy plain
   Of his cold isle, to fill those waking dreams
   That bless the care-worn with their golden gleams;
Fair memories of the things that give no pain.
Those long, bright, summer hours of idleness,
   To which thou, world way-farer, turn'st thy gaze,
Have done for thee what thou nor I can guess;
   Think them not lost, those idle, wandering days,
They are bright colours 'mid that web of gloom
That time is ever weaving for the tomb.

L.

"At the same time the above-named Alfred, king of the West-Saxons,[167] with a few of his nobles, and certain soldiers and vassals, used to lead an unquiet life among the woodlands of the county of Somerset, in great tribulation; for he had none of the necessaries of life …"—Asser's *Life of Alfred*.[168]

Alfred suffered much from sickness during the whole of his life.[169]

---

167 Alfred: Alfred the Great (849–99), king of Wessex and of the Anglo-Saxons (871–99).
168 The quotation is from Asser's *Life of King Alfred*, referring to events in 838, as cited by Giles in *The Life and Times of Alfred the Great* (1848), 170.
169 Asser covers the king's ill-health in detail; J. A. Giles discusses Alfred's health in a chapter of *The Life and Times of Alfred the Great* (1848). The chapter begins: 'It is generally believed, on the authority of Asser, who was Alfred's bishop, biographer, and friend, that our king suffered much, through the whole of his life, from some internal disease, the nature of which was unknown to the physicians of his time' (193).

L.

Alfred the Great.—III. Adversity.[170]

WE wish to those we love skies ever clear,
    Long summer-days, and pathways strewed with flowers:
    Best lessons are not learn'd in such bright hours;
The dark must teach them; through the dimming tear
The spirit-land looks beautiful and near;
    Such hours the soul does to itself reveal,
    And we the mystery of our being feel,
And shapes of beauty from the gloom appear.
No true and noble heart was ever reared
    Amid soft things; it may be pain or want,
Or sorrow o'er the grave of those endeared,
    Or that mysterious woe the soul can plant
Within itself,—but sorrow there must be,
Ere it can struggle to the high and free.

---

[170] This is one of the thirteen sonnets included in the *Manchester Guardian* review of *Sonnets on Anglo-Saxon History* (8 November 1854); see Appendix A.

LI.

THE wife and children of Hastings[171] twice fell into the hands of Alfred;[172] the second time the King was urged to put them to death, to punish Hastings for his perfidy, but Alfred refused, loaded them with presents, and again sent them free to his fierce and persevering foe.[173]

---

171 Hastings: Haesten, ninth-century Viking chieftain.
172 Alfred: Alfred the Great (849–99), king of Wessex and of the Anglo-Saxons (871–99).
173 This is a précis of Turner's account in *History of the Anglo-Saxons*, vol. 1 (1840), 350.

LI.

Alfred the Great.—IV. Releasing the Wife and Children of Hastings the Northman.

>PROUDLY she stood before him, but her eye
>   Was bent upon her children, and she prest
>   Their hands with such a grasp, that they represt
>Scarcely their tears, and turned to ask her why;
>But her fixed look of tearless agony
>   Took away words or motion, and those fears
>   Gave to the child what they refused the mother—tears;
>She gazed with pallid lip and eyelids dry.
>At last she looks on him upon whose tongue
>   Hung death or freedom; on his chair was laid
>An antique book, and by its side was hung
>   His harp and sword. "Lady, be undismayed,"
>He rose and said, "be happy and be free;
>Who ever thought that I could injure thee?"

LII.

For three years Hastings[174] had contended against Alfred,[175] determined, if possible, to obtain a territory in England for himself and his roving band, but the ability of the Saxon King at last compelled him to withdraw: some of his followers settled in East-Anglia, some in Northumbria, and others, escaping to their vessels, crossed the ocean, and sailed up the Seine. Hastings obtained a small territory from the French King.[176] The *Saxon Chronicle* says, "Thanks be to God the army (the Danes) had not utterly broken down the English nation;" but it had suffered much, and also from a mortality both amongst men and cattle.[177]

---

174 Hastings: Haesten, ninth-century Viking chieftain.
175 Alfred: Alfred the Great (849–99), king of Wessex and of the Anglo-Saxons (871–99).
176 This is a précis of Turner's account of Hastings in *History of the Anglo-Saxons*, vol. 1 (1840), 352–5.
177 From the *Anglo-Saxon Chronicle* entry for the year 897, as recorded by J.A. Giles in *The Venerable Bede's Ecclesiastical History of England*, also *The Anglo-Saxon Chronicle* (1847), 364.

LII.

Alfred the Great.—V. Romney Marsh, Kent.[178]

THE fisher's boat rocks idly on the sea,
   The sheep are resting on the grassy hill,
   Where village children wander at their will,
Blithe as the singing birds, almost as free;
And are these all the thoughtful man can see
   Where once intrepid Alfred and his band
   Drove the fierce Northman from the Kentish strand?
Fair is the scene, yet other things there be
Than meet the eye; and with this seeming good
   How much of evil mingles, who may say?
Rightly we shudder at those days of blood;
   But ignorance and crime still bar the way,
And avarice hugs his bags of golden dust,
And long repose brings idlesse and false trust.

---

178 This sonnet is included in the review of *Sonnets on Anglo-Saxon History* in the *Athenæum* (20 January 1855); see Appendix A.

LIII.

DENEWULF, or Denulf, the peasant who sheltered Alfred in his cottage when he was a fugitive amid the marshes of Athelney, was afterwards munificently rewarded by the King, who, observing that Denulf was a man of talent, persuaded him to apply to letters;[179] he became an ecclesiastic, and died Bishop of Winchester in 909.[180]

---

179 Denewulf: (d. 908), bishop of Winchester.
180 This is a précis of Turner's account in *History of the Anglo-Saxons*, vol. 1 (1840), 331–2.

LIII.

Denulf.

From a small lamp a single thread of light
   Fell on the lettered page on which he bent
   A calm, high forehead, and an eye intent:
Thus had he sat for hours, nor marked their flight;
But his mind wandered now, for silent night
   Unrolled for him the records of the past,
   And deeper thoughts came crowding, thick and fast,
Than the old Roman on his page could write;
For none like memory writes for us, and none
   Can read its record but ourselves, and he
Was thinking there, upon that bench of stone,
   Of his rude home beneath the forest tree.—
He sighed; for who unmoved reviews the past,
Which yet he asks not back, nor wished, when here, to last.

LIV.

ETHELFLEDA, or Ethelfled as she is called in the *Saxon Chronicle*, was the eldest child of Alfred the Great;[181] she was one of the most distinguished persons of her time, and greatly assisted her brother Edward, by her courage and ability, in repressing the Danes.[182] After the death of her husband, to whom her father had committed the care of London after it had been rebuilt (it having been nearly destroyed by the Danes), she bore the title of the Lady of Mercia.[183]

---

181 Ethelfleda: Aethelfleda (c. 870–918), ruler of the Mercians (911–18), daughter of Alfred the Great (849–99), king of Wessex and of the Anglo-Saxons (871–99), and Ealhswith (d. 902).
182 Edward: Edward the Elder (d. 924), king of the Anglo-Saxons (899–924).
183 Ethelfleda's husband was Aethelred (d. 911), ealdorman of Mercia and ruler of the Mercians.

LIV.

Woman.—I. Ethelfleda, the daughter of Alfred.[184]

WOMAN hath trodden every path of life,
    Though to her nature strange; priestess or queen,
    To whom men looked in reverence, she hath been;
Leader of armies in heroic strife,
Champion for truth when error hath been rife,—
All these, and more, she hath been, and may be,
And out of these may work in harmony
    That deeper life of hers, the life unseen:
And that true life, how doth the outer touch,
    And make or mar it!—'t is a gift to all,
A solemn gift, that equalises much
    That we think differing, and call great or small.
What are the things that give thee inner might?
These are the great, the rest are rust and blight.

---

184 In writing about Aethelfleda and Aethelgifu, the daughters of King Alfred, this group of three sonnets offers an insightful commentary on the role of women. This is one of the thirteen sonnets included in the *Manchester Guardian* review of *Sonnets on Anglo-Saxon History* (8 November 1854); see Appendix A.

LV.

ETHELFLEDA[185] had been very carefully educated by her father along with her brother Edward.[186] Between the years 910 and 916 she built nine fortresses; the last she erected was one at Runcorn, in Lancashire. She died in 918, after having governed Mercia for eight years, and was buried within the east porch of St. Peter's Church, at Gloucester.[187]

---

185 Ethelfleda: Aethelfleda (c. 870–918), ruler of the Mercians (911–18), daughter of Alfred the Great (849–99), king of Wessex and of the Anglo-Saxons (871–99), and Ealhswith (d. 902).
186 Edward: Edward the Elder (d. 924), king of the Anglo-Saxons (899–924).
187 This section is a summary of Ethelfleda's life as recorded in the Anglo-Saxon Chronicle for the years 912–18: see J. A. Giles, *The Venerable Bede's Ecclesiastical History of England, also The Anglo-Saxon Chronicle* (1847), 369–71.

LV.

Woman.—II. Ethelfleda.

Working 'mid humble cares and petty strife
   The routine of thine unheroic days,
   Things that deserve not aught of blame or praise,
Perhaps they seem, that make the daily life
Of thee as woman, mistress, mother, wife;
So are they, if we look at them alone,
Not at the reflex image by them thrown
   Upon the soul, and lightened by their rays.
Let but thy life be true, nor think it mean,
   Thy home is not the prison of thy soul;
Beyond its narrow bounds fair things are seen,
   And, circling it, eternal oceans roll:
Thine be the beauty that the earth still holds,
And the divine that mortal life enfolds.

LVI.

ETHELGIVA[188] was the third child of Alfred the Great;[189] she became a nun. "... Another monastery also was built by the same King (Alfred) as a residence for nuns, near the eastern gate of Shaftsbury, and his own daughter Ethelgiva was placed in it as abbess. With her many other noble ladies, bound by the rules of the monastic life, dwelt in that monastery. These two (the one for nuns at Shaftsbury, and the other for monks at Athelney) were enriched by the King with much land, as well as personal property."—Asser's *Life of Alfred*.[190]

---

188 Ethelgiva: Aethelgifu, first abbess of Shaftesbury; second daughter of Alfred the Great (849–99), king of Wessex and of the Anglo-Saxons (871–99), and Ealhswith (d. 902).
189 Alfred the Great: Alfred the Great (849–99), king of Wessex and of the Anglo-Saxons (871–99).
190 From Asser's *Life of King Alfred*, which Giles cites in *The Life and Times of Alfred the Great* (1848), 293.

LVI.

Woman.—III. Ethelgiva the Nun.

They had one home, they saw one mother's smile,
    One father blessed them with his deep, strong heart,
    Yet in the world their lives how far apart!
One toiled and thought with men; a convent pile
Was Ethelgiva's narrow world meanwhile;
    Was it too narrow for the gaze it filled,
    And had the heart's loud beatings to be stilled
With many an oft-repeated fruitless wile?
Her life is but a line upon the page
    Of Ethelfleda's story, yet it may
Have left its impress on that distant age,
    For the true-hearted live not for their day,
And words that pure lips breathe, like winged seeds,
May spring in glorious thoughts, or worthy deeds.

LVII.

"891 ... In the same year three chosen men of Hibernian race, burning with piety, leave their country; they privately form a boat by sewing ox-hides; they put into it provisions for a week; they sail seven days and seven nights and arrive on the shores of Cornwall,[191] and set out for the court of King Alfred;[192] from thence they proceed to Rome, and, as is customary with teachers of Christ, they essay to go thence to Jerusalem."—*Ethelwerd's Chronicle*.[193]

They are also named in the Saxon Chronicle; they were called Dubslane, Macbeth, and Maclinmum, and are said to have been skilled in arts and letters.[194]

---

191 Hawkshaw omits the following: 'Here they left their fleet, which had been guided not by the strength of their arms, but by the power of Him who rules all things.'
192 King Alfred: Alfred the Great (849–99), king of Wessex and of the Anglo-Saxons (871–99).
193 *Ethelwerd's Chronicle*: Aethelweard (d. c. 998), chronicler whose work includes material not found in the *Anglo-Saxon Chronicle*. Nineteenth-century publications of the chronicle include J. A. Giles's *Six Old English Chronicles* (London: Henry G. Bohn, 1848), 35. This entry is for the year 891.
194 From the Anglo-Saxon Chronicle entry for the year 891, as recorded by J. A. Giles in *The Venerable Bede's Ecclesiastical History of England, also The Anglo-Saxon Chronicle* (1847), 360.

LVII.

The three Pilgrims.

IN the rude ages, earth had shrines, where men
    Knelt down and prayed; and spots where man forgot,
    Amid the Past's great scenes, the Present's lot.
And Nature needeth them e'en now as then;
In one idea, one age, seek not to pen
    Thy soul, but bid it wander back through time,
    And be in turn the child of every clime,
From the emblazoned hall to the lost outcast's den.
Still earth has shrines, but then we see them not,
    Or marvel where the wondrous beauty lies
That men have seen in many an earth-soiled spot;
    It was the soft lights of the upper skies
That rested o'er them then, and made them bright;
Beams that have paled in artificial light.

LVIII.

"900 ... In the same year King Alfred departed out of this world;[195] that immovable pillar of the Western Saxons—that man full of justice, bold in arms, learned in speech, and, above all things, imbued with the divine instructions. For he had translated into his own language, out of Latin, unnumbered volumes, of so varied a nature, and so excellently, that the sorrowful book of Boethius seemed, not only to the learned but even to those who heard it read, as it were brought to life again.[196] The monarch died on the seventh day after the solemnity of All Saints, and his body rests in peace in the city of Winchester."—*Ethelwerd's Chronicle*.[197]

---

195 King Alfred: Alfred the Great (849–99), king of Wessex and of the Anglo-Saxons (871–99).
196 Boethius: Boethius (c. 480–c. 524), Roman philosopher whose *Consolation of Philosophy* (*Consolatio Philosophiae*) was translated into Old English by Alfred.
197 This section is taken directly from *Ethelwerd's Chronicle* entry for the year 900, as cited by Giles in *Six Old English Chronicles* (1848), 37. Although Hawkshaw states here that Alfred died on the seventh day after All Saints' Day (1 November), the chronicle states that it was seven days before. The date of Alfred's death is commonly recorded as 26 October 899. *Ethelwerd's Chronicle* states that Alfred's body 'rests in peace in the city of Winton', rather than Winchester, as Hawkshaw refers to it: Winton is an archaic name for Winchester.

LVIII.

The Hero-King.[198]

ONE hero fills a century, and the age
    An Alfred filled might well be satisfied;
    He slept within his tomb the Saxon's pride,
And History writ his name upon her page,
And hailed him patriot, statesman, poet, sage,
    And Nature, in his children, bade him still
    Live for the land he loved, and guard from ill
The shores round which the northern sea-steeds rage;
Son, daughter, grandson, echoes of his fame,
    Bore on to after years, until they died
On coward hearts, and not that hero name
    Could rouse to manly hope or noble pride;
Priest-ridden, slavish, down they bow the head
To the proud churchman, or the despot's tread.

---

[198] This is one of the thirteen sonnets included in the *Manchester Guardian* review of *Sonnets on Anglo-Saxon History* (8 November 1854), and one of two sonnets included in the review of the collection in the *Living Age* (6 January 1855); see Appendix A.

LIX.

It is mentioned in the Anglo-Saxon laws that a servile thrael may become a thane, and a ceorl an eorl. The laws of Ethelstan provide that a thane may arrive at the dignity of an eorl, and that a massere or merchant, who went three times over sea with his own craft, might become a thane.[199] Without the possession of a certain quantity of landed property, nobility of birth could not entitle to a seat in the Witena-gemot.[200] The smith or armourer ranked among the lesser thanes.

---

199 Ethelstan: Athelstan, or Aethelstan (c. 895–939), king of England (924–39) and legal reformer.
200 This section is a précis of Turner's discussion of status conferred through property and birth in *History of the Anglo-Saxons*, vol. 3 (1840), 134–5. Witena-gemot: the assembly of the witan, the national council of Anglo-Saxon times (n. 'witenagemot' *OED*).

LIX.

The Thane's Fireside.

The yule log crackles in the ample grate,
    And the rude hall looks cheerful in the light;
      'T is well, for stern the clime and long the night;
Now welcome he who can the tale relate,
How the old sea-king braved his adverse fate;
    Or how the fearful sisters weave the thread
      Of human life amid the ghastly dead,
While grisly demons on their bidding wait.
Strange sounds had each one heard, strange sights had seen,
    For troubled spectres never cease their walk
Till faith grows weak; and years must intervene,
    Aye, years, and ages from that evening's talk
To such an age as this, when earth and sky
And soul, to some, seem scarce a mystery!

LX.

When Athelstan[201] ascended the throne, his brother Edwin[202] was accused of having plotted against his accession: Edwin, who was but a youth, denied the charge, yet Athelstan ordered him, with one attendant, to be put to sea in a boat, without oars. Carried by the winds out of sight of land, the unfortunate prince threw himself into the sea; his attendant afterwards reached the shore in safety. For seven years Athelstan mourned his brother's death, and performed a penance for his own crime.[203]

---

201 Athelstan: Athelstan, or Aethelstan (c. 895–939), king of England (924–39).
202 Edwin: Eadwine (d. 933), son of Edward the Elder (d. 924), king of the Anglo-Saxons (899–924).
203 This section is a précis of Turner's account in *History of the Anglo-Saxons*, vol. 2 (1840), 131–2. Turner cites twelfth-century historian William of Malmesbury as his source for the story of Edwin's death.

LX.

The remorse of Athelstan. —I.

AVAUNT! thou hideous spectre—hence—avaunt!
   Leave me at last! have I not prayed and wept
   In unknown agony, whilst men have slept?
Steal not around me now my heart to daunt,
And freeze mine eyes, or look as thou wert wont
   When we were children,—ah! that would be worse—
   'T would blast my spirit deeper than thy curse,
And that cold, shivering form that doth me haunt.
Is there no penance—long—strange—terrible,
   That will bring peace unto my guilty heart,
As from rough shells we snatch the precious pearl?
   Oh, God! if such there be, to me impart
The secret, and though life itself may fail
In the dread task, my spirit will not quail.

LXI.

"ATHELSTAN[204] educated and established Alan of Bretagne,[205] Louis of France,[206] and Haco of Norway;[207] and these actions are not recorded by English writers, but are attested by the chronicles of the countries benefited by his liberality. Our own authors, by omitting these circumstances, have concealed part of his fame; but this moderation entitles them to credit in other similar events."—See Sharon Turner's *History of the Anglo-Saxons*.[208]

---

204 Athelstan: Athelstan, or Aethelstan (c. 895–939), king of England (924–39).
205 Alan of Bretagne: Alan II, duke of Brittany (d. 952).
206 Louis of France: Louis IV (920–54), king of France (936–54).
207 Haco of Norway: Haakon Haraldsson (920–61), Haakon the Good, king of Norway (934–61).
208 From Turner's account in *History of the Anglo-Saxons*, vol. 2 (1840), 129.

LXI.

Athelstan.—II.

Within the cloister feebler men had sought
   Peace for the guilty soul's great agony,
   But the strong battle on and do not flee:
Perhaps, to his deep spirit came the thought,
In some still, twilight hour of musing brought,
   That proof of sorrow for the past is given
   Best by our love to man, our faith in Heaven:
And in the tangled web of life he wrought
Bright colours round that one dark spot of crime,
   And peace, through him, came to his troubled land,
And men forgot, as onward passed the time,
   That there was blood upon that powerful hand;
But did he, too, forget it?—there are things
The world forgets that yet leave deadliest stings.

LXII.

THE story of Edwy and Elfgiva is too well known to need repetition.[209] Edwy,[210] or Edwin,[211] was but sixteen years old when he succeeded his uncle Edred,[212] in 955, in the government of a kingdom that the priests were filling with discontent and distraction by violently introducing the rule of St. Benedict.[213]

The monkish chroniclers have painted Edwin's character in colours darkened by prejudice, but the more impartial Ethelwerd says that "he was much beloved, and that, on account of his great personal beauty, he was called Paukalus by the people."[214]

---

209 Elfgiva: Elgiva, or Aelfgifu, consort of King Edwy, whose marriage was annulled against their will after clerics found them to be too closely related. The *Anglo-Saxon Chronicle* entry for 958 states: 'In this year archbishop Odo [of Canterbury] separated King Edwy and Elfgiva, because they were too nearly related'; see J. A. Giles, *The Venerable Bede's Ecclesiastical History of England, also The Anglo-Saxon Chronicle* (1847), 380. Frances Burney's five-act tragedy, *Edwy and Elgiva* (1790) is one of several late eighteenth- and early nineteenth-century literary and artistic representations of their story.
210 Edwy: Edwy, or Eadwig (c. 940–59), king of England (955–9).
211 As Turner notes, 'He is commonly called Edwy; but the old authorities are numerous, which express his name to have been Edwin'; he goes on to list references to Edwin in chronicle sources (*History of the Anglo-Saxons*, vol. 2 (1840), 146).
212 Edred: Edred, or Eadred (c. 923–55), king of England (946–55).
213 Benedictine rule was introduced into England during 940s and 950s under Dunstan (c. 909–88), Benedictine monk and reformer, and archbishop of Canterbury (959–88).
214 From *Ethelwerd's Chronicle* as cited by Giles in *Six Old English Chronicles* (1848), 40. Note that the chronicle cites 'Pankalus', and not 'Paukalus' as Edwy's popular name (Edwy All-Fair).

LXII.

Edwy and Elfgiva.

THE times have changed since of a Kentish king
    Augustine humbly begged a ruined pile,
    And saw the moss-grown church with thankful smile,
To thy dark day, poor Edwy, when the ring
Given to thy bride was broken, as a thing
    Worthless and guilty, by a churchman's hand,
    And his proud words woke treason through thy land;
And the vain curse had yet a poisoned sting
That rankled in thy heart; till one short year
    Of love, and grief, and anguish, quenched thy life.
Strange that mere words could cause such crushing fear,
    Or priestly ban wake men to deeds of strife;
Nay, 't is not strange, for words all meaningless
The feeble, shrinking soul yet curse or bless.

LXIII.

THE Anglo-Saxon towns generally arose around the minster; the municipal affairs were managed by a *port-reeve*[215] chosen by the associations called *gylds*[216] which consisted of the freemen of the place. Under princes who carried the influence of the crown to its greatest extent, we find burghers[217] treating as power to power with their king. A symbolic statue in the centre of the market was always a conspicuous object.[218]

---

215 port-reeve: the governor or chief officer of a town or borough (n. 'portreeve' *OED*).
216 gyld: association formed for the mutual aid and protection of its members, or for the prosecution of some common purpose (n. 'gild', OE form 'gyld', *OED*).
217 burgher: an inhabitant of a burgh, borough, or corporate town; a citizen (n. 'burgher' *OED*).
218 This section is a précis of Kemble's *The Saxons in England*, vol. 2 (1849), 312–3.

LXIII.

The Town.

THE daws are wheeling round the minster roof,
    Where priest and bishop in grave council sit,
    While peasant groups, with joke and homely wit,
Gather by the rude market-cross; aloof
Stands the port-reeve, or with a stern reproof
    Chides the ill-doer; or with jealous eye
    Looks on the noble whose gay train sweeps by,
The rough path echoing to his horse's hoof.
Mountains and forests have been Freedom's shrine,
    But not her birth-place; men have worshipped there,
Lonely and sad, the holy and divine,
    That they would love as household things elsewhere;
'T is in the busy street, the crowded mart,
That liberty hath sprung, and man must play his part.

LXIV.

FROM the reign of Athelstan[219] till that of Ethelred the Unready,[220] or from the year 934 until 988, England appears to have been free from the invasions of the northern Vikings; but no wise or powerful princes had filled the throne, and all had been very young at their accession. The violence with which the rule of St. Benedict was forced upon the clergy, alienated the minds of the nobility from the princes who supported its introduction; there was external peace, but no national unity.

---

219 Athelstan: Athelstan, or Aethelstan (c. 895–939), king of England (924–39).
220 Ethelred the Unready: Aethelred II (c. 968–1016), Ethelred the Unready, king of England (978–1013 and 1014–16). He was no older than twelve years when he took the throne.

LXIV.

Disunion.

THE Saxon sun had reached its noontide height,
    And there was peace; but 't was the stifled calm
    That bodes the tempest, but wakes no alarm;
The throne looked fair in that deceitful light,
Yet it was but a pageant, for the might
    Of power was gone, and by religion's shrine
    Stood but a shadow of that thing divine,
Chilling the heart, though glittering to the sight.
While smiled that treacherous sky the priest went forth
    And sowed disunion through the sleeping land;
It had awoke if from the stormy north
    The raven's* scream had sounded—but the hand[221]
That gave the convent dole—the voice, too, heard
In sainted hymn, no heart-forebodings stirred.

---

221 [Poet's Note: *The emblem of the Northmen, whose banner was a raven.]

LXV.

DUNSTAN was born in A.D. 925[222]—the same year that Athelstan ascended the throne.[223] His parents, who were called Heorstan and Cynethryth, seem to have lived near Glastonbury, and were of noble birth. When a child, he often visited the ruins of an ancient British church near his home; tradition had ascribed its foundation to Joseph of Arimathea,[224] the supposed apostle of Britain. The beautiful abbey of Glastonbury was greatly enriched by Edgar[225] when Dunstan had become its abbot,[226] and it had been conformed to the rule of the Benedictines.

---

222 Dunstan: St Dunstan (c. 909–88), Benedictine monk and reformer, and archbishop of Canterbury (959–88).
223 Athelstan: Athelstan, or Aethelstan (c. 895–939), king of England (924–39).
224 Joseph of Arimathea: member of the council of Jerusalem who is said to have buried Christ's body after the crucifixion. Late medieval Christian legend suggests that Joseph was sent as an apostle to Britain and founded Glastonbury Abbey.
225 Edgar: Edgar (943–75), younger brother of Edwy and king of England (959–75).
226 Dunstan: St Dunstan (c. 909–88), Benedictine monk and reformer, and archbishop of Canterbury (959–88), abbot of Glastonbury (940–57).

LXV.

Dunstan.—I. The Boy.

Within an ancient church's ruined aisles
   A boy was idling 'mid the ferns and flowers
   That clothed the crumbling walls; behind, the towers
Of a proud abbey rose; sometimes with smiles
He watched the daws wheel round the antique piles,
   A bird, a beetle, or a butterfly,
   Might for a time arrest his wandering eye,
But deeper thoughts yet filled his soul meanwhiles:
No common soul was his; for good or ill
   There was a mighty power; yet who that saw
The truant dreaming there, so calm and still,
   Could omens from it of his future draw?
That child's heart, like the veiled Egyptian shrine,
The monstrous might conceal, or the divine.

LXVI.

It was during one of Dunstan's visits to the old British church that he had, according to the monkish recorders of his life, a vision of his future greatness.[227] Some Irish ecclesiastics had settled at Glastonbury, and were teaching the liberal studies to the children of the nobility; from them Dunstan received his first instruction: during his studies in the monastery he had a severe illness, and during the night, in a fit of delirium, he climbed upon the roof of the church, and, descending through a hole left by some workmen, was found the next morning asleep in the edifice. This adventure was converted into a miracle.[228]

---

227 Dunstan: St Dunstan (c. 909–88), Benedictine monk and reformer, and archbishop of Canterbury (959–88).
228 This section is a précis of Turner's account. In his footnotes, Turner draws a distinction between chroniclers' accounts and later biographical interpretations. The former, he notes, 'shows us the simple and natural truth of an incident which the future biographers of Dunstan have converted into an elaborate and ridiculous miracle' (*History of the Anglo-Saxons*, vol. 2 (1840), 151).

LXVI.

Dunstan.—II. The Dream.

He had been thinking how, in earth's first day,
   Men had built cities and been great; he slept,
   And his mind still its waking musings kept,
But mixed with visions of what round him lay—
The abbey's towers—the ruins, mossed and grey;
   He saw a lordly monastery rise,
   With towers and chapel there before his eyes,
And down each aisle deep music found its way;
He saw the abbot in his costly chair,
   Attended like a prince; and then there came
Voices, he knew not whence—as if the air
   Grew vocal with one word—it was his name:
He woke—the dream of sleep had passed away,
But it came back in waking dreams by day.

LXVII.

THE parents of Dunstan encouraged him in study, and his great abilities soon enabled him to master all the learning and science of the times; he excelled in music and in the mechanical arts, and also in painting, and copying manuscripts.[229]

His uncle Aldhelm, Archbishop of Canterbury,[230] introduced him at the court of Athelstan,[231] and that King often pleased himself with the young courtier's musical talents.[232]

---

229 Dunstan: St Dunstan (c. 909–88), Benedictine monk and reformer, and archbishop of Canterbury (959–88).
230 Aldhelm: Athelm, or Aethelhelm (d. 926), archbishop of Canterbury (c. 923–26).
231 Athelstan: Athelstan, or Aethelstan (c. 895–939), king of England (924–39).
232 This section is a précis of Turner's account in *History of the Anglo-Saxons*, vol. 2 (1840), 151–2.

LXVII.

Dunstan.—III. The Youth's aspirings.

He would be great, and hard he toiled for fame:
   His one desire was to outstrip his race,
   Or with the first to keep an even pace.
Manful the toil, and noble was the aim—
But God and man a something higher claim
   From man than this; a name may be a power
   To aid the right cause in the adverse hour;
If that the motive, none the wish may blame:
Dunstan! perchance that holy wish was thine;
   Amid the pure aspirings of the youth
How much of faith and love with all entwine—
   Love that may lead, and faith that points to truth:
Ah! had he followed then where nature led,
Her light had gladness o'er his pathway shed.

LXVIII.

"No circumstance can more impressively attest the superiority of Dunstan's attainments than his having been accused, while at court, of demoniacal arts.[233] The charge of magic was of all others the most destructive, because the most difficult to repel. Every exertion of superior intellect in defence was misconstrued to be preternatural, and confirmed the imputation. His enemies were successful—Dunstan was driven from court, and, not content with his disgrace, they insulted him, pursued, and threw him into a marsh; he extricated himself, and retired to a friend's house."—Sharon Turner's *History of the Anglo-Saxons*.[234]

---

233 Dunstan: St Dunstan (c. 909–88), Benedictine monk and reformer, and archbishop of Canterbury (959–88).
234 Dunstan was expelled from the court of King Athelstan in 935. Hawkshaw omits sections from Turner's account, which is here quoted in full: 'No circumstance can more impressively attest the superiority of Dunstan's attainments than his having been accused, while at court, of demoniacal arts. Such charges give demonstration of the talents and knowledge of the person so accused. In the very same century another man of eminence suffered under a similar imputation, because he had made a sphere, invented clocks, and attempted a telescop [sic]. The charge of magic was of all others the most destructive, because the most difficult to repel. Every exertion of superior intellect in defence was misconstrued to be preternatural, and confirmed the imputation. His enemies were successful. The king was influenced against him, and Dunstan was driven from court;—from that Eden of his hopes, where, like another Wolsey, he was planning to be naturalised. His courtly rivals were not content with his disgrace: they insulted as well as supplanted him; they pursued and threw him into a miry marsh. He extricated himself on their retreat, and reached a friend's house about a mile distant' (*History of the Anglo-Saxons*, vol. 2 (1840), 152–3).

LXVIII.

Dunstan.—IV. The Trial.

BELIEVE not him whose creed thy heart denies
   In all its better moments; when the tone
   Of others' gladness wakes one in thine own,
Or when beneath the blue o'er-arching skies
Earth in the blessedness of sunshine lies,
   What thou think'st then, of God, the universe,
   Of men and of thyself, oh, think no worse
When man with sophistries thy spirit tries.
His hour of trial came, as come it must,
   To every heart, though wearing different forms;
All faded upon which he placed his trust,
   Like mirage pictures in the desert storms,
From where he entered blithesome, frank, and gay,
Gloomy, suspicious, sad, he takes his lonely way.

LXIX.

AFTER Dunstan's[235] retirement from the court of Athelstan,[236] he became attached to a young maiden whom he wished to marry; a relation whom he had in the church,[237] opposed his wishes, and pronounced them suggestions of the devil to lead him from a monastic life. Dunstan at first strongly objected; but his relative still continued his importunities, denouncing the vengeance of Heaven upon him if he persisted in his refusal.[238]

---

235 Dunstan: St Dunstan (c. 909–88), Benedictine monk and reformer, and archbishop of Canterbury (959–88).
236 Athelstan: Athelstan, or Aethelstan (c. 895–939), king of England (924–39).
237 Aelfheah 'the Bald' (d. 951), bishop of Winchester (934–51).
238 This section is a précis of Turner's account in *History of the Anglo-Saxons*, vol. 2 (1840), 153–4.

LXIX.

Dunstan.—V. Love.

ALL is not lost, for Nature still survives
   Within the heart, and she can build afresh
   What courts have spoiled, e'en as her broken mesh
The gossamer re-weaves, once in our lives
Love comes, and all the beautiful revives;
   And noble thoughts we never dreamed to feel,
   It wakens in us, as sunbeams reveal
The sparry cave; 't is love the spirit shrives.
He loved as passionate natures only can,
   And then the tempter came, not as they tell,
Who, knowing little of the life of man,
   Think we can sin by loving him too well;
No, from his creed, not from his heart, it came,
To blast and scorch him with unhallowed flame.

LXX.

AMIDST the agitation of contending passions, the health of Dunstan gave way;[239] he was attacked by a dangerous disease, and his life was despaired of; at length he slowly recovered, assumed the monkish habit, and renounced the world.[240] During the reigns of Edred,[241] Edwy,[242] and Edgar,[243] his power was unbounded. His illness, subsequent austerities, and great ambition, remind us of Ignatius Loyola.[244]

---

239 Dunstan: St Dunstan (c. 909–88), Benedictine monk and reformer, and archbishop of Canterbury (959–88).
240 This section is a précis of Turner's account in *History of the Anglo-Saxons*, vol. 2 (1840), 154.
241 Edred: Edred, or Eadred (c. 923–55), king of England (946–55).
242 Edwy: Edwy, or Eadwig (c. 940–59), king of England (955–9).
243 Edgar: (943–75), younger brother of Edwy and king of England (959–75).
244 Ignatius Loyola: St Ignatius of Loyola (1491–1556), Spanish theologian and founder of the Society of Jesus (Jesuits). The comparison is Hawkshaw's, rather than Turner's.

LXX.

Dunstan.—VI. The Fall.

Love God the more by loving man the less;
   By outraging the nature He has given,
   Win thou a brighter pathway to his Heaven;
Call his fair world a howling wilderness,
And man, whom Jesus came on earth to bless,
   Heir of perdition; leave thy soul to those
   To whom thou can'st not, if thou dar'st, disclose
Its doubts, for strives it not in mute distress?
This was the trial that assailed his heart,
   And crushed the truthful from it; from that hour,
Deceiver and deceived, he played his part,
   On love and Nature's ruins rose to power;
His life, henceforth, a falsehood, till the light
That once had guided, did but dim his sight.

LXXI.

"He made with his own hands a subterraneous cave or cell, so unlike anything of the sort, that his biographer, who had seen it, knew not what to call it ....[245] Dunstan[246] carried to his cell[247] a fragment of his former disposition; he exercised himself in working in metals."— Sharon Turner's *History of the Anglo-Saxons*.[248]

His miracles may be passed over in silence, as the effects of a credulous age, and, perhaps, of a deranged mind.

---

245 Turner footnotes 'Osberne' as the biographer: Osbern (d. c. 1090), Benedictine monk and hagiographer.
246 Dunstan: St Dunstan (c. 909–88), Benedictine monk and reformer, and archbishop of Canterbury (959–88).
247 Turner refers to a 'sepulchral cell'.
248 This section is a précis of Turner's account in *History of the Anglo-Saxons*, vol. 2 (1840), 155.

LXXI.

Dunstan.—VII. Nature's Revenge.

But the death-struggles of that fiery soul,
   The grave-like cell the haggard brow revealed,
   For Nature without conflict did not yield:
Not to uproot all passion, but control,
And make the spirit one harmonious whole,
   Religion aims; the harp she tunes again,
   By earthly damps unstrung, a loftier strain
It then can give than e'er from Eden stole.
He who foresees the destinies of men,
   Gives them the passions suited to their task,
Not one too many, or too few; who, then,
   Shall proudly murmuring dare of Him to ask,
Why was I thus? seek, rather, through the strife
Of conflict, to work out thy end of life.

LXXII.

"I BELIEVE Dunstan's monkish and very vulgar-minded panegyrists to have done his character and memory great wrong;[249] and that they have measured the distinguished statesman by the narrow gauge of their own intelligence and desire. Whatever may have been the Archbishop's private leaning, he appears to have conducted himself with great discretion."—Kemble's *Saxons in England*.[250]

It is said he refused to crown Ethelred, judging, no doubt, that it was impolitic to raise a mere child to the throne, and under such equivocal circumstances as those which attended his accession.[251]

---

249 Dunstan: St Dunstan (c. 909–88), Benedictine monk and reformer, and archbishop of Canterbury (959–88).
250 Taken from Kemble's *The Saxons in England*, vol. 2 (1849), 459–60, with omissions.
251 Ethelred: Aethelred II (c. 968–1016), Ethelred the Unready, king of England (978–1013 and 1014–16). The young Ethelred came to the throne following the murder of his half-brother, Edward (c. 962–79), later known as Edward the Martyr (975–8), who had taken the crown after the death of their father, Edgar (943–75), king of England (959–75). Edward's reign was challenged by supporters of Ethelred, and he was murdered at Corfe Castle, Dorset. Some sources implicate Ethelred's mother, Queen Aelfthryth, in the murder of her stepson.

LXXII.

Dunstan.—VIII. Refusing to crown Ethelred.

BOWED down with years, but unsubdued in will,
 Stood the stern monk beside the boyish king,
 While nearer pressed around the gazing ring
Of priests and thanes, who the old chapel fill:
The chant had ceased, and all was still; so still,
 That the breeze, sighing through the cloisters, came
 Weird-like; and through each mailed warrior's frame
Shot with an undefined but fearful thrill.
"I crown thee not, I bless thee not;"—the word[252]
 Fell as a prophet's on the listening throng,
And sad forebodings in their hearts it stirred,
 Dark fears that would be darker truths ere long:
And ere the spell was gone that on them lay,
From the hushed chapel Dunstan passed away.

---

252 In *History of the Anglo-Saxons* (1831), Francis Palgrave suggests the following words from Dunstan on the occasion of Ethelred's coronation: 'Even as, by the death of thy brother, thou didst aspire to the kingdom, hear the decree of Heaven. The sin of thy wicked mother and of her accomplices shall rest upon thy head; and such evils shall fall upon the English as they have never yet suffered, from the days when they first came into the isle of Britain, even until the present time' (281).

LXXIII.

"SIRIC[253] the successor of Dunstan,[254] reasoned that as they (the Danes) only came for booty, it would be wiser to give them what they wanted .... Whether the King's ecclesiastical advisers were afraid of calling out the chiefs of the country, with their military arrays; or, like most clerical statesmen, were incompetent to advise[255] the wisest public measure; or whether the nobles, in their contempt for the King and his administration,[256] were not displeased at the invasion, and therefore did not oppose the payment, cannot now be certainly known."—Sharon Turner's *History of the Anglo-Saxons.*[257]

---

253 Siric: Sigeric (d. 994), archbishop of Canterbury (990–994).
254 Dunstan: St Dunstan (c. 909–88), Benedictine monk and reformer, and archbishop of Canterbury (959–88).
255 Turner has 'devise' rather than 'advise'.
256 The King: Aethelred II (c. 968–1016), Ethelred the Unready, king of England (978–1013 and 1014–16).
257 This section is taken from Turner's account in *History of the Anglo-Saxons*, vol. 2 (1840), 192–3.

LXXIII.

Ethelred the Unready.

DARK clouds are glooming o'er the Saxon land,
   Its King a churchman's tool, and gold alone
   Buys from the Danish chief the tottering throne.
Woe to the land whose priests are kings; no hand
Can bear a heavier scourge than their slight wand;
   Minster and convent rise amid the woods,
   And vesper chimes float o'er the solitudes,
But mix with shouts from many a pirate band.
It was a time for deeds, not words though pure,
   The fortress, not the chapel; and the arm
Swinging the censor with a childish care,
   Had helped to save a nation; there is balm
Sweeter than incense in the grateful tear
Of the weak saved from agony and fear.

LXXIV.

"A.D. 1002, and in that year the King[258] ordered all the Danish men that were in England to be slain; this was done on St. Brice's Mass-day."[259]

"A.D. 1005. In this year was the great famine throughout the English nation; such, that no man ever before recollected one so grim."—*Anglo-Saxon Chronicle*.[260]

---

258 The King: Aethelred II (c. 968–1016), Ethelred the Unready, king of England (978–1013 and 1014–16).
259 St. Brice's Mass-day: St Brice's Day massacre (13 November 1002).
260 From the Anglo-Saxon Chronicle entries for the years 1002 and 1005, as recorded by J. A. Giles in *The Venerable Bede's Ecclesiastical History of England, also The Anglo-Saxon Chronicle* (1847), 396–7.

LXXIV.

Massacre of the Danes.

THINK not thy crooked policy will save
    Thy crown or kingdom, weak and cruel chief,
    It will but give to thee a deadly grief;
Crimes do not go unpunished to the grave,
The avenging furies back the culprit wave
    From its repose, and hunt him o'er the earth,
    Shouting in silent hours, whispering in mirth,
Words that will make a coward of the brave.
The blighted harvest withers in the field,
    The house-dog watches by a fireless home,
In Wolfnoth's hall are neither sword nor shield;[261]
    And herds untended through the forest roam,
And in men's hearts died love, and hope, and trust,
Things that will raise a nation from the dust.

---

261 Wolfnoth: a likely reference to Wulfnoth Cild, a thegn of Sussex and thought to be the father of Godwine (1001–53), earl of Wessex.

LXXV.

"ETHELRED[262] was liberal to poets who amused him. Gunnlaugr, the Scalld, sailed to London, and presented himself to the King, with an heroic poem on the royal *virtues*. He sang it, and received in return a purple tunic, lined with the richest furs, and adorned with fringe; and was appointed to a station in the palace."—Sharon Turner's *History of the Anglo-Saxons*.[263]

---

262 Ethelred: Aethelred II (c. 968–1016), Ethelred the Unready, king of England (978–1013 and 1014–16).
263 This section is taken from Turner's account in *History of the Anglo-Saxons*, vol. 2 (1840), 198.

LXXV.

The Poet.

Rust gather on that harp from aye that rings
    The false praise of the worthless; or is still
    When the oppressor vaunts his deeds of ill;
'T is sad as if an angel's starry wings
Bore him to Erebus.[264] What! can the things
    Of earthly tinsel dazzle eyes that see
    Beneath the surface of humanity,
How the dark deed, from a mean heart upsprings?
Shall there be none to live the spirit-life,
    No priest of nature, and no seer of time?
Still, let some whisper 'mid this deafening strife,
    That earth yet keeps her grasp of the sublime,
That Time still touches on Eternity,
That faith, and life, and death, are things that ever be.

---

264 Erebus: the proper name of a dark region between Earth and Hades, and as such a place of blackness and gloom.

LXXVI.

EDMUND Ironside,[265] the brave son of the weak Ethelred,[266] succeeded to the government of the distracted kingdom, half of which was now in the possession of the Danes, in A.D. 1016. Before the battle of Scearstan,[267] addressing the English, he conjured them to remember their country, their families, their homes, for which they were fighting.

During the conflict, a report was spread by the enemy, that he was killed; but ascending an eminence, he took off his helmet, and exposed his unarmed head to undeceive his people: but the panic had spread; his efforts were unavailing; the battle was lost.[268]

---

265 Edmund Ironside: Edmund II (c. 988–1016), king of England (1016).
266 Ethelred: Aethelred II (c. 968–1016), Ethelred the Unready, king of England (978–1013 and 1014–16).
267 Scearstan: battle between Edmund II and the Danes, led by Cnut, at Sherston, Wiltshire (1016).
268 This section is a précis of Turner's account in *History of the Anglo-Saxons*, vol. 2 (1840), 203–5.

LXXVI.

Edmund Ironside.

He thought his hero-soul could animate
   For a brief space that flying host—'t is vain;
   Wildly they rush across the fatal plain—
All that they highest, dearest, held of late,
In one mad wish for life they leave to fate;
   Their country seemed but as another—fame
   A thing unthought of—freedom but a name;
Within their craven hearts died even love and hate.
Clasp the plumed helm again upon thy brow,
   And turn thee from that field where all is lost;
And yet it is not so; not then, nor now,
   Does that which so much heart and mind hath cost
Perish for ever from one blow.—He passed
From the night-shadowed plain, the proudest and the last.

LXXVII.

"Canute,[269] from his warlike ability, surnamed the Brave; from his renown and empire, the Great; from his liberality, the Rich; and from his devotion, the Pious."—Sharon Turner's *History of the Anglo-Saxons*.[270]

"1017. In this year King Canute obtained the whole realm of the English race. And he banished Edwy the Etheling,[271] and afterwards commanded him to be slain, and Edwy, King of the Churls."[272]

"1029. This year King Canute gave to Christ Church, at Canterbury, the haven at Sandwich, and all the dues that arise thereof on either side of the haven."—*The Anglo-Saxon Chronicle*.[273]

---

269 Canute: Canute, or Cnut (d. 1035), king of England (1016–35), Denmark (1018–35) and Norway (1028–35).
270 This section is taken from Turner's account (*History of the Anglo-Saxons*, vol. 2 (1840), 208.
271 Edwy the Etheling: Eadwig, son of Aethelred II (c. 968–1016), Ethelred the Unready, king of England (978–1013 and 1014–16).
272 Edwy, King of the Churls: Eadwig, English nobleman. Churls: in the Old English constitution, men without rank (n. 'churl' *OED*).
273 From the *Anglo-Saxon Chronicle* entry for the years 1017 and 1029, as recorded by J. A. Giles in *The Venerable Bede's Ecclesiastical History of England*, also *The Anglo-Saxon Chronicle* (1847), 409, 412.

LXXVII.

Canute the Great.

C<small>ANUTE</small> the Great!—the great in what? in crime?
    I know no title that he hath to be
    Ennobled thus by flattering history;
A massive figure through the mists of Time
He looms upon us, but the true sublime
    Is not in him: 't is easy to forgive
    Those whom we envy not; permit to live
Those whom we fear not to our height can climb:
Easy to put aside the glittering toy
    That symbolized the power his stern red hand
Clutched with a grasp death only could destroy;
    And to heap offerings of a plundered land
Upon the church's altars, ne'er can be
Accepted sacrifice to Deity.

LXXVIII.

During the troubles that followed the withdrawal of the Romans from Britain, a great portion of the land had gone out of cultivation and was again covered with forest.

"Half a century in an unexhausted soil is ample time to convert the most flourishing district into thick brushwood and impervious *bush*. Beech and fir[274] do not require fifty years to become large trees; the elm, the alder, and even the oak, are well-sized growths at that age."—Kemble's *Saxons in England*.[275]

---

274 Hawkshaw omits the following: 'which, though said by Strabo to be not indigenous, must have been plentiful in the fifth century'.
275 From Kemble's *The Saxons in England*, vol. 2 (1849), 289.

LXXVIII.

The Forest.

PAUSE for a while upon those gentler things
    History deems worthless 'mid her deeds of strife
    (Though blood and tears ne'er made a nation's life).
O'er the still lake its way the heron wings,
Close to the swineherd's cot the redbreast sings,
    While he by gurgling brook or forest tree
    Stretches his limbs in idle liberty,
While through the glades the hunter's bugle rings.
The forest! 't was our Saxon fathers' home,
    Girdling with leafy walls each cultured spot;
No wonder that we love the gothic dome,
    Impressions of that past we have forgot
Rest on us still, though, mindless of their power,
We think ourselves the offspring of the hour.

LXXIX.

"THAT Godwin[276] was the son of a herdsman is a fact recorded in the MS. Chronicle of Radulphus Niger.[277] This author says explicitly what no other has mentioned—Earl Godwin was the son of a herdsman."[278]—Sharon Turner's *History of the Anglo- Saxons*.[279]

Godwin was handsome and eloquent: he married Gyda,[280] the sister of Ulfr,[281] the Danish Jarl, whose life he saved, and they were the parents of Harold, the last Saxon king.[282]

---

276 Godwin: Godwine (1001–53), earl of Wessex.
277 Radulphus Niger: Ralph the Black (c. 1140–c. 1217), Anglo-French theologian and one of the English Chroniclers.
278 Although details of Godwine's ancestry are uncertain, it is now thought that he was the son of Wulfnoth Cild, a thegn of Sussex.
279 This is taken from Turner's account in *History of the Anglo-Saxons*, vol. 2 (1840), 207.
280 Gyda: Gytha, wife of Godwine (1001–53), earl of Wessex, and mother of Harold II, king of England (1066).
281 In his footnote, Turner draws on the thirteenth-century Icelandic Knytlinga saga for an account of Godwine saving Ulfr, his subsequent marriage to Gytha and his acceptance into the court of King Cnut (*History of the Anglo-Saxons*, vol. 2 (1840), 207–8).
282 Harold: Harold Godwineson (c. 1022–66), reigned as Harold II, king of England (1066).

LXXIX.

Godwin.—I. Childhood.

A boy through that old forest wends his way,
   Driving his cattle to the upland side,
   Where through the livelong day he will abide,
Nor chide the sun for its too long delay;
Though brother he hath none, nor social play;
   But woods, and streamlets, and the grassy hills,
   O'er which the fresh breeze wanders as it wills,
And clouds are chased by every sunny ray,
Have been to him as friends from infant years;
   And with his thoughts and them he lives alone,
Nursing in solitude his hopes and fears,
   King of a little world, and that his own:
The night shades gather, and then son to sire
Sings the wild saga by the cottage fire.

LXXX.

AFTER the battle of Scearstan,[283] a Danish chief,[284] having lost his way in a wood, met a youth driving his cattle to pasture, and asked to be directed to the camp of Canute,[285] offering the boy his ring if he would show him the way.—"I will not accept your ring, but I will try to lead you to your friends," was Godwin's answer[286]—and taking Ulfr to his father's cottage, he gave him refreshment.[287]

---

283 battle of Scearstan: battle between Edmund II and the Danes, led by Cnut, at Sherston, Wiltshire (1016).
284 Danish chief: Ulf (d. 1026).
285 Canute: Canute, or Cnut (d. 1035), king of England (1016–35), Denmark (1018–35) and Norway (1028–35).
286 Godwin: Godwine (1001–53), earl of Wessex.
287 This is a précis of the account of Godwine in the Knytlinga Saga, as cited in Turner's footnotes (*History of the Anglo-Saxons*, vol. 2 (1840), 208).

LXXX.

Godwin.—II. The meeting with Ulfr.

The forest echoes to another tread
    Than the lone herd-boy's, and with headlong speed,
    Through bush and fern brake, as in utmost need,
A warrior presses, turning oft his head,
Listening, but pausing not; the sun-beams shed
    Their golden arrows on his mossy path,
    But the wild tempest in its fiercest wrath
Had waked within his heart far less of dread.
He is perceived;—there stands the peasant youth,
    But the frank bearing of his noble face
Forbids distrust; so truth gives birth to truth,
    Ulfr to Godwin tells his name and race,
"Give me protection, lead me to my king,
And thy reward shall be this priceless ring."

LXXXI.

As soon as it was dark, the horses were provided, and the fugitive and his guide proceeded to the Danish camp, which they reached in safety the next day. The grateful jarl treated Godwin as his own child,[288] and, after some time, Canute,[289] to gratify Ulfr, raised the young herdsman to the rank of jarl.[290]

---

288 Godwin: Godwine (1001–53), earl of Wessex.
289 Canute: Canute, or Cnut (d. 1035), king of England (1016–35), Denmark (1018–35) and Norway (1028–35).
290 This is a précis of the account of Godwine in the Knytlinga saga, as cited in Turner's footnotes (*History of the Anglo-Saxons*, vol. 2 (1840), 208).

LXXXI.

Godwin.—III. The Flight.

"I NEED not that—take back thy glittering bribe,
   I sell not favours to a man in need,
   Nor is gold payment for a worthy deed,"
Replied the youth, and put the gem aside;
"Yet in my father's cottage thou canst 'bide
   Till the night shadows darken o'er the sky,
   Day is no time for fugitives to fly,
And if need be, I will be Ulfr's guide."
Oh, 'mid the gloom and darkness of the past,
   This story gathers light around it,—one
Perchance of many like it, that would cast
   Hope on the future, light on ages gone,
Making us turn with loving eyes, and trust,
To Him, who hath to all mankind been just.

LXXXII.

THE favour showed by Edward the Confessor to the Norman nobles,[291] amongst whom he had passed his youth, was particularly distasteful to Godwin;[292] it was owing to his having armed to punish Eustace, Count of Bologne,[293] and his followers, for having killed some of the citizens of Dover, which was in Godwin's earldom, that he and his family were banished, the King having taken the part of his Norman favourites.[294]

---

291 Edward the Confessor: St Edward (c. 1003–66), Edward the Confessor, king of England (1042–66).
292 Godwin: Godwine (1001–53), earl of Wessex.
293 Eustace, Count of Boulogne: Eustace II (d. 1087), count of Boulogne.
294 This is a précis of Turner's account in *History of the Anglo-Saxons*, vol. 2 (1840), 221–4.

LXXXII.

Godwin.—IV. The Earl.

THAT care-worn man, amid his stately sons,
    Who guides the sceptre for the feeble hand
    That holds it; hero of his Saxon land,
Whose frowning look the Norman courtier shuns,
Whose eloquence the hostile Witna stuns,[295]
    Is the Earl Godwin; time hath changed that face,
    But the soul's current there hath left a trace
More marked, though silent and unknown it runs;
The thoughts of lofty and far-seeing souls
    To others' ears they seldom can reveal,
Or the strong will the social love controls;
    Thus, smaller minds guess little what they feel,
Till in the outer life the thought appears,
Deed of a day, but product of long years.

---

295 Witna: the assembly of the witan, the national council of Anglo-Saxon times (n. 'witenagemot' *OED*). Turner's account makes reference to the assembly of the witenagemot which banished Godwine and his family (*History of the Anglo-Saxons*, vol. 2 (1840), 223).

LXXXIII.

"A.D. 1053. In this year was the King[296] at Winchester, at Easter, and Godwin,[297] the earl with him, and Harold,[298] the earl, his son, and Tosty.[299] Then on the second day of Easter, sat he with the King at the feast; then suddenly sank he down by the footstool, deprived of speech, and of all his power, and he was carried into the king's chamber, and they thought it would pass over, but it did not so; but he continued on, thus speechless and powerless, until the Thursday, and then resigned his life, and he lies there within the Old-Minster."[300]—*Anglo-Saxon Chronicle.*[301]

Some say Godwin was denying his share in the murder of Alfred,[302] the King's brother, when he was seized with his fatal illness.[303]

---

296 The King: St Edward (c. 1003–66), Edward the Confessor, king of England (1042–66).
297 Godwin: Godwine (1001–53), earl of Wessex.
298 Harold: Harold Godwineson (c. 1022–66), reigned as Harold II, king of England (1066).
299 Tosty: Tostig Godwineson (d. 1066), earl of Northumbria.
300 Old-Minster: the Old Minster, Winchester.
301 From the Anglo-Saxon Chronicle entry for the year 1053, as recorded by J. A. Giles in *The Venerable Bede's Ecclesiastical History of England, also The Anglo-Saxon Chronicle* (1847), 431.
302 Edward's younger brother, Alfred the Atheling, had been murdered in 1036 on his return from France.
303 Turner includes these suggestions in his account of Godwin's death in *History of the Anglo-Saxons*, vol. 2 (1840), 226.

LXXXIII.

Godwin.—V. The Death-Feast.

When on the fields of fight he braved his foes,
    He knew death tracked him; and across his bark
    Its shadow crept, when through the billows dark
Of a wild sea he fled; and 'mid repose,
When the night-glooms around all nature close,
    And immaterial things assert their sway,
    To his unlistening ear its voice found way,
Hollow as from earth's sepulchres it rose.
But no shades darken o'er that festive hall,
    No voice sounds ominous amid the throng,
And proudly through that crowd, erect and tall,
    To meet his King Earl Godwin moves along;
But there, unseen, beside him glides that form,
Whose shadow he had felt in fight and storm.

LXXXIV.

WHEN Godwin[304] and his family were restored to their country and honours, after defeating the machinations of the Norman favourites of the King, Sweyn,[305] his eldest son, was not allowed to share in the privileges granted to the rest of his relations; he was outlawed for a murder committed six years before.[306] Stung with remorse for his crime, he set off to walk with naked feet, from Flanders, where he then was, to Jerusalem; he died on his way back at Constantinople.[307]—*Anglo-Saxon Chronicle.*[308]

---

304 Godwin: Godwine (1001–53), earl of Wessex.
305 Sweyn: Sweyn Godwineson (d. 1052).
306 Hawkshaw refers to the murder of Beorn in the prose accompanying sonnet XXXI, using Turner's account as her source (*History of the Anglo-Saxons*, vol. 2 (1840), 225).
307 Hawkshaw refers to Sweyn's pilgrimage in the prose accompanying sonnet XXXI, using Turner's account as her source (*History of the Anglo-Saxons*, vol. 2 (1840), 225).
308 Although Sweyn's pilgrimage is mentioned in the Anglo-Saxon Chronicle entry for the year 1052, as recorded by J. A. Giles in *The Venerable Bede's Ecclesiastical History of England, also The Anglo-Saxon Chronicle* (1847), 429–30, Hawkshaw's wording is closer to the account of Turner in *History of the Anglo-Saxons*, vol. 2 (1840), 225.

LXXXIV.

Sweyn, the Outlawed.

WITHIN the garden where the Saviour prayed,
   Sits a lone man; upon his shaded face
   Are sadder lines than time alone can trace;
From the fierce setting sun an olive's shade
Screened his o'er-wearied frame, the cool breeze played
   Through the old branches on his heated brow,
   But nought of what is round him recks he now;
Before the past, the now, the future, fade.
Barefooted he hath reached that sainted earth
   That was to give him peace,—the goal is won;
But memories of the spot that gave him birth,
   Thoughts, dreams, regrets, he would forever shun,
Press on him in that moment, when he deemed
The present had the darkened past redeemed.

LXXXV.

"A.D. 1052. Then soon came William, the Earl,[309] from beyond sea, with a great band of Frenchmen; and the King received him, and as many of his companions as it pleased him."[310]—*Anglo-Saxon Chronicle*.[311]

This visit of William of Normandy took place during the exile of Godwin and his family;[312] the short-sighted King showed him his cities and castles, and loaded him with presents.

---

309 William, the Earl: William (1028–87), duke of Normandy, later William I, or William the Conqueror, first Norman king of England (1066–87).
310 The King: St Edward (c. 1003–66), Edward the Confessor, king of England (1042–66).
311 From the Anglo-Saxon Chronicle entry for the year 1052, as recorded by J. A. Giles in *The Venerable Bede's Ecclesiastical History of England, also The Anglo-Saxon Chronicle* (1847), 429.
312 Godwin: Godwine (1001–53), earl of Wessex.

LXXXV.

The Visit.

He came an honoured and a peaceful guest,
   No omens marked his way, no bloody sun
   Glared on the earth, no stars did backward run,
But bright in gold and crimson glowed the west,
And men awoke, and toiled, and went to rest
   The same as ever, and gay pomp and glee,
   Unwonted, broke the dumb monotony
That o'er the monkish King and convent-palace prest;
With courtly words he soothes the monarch's ear,
   With sacred trifles wins his feeble heart;
Of guest and kinsman who can feel a fear,
   Or lack frank bearing, or free speech?—they part;
The one beside his crucifix forgets
All that hath past; his sword the other whets.

LXXXVI.

EDITHA,[313] "the rose of England," the daughter of Godwin,[314] and wife of Edward the Confessor,[315] is described by Ingulf,[316] who knew her, as very beautiful, meek, and modest, faithful, virtuous, and the enemy of no one; she was also a learned woman.[317] During the exile of her family and friends, she was confined by Edward in the Convent of Wherwell, but was restored to her regal honours upon their return.[318]

---

313 Editha: Edith, or Eadgyth (d. 1075), queen of England, consort of Edward the Confessor.
314 Godwin: Godwine (1001–53), earl of Wessex.
315 Edward the Confessor: St Edward (c. 1003–66), Edward the Confessor, king of England (1042–66).
316 Ingulf: Ingulf (c. 1045–1109), Benedictine Abbot of Crowland (Croyland) Abbey.
317 Taken from Turner's footnote which cites Ingulf; Turner notes that Editha was named 'fair rose' by English chroniclers (*History of the Anglo-Saxons*, vol. 2 (1840), 220).
318 The *Anglo-Saxon Chronicle* entry for the year 1048 refers to Editha's confinement at Wherwell (Giles, *The Venerable Bede's Ecclesiastical History of England*, also *The Anglo-Saxon Chronicle* (1847), 420–22), as does Francis Palgrave in *History of the Anglo-Saxons* (1831), 342.

LXXXVI.

Editha in the Monastery at Wherwell.

THE morning sun crept through the quiet room,
   And fell upon the web her fingers wrought
   With womanish skill; a task that left each thought
Unfettered, and yet stole away its gloom;
"I scarcely could regret my altered doom,"
   She said, "but that injustice hath its smart,
   And fears for those I love oppress my heart;
O'er Godwin's house the shades of evening loom,
Else were the joyless palace for the cell
   An outward change alone; and I more free
Within this convent shade, than when I dwell
   In regal halls, unloving King, with thee;
Here of my heart, and mind, and time, am I
Still Queen, and Edith loves her destiny."

LXXXVII.

EDWARD,[319] the son of Edmund Ironside,[320] had been brought up in Hungary, Canute having attempted his life;[321] he had married Agatha, the daughter of Henry, the German Emperor;[322] Edward the Confessor sent for him, to make him his successor, but he died, the year following his arrival, much to the grief of the nation.[323]

> "A.D. 1057. Alas! that was a rueful case,
>   and harmful
>   for all this nation,
>   that he so soon
>   his life did end,
>   after that he to Angle-land came,
>   for the mishap
>   of this wretched nation."
>   *Anglo-Saxon Chronicle.*[324]

---

319 Edward: Edward the Exile, or Edward Atheling (d. 1057).
320 Edmund Ironside: Edmund II (c. 988–1016), king of England (1016).
321 Canute: Canute, or Cnut (d. 1035), king of England (1016–35), Denmark (1018–35) and Norway (1028–35).
322 Henry: Henry III (1017–56), king of Germany (1039–56) and Holy Roman emperor (1046–56). The lineage of Agatha is unproven, although the connection to Henry III was commonly suggested by chroniclers.
323 This is a précis of Turner's account in *History of the Anglo-Saxons*, vol. 2 (1840), 209, 230.
324 From the *Anglo-Saxon Chronicle* entry for the year 1057, as recorded by J. A. Giles in *The Venerable Bede's Ecclesiastical History of England*, also *The Anglo-Saxon Chronicle* (1847), 435.

LXXXVII.

Death-Shadowings.—I. Edward the Etheling.

Exile, thou tread'st thy native shores again!
   But the death-shadows on thy regal brow
   Are resting, dark and ominous, e'en now;
But with thy life, far more than it, will wane—
Thy ebbing pulse shall through a nation's vein
   Send back the life-blood; in thy grave will lie
   The shades of what had been a dynasty;
A people to its heart will feel thy pain.
'T was even so; and yet they knew him not;
   But he was symbol of a higher thing,
And in the weakness of our mortal lot,
   And 'mid the darkness earthly shadows fling;
Better the emblem see, than but a place
That our own image fills—or formless space.

LXXXVIII.

"IN 1057 England lost Leofric,[325] by whose wisdom the reign of Edward was preserved from many perils and disorders .... Leofric was the father of Hereward,[326] whose life seemed devoted to the task of supplying incidents to the genius of romance and heroic song."—Sharon Turner's *History of the Anglo-Saxons*.[327]

"A.D. 1057. In the same year (in which Edward Etheling died) died Leofric, the Earl; he was very wise for God and also for the world, which was a blessing to all this nation. He lies at Coventry."—*Anglo-Saxon Chronicle*.[328]

---

325 Leofric: Leofric, earl of Mercia (d. 1057).
326 Hereward: Hereward the Wake (d. c. 1071), semi-legendary Anglo-Saxon rebel leader.
327 Taken from Turner's account in *History of the Anglo-Saxons*, vol. 2 (1840), 229. The reference to Hereward relates to Turner's footnote rather than the body of the text. With various contemporary or near-contemporary sources making competing claims for Hereward's ancestry, his parentage remains uncertain.
328 From the Anglo-Saxon Chronicle entry for the year 1057, as recorded by J. A. Giles in *The Venerable Bede's Ecclesiastical History of England, also The Anglo-Saxon Chronicle* (1847), 434–5.

LXXXVIII.

Death-Shadowings.—II. Leofric.

A wish, an unsubstantial hope—a beam,
   Perchance, but like a spring-day morning's, fled,
   When o'er the Etheling's brow the death-glooms spread;
'T was but the fading of a glittering dream,
The passing of fair things that did but seem,
   And yet were not,—but now the shadows creep
   O'er a great life, a truth that Time will keep,
A fact, with whose results the ages teem.
He died; men did not marvel, for the thing
   Was common as the setting of the sun:
But when the midnight's spectral voices ring,
   And the cold mists roll heavily and dun
Across their path, 't is common things they feel
That make of every day the woe or weal.

LXXXIX.

LEOFRIC[329] appears to have had less ambition than Godwin,[330] and to have been more concerned for the good of the nation than his own advancement: it was his moderation, and that of some others, that prevented a civil war in 1052.

"… Then thought some of them that it would be a great folly that they should join battle; because there was nearly all that was most noble in England in the two armies, and they thought that they should expose the land to our foes, and cause great destruction among ourselves. Then counselled they that hostages should be given mutually; and they appointed a term at London."—*Anglo-Saxon Chronicle*.[331]

---

329 Leofric: Leofric, earl of Mercia (d. 1057).
330 Godwin: Godwine (1001–53), earl of Wessex.
331 From the Anglo-Saxon Chronicle entry for the year 1052, as recorded by J. A. Giles in *The Venerable Bede's Ecclesiastical History of England, also The Anglo-Saxon Chronicle* (1847), 427–30.

LXXXIX.

Death-Shadowings.—III. Leofric.

WISE, moderate, reverent!—when he died, a tie
   That bound discordant souls together broke;
   The haughty listened when the noble spoke,
And the weak looked to him confidingly
Who counselled peace; and when he bent his knee
   Before the shrine of God, the poor one saw
   A fellow-mortal only, and the flaw
Of riches and of power he did not see.
Clear-shining, but not dazzling, on he moved,
   To set in peace; but his far-seeing eye
Discerned the storm-clouds o'er the land he loved,
   Yet saw beyond them, too, a brighter sky;
And hope and courage for the future grew
Out of the present's gloom: the true soul sees the true.

XC.

EDWARD[332] was the son of Ethelred[333] and Emma,[334] the sister of Robert, Duke of Normandy, the father of William the Conqueror:[335] in A.D. 1013, Ethelred, being severely pressed by the Danes, sent first his queen and afterwards his two youngest sons, Edward and Alfred,[336] to Normandy, where they were kindly received by their relative Robert, and where Edward remained until A.D. 1040, when he returned to England in the reign of his half-brother, Hardicanute,[337] who appears to have treated him kindly: he was chosen King by the English on the death of Hardicanute in the following year.

---

332 Edward: St Edward (c. 1003–66), Edward the Confessor, king of England (1042–66).
333 Ethelred: Aethelred II (c. 968–1016), Ethelred the Unready, king of England (978–1013 and 1014–16).
334 Emma: Emma, or Aelfgifu (d. 1052), queen consort of England.
335 William the Conqueror: William (1028–87), William I, or William the Conqueror, first Norman king of England (1066–87).
336 Alfred: Alfred the Atheling (d. 1036).
337 Hardicanute: Harthacnut (c. 1018–42), king of England (1040–1042).

XC.

Edward the Confessor.—I.

In monkish cowl, or in the hermit's cell,
   In pious trifling might his days have fled;
   But among living men, with spirit dead,
He dwelt and moved a mockery; and there fell
A blight around him, making home a hell;
   In all life's solemn duties he could see
   Nought but the traces of mortality,
In earthly beauty but a demon's spell.
The mystic splendour of the silent skies,
   The wondrous beauty wheresoe'er we tread,
Earth's kind humanities and household ties,
   Must they but fill the soul with secret dread,
As if the purest breath of love were sin,
And poison lurked each flower of life within!

XCI.

WEAK in intellect, alienating the minds of the English by his attachment to Norman favourites, expending money on relics and churches that should have been spent in fortifying his kingdom, Edward[338] paved the way for the subversion of the Saxon dynasty: he is described as tall and well made, with a fair complexion; his time was chiefly passed between prayers and hunting: he was canonized, and many miracles attributed to him.[339]

---

338 Edward: St Edward (c. 1003–66), Edward the Confessor, king of England (1042–66).
339 This is a précis of Turner's account in *History of the Anglo-Saxons*, vol. 2 (1840), 230.

XCI.

Edward the Confessor.—II.

No neutral character will nature own;
    For good or evil we must live and die,
    And vain it is the destiny to fly;
Unknown, unfelt, no life hath ever flown,
Though it may seem a drop to oceans thrown;
    Power unemployed, as power misused, may tell
    On the world's progress; in the monkish cell
Have mouldered men that should have graced a throne.
And the last Edward of the Saxon name
    Died, and was buried in that stately pile
His piety had reared,—the way to fame,
    And heaven as well, men thought: nor need we smile;
The feeling lingers with us still,—men give
Their gold for that for which they ought to live.

XCII.

"A.D. 1060. In this year there was a great earthquake ... A.D. 1066. Then was over all England such a token seen in the heavens as no man ever before saw. Some men said that it was cometa, the star, which some men call the haired star; and it appeared first on the eve Litania Major,[340] the 8th before the Kalends of May,[341] and so shone all the seven nights."—*Anglo-Saxon Chronicle*.[342]

This comet is represented in the Bayeux tapestry; it appeared in the year in which the battle of Hastings was fought.[343]

---

340 Litania Major: procession of Christian devotion to invoke God's mercy, observed on 25 April.
341 Kalends of May: the first day of the month.
342 From the *Anglo-Saxon Chronicle* entries for the years 1060 and 1066, as recorded by J. A. Giles in *The Venerable Bede's Ecclesiastical History of England, also The Anglo-Saxon Chronicle* (1847), 436, 439–44.
343 From Turner's account in *History of the Anglo-Saxons*, vol. 2 (1840), 237.

XCII.

The Eventide.—I.

The night was closing round the Saxon's throne,
    The signs of change were all around, yet few
    From the right omens faithful augury drew;
There was no omen in the hollow moan
Of blighting winds in summer, or the tone
    Of earthquake or of tempest, yet with fear
    These shook the unthinking, as they reached his ear
With fearful tidings of a land o'erthrown.
Not Sybil-like doth Nature stand to warn
    Kings and their people of their destiny;
She wraps her head in clouds by mountain tarn,
    But there she speaketh but of Deity,
And the immortal, not of earthly things—
The fate of empires, or the doom of kings.

XCIII.

"A.D. 1054. This year went Seward the Earl[344] both with a ship-force and a land-force, and put to flight King Macbeth;[345] … but his son Osborn and his sister's son Seward, and some of his house carls[346] and also of the King's were slain."

"And in this year there was so great a murrain among cattle as no man remembered for many years before."[347]—*Anglo-Saxon Chronicle.*[348]

---

344 Seward the Earl: Siward, earl of Northumbria (d. 1055).
345 King Macbeth: Macbeth (d. 1057), king of Scotland (1040–1057).
346 house carls: retainers, or members of the household of troops of a king or noble; in late Anglo-Saxon England a housecarl was a man of thegn's rank (n. 'housecarl' *OED*).
347 murrain: infectious disease, plague, pestilence (n. 'murrain' *OED*).
348 Although not an exact transcription as the quotation marks suggest, this is taken from the *Anglo-Saxon Chronicle* entry for the year 1054, as recorded by J. A. Giles in *The Venerable Bede's Ecclesiastical History of England, also The Anglo-Saxon Chronicle* (1847), 431–2.

XCIII.

The Eventide.—II.

PALE famine, with her nerveless hand, had stood
    By many a forest home, and plague had spread
    Her dark wings o'er the marts where merchants tread,
And war had quenched the noble's hearth in blood,
And the best ships were sunk in ocean's flood,
    And strangers stood around the monarch's throne,
    Who loved their country better than his own,
That King too pious to be just or good.
These were the omens that men should have read;
    And some there were who spelt the signs aright,
And saw the crown upon the Norman's head,
    And the dark battle-field of Hastings' fight;
A people's common deeds and words are signs.
The future's prophet asks no plainer lines.

XCIV.

THAT it was the wish of Edward the Confessor[349] that Harold[350] should succeed him is expressly stated in the *Saxon Chronicle*;[351] his character was full of promise; he had on many occasions showed great talents, moderation, and undaunted bravery; he was beloved by the people, and had made himself feared by the turbulent nobility: if Harold had not fallen, the fight of Hastings would have been but a barren victory to William,[352] but his death left the English without a leader suited to the emergencies of the times.[353]

---

349 Edward the Confessor: St Edward (c. 1003–66), Edward the Confessor, king of England (1042–66).
350 Harold: Harold Godwineson (c. 1022–66), reigned as Harold II, king of England (1066).
351 Harold's succession is detailed in the Anglo-Saxon Chronicle entry for the year 1065, as recorded by J.A. Giles in *The Venerable Bede's Ecclesiastical History of England, also The Anglo-Saxon Chronicle* (1847), 437–9.
352 William: William (1028–87), William I, or William the Conqueror, first Norman king of England (1066–87).
353 This is a précis of Turner's account in *History of the Anglo-Saxons*, vol. 2 (1840), 230–37.

XCIV.

Harold.—I.

AND now there rises from the shadowy past
   A kingly figure, on whose mournful brow
   The Norns have written doom,—and who art thou?[354]
"Of a wrecked bark the tall but shattered mast
Of England's Saxon kings and heroes, last,
   The embodiment of systems passed away,
   The type of principles, some far-off day,
The Anglo-Saxon will to death hold fast."
A herdsman's grandson, but a people's choice;
   Harold, thou hadst a right divine to reign,
A right divine to die: there is a voice
   That never speaks from patriot-graves in vain;
Thy single arm thy country could not save,
And the throne was less noble than the grave.

---

354 Norns: in Scandinavian mythology, each of the three Fates, or goddesses of destiny (n. 'Norn' OED).

XCV.

"… AND William[355] came against him (Harold) unawares, before his people were set in order. But the King, nevertheless, strenuously fought against him with those men who would follow him; and there was great slaughter made on either hand. There was slain King Harold,[356] and Leofwin, the Earl,[357] his brother, and Girth, the Earl,[358] his brother; and the Frenchman had possession of the place of carnage, all as God granted them for the people's sins"—*Anglo-Saxon Chronicle.*[359]

---

355 William: William (1028–87), William I, or William the Conqueror, first Norman king of England (1066–87).
356 King Harold: Harold Godwineson (c. 1022–66), reigned as Harold II, king of England (1066), last Anglo-Saxon king of England, died at the Battle of Hastings, 14 October 1066.
357 Leofwin: Leofwine Godwineson, earl (d. 1066).
358 Girth: Gyrth Godwineson, earl of East Anglia (d. 1066).
359 From the Anglo-Saxon Chronicle entry for the year 1066, as recorded by J. A. Giles in *The Venerable Bede's Ecclesiastical History of England, also The Anglo-Saxon Chronicle* (1847), 439–44.

XCV.

Harold.—II.

AMID the bloody haze of Hastings' fight
    The Saxon sun went down when Harold died,
    And his brave brothers perished at his side;
He who from chaos order draws, and light
To spring from darkness, maketh right of might
    In a world's history; but no finite power,
    Whose sight and sway are bounded by the hour,
To claim such high prerogative hath right:
Years of oppression passed, and race with race
    Waged fierce, unceasing war; peace came at last,
When time had softened down each hostile trace,—
    But was there progress till the warfare passed?
That Normandy to England joined, became
Her curse, almost her ruin, not her fame.

XCVI.

It is said that Gyda, or Githa,[360] the mother of Harold,[361] offered to William the Conqueror[362] the weight of her son's dead body in gold if he would give it her to bury, but that he refused.[363]

"A.D. 1067. This year Harold's mother, Githa, and the wives of many good men with her, went to the Steep Holmes, and there abode some time; and afterwards went from thence over sea to St. Omer's."—*Anglo-Saxon Chronicle*.[364]

---

360 Gyda, or Githa: Gytha, wife of Godwine (1001–53), earl of Wessex, and mother of Harold II, king of England (1066).
361 Harold: Harold Godwineson (c. 1022–66), reigned as Harold II, king of England (1066).
362 William the Conqueror: William (1028–87), William I, or William the Conqueror, first Norman king of England (1066–87).
363 This is a précis of Turner's account in *History of the Anglo-Saxons*, vol. 2 (1840), 255–6.
364 From the Anglo-Saxon Chronicle entry for the year 1067, as recorded by J. A. Giles in *The Venerable Bede's Ecclesiastical History of England, also The Anglo-Saxon Chronicle* (1847), 444–6.

XCVI.

The Mother of Harold.

Around that grief-struck woman silently
   They stood, yet gave her not of words or tears,
   For each one had her load of woes and fears,
Beneath whose weight she bent; it was the tie
Of sorrow, scarcely that of sympathy,
   That bound the orphan and the widowed bride
   In that dark hour to childless Githa's side;
She raised at length her sunk and stony eye
And gazed her last on England—and "Farewell"
   Came deep and hollow from her moveless lip,
"I cannot bless the land where Harold fell,
   And where the cup of woe to its last sip
The mother drained—nor will she curse where rest
Her children's graves, and where she once was blest."

XCVII.

HAROLD fell by the great standard that he had defended to the last, as the shades of an autumnal night were closing over the field of Hastings:[365] the force of the Anglo-Saxons was very inferior to that of the Normans—one author says not more than a fourth; they had engaged and defeated Harold Hardrada and the Norwegians a few days before:[366] so fearful were the monks of Waltham Abbey that the battle would be fatal to Harold, that they sent two of their number, Osegod Cnoppe and Ailric the Childemaister, to the field, to secure his body if he fell.[367]

---

365 Harold: Harold Godwineson (c. 1022–66), reigned as Harold II, king of England (1066).
366 Harold Hardrada: Harald Hardrada (1015–66), king of Norway (1046–66), defeated by Harold II at the Battle of Stamford Bridge on 25 September 1066.
367 This account of the monks of Waltham Abbey is a précis of a footnote in Turner's *The History of England during the Middle Ages*, vol. 1 (1825), 62.

XCVII.

Night after Battle.[368]

SILENCE and death! how hideous or how fair
   These two may be; soft as in angel's sleep
   The dead may look, and grief forget to weep;
And on the mountains there are moments, rare
And precious, when the earth, and sky, and air,
   Are hushed in breathless stillness, as if God
   Amid their mighty solitudes had trod.
And not a tone did awe-struck nature dare;
And death, and night, and silence settled down
   Upon that field of fatal fight; and not
A requiem sighed the wind; with sullen frown
   The clouds hung moveless o'er the accursed spot,
But bursting storms, less fearful, had seemed there
The death was doom, the silence was despair.

---

[368] This is one of the thirteen sonnets included in the *Manchester Guardian* review of *Sonnets on Anglo-Saxon History* (8 November 1854); see Appendix A.

XCVIII.

IN England the conquering race have been fused into the conquered: the name of Conqueror can, however, scarcely be applied with propriety to William, who "waited" until the people, left without a leader fit to govern so distracted a kingdom, offered him the crown, on condition that he swore to govern them according to their ancient laws;[369] and it was not until that promise, unfaithfully kept by himself, was gradually observed by his successors, that peace was restored to the land.

---

369 William: William (1028–87), William I, or William the Conqueror, first Norman king of England (1066–87).

XCVIII.

The Anglo-Saxons.[370]

CONQUERED, but unsubdued in spirit still,
   The sullen Saxon tilled the Norman's field,
   Chained down to earth he still refused to yield,
The conqueror's foot could never crush his will;
With a slave's hand he might his tasks fulfil,
   But no slave's heart was his, and daily toil
   Wound not around his soul a deadening coil,
Its higher hopes and faculties to kill.
And so the conquerers had to yield at last,
   E'en to the conquered language, laws, and name;
And as their sons in freedom grow, that past
   Is looked upon with reverence, not with shame,
And hearts that beat beyond the Atlantic tide,
Turn to that far-off time with love and pride.

---

[370] Paul Hill cites this sonnet in his discussion of Hawkshaw's sonnet sequence in *The Anglo-Saxons: The Verdict of History* (Stroud: Tempus Publishing, 2006), 146.

Conclusion.[371]

AND now the task I planned in days gone by
    Is finished; and I turn mine eyes once more
    From their long looking on the things of yore
Unto the future's veiléd mystery,
Or the all-pressing present, wherein lie
    The truth-grains of that past—atoms enwrought
    With stately forms, or household words and thought,
And mixed for aye with England's destiny.
Farewell, then, country of my Saxon sires!
    By Edward's shrine I bid thee now farewell;[372]
In thee were lighted first those household fires
    Where loving hearts and truthful spirits dwell;
Each summer glade beneath the forest tree,
To me, old Saxon-land, shall speak of thee!

---

371 This is one of the thirteen sonnets included in the *Manchester Guardian* review of *Sonnets on Anglo-Saxon History* (8 November 1854); see Appendix A.
372 Edwards's shrine: shrine to Edward the Confessor in Westminster Abbey, London.

1871

CECIL'S OWN BOOK

Cecil's Own Book was printed for private circulation in 1871. There is no record of where it was printed, nor of how many copies were produced.[1] The collection's three short stories and ten poems are accompanied by eight monochrome watercolours which have been pasted in after printing: four of the illustrations are signed 'H. M. M.' It is likely that the books were presented as gifts to family and friends, with the primary recipient Cecil Wedgwood, the Hawkshaws' young grandson, who was eight years old in 1871. Cecil had been born at Hem Heath, Trentham, near Stafford on 28 March 1863 to the Hawkshaws' eldest daughter Mary and her husband Godfrey Wedgwood.[2] Mary contracted puerperal mania and lived for only 11 days following Cecil's birth. She died at Hem Heath on 7 April 1863. In the weeks following her daughter's sudden death, Ann herself became ill, and in letters written to her son Henry she speaks of her illness and of Godfrey's loss and his dependence on the Hawkshaws for emotional support.[3] As expressed in 'In Memoriam', the poignant elegy of remembrance which draws *Cecil's Own Book* to a close, the loss of three of her six children, and particularly Mary, affected Hawkshaw deeply.

As he grew up, Cecil spent a good deal of time with his grandparents and extended family: the Hawkshaws' eldest son John Clarke had married Godfrey's sister Cecily Wedgwood in 1865 and they went on to have several children.[4] *Cecil's Own Book* was undoubtedly written to amuse and educate Ann's young grandson, but also, as the book's dedication suggests, as a memorial to her daughter: 'To the Memory of Mary, the Mother of Cecil'. Written whilst at Hollycombe, the four-thousand-acre estate in West Sussex purchased by John Hawkshaw in 1865, *Cecil's Own Book* is an intimate collection brought alive by Cecil featuring either by name, in the poems 'The Squirrel that forgot that it would be Winter' and 'The Ambitious Water-Lily', or by implication through the inclusion of motherless boys as protagonists in the collection's three short stories. With one story written in the tradition of the *Arabian Nights*, featuring adventures with mystical magic rings and genies in Bagdad, and then set underwater in an echo of Charles Kingsley's *The Water-Babies*, another which names its characters in the style of Kingsley's Mrs Doasyouwouldbedoneby, and a third featuring crockery and cruet that dance and entertain at grand dinners, as in Lewis Carroll's *Alice's Adventures in Wonderland*, Hawkshaw's blend of gentle didacticism and humour is inspired by familiar children's stories which she reworks through her original tales to delight and entertain her young grandson. Moreover, the subtle allusions

---

1 The title page reads: 'Cecil's Own Book, by "Granny" (Mrs Hawkshaw). Printed for private circulation, 1871.'
2 Mary Jane Jackson Hawkshaw and Godfrey Wedgwood (1833–1905) were married at St Peter's Church, Pimlico, on 24 June 1862. Godfrey was the son of Francis Wedgwood (1800–1888) and Frances Mosley (1807–74) and great-grandson of Josiah Wedgwood (1730–95), founder of Wedgwood pottery. Godfrey was a partner in the Wedgwood pottery firm from 1859 to 1891.
3 See the biographical introduction for further details of this correspondence.
4 John Clarke Hawkshaw and Cecily Wedgwood (1837–1917) were married at Barlaston, Stafford, on 12 October 1865.

to death and loss in these short stories look to reassure Cecil of the continued presence of loved ones, even after death.[5]

As with much of Hawkshaw's poetry, the ten poems in this final collection are anchored in the natural world. Yet there is a departure from Hawkshaw's previously unequivocal representation of nature as an embodiment of God's goodness. Whereas in her earlier work, each aspect of the natural world served as evidence of a benevolent and loving God, in *Cecil's Own Book* Hawkshaw characterises anarchic and wasteful nature in poems such as 'The Selfish Toad', 'The Discontented Stream', 'The Ambitious Water-Lily' and 'The Squirrel that forgot that it would be Winter'. In a collection written specifically for a child there are clear moral messages in the didactic tone of these poems, but even to consider these attributes in nature would have been unthinkable in her earlier writing. Whether this shift in tone can be accounted for in the loss of three children, or in an increased awareness of scientific explanations of the natural world, is uncertain, but the change in Hawkshaw's representation of nature is striking.

The final poem in the collection, 'In Memoriam', is a poignant elegy of remembrance which expresses Hawkshaw's dismay at the untimely deaths of three of her six children. For a detailed reading of the poem and its references to the Hawkshaw children, see the biographical introduction.

---

5 Cecil Wedgwood became a man of some note. Having joined the family pottery firm he was made a partner of Wedgwood in 1884, aged 21. He was first mayor of the Federated County Borough of Stoke-on-Trent in 1910 and 1911. As Major Cecil Wedgwood he fought with 8th Battalion, North Staffordshire Regiment in the First World War: he died during the Battle of the Somme on 3 July 1916.

Part I.

The Wonderful Adventures of Hassan the Younger, the Son of Hassan-el-Alfi the Camel Driver

When the Caliph Omar[6] reigned in Bagdad there lived by the Wells of Mousa[7] a certain camel driver, called Hassan-el-Alfi, who had seven sons, and the youngest was named Hassan the little, or Hassan the younger, to distinguish him from his father. The six elder sons went long journeys with their father across the desert, but the little Hassan went not, but remained at home with an old woman who had been his nurse, and he played in the garden by the fountains, and amused himself on the sea-shore gathering shells, of which there were many of strange shapes, and of most beautiful colours.

One day when his father and brothers were absent, the old woman said to Hassan, "I must go away for two days to buy some clothes of which I am in need, go not away to the sea-shore, but stay in the house and the garden, for it may happen that thy father and thy brothers may return in my absence, and if they came back and found no one to prepare them food they would be greatly displeased." So Hassan promised the old woman he would remain in the garden till she returned; so she departed, taking a bottle of water to drink and some dates to eat on her journey, and Hassan sat down under the tall palm trees by the side of the large fountain to read in the Koran, for his father would not allow his sons to remain ignorant of the arts of reading and writing.

When he had finished reading he looked up, and to his great astonishment he saw an old man standing by the fountain, for he had heard no one come up the garden; the old man had a long white beard that reached down to his girdle, his dress was a long lined tunic fastened with a leather belt, from which hung a small red earthen dish like a little shallow basin, he had in one hand a bottle made of the same sort of red earth, and in the other a long bamboo stick on which he leaned heavily, as if he had walked long in the desert and was weary.

Now Hassan knew at once that he was a holy man who had been on a pilgrimage to the tomb of the Prophet, and he laid aside his book and rose up from under the trees, where he had been sitting, and saluted the old man, by bowing down with his face to the ground, and said, "My father, will you drink of the waters of Mousa, and repose under the aged palm trees where our great ancestor Ishmael hath sat;" and the old man replied, "I will, my son:" then Hassan spread a mat under the tree, and fetched water from the well, and hastened and put dates and oranges, and custard apples, in a basket made of palm leaf, and strewed sweet scented Henna flowers over them, and when he had brought them to the pilgrim, he said, "Eat, my father, and leave a blessing on the house of Hassan-el-Alfi, even the blessing of one who hath prayed at the tomb of the Prophet; praised be Allah!"

---

6 This reference to Caliph Omar (c. 581–644) sets the story between 634 and 644, when Omar was caliph: the caliph being the chief civil and religious leader, successor of Muhammad.
7 The Wells of Mousa are located some eight miles from Suez, Egypt. Ann and her daughter Editha had accompanied John Hawkshaw on a trip to Suez in October 1862, on the invitation of Said Pasha, viceroy of Egypt, who had invited John to report on the proposed plans for the Suez Canal.

For so he had been taught by his father, to welcome all holy men when they came to drink of the wells of the desert.

So the old man eat, and drank, and lay down and slept under the cool shade of the palm trees, overcome by the fatigue of his long journey, and by the heat of the day; for the sky was without a cloud, and of the colour of burnished copper; and the fierce heat of the sun, was like the heat of a great oven: and the long leaves of the palm trees moved not, for there was not a breath of air to stir them; and the sweet scented flowers drooped as if they were dying; and the bundles of hay ready for the camels when they came home, were dry as the shavings of wood; and the sand of the desert that surrounded the gardens and the wells, glistened and shone in the glare of that terrible noonday heat; even the lizards clung to the mud walls, silent and sleepy, and did not run nimbly about, and in and out of the cracks, as if they were playing at hide and seek with one another, as is the wont of lizards to do. There was not a sound of man or beast, of bird or insect, wind or water, for the silence was complete. All things seemed burnt to brick, and baked into hardness; and Hassan, as well as the old man, overpowered by the heat, slept till the sun began to go down in the west, and a breeze began to stir the branches of the trees, and the flowers revived in the pleasant coolness.

Then Hassan awoke, and looked to see if the pilgrim was sleeping; but lo! he was gone! but on the mat where he had slept, were two leather bags, tied with strings; then Hassan got up with haste, and ran round the garden, and looked in the garden-house, built by the great fountain, but he could not find the old man, then he climbed to the top of a tall tree from which he could see for miles into the desert, but he saw nothing but a great dust, which he knew must be caused by a troop of camels, and he rejoiced at the sight, and his heart was glad, for he thought it must be his father and brothers who were coming home; so he came down quickly, and prepared the hay for the camels to eat, and water for them to drink, and spread a mat for his father, and got ready food for supper.

And when all things were in a state of readiness, he remembered the bags that the old man had left; and opened one to see what was in it; and when he had looked into it, he was amazed, for it was full of pieces of gold: then he opened the other, and behold! it was full of diamonds, and rubies, and emeralds!

Then Hassan clapped his hands and danced round the bags with delight, and cried, "I will go to Bagdad, and live as doth the Weezer of Caliph, and wear a robe of silk, and drink sherbert out of a golden cup." Then he took out some of the diamonds, and rubies, and emeralds, and admired greatly their beautiful colours, and held up the diamonds to the light, to see how they glittered, and whilst he was searching amongst them, he saw there was a piece of paper with some words written thereon, and looking with attention he perceived that it was addressed unto himself, for on the outside was written, in beautiful Arabic writing: "To Hassan the little, the son of Hassan-el-Alfi;" then he unrolled the paper, and then he saw that there was more writing inside, and he composed himself attentively to read, and the words were as follows:

"The blessing of the old man, even the aged pilgrim from Mecca, who was wearied with journeying, and fainting for lack of bread and of water, and who drank of the Wells of Mousa, and eat of the fresh dates of the garden, and slept safely under the palm trees in the hot noon-tide, rest on the house of Hassan-el-Alfi, and a double blessing rest on the head of Hassan the little, for he reverenced the aged man, even the aged pilgrim from Mecca, and made obeisance unto him, and tended him like a son. Now the old man, believing that the boy Hassan is one in whose heart dwelleth truth, leaveth in his care two leather bags, filled with precious treasure, until he cometh again to claim them; and at the time appointed by Allah he will come again, and ask of Hassan the little to deliver up the gold and the gems; he also giveth to Hassan a ring, that is sewed up in a small bag of silk of Damascus, which is concealed at the bottom of the bag of gold. Praised be Allah!"

Now when Hassan had read these words, he emptied the bag of gold on the mat, and found at the bottom a small silken bag, such as the writing had described, and it was carefully sewed up; then he took from his belt a knife and cut the stitches, and there appeared at the bottom of the bag a ring: then Hassan took out the ring, and behold! it was but a ring of copper; and he threw it down on the ground, and said, "It is but a ring of copper, such as the very water-carriers of Cairo would not gather out of the dust;" and when he looked at the gold and the precious stones, he despised the copper ring, and left it lying on the ground, and sat silent and sad.

Now near him was a henna tree covered with white sweet-scented blossoms, and a bird of dull plumage that had no beauty, came and perched on the branches, and began to sing, and it sang these words, to the great astonishment of Hassan, as he sat with all the treasure of the sacks poured out around him, and the ring thrown down on the mat:—

> Look not on the treasure, Hassan,
>   Hide it quickly from thy sight;
> Watch me as I float away,
>   Far above these realms of night;
> Homeliest things are not the meanest,
>   And the dull can change to bright.
> Watch me as I float away
>   To the skies of pearly light.

After that, the bird with the dusky wings flew away, and as it flew far away, it seemed to Hassan no more a bird, but a Peri with wings of gold and azure.[8]

Then Hassan arose before the words of the wonderful creature had escaped his memory, and gathered all the gold and the precious stones, and put them into the bags, and tied them with the strings, and sat down on the mat; but he was sad, and sighed frequently and said, "Of what use is all this treasure to an old man whose time on this earth will be short, and whose days are spent in pilgrimages to the Holy Places, and in ceaseless prayers to Allah, and that bread and water sufficeth for food. I will take the bags and hide them in the earth, and when some weeks had passed by, and my father and my brothers are about again to depart, I will secrete some of the treasure in my belt, and I will go with them, and when I reach some great city I will leave my father and my brothers, and will sell the precious stones and buy silk robes and a palace like the palace of the Weezer, and no one will know, and when I want more money, I will return hither secretly, and take more of the treasure;" and he rose and prepared to carry away the bags and hide them, but again he heard words come from the henna tree, and he stopped and beheld, and there sat a bird of

---

8 Peri: from Persian and Iranian mythology, the Peri are descended from fallen angels who have been denied paradise until they have done penance.

most brilliant plumage in the branches, its wings glittered like the jewels in the turban of the Caliph, and Hassan was astonished at its great beauty, and it said:—

> Take the treasure, take it, Hassan,
>   It will make thee rich and great;
> There is no one here to see thee,
>   I will not the deed relate;
> Am I not of wondrous beauty,
>   Would'st thou like to share my fate?
> Take the treasure, seize it quickly,
>   And for ever be my mate.

Then Hassan began to dig a hole to bury the bags, and while he did so, he thought he heard a laugh of derision from the glittering creature, and he was afraid and trembled exceedingly, for he knew he was doing an evil deed in taking the treasure of the old man to be his own: now it was the hour of sunset, and he remembered he had not washed, so he put down the bags and washed in the well, and spread his carpet, and knelt down to pray, with his face towards Mecca, and as he prayed the bird changed its form, and became a loathsome creature, with wings like a bat, and long sharp claws on its feet, and round staring eyes, that were like sparks of fire, that scorched Hassan as he looked at it, and its voice became like the voice of the cruel Hyena of the desert, and Hassan was terrified beyond measure, and he said, "I will not take the treasure of the old man, I will only take the ring that he gave me, and the blessing he inscribed on the paper will rest on me, and on the house of my father."

And he sought for the ring, and put it on the forefinger of his right hand, and when he did so the ugly creature gave a loud scream and flew away, and Hassan shuddered with exceeding fear.

Then he took the bags into the garden house, and sat down to wait till his father and brothers should arrive, and his heart was at peace.

And now outside the hedge of the garden he heard the loud voices of men, and the voices were not the voices of his brothers, but those of strangers, and their words were violent, and they uttered not the name of Allah, and Hassan was afraid, and he sat still on the mat and trembled.

Then six men entered the garden and took the hay and the water, that Hassan had prepared for his father's camels, and gave them to their own camels, and when they had taken the loads off the beasts, they left them fastened to a palm-tree outside the garden, and came themselves to the place where Hassan sat.

Now they were fierce robbers from the desert, who feared not Allah, and had no pity on any living thing. When they saw Hassan they said, "Oh! here is a slave who will procure us food and water, for doubtless he hath them by him, for is not this the house and garden of Hassan-el-Alfi the rich camel driver, whom we robbed on the way to Bagdad?" Then he who was the chief said to Hassan the little, "Rise, and bring us quickly some food and water, and spread mats under the trees, for we will rest and eat in this place, and afterwards thou shalt go with us, and be our slave and attend to the camels."

Then poor Hassan the little rose trembling, and went to fetch water and food, and he wept and said, "Alas! alas! I shall see my father and my brothers no more, but must be a slave to the robbers of the desert," and he wrung his hands and wept bitterly; but the men had no pity on him, but said, "If thou makest not haste, oh slave! we will beat thee as the carpets are beaten in the palace of the Caliph."

Now one of the robbers went into the garden house to see if there he could find clothes or money to carry away, and as he was searching he espied the two bags that Hassan had put on the divan, and he took them, and carried them to the other robbers under the palm trees, and they said:

"Oh! what have we here, what hath this boy hidden in these leather bags, that are so carefully tied up?" and when they had opened them, and saw the treasure, they rejoiced excessively and said, "This exceedeth all the treasure we have taken from the caravans this year."

Then the Sheik said, "Tie up the bags, and tomorrow when we rest at noon I will divide the gold and the precious stones, to each his right proportion, but the boy I will keep to be my slave."

When Hassan heard these words he fell on his face, and entreated them not to carry him away, nor to take the bags, and he told them the whole story about the Old Man, and he shewed them the writing to prove that he spoke words of truth, and they read the paper, and saw that it was as he had said: then they laughed and mocked at Hassan and said, "Let us look at this ring;" and when they saw it they laughed yet the louder, and the Sheik said, "Thou mayest keep thy copper ring, for it is fit only for the finger of a slave; but we will have the bags, and I will keep also the writing for it may be a charm of great value, as it is the writing of a Dervish."

And when Hassan entreated them to have pity on him, they beat him with a bamboo cane, put him into the garden house, and fastened the door; and he wept all night and could not sleep, and continually lamented, and said, "Oh! my father, oh! my brothers."

And as he sat weeping and lamenting, behold the ring came off his finger, and it rolled along the floor, and as it rolled, it grew bigger and brighter, till it shone like molten iron, and grew yet larger and larger and then it fell over, and Hassan was sitting in the centre of the great circle that it made, and it appeared like fire all around him, but it scorched him not; and outside the circle of fire he saw the vile creature that tempted him to take the bags, and also evil genii, and ugly crawling creatures, and loathsome animals, that tried to get at him, but they could not because of the wonderful belt of flame that surrounded him, so after a time they fled away, and when they were gone the ring shrunk again to its former size and appeared but as a ring of copper, and Hassan took it up, and put it on his finger, and said, "Doubtless this ring hath wonderful properties, and is a talisman of great value, praised be Allah!"

And he rejoiced that the robbers had despised it, and that they had left it with him. And after that his heart was less sorrowful, and he slept and was refreshed.

Now early in the morning the robbers unfastened the door of the garden house, and called to Hassan to come out, and to load the camels; and when all was ready, they took the two bags of treasure and departed; the Sheik rode on a fleet dromedary, and he made Hassan lead the camels that were laden with water, for they had filled all their water-skins with the sweet water from the Wells of Mousa, for they were going many days' journey into the desert where they would find no water, nor grass nor herbs save the bitter herbs of the wilderness that no man can eat; they took the way to the Red Sea, and at noon they stopped to shelter from the extreme heat of the sun, under a great rock, and the camels lay down to rest; then the Sheik said, "Bring the sacks, and I will divide the gold and the precious stones;" and Hassan was compelled to bring them; and they opened first the sack that contained the gold, and lo! instead of gold it was filled with sand; then they opened the other that contained the diamonds, and the emeralds, and the rubies, and lo! they had been changed into little white and coloured pebbles, such as are on the sea shore.

Then the Sheik said, "It is thou that hast done this, oh! Hassan the little; thou shalt die, thou deceitful and wicked slave, if thou dost not immediately reveal where thou hast hidden the treasure that was in these sacks yesterday;" then Hassan replied, "Oh! my Master, I know not how this hath taken place, I am ignorant of what hath become of the treasure;" but they would not believe him, and were exasperated beyond measure because the treasure was gone; so they took up Hassan and threw him into the sea; and he sank out of their sight in the clear water, and they left the bags under the rock and departed on their journey.

Now Hassan, at the first, when he was thrown into the sea, was stunned, and his mind was confused with fear, but after awhile he found to his great joy, and extreme wonder, that he could live in the water as well as on the land; and he went down to the bottom of the sea, and it was as a lovely garden. The corals and the sea plants, amongst which the shining little fishes swam, or rested, were beautiful to his sight, and the coolness of the water was refreshing to his heated limbs, and he said, "Praised be Allah! who hath bestowed on me this wonderful ring, for it is no doubt by its power that I have been preserved, and that I can live at the bottom of the sea. I will sit awhile on this ledge of rock, that looks like a couch, with a carpet of Ispahan spread over it; for this sea moss is beautiful as embroidered work from the looms of Iran, and I will watch the strange creatures of the sea, as they swim about me."

So he sat down on the rock, and the water was like a vault of emerald above him, and he saw the oysters opening and shutting their shells, and he saw the pearls glistening within them, and he watched the sea hedgehogs moving about, and he gathered shells of great beauty, such as he had never found on the shore, whose colours were like the colours of the rainbow, in which one colour mingles with another. And Hassan said to himself, "This place is lovely as the gardens of Damascus, of which my father hath told me."

Then he found a large shell that resembled a trumpet, and he put it to his mouth and blew into it, and it produced a sound like that of a silver trumpet, and he had amused himself with blowing into it; but after he had amused himself so for some time he heard a similar sound proceeding from a distance; and the sound came nearer and nearer, and he beheld a troop of creatures coming towards him; their faces were beautiful as the moon, and their eyes lovely as the eyes of the gazelles of the desert, and their arms were fair as alabaster, but from their waists they resembled fishes; now they were the sons and daughters of the old Merman who lived in the cavern underneath the rock on which Hassan was sitting; they had heard the sound of the trumpet shell that he had been playing upon, and had come up to see who it was that had taken one of their instruments of music.

"It may be," Hassan heard them say as they came on, "one of our cousins from Iran who hath brought us the large pearls that our Uncle promised us so long ago, or perchance it is a messenger from the Sea King to enquire after the health of our father, for he is now the oldest and most venerated of all the sons of the sea."

But when they saw Hassan they were overcome with astonishment and wonder, and were silent from amazement; after awhile they recovered from their great surprise and swam close up to him, and one of them said, "This is one of the strange creatures who live on the land, to whom Allah hath not granted a tail, but who move about on two pegs;" and they began to laugh immoderately, and they said, "Let us take the tailless creature to our father, it will amuse him greatly to see him."

Then one of them said to Hassan, "Can'st thou speak, oh! thou tailless creature, or art thou dumb like the fishes? what is thy name?"

Then Hassan said, "I am called Hassan the little, and the name of my father is Hassan-el-Alfi, the camel driver, and because of a charm I have about me, I can live in the water, and I will go with you, for though you are but sea-monsters, and I am of the superior race of men, I think you are kind in heart, and will not hurt me:"—then they said, "No, we will not hurt thee;" but they laughed excessively when they heard him call them sea-monsters, and said, "This poor creature from the land hath not much intelligence, for he thinketh he is greater and wiser that the Mermen who have tails covered with shining scales of gold and green and azure, but Allah hath not granted to all creatures the same amount of sense; so we will have pity on him."

When they saw Hassan stand on his two legs, they laughed again, and said, "Do all the creatures on the land move as thou doest on two pegs?" And Hassan answered, "No, some of them go on four," then they laughed again more immoderately, and said, "Certainly the old man of the sea, who composeth the songs and the histories, never imagined any creatures so strange as these, of whom this mortal speaketh, and he hath lived for a thousand years, and is the most learned of all the children of the sea; we think in this matter, thou tellest not the truth, oh! Hassan the little, but now we will go to our father, the old man of the sea."

Then Hassan floated with them through the clear water, till they came to a cavern, and they swam into it, and Hassan was oppressed and bewildered with the extreme beauty of the place when he examined it, there were on each hand a thousand pillars of emerald, that supported the roof that was inlaid with the scales of gold and silver fishes curiously wrought together; and between each pillar was suspended a globe of pure white crystal, filled with the phosphorescence of the sea, which gave light to the hall of the thousand pillars. The floor was of pale pink coral, of the most delicate colour, and the divan was formed of mother-of-pearl, and on it reclined at the upper end of the hall, the wise old man of the sea.

Then the mermen and mermaidens brought Hassan to him and said, "Oh! our father, we have found this strange creature of the land, and have brought him, that thou mayest amuse thyself with him, and he shall tell us his history, though he is not beautiful to behold, and seemeth to lack intelligence."

Then the old Merman regarded Hassan, and said, "Tell us thy story, and after I have heard thee speak I can judge of thy sense." And Hassan told them all his history, he disguised nothing, and when he had finished the old Merman said, "I am the oldest son of the sea, yet I cannot decide whether the things thou tellest, oh! son of the land, are truth or falsehood; I will consider the matter for a whole moon, and thou shalt dwell here with my sons and my daughters, and no one shall say that thou art a liar, or shall mock thee." And his children were abashed before him, for they knew he was wise, with the wisdom of many years, and they were very young; yet had they given an opinion immediately they had seen Hassan, that he was a creature of little sense, and spoke falsehoods, but their father had decided that he must consider the subject for one whole moon, and they said one to another, "We will not laugh any more at the tailless creature, but will call him Hassan, as he saith that is his name."

So they were kind to him, and his heart was at peace, and they shewed him every day some new plant or new creature of the sea, and he was every day more astonished at the wonderful things he saw; and when a moon was nearly past, Hassan said to one of the maidens of the sea, who was the most loved of them all, "I wonder not, oh! dear maiden of the sea, that thy brothers believed in their hearts that I spoke falsehoods, when I told them of the strange creatures of the land, for if any one had informed me when I dwelt by the Wells of Mousa, of the strange things that I see here day by day, I should have said that they spoke not the truth; I perceive that it becometh the young and the ignorant to be silent and to learn."

Now at the end of a full moon the old Merman of the Hall of the Thousand Pillars, sent for Hassan and said to him, "Oh! son of the land, I have pondered over thy words, and have observed thy deeds, for one whole moon, and I am convinced that thou speakest the truth, so dwell with us as long as thou art content to do so, and tell us of the strange adventures that have come to thy knowledge, respecting the children of the land;" so Hassan was glad that his words were believed, and he told them of his home by the Wells of Mousa, and of the beautiful things he had heard described by his friends who had visited strange countries. And when he had finished, some of the children of the sea sighed and said, "It were better to live on the land than in the sea." But the old wise man said, "Allah, whose name be praised, hath appointed to all creatures the lot that is best for them, and a change will come for you, oh! you children of the sea." Then the sea maiden, who was the best beloved, said, "Yes, oh! my father, we shall assuredly go to the Isle of the Sweet Fountains, when the time that Allah hath appointed shall come."

Now it came to pass that in seven days the dear maiden of the sea, who was the most beloved, died, and they all lamented for her bitterly, and Hassan also, though he was not of their race nor of their kindred, wept for the loss of the maiden of the pure and loving heart, and the Hall of the Thousand Pillars became sad to him, and he wandered from it, until he lost all means of finding his way back again, and he floated into the deep ocean, and sank deeper and deeper into its silent and measureless abysses, and he became afraid as he went downward and downward into its silent depths. For as he descended lower and lower, all the beautiful things he had seen in the Hall of the Merman disappeared, and the silence and the solitude became insupportable to Hassan, and his heart became as a stone within him, as he sank deeper and deeper, and he said, "Perchance it is ordained that I am to live for ever amid these silent waters; oh! would that I had died like the dear maiden of the sea," but his lamenting was of no avail, for he sank yet deeper and deeper, till at last his feet rested on a vast mountain that rose from the bottom of the nethermost ocean, and he was glad even of that change, though the mountain was full of deep pits and horrible caverns, and he would have rejoiced at the sight of the smallest fish, or of a piece of sea-weed clinging to the rocks, but there was no living thing to be seen. But he said, "Perchance, in that immense cavern that I see in the side of the mountain there may dwell some kind creatures of the race of the Merman, who will direct me how to find my way to the land, for I wish now to return to my father's house." So he descended and looked into the cavern, and he could not move from the spot, but stood like one entranced, and his eyes were dilated with astonishment and wonder, and fear. He saw that the cavern was of great extent, and was supported on pillars of adamant, and the floor and the roof were of marble, black as the night sky when no stars shine in it; to each pillar was a ring and an iron chain; at the further end of the cave was a door of open iron, curiously wrought with figures of a serpent, with a crown of gold and of carbuncles on his head, and through the open work of the door he saw another cave, more wonderful than the first, for in the middle was a fountain of fire, and the flames kept shooting upward, and then falling down again like streams of liquid amber. And by the light of the fire fountain,

Hassan saw, reclining on a divan of black stone, the Great Sea Serpent King, and he knew who he was, because the wise old man of the sea had spoken of him, but always with abhorrence, because he did evil to the mermen and enchanted them, and they avoided him and feared him greatly. Hassan could not see his great length, for he was coiled round and round till he formed as many circles as sailors make of a thousand fathoms of cordage, but he saw that he had on his head a great crown of gold, and had round his neck a collar of carbuncles of the size of ostrich eggs, and they glimmered and shone in the light of the fountain of fire.

When Hassan had observed all these things, he said, "This is a vile place, and this is an evil disposed creature, I will not tarry any longer near him, though I perceive that he is asleep now, but if he wakes he may entrance me, and turn me into a pillar of adamant, for now I see that all the pillars in this cave are in the likeness of living things of the sea or of the land, and doubtless by his magic he hath entranced them."

So Hassan turned and fled quickly. Now as he was passing out he saw that there were two strange sea-monsters, chained by their necks to the two pillars nearest the entrance, and as he looked on them, he saw that they were weeping, and they opened their mouths, as if they would fain speak to him, but they could not utter a sound; but they continued to gaze at him, with eyes full of tears.

Now Hassan was compassionate, and he said, "Who are ye?" but they only looked the more sorrowfully and beseechingly at him, but could not utter a word, then Hassan perceived that they were dumb, but that they were not without intelligence, and he said, "I will at the least unchain them, and perchance they will find, by the mercy of Allah, some way out of their enchantment;" so he went to the one on the right hand, and undid his chain, and while he did so, he touched the strange creature with his ring, and lo! it was changed immediately into a young merman; then Hassan was glad, and unfastened the one on the left hand, and touched it also with his ring, and lo! it became a beautiful maiden of the sea, and they said, "O beneficent one, let us hasten away from this abominable cave, praised be Allah, who hath had pity on us, and sent thee to deliver us, for we have been enchanted for many years, and hope of deliverance had died in our hearts."

So they and Hassan went out of the cave and began to float upward through the waters, but they grew weary and decided to rest, so they reposed on a ledge of the great mountain, at the foot of which was the Hall of Adamant, and while they reclined on the rock, Hassan said, "Tell me your adventure, oh! ye children of the sea, and by what misfortune ye became enchanted;" and they replied to him, "Oh! good creature of the land, we are of the children of the sea who dwell in the Gulf of Oran, and our home is in the Palace of Pearl; for it is built of Mother of Pearl, that glistens in the clear waters with the colours of the rainbow, and it is surrounded by a grove of pink coral, beautiful to behold; now it happened by the disposal of Allah, whose name be praised, that our father said, 'Take these pearls to our cousins, the children of the old man of the sea, who dwelleth in the Hall of the Thousand Pillars;'" then Hassan interrupted them and said, "My heart is glad, and I rejoice greatly, that I have delivered you from your enchantment in the Hall of the Serpent King, for you are the relations of those whom I respect greatly, and with whom I have dwelt more than one whole moon: but proceed with your adventures, for I would fain hear them to the conclusion."

"Oh benevolent stranger," they said, "We took the pearls from our father, and we replied, 'Oh! father, to hear is to obey;' but when we had left him, and were swimming on to the Hall of the Thousand Pillars, we said to each other, 'What use is it to go directly to the old man of the sea, let us amuse ourselves by going downwards, to see what things and creatures are in the abysses of the great ocean, for doubtless they are many and wonderful to behold'. But, alas! after a time we lost all power over our motions, and were drawn down rapidly with great force, till we reached the Hall of Adamant, and were drawn by enchantment into it, and up to the place where reclined the Serpent King of the Sea, and he hissed at us, and said; 'Oh! disobedient children of the sea, ye are in my power now, and I will enchant you, and ye shall lose all that is beautiful about you, and become monsters.'

"Then we feared greatly and wept, but he only laughed and hissed at us, and as he looked at us with his red fiery eyes, we felt ourselves changed into the ugly creatures thou sawest, oh, good stranger, and then he chained us to the pillars at the entrance of the cave, and the power of speech was taken from us, we could only weep and lament our fate in our hearts, for it was not in the power of the evil Serpent King to change our minds, and though we could not utter words, we could pray to Allah in our thoughts and entreat him to have compassion on us; but our hearts grew every moon more sorrowful, and we despaired of deliverance, when thou camest and released us.

"Oh! beneficent stranger; wilt thou tell us thy name, that we may retain it for ever in our memories, and inscribe it in the most honourable place of the Palace of Pearl."

And he said, "My name is Hassan the little, the son of Hassan-el-Alfi, the camel driver of the Wells of Mousa."

And they replied to him, "During the whole of our existence we will not forget thee, Oh! Hassan, for the ungrateful are an abomination to Allah!"

Then they proceeded upwards, and at last the children of the sea uttered a cry of joy, and said, "We know now that we are not far from our home, for these rocks are familiar to us," and they parted from Hassan with many kind words and thanks, and he continued his way towards the shores of Arabia.

It was at the time of sunset when he came to the top of the sea, and he saw at a little distance from him an island beautiful as the gardens of Paradise. At first he thought it was only the reflection of the gold and purple and rose colours of the sky, which made the appearance of a glorious island of light in the clear waters of the sea; but as he considered it with attention he became convinced that it was the Island of the Sweet Fountains, that the dear maiden of the sea loved to converse about, and he said, "I will go and examine more nearly the island of beauty and loveliness that Allah hath placed in the sea."

And he drew near, and landed in a garden where all the flowers of the world were blooming, and where the sound of fountains that fell into marble basins, curiously carved, and the murmuring of running streams were heard perpetually; and Hassan's heart was dilated with joy at the sight of the garden, and he said:—

"I will repose here one night before I proceed to my father's house; I am astonished that I never heard from any of the dwellers by the Wells of Mousa of this beautiful island, for it seemeth to me very nigh to the land of the sons of Ishmael."

And it was even so, but to the generality of persons it only appeared as the colours of the sunset, and they passed it by with indifference.

So Hassan wandered about the garden, and drank from the fountains, and lay down to sleep, and when he awoke from a sweet and refreshing slumber, the full moon was shining, and he looked up, and lo! beside him stood a beautiful creature of the children of the Genii; her eyes were like the eyes of the gazelle of the desert, and her form was like the palm tree in its beauty and grace, and Hassan arose and bowed with his face to the ground, and made obeisance, for he was overwhelmed with astonishment and wonder, and reverence; then he heard a voice sweet as the wind of the south through the curves of a sea shell, that said:—

"Hassan, son of Hassan-el-Alfi, dost thou not know me;" and he gazed on the beautiful genii, and he knew in his heart that it was the dear maiden of the sea whom he had loved so much when he lived in the Hall of the Thousand Pillars. Now she was changed into wondrous beauty and loveliness, but it was only the change from the seed to the full grown flower; so Hassan knew her to be the same dear maiden who had been so kind to him before she was changed, and became one of the genii of the Island of the Sweet Fountains, and his heart was filled with joy, that found no words to express itself, so he only gazed at her with pleasure in his eyes, and with his hands clasped in reverence, for he felt he was in the presence of a being greatly superior to himself, and he remembered with shame how often he had despised the discourse he had heard from her, of the things that would be in the Island of the Sweet Fountains, to which she always said she should go after her life as a maiden of the sea had finished; for the words had seemed to him but as fables, so now he bowed before her, and was silent.

Then she smiled on him, and said softly, "I know what thou hast done for the disobedient children of the sea, whom thou hast released from a long enchantment; the blessing of Allah, whose name be praised, be on thee, Hassan. And now thou must return to thy father's house, and perform all the duties that pertain to thy station, as the son of the good camel driver, Hassan-el-Alfi, whose misfortunes have been many and grievous; and when thy task is completed thou wilt see me again."

Then Hassan found words to speak, and said, "Oh, beautiful daughter of the Genii, cannot I benefit thee in some measure; can I not go to the Hall of the Thousand Pillars, and bring thee tokens of the welfare of thy father and of those whom thou lovest?"

Then replied the lovely child of the Genii, with a smile that made the heart happy, as a ray of sunshine maketh gladsome a dark cavern, "It is good that thou hast thought of this, oh! Hassan, but I need it not: every day I see them, and know of their welfare, for when the last ray of the sun toucheth the sea, I go down upon it and visit my kindred; they are not aware of my presence, for so Allah hath decreed, except that they feel in their hearts an ineffable calm for which they can assign no reason, and I shall watch over them till the time that is fixed shall come, and they too shall join me in the Island of the Sweet Fountains, and the time will not be long."

When she ceased speaking, Hassan felt a wonderful drowsiness come over him, and he fell into a deep sleep. How long he slept he never could discover, but when he awoke it was noonday, and he was laid under the rocks, where the robbers had examined the sacks and found them full of stones and sand, and where they had determined to throw Hassan into the sea. And now when he had opened his eyes, behold! he saw the two sacks beside him; and he was overwhelmed with astonishment, and said, "The beautiful child of the Genii hath conveyed me hither during the night; now I will return immediately as she desired me to do, unto the Wells of Mousa, and serve and comfort my father,"—and he prepared to depart; when lo! he saw before him the aged pilgrim who had given him the ring and the bags, so he bowed to the ground and said:—

"I have nothing to offer thee, holy Dervish, not even a cup of water, for my adventures have been strange since I entertained thee at my father's house, and I am straitened in my heart, because I have not fulfilled the trust thou gavest to me; here are the bags committed to my keeping, but they are filled with sand and pebbles."

Then the old man touched the bags with his staff, and said, "Open the bags, oh! Hassan the little, and let us see the change that has befallen the treasure."

So Hassan opened them, and they were filled with gold and diamonds, and rubies and emeralds as before, and he was silent with wonder and joy. Then he said, "I restore to thee, oh! holy pilgrim, that thou leftest with me, and I thank thee above all for this wonderful talisman that thou gavest me, which hath been the means of teaching me many things I should not have discovered without it."

Then the Dervish said, "I give thee the sacks of treasure, but thou must give me the ring, for I need it to give to others of thy age, and who require to be taught as thou hast been." So Hassan took the copper ring from his finger, and gave it to the Dervish, and he blessed him and departed, and Hassan saw him no more.

Then Hassan took a few pieces of gold from one of the sacks, and put them in his sash, and he hid the bags of treasure in a hole in the rocks, and departed to the house of his father; and the way was toilsome over the hot sand of the desert; and when he arrived he found no one there; and the garden was overrun with weeds, and the channels for the water round the garden of herbs was dry, for no one had replenished them from the well, since he had been taken away by the robbers, and the fence was broken down, and the ripe dates were dropping from the trees, for there was no one to gather them; the only thing that remained unchanged was the great well, for the water still bubbled up in it, and ran over the side of the basin into a little canal it had made for itself, and along the side of this channel the flowers and the trees were green and beautiful. So Hassan drank of the water, and did eat of the fruit, and was refreshed, and lay down to rest in the garden house.

Now Hassan arose as soon as it was day, and began to draw water, and pour it into the channels to refresh the trees and the herbs, and while he was at work a family came by of poor Arabs who had been robbed of all they possessed by the Bedouins of the desert; and the father and his three sons asked charity of Hassan in the name of Allah, and he gave them some dates to eat and gave them water from the well, and then he said: "Be content to abide here, and to assist me to restore the garden to its former state of usefulness and beauty, and I will pay you with liberality for your work, for I am desirous to have it in order before the return of my father, who hath been long absent; and I too, though I am so young, have had strange adventures, and have been far away from this place where I was born; perchance some day if ye consent to dwell with me, I may tell you of the wonderful events that have occurred to me."

Then the men rejoiced and said, "We will stay and work for thee, oh! master, and thou shalt pay us for our labour." Then the work of restoring all things to perfection proceeded rapidly, and after a while Hassan went to the place where he had hid the sacks, and took out more gold, and bought camels and sheep, and carpets to cover the divans, and made all ready to receive his father and his brothers, but they came not, neither had he any tidings of them; and he went out, and sat down in the desert and wept, and said, "Alas! my father; alas! my brothers."

And as he sat and lamented, there came to him a poor man whose robe was worn and tattered, and whose face betokened hunger and sickness, but he no sooner saw Hassan than he cried out, "Oh! Hassan, my son." And he embraced him, and they wept for joy, for it was Hassan-el-Alfi, the father of Hassan the little. Then he reverently led his father home, and brought him water to wash, and took off his soiled robe, and put on him one of silk, and made him recline on the divan, and the servants came and served him with food and sherbet.

When he was refreshed, Hassan inquired respecting the welfare of his brothers, and his father answered, "Alas! my son, we have been robbed of all we possessed, and thy brothers were compelled to hire themselves as servants to a rich merchant of Bagdad; but I was too old to work, so they gave me some water and food for my journey, and I have with great toil and labour travelled home, and I am greatly astonished at all the abundance and beauty that I see around me, and I know not from whence it hath come."

Then Hassan the younger told his father of all his strange adventures, and the night was far advanced before he had narrated them all. Then they praised Allah, and lay down to sleep.

On the morrow Hassan sent two of the servants with camels and gold and jewels to Bagdad for his brothers, that they might be relieved from their servitude; and at the end of two moons they returned, and there was rejoicing in the house of Hassan-el-Alfi, such as had not been remembered by any man that dwelt by the Wells of Mousa.

The Selfish Toad

There was once an old Toad,
Lived under a stone;
He had lived there for years,
All alone, all alone.

Sometimes he went out
To look for a dinner;
He knew when the time came,
Because he was thinner.

So when he had eaten
   A few worms and snails,
(He quickly munched them up,
   Heads, bodies, and tails.)

He slowly crawled back,
   To his home by the stone;
And said, "It is pleasant,
   To live here alone;

"I've no one to tease me,
   And no one to feed,
To live all for oneself,
   Is a very good creed:

"There's that drudge of a Field-mouse,
   With six babies to keep;
I wonder if ever,
   She gets a night's sleep;

"I wish that their house
   Was away from my door,
They are squeaking for breakfast,
   When I want to snore.

"And there are the Bees,
   The ridiculous things,
Always working and buzzing,
   And shaking their wings.

"I have got an attack
   Of the nerves, with their humming;
It is almost as bad,
   As the Woodpecker's drumming.

"Around me is ever
   This worry and din,
Then I live in a fright
   That my floor will fall in:

"For Engineer Mole
   With his sharp scratching claws,
Is making a tunnel,
   Right under my paws."

Just then a small voice,
    From underground said,
"Good morrow, old grumbler,
    I am under your bed:

"When you miscall your neighbours
    So loudly don't speak,
I have very good hearing,
    Though my sight's rather weak."

He had scarcely done talking,
    When down from the hill
Came sliding some gravel,
    And when it stood still—

It had filled up the doorway
    Of Mr. Toad's house,
And fastened him in
    As a trap holds a mouse.

He panted and struggled,
    And thought he must die,
When up came the Mole
    At his piteous cry;

"Oh! dear Mr. Mole,"
    Said the Toad with a groan,
"Can you tunnel a way
    From under this stone."

"Oh! oh!" said the Mole,
    "You are growing polite,
When you want me to help you,
    Here out of your fright;

"I have heard that your people
    Can live in a stone,
You would like that, no doubt,
    You like living alone."

"Oh! dear Mr. Mole,
    Don't stand talking, but try
To make a hole out,
    Or I surely shall die."

"Well, well," said the Mole,
  "I will do what I can."
And to scratch a way out,
  In right earnest began:

And after a great deal
  Of panting and puffing,
And squeezing and groaning,
  And sighing and huffing,

The Toad made his way
  Through the dark narrow hole;
And waving his paw,
  Said, "Oh, dear Mr. Mole,

"You're the cleverest and kindest
  Of creatures I know,
I wish I had more
  Than mere thanks to bestow,

"But one thing I've learnt,
  It's a good thing to work,
And never a neighbourly
  Action to shirk;

"And the Field-mice may squeak,
  And the Bees they may hum,
And you may make tunnels,
  And I will be dumb."

The Discontented Stream

Far away amid the mountains,
    Underneath an aged thorn,
'Mid a tuft of emerald greenness,
    Once a tiny stream was born.

With no noise it bubbled upward,
    Then it gently slid away,
Hollowing out its rocky channel,
    Through long ages day by day.

Sometimes round the stones it fretted,
    Turning, twisting, here and there,
Sometimes over pebbles rippling,
    Making them as jewels fair.

Then again, 'twas almost hidden
    By the heather and the fern;
And the shy birds of the moorland
    Drank from out the tiny burn.

Wider grown, through fields it wandered,
    And beside its grassy edge,
The reed warblers built their nests
    Amongst the bulrush and the sedge.

Underneath moss covered bridges,
    Past the village and the farm,
Still it hurried onward, onward,
    Never resting, never calm.

From its home amid the mountains,
    Underneath the old thorn tree;
Through the moorland and the meadow,
    On it went to find the sea.

Thus for ages, long, long ages,
    It had wandered on its way;
When one hot and sultry summer
    The reed warblers heard it say:

"Ever flowing, ever flowing,
    To the wild and solemn sea,
Am I never to be tranquil,
    All things seem to rest but me.

"I am weary of this movement,
    Of this never-ceasing flow;
I should like to stop and listen,
    Or watch the flowers and rushes grow."

Then a voice came murmuring softly
    From the willow over head,
"Think not of thy pleasure, streamlet,"
    Thus the bending branches said:

"Thou wert made for ceaseless motion,
    Ever to the sea to tend;
I was made, nor murmur at it,
    All my life o'er thee to bend."

But the stream still murmured sadly,
    "Would, oh! would that I might rest,"
"To lie stagnant, dull, and weedy,
    Streamlet, would not make thee blest,"

Said the yellow globe flowers to it,
    As it hurried murmuring past;
But the day, so longed for, hoped for,
    To the streamlet came at last.

It was turned into a hollow,
    Banked and hidden from the view;
And no more the waving willow,
    Or the wild flowers near it grew.

It was still, and black, and silent,
    Slimy weeds upon it spread;
Loathsome newts and tadpoles filled it;
    But fair creatures from it fled.

Wicked Jack-o-lanthorns loved it,[9]
    And on dark and misty nights
Danced, and gambolled round, and o'er it,
    With their false and flitting lights.

And if poor benighted wanderers,
    Thinking it was cottage fire,
Trusting, followed the bad elfins,
    They were lost amidst the mire.

Noisome vapours o'er it hovered,
    And men shunned the doleful spot;
Thus was lost the mountain streamlet
    That had murmured at its lot!

---

9 Jack-o-lanthorns: sometimes called Will-o'-the wisp, this is a popular name for the phenomenon properly called ignis fatuus, a phosphorescent light seen hovering or flitting over marshy ground caused by the combustion of flammable gasses released from decaying matter (n. 'ignis fatuus' OED).

Little Prince Bepettedbyall[10]

Once upon a time, there lived a little boy who was called Prince Bepettedbyall; his house was in one of the Fairylands,—for you must know there are a great many Fairylands besides that you read of, in the dear old books, that all children love so much,—all except those very dull boys and girls, who can only read the very biggest fact print, and can never look inside anything.

Oh! yes, there is the Fairyland of the dear old books, where the trees are made of emeralds and the apples are gold, and where the lady fairies sleep on rose leaves, and the baby fairies swing in hammocks of gossamer, and the fairy soldiers have arms of thistle down, and rise on dragon flies when they go to battle.

Then there is the Fairyland of the brave-hearted Northmen, where the palaces are built of glittering Icebergs, and the little Gnomes dig and hammer in the mines of silver and gold, and laugh and grin at any unlucky mortal who has strayed into their caverns; and threaten to pour molten metal down his throat, or to pinch off his nose with their hot tongs,—all in joke you know, for they are very good natured little dwarfs after all, with their big heads, and funny short crooked legs, at which they laugh themselves quite as much, as they laugh at anybody else.

Oh! they are merry mischievous little fellows, these Gnomes of the Northern Mountains; and they watch year by year the beautiful metals and the glittering crystals as they grow deep down in the caverns of the rocks; and they dig them out, and make jewels and drinking cups of them for the King of the Gnomes, who lives in the middle of a mountain near the North Pole; and sometimes they make channels in the mountains, and pour metal into them, and then if any men find it they dig it out, and are very glad they have discovered it; and one learned man says it was made so and so; and another learned man contradicts him, and says, "No! these rocks and metals have been made 'so and so,'" and they get angry and quarrel about it, and all the time the little Gnomes laugh and chuckle, and say, "Listen to these mortals, who think themselves so wise, what nonsense they talk, and how they quarrel and contradict each other."

Sometimes, when they are in a very good humour, they will take a pocket full of precious stones, and pour them into a stream, or put them in a hole for some poor man to find and sell, to buy food for his little children. Oh! they are not bad fellows, the little crooked legged Gnomes.

Another Fairyland is the Fairyland of the Greedy Children; where the houses are built of sugar-candy, and the walls are of hardbake and butter-scotch, and the trees are all of barley-sugar, and the streams are ginger beer and cowslip wine, and the snow turns to whipped cream, and the rain to new milk!

But that Fairyland is very near the country of Physic-cum-headache,—a very ugly place indeed, where the sand is Gregory's powder,[11] and the lakes are filled with Black

---

10 The name of 'Little Prince Bepettedbyall' and the place name 'Allroundaboutus' echo the naming of Mrs Doasyouwouldbedoneby and the Doasyoulikes by Charles Kingsley (1819–75) in *The Water-Babies* (1863).

11 Gregory's powder: a compound powder of rhubarb, magnesia and ginger, prescribed as a laxative and unpleasant to taste.

draught,[12] and smell worse than the Thames or the Cam at Cambridge, or the fountains in Kensington Gardens![13]

And last of all, there is the country of Allroundaboutus, the most lovely of all the Fairylands; only so many people who live there are blind, and never see any of the beautiful things that surround them, or hear the sweet sounds that are for ever murmuring round them: for the winds make Æolian harps of the trees, and play, oh! such pleasant music on them; and the mountain streams do the same with the rocks they run over; and the flowers talk to each other, especially in an evening, just before they go to sleep in the twilight. The little blue "Forget-me-nots" on the edges of the still calm lakes, sing songs to the beautiful Water-lilies, as they float near them; and the words are about those who used to love them, perhaps most of all, for their sweet name: and when the oldest, the pink ones, have sung a verse, all the young blue ones then join in a chorus, and sing, "Forget-me-not, Forget-me-not." And the Water-lilies say, "No! we will not forget you, for you tell us of those who have passed away to the land of all Blessedness; those who always understand the music of the Fairyland in which they dwelt while here."

And so they all talk about the things they like the best, and that they think the most about. And some are very merry, and sing such funny songs; but it is only the very good tempered and happy children who can hear them.

The red Poppies throw their scarlet caps at the blue corn flowers, when the Harvest Moon is shining bright and clear, and say, "Come, you little blue jokers, practise the Harvest-Home song, and let us have a night of it." And then they get so noisy and play each other such jokes, that the grave ripe corn (especially the barley, which ought to be serious you know, for it is bearded like a patriarch), can scarcely get any sleep.

And then the trees, and flowers, and waters in the land of Allroundaboutus are so clever, they always tell the tales and sing the songs that suit the people best, who can hear them; I told you many people never can hear them, not in all their life, and will not believe that any one hears them; I wonder if you will hear their pleasant talk; I hope so, for it is a great pleasure.

Well, I was saying they are so clever in always talking at the right time and about the right things; they never tell sad stories to happy little boys and girls; nor joking ones to those who are in sorrow; they speak gently, oh! so gently, and sadly to those whose dear ones have gone away, and who will see them no more, till after many tears have been wept. Nor do they tell laughing tales to those who are studying the nature of wonderful plants, and rocks; and to some they sing grand hymns about the beginning of things; and to some they tell the story of the past, of the long, long ages gone, of that far off time when monstrous creatures alone lived on this earth, and men were none.

But I was going to tell you about the little Prince Bepettedbyall, and instead of that I have been telling about Fairy lands; so now I will begin again, and tell you about him.

Well, I think it must have been in the land of Allroundaboutus that he lived. He had a great many people to take care of him, as a little Prince Bepettedbyall was sure to have, and better far than most little Princes, he had a great many people who loved him.

There were the three head Gouvernantes,[14] the first of whom was the Lady Cecilia, who saw that he was properly clothed and fed. He was never allowed to go into the Land of Greedy Children, to chip bits off the rocks of hardbake, and break the branches

---

12 Black draught: a commonly used saline purgative.
13 [Poet's Note: Written before the improvements.]
14 Gouvernantes: governesses, or female teachers (n. 'gouvernante' *OED*).

of the sugar-candy trees, because if he had, a creature all covered with black cloth, who drove about in a sort of chariot, would have carried him away to the land of Physic-cum-headache, and perhaps have kept him there for several days, or even it might be weeks, for it is often very hard indeed to get away from that ugly country. She had also to watch lest the Ice-King or the Frost-Giant should touch him, and pinch his hands and feet, till they were stiff and red, which they will do if they can catch little children out of doors at Christmas without their warm gaiters and mittens on. And if the North-Wind,—or his worse brother, the East-Wind came holloaing by, frightening all the poor little Spring flowers that had just peeped out of the ground to look at the sun, and say, "Good day, little Bepettedbyall;" Lady Cecilia would say, "You must ride on your rocking-horse to-day, and I will tell you stories, but you must not go out, to fight with the North-Wind: why he has just come back from freezing the sea for the Ice-King at the North Pole, and getting his fleet of ice-bergs ready for him to sail down and crush the whale ships,—once they nearly crushed to pieces the ship in which one of your Uncles was going to a country a long way from here; so we do not like the Ice-King's fleet, though they are beautiful to look at."

Then there was the Lady Bienaimée, who taught him what things he might play with, and what things he was not to touch, and he soon learnt to know that he was not to take the King his father's books off the shelves in the library, and build houses of them, as he did with his wooden bricks; and she taught him too, not to begin to scream when he saw the sous-gouvernante, Mananeta, descend the staircase to conduct him to his own apartments.

The Lady Rosina's principal duty was to play and sing to him when he was too tired to care for his toys.[15]

He had a wonderful animal, on which he rode when the weather was fine; it had four legs, and a long tail to switch off the flies, and soft short grey hair, and a brown mark across its shoulders, and *rather* long ears: I am obliged to say also that it had not a pleasant voice; but Bepettedbyall was very fond of it, though sometimes I am sorry to say, if he had a cane in his hand—for he did not always carry a sceptre about with him, as little Princes do in the Fairylands of the dear old books;—no, he only carried a cane, and sometimes he struck Asswoolly—that was the animal's name—a sharp blow on its head, that made it put its rather long ears down and start off quite suddenly, so fast that Prince Bepettedbyall would fall upon its neck, and have to clutch at the housings that covered it, lest he should come tumbling down upon the ground; and you may imagine what a fright he looked, doubled up on Asswoolly's back like a bundle made of a pillow, and a hat and jacket, and a pair of boots!

Then Lady Bienaimée would say to him, "You are justly punished for being so unkind, and I hope whenever you are cruel, as you were just now, that Asswoolly will treat you in the same way."

But I think he was not often unkind to anything, or the beautiful little creature with wings, that lived in the grove near the Palace, would not have come to him, ye it did so, and whenever he came near its home it would spread out its pretty wings and come to look at

---

15 If Little Prince Bepettedbyall is read as being Cecil Wedgwood, it is likely that the names and characters of these 'Gouvernantes' are based on female companions of Cecil and the Hawkshaw family – possibly Cecil's aunts. For instance, it is feasible that 'Lady Cecilia' is a reference to Cecily Hawkshaw, wife of Ann's eldest son, John Clarke, and therefore Cecil's aunt. 'Bienaimée' translates as 'beloved', and with Ann's youngest daughter Editha referred to as 'beloved' in *Poems for My Children*, it is possible that 'Lady Bienaimée' is a reference to Editha – also Cecil's aunt. No immediate connection can be made between the Hawkshaw or Wedgwood families and the name 'Rosina'.

him and speak to him; its voice was very sweet, but he could not understand what it said, because it belonged to another world, not to his world, of which he had not yet learned the language, but he liked its pleasant voice.

Sometimes he was taken for a short time to stay in the City of the World[16]—an immense City, and containing more wonderful things than were to be found in the Cities of the Arabian Nights; I think even Sinbad, who had seen so many strange places, would have been astonished if he had been taken by some Jin and put down in the middle of the City of the World, and would have exclaimed, "By Allah, this is wonderful! the noise of this multitude of people is like the sound made by the Army of the King of the Jins as they pass over the desert."[17]

But the soft low voices of the land of Allroundaboutus are almost lost in the great sounds of that mighty City, and I think the little Prince, when he was very young, liked better to be in his own Fairyland, amongst the trees and flowers that he understood.

I think this is all I can tell at present about Prince Bepettedbyall; he is now growing so tall that I fear he will soon have to leave his own pleasant land: and if he does, I hope he will go and live in the country that many of his relations inhabit, which is a very beautiful land too, and where he can listen to the stories that the rocks and the forests tell.

The Noontide Dream

A little child sat on the grass,
And as he watched the shadows pass,
From the clouds above his head,
Softly to himself he said:
"I do not like the shadows flitting

---

16 City of the World: London.
17 Jin: in Muslim demonology, an order of spirits lower than the angels, said to have the power of appearing in human and animal forms, and to exercise supernatural influence over men (n. 'jinn' *OED*).

O'er the place where I am sitting;
Chasing the sunbeams up the hill,
And making all so sad and chill;
What were clouds made for I wonder,
Are they meant to hold the thunder,
Or palaces the Rain-King makes,
And the angry North-Wind breaks—
When the Ice-King sends him forth,
From his snow-lands in the north,—
Where the walrus has its home,
And the savage white bears roam."
    Softly to himself thus talking,
While the shadows danced and played;
    Sleep came o'er him gently stealing,
On the thyme his head was laid:
And a thousand fairy faces,
That were ever changing places,
Dancing here, and resting there,
    Flitted round him, whispering wonders,
That they saw on land and sea;
    "Where Niagra foams and thunders,"
Thus they say: "At home are we,
On the crest of ocean billows,
On the dancing stream, where willows
    In the summer noontide quiver,
On the dewdrops of the morning,
    That the gossamer hath strung;
When the autumn day is dawning—
We can dance, if but our King
Far away the clouds will fling:
For we vanish, one and all,
When cloud-shadows o'er us fall;
All the flowers our empire own
    Pale, and colourless, and weak,
They will tell you, they must be
    Without us; could you hear them speak:
Listen, mortal child, and try
To hear the voices passing by:
Voices, that for ever sound
All this wondrous world around."
Then he saw them, hand-in-hand,
On the bank beside him stand;
One was clothed in robe of blue,
Another had the rose's hue,
And for ever mixing, blending,
Each to each her colours lending,
Till at last they all were blent

In one dazzling element;
And they smiling, sped away—
And a warm and sunny ray
Woke the child from out his sleep
That had been so soft and deep.

The Squirrel that forgot that it would be Winter
A Story of Hollycombe in 1866[18]

There was a little Squirrel once,
    Lived in a Tulip-tree;
As merry a little fellow
    As ever you did see:

His tail was long and bushy,
    His fur was thick and soft,
And he had a nest within a hole,
    In the branches up aloft.

All summer he had played about,
    And never food had wanted,
Though he did not meddle with the trees
    That Grandpapa had planted:[19]

---

18 Hollycombe House, the Hawkshaws' country residence, is pictured in the line drawing accompanying this poem. As a child Cecil Wedgwood spent time here with his grandparents.
19 Grandpapa: John Hawkshaw (1811–91).

He did not nibble off the shoots
    Of Dolly's cedar tree,[20]
Or gnaw the Wellingtonia
    That dear Cecil's is to be.

But he cracked the nice sweet beech nuts,
    And scampered o'er the grass,
And gathered up the acorns brown—
    But then, alas! alas!

He quite forgot that summer days
    And autumn nuts don't last;
And quite forgot how he must live
    When the pleasant time was past.

November days were short and chill,
    But yet upon the ground
An acorn, or a chestnut,
    By searching well he found.

But after that, December came,
    And the wind sighed wild and drear;
He listened, but no Robin's song
    Could little Frisky hear:

Nought but the sighing of the wind
    The leafless branches through,
Or the whirring of the pheasant cock
    As past his hole it flew.

Then Christmas came, and white and thick
    The snow lay on the ground,
And not an acorn or a nut
    Could anywhere be found.

He tried to sleep—but in the morn
    A faint and sickly ray
Of sunshine, crept into his hole,
    And told him it was day.

So down the tree he slowly came,
    And crept along the snow,
And o'er the lawn, and o'er the fence
    To where the beech trees grow—

---

20 Dolly: this is a likely abbreviation of Dorothy; a reference to the Hawkshaws' young granddaughter Dorothy (b. 1866), daughter of John Clarke and Cecily Hawkshaw, and thus Cecil's young cousin.

Beside the croquet ground—for there
    His cousin Flosky dwelt;
And very humbly on the snow,
    Poor little Frisky knelt.

"I'm very hungry, cousin Flos,
    And you have such a store
Of nuts and acorns in your hole,
    Do let me have a score:

"I'll pay them back next year, dear cos,
    I will indeed, and try
Not to forget in summer days
    How quickly they go by."

When Flosky heard his cousin call,
    He never said a word,
Pretending to be fast asleep,
    And that he nothing heard.

He crept down farther in his hole
    Among the nice warm hay,
And thought: I will not make a noise,
    And then he'll go away.

Poor Frisky listened,—but in vain,
    He pricked up both his ears,
His heart grew very sad indeed,
    His eyes were full of tears.—

He wiped them with his furry tail,
    And then he said, "I'll try
To find a bit of twig to eat:
    None can me that deny."

So slowly o'er the fence he crept,
    And o'er the lawn again,
He was so hungry, and so cold,
    To walk was quite a pain.

But Frisky, when he reached his home,
    Screamed out in pure delight,
And clapped his little paws, and danced
    Quite frantic with delight.

For Bridger, with his broom had swept
    A place quite clean and bare,
And Grandpapa had put a heap
    Of maize and barley there.

He ate a little barley first,
    And then he tried the maize;
"Oh dear," he said, "I have not had
    Such food for many days."

Then up into his hole he took
    A store, to last till spring,
When well he knew the buds would burst,
    And the little birds would sing;

And the sunshine on the soft green leaves,
    Would play and rest by turn,
And noiselessly unfolding too,
    Would grow the lady fern.

"How good," he said, "it was to put
    That nice sweet food for me,
I'll never nibble off a shoot
    Again of any tree."

The Ambitious Water-Lily

Once embosomed by high mountains,
    On which giant pine trees grew,
Lay a lovely quiet lakelet
    With its waters of deep blue.

Water-fowl from many countries,
    Built their nests upon its shore,
For by man 'twas unfrequented,
    Nor disturbed by dipping oar.

On one side high crags enclosed it,
    That the ivies clothed with green,
And in every nook and crevice
    Tufts of feathery fern were seen.

Stones, that centuries had rounded,
    Were upon the other hand;
And like gold dust in the sunshine,
    Glittered the low banks of sand.

There the bramble's* shining berries,[21]
    And its graceful leaves were spread,
While the hardy mountain ashes,
    Waved their branches over head.

But though mortal never crossed it,
    Oft was seen a fairy boat—
By the wild birds in the twilight,
    O'er its stilly waves to float.

In it stood a tiny lady:
    Not more beautiful than she
Were the daughters of the Genii,
    Or the Peris of the Sea.

Shining, glistening, in the sunset:
    Gleaming pale when moonlight fell,
Skimmed her pearly vessel onward,
    Fashioned like an Ocean Shell.

---

21 [Poet's Note: *The beautiful Stone Bramble.]

All things knew her, all things loved her,
   Birds and wild flowers of the glen;
All like her that lived with nature,
   Far away from haunts of men.

In the shallows of the lakelet
   Was the Water-Lily's home:
There for years had she been floating,
   And had never wished to roam.

But one day she drooped in sorrow,
   Closed her flowers, and sighing, said:
"Wasted life, to dwell for ever
   On this lake's unnoticed bed."

"Lily of these lovely waters,
   Art thou weary of thy lot,
That all other flowers have envied?"
   Said the meek Forget-me-not.

"Ah! thou know'st not, simple floweret,"
   Said the Water-Lily then,
"That my kinsfolk live in splendour
   Where are found the haunts of men;—

"One wears a Crown Imperial,—one
   Is Royal, the proud Fleur-de-lys;
A Sultan's cap another boasts,
   And I am—what? alas! for me—

"I am but Nymphea Alba,—only
   The White Maiden of the lake!"
"And what sweeter, dearer title,
   Could men give, or could'st thou take?

"But who told thee of thy kindred,
   And about the homes of men:
I have come all down the burnside
   From the source above the glen—

And I never heard these histories?"—
   Then the Lily waved with pride,
And turned scornfully, and proudly,
   From the pale flower at her side.

"What shouldst thou know of the great world?
   Who would care to tell to thee
Of the lands o'er which they wander,
   Or the wondrous things they see?

"When the Wild Geese came last season,
   To encamp beside our lake,
One of them came swimming near me,
   First he bowed, and then he spake:

"Princess!—Yes, he called me Princess,—
   What a dreary lot is thine,
I should pine away and perish
   In a month—if it were mine.

"Then he told me of the countries
   Where my noble kinsfolk dwell,
In the garden of the Rose Queen,
   For she loves them passing well.

"And he said that I was fairer
   Than the fairest of them all,
Lovelier that the Royal Lily—
   Though perhaps not quite so tall."

"So it was the Wild Goose told thee
   Of the countries far away,
If they are so grand and glorious,
   Had he not there better stay?

"Do not listen to his gossip,
   Babbler he hath ever been:"
Then she paused—"See, down the waters
   Comes our lovely Fairy Queen."

"It is well," the Lily answered,
   "I will ask of her a boon,
And if granted, in the great world,
   Oh! what joy, I shall be soon."

When the Queen heard her petition,
   Mournfully she turned away,
Sighing said, "Thy boon, oh! Lily,
   Shall be granted in a day."

The next morning, down the mountains,
    Ere the flowers were half awake,
Came a man, the first that ever
    Had approached that lovely lake.

Eagerly he seized the Lily—
    Then for miles and miles he sped,
Till at last he smiling placed it
    In a garden fountain's bed.

Dark and muddy was the water,
    Thick and sooty was the air,
For the smoky, giant city,
    Blighted all of beauty there.

One by one the Lily's petals
    Browned and withered ere they spread,
And its leaves discoloured, shrivelled,
    Sank within their muddy bed:

And the owner of the garden
    Seized and flung it o'er the wall,
And amid a bed of nettles
    Did the Water-Lily fall.

There it very soon had perished,
    But a little boy (I think
It might be Cecil) saw and took it
    To a pretty brooklet's brink:

And there threw it in the water,
    Where it grew—but never more
Did it bloom in snowy beauty,
    As beside the still lake's shore!

The Fairy Gift; or, The Iron Bracelet

Once upon a time;—that is the way all Fairy Stories used to begin,—once upon a time, there lived a little boy called Fritz, his home was on the banks of the beautiful stream that came tumbling over the rocks at the back of the hut in which he and his Grandfather dwelt, for Fritz had no parents, but had always lived with his Grandfather, who earned his livelihood by catching fish in the stream, and selling it to the great lords and ladies who lived in the castles in the neighbourhood; when he was not fishing, he cultivated a small garden, in which Fritz helped him: that was their work in summer, but after all the vegetables had been stowed away, and the dried fish had been hung up on the rafters of the hut, for it was but a hut in which they lived, though it was always very clean, they sat by the fire during the long evenings, making wooden toys for children.

But Fritz never found it dull, for his kind old Grandfather told him stories of all the wonderful countries he had seen when he was a young man, and a soldier; he taught Fritz to read and write, as well as to make the little wooden toys which he sold in the spring to the children at the castles around, and Fritz was very obedient to his dear old Grandfather whom he loved very much.

He had one pet, a beautiful cat, he had found it one day when it was a kitten, nearly starved and half drowned, for some cruel person had thrown it into the stream, but it had fallen amongst the reeds and rushes near the bank, and so Fritz was able to get it out; it was nearly dead with wet, and hunger, and fright, but he took it home and gave it some warm milk, and wrapped it up in an old jacket, and put it near the fire, and it soon got well, and grew to be the most beautiful cat that was ever seen in that country; and the cruel man who had thrown it into the stream wanted to buy it, that he might give it to the Wife of the great Lord under whom he lived, in order to gain her favour, but Fritz would not part with his favourite for any money, though he was poor, and money would have bought him many things he would have liked to have.

It happened one day, as Fritz was playing by the side of the stream, he saw something bright, glittering in the sun; it was hanging on a reed by the edge of the river, where he was just able to reach it with a little stick he had in his hand, when he got it on to the bank and looked at it, he clapped his hands and quite shouted for joy: it was a small gold girdle, most beautifully made, for it was as soft and flexible as a ribbon, though it was set with the finest diamonds and emeralds and rubies. Fritz knew that they were precious stones, for sometimes when he went to sell fish or toys at the castle, he saw the great lady there, and she wore a girdle round her waist, and a circlet on her head, set with pearls that were very beautiful—but they were not to be compared with these.—It was not likely that they should be, for this tiny belt belonged to the Queen of the Fairyland nearest to Fritz's home, and the Gnomes of the mountains had been twenty years collecting them for her; but Fritz did not know that till long afterwards, he only thought what a great deal of money he could sell them for, and what a nice cottage he would build for himself and his Grandfather, and how he would hire a man to fish and to dig the garden, and let the poor old man rest all the remainder of his life.

So he took the beautiful girdle and wrapped it up in his blouse, and ran home as fast as ever he could. His Grandfather had gone to a town some miles off to buy twine to make fishing nets of, and would not return that night, so Fritz had no one to shew his treasure to but Pussy, who was asleep on his Grandfather's easy chair; he called out as soon as he got into the house, "Wake up, Silky Paws," that was her name, "wake up and see what I have found, and when I have sold the gems, you shall have a red collar with a silver bell to it, that you shall, dear old Silky Paws."

And Pussy got up and pawed, and opened her great round eyes, and stared as he shook the glittering thing before her, but I do not think she understood anything about it, and would have thought a nice shining fish just caught in the stream a much lovelier sight. For a cat, however handsome and good it may be, can only have a cat's mind, and a cat's taste.

Finding that Pussy did not care to look at his treasure, he took it into the little closet in which he slept, and put it on the window seat close to his bed, and then gave Silky Paws her supper, which she liked much better than fine jewels.

It was a beautiful moonlight night, and the last thing Fritz saw before going to sleep was the moonlight streaming through the window, and falling on the fairy girdle. He had not been long asleep before he was awakened by some one quite close to him repeating his name; the voice was very low and sweet, yet it awoke him completely, and he started up in bed, and looked in the direction from which the sound came, and in the window seat where lay the girdle, he saw, standing upon the moon-beam, on which she had glided down from Cloudland, where she had been to visit some of her distant relations,—the Fairy Queen herself. She was so beautiful, and smiled so sweetly, that Fritz was not at all afraid, though he had never seen any lady before so very, very small, or dressed in such curious clothes, for her robe was of gossamer, worn over a petticoat of the rarest pink rose petals, her mantle was of the richest purple heartsease, trimmed with the white silky down of the marsh cotton grass, necklace of dewdrops, with a photograph suspended from it of the Fairy King, done on water by a new process, head-dress of humming-bird plumes, train of the phosphorescence of the sea—a perfectly new discovery of the court milliners—hair powdered with star dust, to give the fashionable tint. I know I am quite correct about her costume, for it had appeared in the Fairy Court Journal just before.

Fritz waited respectfully for her to speak first, and at length she said, after looking at the girdle at her feet: "I have come, little boy, to ask you to give me back the girdle that you found by the river to-day, for it is mine."

Fritz ventured to say, "But, Madam, who told you I had found it, there was no person near when I took it off the reeds?"

"Oh!" she replied, "I do not need mortals to tell me what I want to know. I am the Fairy Queen, and I understand the language of the birds, and the insects, and the flowers, and the trees, and I ask them when I want to know anything. A King-fisher, who was standing on a stone in the middle of the river, watching for minnows, saw me drop my girdle as I was floating past to visit my cousins in Sunset land; as it was nothing he could eat, the greedy creature, he told a Water-Ouzel about it, and he, glad to have a bit of news to repeat, told it to the Sky-lark, who was just quitting her nest to take her daily exercise high up in the soft evening air, and she waited to tell me as I came down,—for, though she flies high, she cannot reach Cloudland, as we fairies can; but when I came to the river, my girdle was gone, so I enquired of the reeds what had become of it? but the reeds are more clever at singing or sighing than observing, and they sung something, of which the only words I could distinguish, were 'Lost, lost, lost,'—so I turned from them, to the bright, wide-awake, yellow water-lilies, that keep their heads above the water, and their eyes open, and they told me at once that the little boy Fritz, who lived in the hut close by, had taken it away."

Fritz thought: I will pull up those tattling water-lilies to-morrow, and throw them on the bank for telling, but he did not dare to say so,—and it was wrong of him to want to keep the jewel now that he knew to whom it belonged; but you see it was a great temptation for him to wish to keep it, for he was very poor, and wished so much to get nice things for his old Grandfather; but it was only for a moment or two that these bad thoughts remained in his mind, and he took up the girdle and held it to the Fairy, saying, "It is yours, I must not keep what is not my own."

Then she smiled very pleasantly on him, and clasped it round her waist, and said, "I will leave you a gift, which you must never part with until you are a very old man." And then she glided up the moonbeam and was gone.

When she was out of sight, Fritz jumped out of bed to see what she had left him instead of the beautiful belt, and he was very much disappointed and ready to cry when he saw it was only an iron bracelet; it was made with great care, but still it was only iron. He threw it down on the ground at first, but after a while he thought, the Fairy Queen would not give me a thing that was worthless, she is too good to ridicule and insult me, when I have given her back the girdle she prizes so much. I will do as she told me, and put this bracelet on, and never part with it till I am a very old man, too old to work.

So Fritz clasped it on his right arm and fell asleep again, and dreamed wonderful dreams of gold and gems hidden in the mountains, of which he was filling a basket—when, with a tremendous noise, a side of the cavern fell down, and a door made all of one diamond flashed on him, and he awoke with a great start, and found the morning sun shining full on his face through the little window, and his Grandfather knocking with his big oak stick on the door. Then Fritz jumped up quickly, and opened the door for the old man, who wondered to have found him asleep after the sun had risen, for he did not know the boy had been kept awake in the night talking to the Fairy.

Now it happened some weeks after this, that the old fisherman died, and Fritz was left all alone in the hut, with no one in the whole world to care for him. And after the people in the valley had buried his Grandfather, he sat down by the fire very sad, wondering what he must do;—at last he determined to go to the castle and ask if they would give him work, he did not mind how hard he worked if he could only earn enough to buy him food and clothing, for he was strong and hated to be idle; but during that night, a terrible thunder-storm came on, and the river, swollen by the heavy rain, overflowed its banks, and the water began to pour into the hut, and at the same time a flash of lightning set fire to the thatch; poor Fritz had only just time to escape through the window, and began to scramble up the rocky hill at the back of the house, when he saw Silky Paws near the door, who was so terrified at the sight of the water that she could not move for fear, but stood on a stone mewing piteously. Fritz saw her from the place he had climbed to, and could not bear to watch his poor favourite perish, so he slid down the hill again, and waded to where she was, he was only just in time to save her, for the water was commencing to wash over the stone on which she stood, and in a few minutes she would have been drowned; the water reached now as high as Fritz's knees, and he sometimes feared he should be washed away, but he struggled on, and at last got to the top of the hill, and sat down to rest; the sun had just risen, and Fritz took off his wet clothes and spread them on a rock to dry, and then he looked round to see if there was any way for him to cross the valley, but he could discover none, it looked like a great lake instead of the fertile place he used to know so well: all the corn had been washed away, and great trees torn up by the roots; the torrents were dashing down with a frightful noise, and soon he saw his old home, where he had been so happy for years, washed down, and whirled away by the roaring waters.

From the top of the rocky hill up which Fritz had with difficulty climbed, stretched a wild desolate plain, covered with broken masses of stone, among which grew here and there furze bushes, tufts of heather, and some plants of bilberries, whose fruit was then ripe. It was a dreary prospect Fritz had to look at, when the sun was high enough in the sky for him to see objects distinctly:—on one side, the roaring, foaming waters, twirling round the uprooted pine trees, that had got fast together in great heaps, or bearing onward fragments of peasant's cottages that had been washed away; on the other side of him, further than his eye could reach, lay the barren, pathless heath, quite unknown to him, but which was nevertheless his only way of safety.

But he was a brave boy, and had been accustomed to a life of hardship, so when the sun had dried his clothes, he put them on, and taking pussy under his arm, he started off. In the pocket of his jacket he found a piece of bread, and when he was tired with walking, he sat down on the dry heather, and having gathered some bilberries, made a hearty meal—at least he thought it one. Silky Paws sat on a stone in the sunshine purring so contentedly that I suspect she too had found a dinner of a field mouse or little bird, however I cannot be sure about that, at all events she did not seem to want any of her master's.

Then they trudged on again, and after some hours walking, they found a narrow footpath, the sight of it cheered Fritz, for he thought rightly that it must lead to some dwelling, and so it did; after a while it became wider and more trodden, and just as it began to grow dark he saw before him a bright light: such a light as he had never seen before. His Grandfather had told him of burning mountains that he had seen when he was in distant countries, and at first he thought the flames he saw shooting up to the dark sky must come from a volcano, but as he drew nearer, he saw it was not a mountain, but a large building that was before him, and the fire came from large furnaces; he crept slowly and quietly to the door and peeped in.—He saw a number of men watching the iron that was being smelted in the furnaces, big strong men, with faces and hands very black indeed. Fritz was at first rather frightened when he saw them, but he had become very cold and hungry, and so at last he ventured in, and asked very humbly if he might warm himself near one of the fires? One of the men asked him gruffly, "What he wanted, and where he came from?" So he told them his sad little story, and shewed them his beautiful pussy, who had jumped out of his arms and was sitting winking with her large green eyes at the great fire.

The men, though they were rough in manners, and had loud voices, were not unkind in heart, and one of them, who had a boy about the age of Fritz, who had gone to be a sailor, and was then far away on the seas, felt pity for the poor friendless boy, and said, "Here, my lad, sit down on this old rug and rest yourself, and you shall have some supper,—for I will answer for it that you are ready for a good meal,—for a crust of bread and bilberries makes but a poor dinner."

The tears came into Fritz's eyes at such unlooked-for kindness, and he sat down by the fire and ate his supper, and the good man gave some to Silky Paws: and then told Fritz he might sleep there if he did not meddle with anything, which he promised not to do, and soon he was fast asleep.

The next morning the master of the workmen came, and seeing Fritz, asked who he was, and having heard his history, said he might stay and work for him; at this Fritz was very glad, and though at first he was rather awkward and often got scolded, he tried so hard to do right, and was so wishful to please everybody, and was so truthful and honest, that he became a great favourite with the men and with their master too; every one liked him—except one surly, dark browed man, who was indeed a thief, though no one suspected him of being one. The reason he hated Fritz so much was, that one day when he was hiding some pieces of metal which he intended to take away when it was dark, Fritz came by the place, and the bad man thought the boy must have seen what he was doing, and would perhaps tell of him; he could not, however, be quite sure that Fritz did see him, or I am afraid he would have taken some cruel means to have got rid of him that very night,—but settled in his own mind that he would soon get rid of the poor stranger. Now it happened that Fritz had not seen what the man was doing, and was besides so honest himself that he never thought of suspecting others of stealing; so for some time everything went on as usual;—but one morning there was a great consternation at the foundry, the men and boys were talking together in groups, and the master was in earnest conversation with Fritz's enemy in a distant part of the works: Fritz asked one of the boys what was the matter? who answered him very rudely: "Oh! you will know soon enough, little hypocrite!" and then turned away from him; at that instant, the man who had been first kind to him came up, and with grave and sad face told him to come along,—the master wanted him. When he came to where the master was, he was told, in a stern voice,—that he must instantly quit the works: "and, if it had not been for the entreaties of your good friend, who is one of my best and most honest workmen, I should have sent you to prison, you ungrateful, thievish boy!" said the master.

Poor Fritz was quite amazed, and for some time could not speak, but at last asked, in a trembling voice, what he had done wrong? "Perhaps you do not call it wrong to steal, look at these things:"—and he shewed him several valuable articles,—one a hunting knife, beautifully chased and enamelled, the master had lost some weeks before, and thought he had dropped it on his way home from the works at night. Fritz looked at the things, but did not understand any better than before what it all meant; when turning, he saw the eyes of the real thief fixed on his with a look of hatred, while a wicked smile was on his face, as he said to the poor boy: "Oh! oh! my fine lad, you do not know these pretty things, nor how they got into your box, tied up in an old handkerchief: they did not walk in of themselves did they? or maybe you will say Mrs Silky Paws put them there;—cats do quite as queer things as that, if all is true that the cooks say about them!"—and then he gave a cruel little laugh, which made poor Fritz's heart sink within him. "Indeed, indeed, I do not know how these things got into my box, Sir," he said humbly, but firmly, to his master; but no one believed him, and his master told him to begone instantly, to take his clothes and be off in ten minutes, or he should go to prison.

Before the ten minutes were passed, with his little bundle in his hand, and Silky Paws walking solemnly beside him, as if she knew he was in sorrow, poor Fritz again set out on his wanderings; his heart almost burst with indignation when the boys shouted and sneered at him as he passed: but what brought the tears into his eyes, was not their rudeness, but it was to see his kind old friend shake his head mournfully as he went by, for Fritz had hoped till then, that he at least would not believe him to be a thief!

When he got out of sight, he sat down on a stone and cried, and thought how forlorn and desolate he was: but that did not last long: "It is better to be wrongfully blamed," he said to himself, "than to be suffering now in my own mind for having *done* wrong; I have the fairy's gift yet, and somehow I think as long as I have that, I shall not starve or be very unhappy."

So Fritz took up Pussy, and putting a short stick through his bundle, he swung it on his shoulder and began to ascend a steep rocky hill; he was soon miles away from the foundry. He felt more cheerful as he went along; the day was fine, and the air that came blowing over the wide stony plain he had now reached was pure and bracing, and now he felt what a good thing it was that he had not been brought up in a life of idleness and luxury; the homely provisions in his bundle tasted delicious, as he sat on a stone at noon by a mountain-stream eating his dinner, while Pussy sat washing her face with her paws, and looking very contented, for she had shared her master's meal: and I have no doubt cats take a more cheerful view of cat-life when they have had a nice plentiful dinner,—and most little boys and girls are like them in that respect;—one cannot be very merry if one be very hungry.

Refreshed with his dinner and rest, Fritz started again: but the further he went, the wilder the country grew; he was on a great plain, strewn with huge pieces of rock, and full of noisy dashing streams that came down from the mountains that bounded his view; after walking a long time, he came to a narrow valley which formed an opening in the hills, and down which roared a wide deep river; he kept walking along the side of the water for some hours, and as night was coming on, and he saw no sign of any human being, for the first time he began to be afraid he should die of hunger and cold in that desolate place. Just as the twilight was darkening into night, and the stars were one after another peeping through the clear, dark, blue sky, he suddenly came to the end of the valley;—the mountains, far too high for him to climb, walled it in, and the river, on whose banks he had been walking, came down them with a noise like thunder,—and which he had thought, as he came up the valley, was thunder,—down it rushed, from ledge to ledge of rock, foaming and dashing as it had done for thousands of years; he saw there was no getting out of the valley that way, and with a sigh turned round to retrace his steps:—when, what was his astonishment and terror, to see no outlet now at the other end! It seemed as if the mountains had suddenly closed, and fastened him in.

Now he was really terrified, and the old Eastern stories his Grandfather used to tell him of wicked Jins and Efreets came into his mind,[22] and he thought some of them must have got out of the bottles in which Sulyman the Wise had fastened them up, to hinder them from doing evil;[23] and they have come to live in this dismal place, and will make a slave of me, and perhaps will kill poor Silky Paws:—oh! what shall I do? And for a while he wrung his hands in despair, and cried bitterly ... But catching a sight of his bracelet, his courage revived—"The good and beautiful fairy," he said to himself, "would never have given me this if it was not to be of some use to me: it may be a talisman against all the horrors of this place, or of the creatures that are in it.—I will walk quite to the end of the valley and see what is there." He did so, and found in the side of the mountain a large cavern, and going into it, saw a passage from it into another but smaller cave, into which he went, intending to sleep there, and then to try in the morning to find some opening through the mountains. So, putting his little bundle under his head for a pillow, he fell asleep—he was very tired and hungry, but he did not eat the piece of bread he had left, because he knew he should want it still more in the morning.

He had not been asleep long before he was awakened by a strange noise, that seemed to come from some cavern near him,—it was a sound of hammers: at first he thought he had been dreaming of working in the foundry, but listening a short time, he became certain it proceeded from some place near him; it was now evening, and twilight outside, but the cave in which he had taken shelter was quite dark; he raised his head, and then saw, at a great distance, a light, that looked scarcely bigger than a star, and the hammering came from that side: he got up, and felt with his hands all round the cave, till he came to an opening he had not noticed before; it was an archway in the rock, and led into a longer and loftier passage than the one he had come by, and at the end he saw the light gleaming and heard the noise more distinctly. Feeling his way along the side of the passage very carefully, he came at last to a small but beautiful arch, made of rock-crystal, to which the fire inside gave the appearance of ruby. Fritz was very much astonished, and looked cautiously into the cavern—to which the crystal arch was the entrance: and there a wonderful sight met his eyes, the cavern was of great size and very lofty, and many smaller ones opened into it, and before each of these hung curtains of woven gold, with borders of glittering gems: Fritz thought they were pieces of coloured glass when he saw them first, but he afterwards learned they were precious stones found in the middle of the mountains; in the large cavern were many little furnaces: it was from the fires underneath these that the light he had seen came from, though high above his head, swinging by golden chains, was a large lamp of the clearest crystal, in which rock oil was always burning.

---

22 Jins and Efreets: shape-changing spirits of Muslim demonology, referred to in short stories and folk tales from the Middle East such as *The Thousand and One Nights*, translated by Edward William Lane (1801–76) and published in three volumes between 1839 and 1841.

23 In *The Thousand and One Nights* the prophet Suleymán punishes Jins and Efreets by imprisoning them in bottles and casting them into the sea.

But it was not these strange sights that amazed him the most, it was the curious little beings who were busy working at the furnaces, poking at the fires, or taking up ladles full of the melted metal to see if it was ready to work; they had big heads, short bodies, and little crooked legs, and they laughed and chattered so much that they never heard Fritz's footsteps; and he was so surprised at what he saw, and at the funny appearance of the Gnomes, that he could not help laughing; at last one of them began to dance round and round, waving his ladle over his head, and he looked so comical that Fritz could restrain himself no longer, but burst into a loud laugh, which the echoes of the cavern repeated, till it seemed as if a dozen Fritzes were laughing: immediately there was a profound silence, and poor Fritz was frightened at what he had done, and sorry at being so rude; therefore, mustering all his courage, he walked into the middle of the cavern, and taking off his cap, made a very low bow to the Gnomes, who had all left their fires, and were standing together in a group:—"Who are you, and how did you get into the regions of the King of the Gnomes?" said one. Then Fritz told them his story, to which they listened very attentively. "We must take you to the King, and he will know whether your story of the Fairy Queen's gift is true or not, for he is a great friend of hers, and he is acquainted with the sort of gifts she bestows on mortals; it is about time for supper, so we will leave off work, and take you to his Majesty."

Then each one went behind one of the golden curtains to wash and dress, and they told Fritz where he could find some water to do the same, and by the time the Gnomes were ready he had put on his best clothes; and the little dwarfs seemed quite to approve of him, for he was a handsome, good-natured boy, and they nodded their big heads, and smiled, as much as to say, "We think he will do." Then they told him to follow them; and they passed behind the largest curtain that hung at the upper end of the cave; the cavern they now entered was entirely made of crystals of all colours, in the middle was a small fountain of pale green malachite,[24] full of the clearest and purest water, at the end of the cavern sat the King of the Gnomes, on a throne of gold, made in the shape of a dragon; its body made the seat, the two wings made the sides, and the scaly turned-up tail the back, and on the head with its wide open mouth the funny Gnome King rested his little feet; he had a sceptre that looked exceedingly like a shovel, and the shape of his crown was so much like the top of a pair of tongs that Fritz could not help thinking that the good dwarfs had borrowed the patterns for their regalia from the fire irons! Indeed, I believe the mischievous little fellows thought it was a good joke to make their sovereign have for ornament, what they had for use; before the King was a table, made of lapis lazuli,[25] covered with dishes, from which came very savoury odours, that made poor Fritz feel ten times more hungry than before; there was a great flagon of wine in the middle of the table, and beautiful cups placed by each plate, they were all alike except the King's, he had a goblet that blazed with rubies:—all the plates and dishes,—indeed everything on the table was of gold, and of the oddest forms! One great dish was like a turtle, and when you took off the upper part, you found it was full of turtle soup: another was like an ostrich egg in the middle of a dish of sand,—it was not sand, but gold dust, that had an omelette in it: the salt-cellar was in the shape of a nautilus shell: the pepper-box was the head of a man sneezing, as if he had got some of the pepper up his nose: and the vinegar-cruet was like a very thin woman, with such a long, spiteful, cross face, that one of the Gnomes, as soon as they were seated at table, turned it round, and hid it with the oil-flask, which was a jolly fat

---

24 malachite: a green-coloured, copper-based mineral (n. 'malachite' *OED*).
25 lapis lazuli: a bright-blue silicate mineral, containing sulphur (n. 'lapis lazuli' *OED*).

little Puck, with a basket of ripe olives. "The sight of that vinegar face would take away my appetite," said the Gnome, laughing;—"it was made, you must know, Master Fritz, by my brother yonder, when he had a fit of indigestion from eating too many brandy-balls, into which pounded diamonds had been put for loaf-sugar." Fritz looked very much astonished at any cook even in Gnomeland making such an odd mistake,—he had not learned what joking fellows the Gnomes were.

But before they sat down to supper, they all went and bowed to the King, one after another, at last came Fritz,—rather frightened. "Oh! oh!" said his Majesty, "whom have we here? how have you found your way to my dominions without a guide? I have sent no one lately up to that fool's land you come from, so you could not have had any one to shew you the way down here, young master."

Then Fritz, bowing very low, told his story; all the dwarfs stood round him and looked very pitiful, and hoped the King would believe him, as they did. "Let me look at the bracelet," said the King; so Fritz shewed it to him. "All right," exclaimed his majesty, "I have known that for many a year; the Fairy Queen will want it back some day, it has gone through many hands already. I dare say that respectable old antediluvian Tubal-Cain, who worked like us in metals, had it once on his brawny arm;[26]—but now it is time to sup, and the smell of that soup is enough to give any one an appetite without a twenty-four hours' fast, like thine, Fritz."

Then they sat down, and such a merry party they were: how they did laugh, and told such funny stories of the tricks they had played ill-natured people when they went up on the earth: they never teased the kind and good ones;—"We will pay off thy old enemy some day, Fritz," said one of them; but he answered he had rather they would help the workman who had been so good to him. "Oh! thou shalt do that thyself some day if thou canst keep thy bracelet," said the King. Fritz thought it was very unlikely that he should ever be able to assist anyone, but as it would have been unpolite for a boy like him to contradict the Gnome King he contented himself with thinking it only.

At last this merry supper was over, and as Fritz was wondering who would clear away the things, and was going to offer to do it himself, he saw the table move itself gently on one side; a table running about was not at all a wonderful thing down in Gnomeland, but as Fritz did not live in our country, and had never heard of Mr. Home, he was very much astonished.[27] As soon as the table was on a nice slope, all the dishes began to move off,—the great soup dish went flapping and floundering away first, then the omelette dish rolled off, but went so fast that it knocked over a neat little frog dish that was hopping quite gracefully away; the fowl dishes flew off, so they could have done without the table being tilted; the cruet tumbled head-over-heels as if he were a real Robin Goodfellow,[28]

---

26 Tubal-Cain: a descendant of Cain in the Old Testament, Tubal-Cain is referred to as 'an instructor of every artificer in brass and iron' (Genesis 4:22).

27 Mr Home: Daniel Dunglas Home (1833–86), spiritualistic medium. Participants in his séances reported a number of phenomena, including the moving of furniture and objects that moved unaided through the air. Invitations to his sittings were in high demand. Elizabeth Barrett Browning and her husband Robert were amongst those who attended Home's séances in London during the 1850s: Robert Browning later lampooned Home in 'Mr Sludge, "the Medium"' (1864).

28 Robin Goodfellow: a mischievous sprite or goblin believed to haunt the countryside (n. 'Robin Goodfellow' OED).

the pepper and mustard went one after the other sulkily, and the sour-faced vinegar-cruet marched off alone, the salt-cellar sailed past her without notice;—you see these five were often compelled to be together against their inclinations: indeed they had often to be beaten to make them agree at all.

When all had gone off to the pantry, the table turned itself upside down, slowly ascended to the top of the cave and rested there, till it should be wanted again next day. How very convenient it would be in small London rooms if the furniture would put itself away as it does in Gnomeland, and give people a little more space at evening parties!

When the table was gone, Fritz saw a gold couch walk in from a cavern behind the King's seat—which was indeed his dressing-room, but it was so small that he could only use it after the couch had come out; as soon as the couch had jumped and wriggled itself into the front of the throne, all the dwarfs bowed to the King and went to bed, and Fritz with them, and in ten minutes he was fast asleep, which was well for him, or the snoring of his Majesty might have kept him awake; the Gnomes were used to it, and snored in a lower key. So ended Fritz's first evening in the cave of the Gnomes.

The next morning, before breakfast, the dwarfs began to work: they were making a gold dinner-service for the Fairy Queen, and as the time for her annual visit was drawing near, they were working very hard to get it finished before her arrival. Fritz stood and watched them for some time, and then offered to do anything he could to help them, he thought he could do some of the courser parts of the manufacture, and at least, he said, "I can attend to the fires;" so every day for many months he lived with them, and they taught him to work in metals, and as he was intelligent and industrious he soon became a skilful workman, and was happy and contented; but sometimes he sighed and said to himself that he should like to go up to his own world again after a while, but he did not say it to the kind little dwarfs, fearing they might think him ungrateful for all their goodness to him.

At last the dinner-set, which was to be a present from the King of the Gnomes to the Queen of the Fairies, was finished, and very beautiful it was; you, I dare say, if you had seen it, would have thought it a doll's dinner-service, it was so small, but it was quite large enough for fairies, they are so tiny, you know. The plate-chests were made of ivory, bound with bands of gold and lined with quilted satin—a beautiful Salamandrine had done that for the Gnomes because they could not sew, she was a great friend of theirs, and often came to see them when the weather was warm, for she could not bear cold, as you may imagine when I tell you that she lived inside a volcano, and instead of water to bathe in used fire, just sitting down in the flames when she thought she wanted a bath.[29] Fritz was very anxious to see her, he had heard the dwarfs talk so much about her goodness and wonderful beauty; and one day when he had made a very bright fire, and the flames were blazing up the fissure in the rock that served for a chimney, he saw a lovely creature come gliding through them, and then sit down on the edge of the furnace, where the gold was bubbling and hissing; he knew at once that it must be the Salamandrine come to see her friends. As soon as they saw her they all crowded round to welcome her, and invited her to come down and sit near the King: "You shall have your own chair of state near his throne," they said to her;—"we will put some burning charcoal in the asbestos cushions to make it comfortable: but we cannot join you up there on the furnace," they said, laughing. She wore a robe of changeable colour, sometimes it looked like flame, sometimes blue, like

---

29 Salamandrine: a lizard-like animal that is said to be able to live in, or endure, fire (n. 'salamandrine' OED).

the beautiful colours you see in the fire on a frosty night; her girdle was of diamonds, and she had a band of diamonds on her head, and her long golden hair fell in ringlets on her shoulders: she was tall and slender, and all her movements were graceful, like the flames when they bend and waver round a burning piece of wood. Fritz stood gazing at her with wonder and delight, he had never seen anything so lovely in his life before, and the little dwarfs seemed as if they would kneel down and worship her: she smiled very sweetly, and then said: "Thanks, kind friends, I will come down, though this seat is certainly very warm and pleasant; but I want a chat with the King, and I have brought you some metal ready melted, I found it near my drawing-room fire yesterday. The fires in my house are rather large you know, and as they have been burning a few thousand years, the place is comfortably aired by this time;"—the Gnomes laughed, and said they thought it must be so. Then she stepped down and walked towards the King, four of them carrying her chair, which was a large piece of furniture for them to carry, and had taken them a long time to make, but they thought nothing a trouble that they could do for their favourite. The little King jumped up in such a hurry when he saw the Salamandrine coming that he let his sceptre fall, and knocked his crown all awry; she smiled, and after she and the King had shaken hands, she sat down in her chair of state and told him what was going on in the volcano, in which she had her palace, and about her last visit to Iceland to see her relations, who lived in Mount Hecla,[30] and of the delicious baths she had while there in the hot springs. Then refreshments were brought, but the wine was so hot that the poor King scalded his tongue, while drinking her health, but she sipped it, and said it was delicious; then she examined the Fairy Queen's dinner-service, and admired it very much: but said gold dishes would not do for her, they would melt in her warm kitchen, even her crystal was often cracked with the heat. Then bidding them all good bye, she stepped on to the furnace, and ascended with flames through the fissure in the rocks.

 The beautiful fire spirit had scarcely gone away before a noise was heard in the long passage leading to the caverns. "What can that be," said Fritz, "it sounds like the buzzing of bees?"—and he went to the entrance to look: and who should he see but the good Fairy Queen and all her train: such a long procession,—but all so small,—first came six out-riders mounted on wasps, which they had tamed and rendered gentle, then the Queen on her pearl chariot, drawn by eight dragon-flies, whose beautiful gauzy wings of blue and green and gold, made the buzzing noise Fritz had heard, as they flew swiftly along with the carriage,—they were difficult steeds to drive, but the coachman could keep them in order, troublesome as they were, he was a cunning old mosquito from Java, and if they would not obey him he would just let them feel his sting, which did better than a whip; the footmen were butterflies, there would not have been room for three to stand, but they kept their wings shut when behind their Mistress, and only shewed their gorgeous liveries when they flew down to open the chariot door with their antennae, for the Queen to alight,—the damp would have spoiled their feather coats, so it was convenient for two reasons, it saved Her Majesty the expense of water-proof over-coats and carriage umbrellas! After the royal chariot, came six more, each with four small dragon-flies to draw them, filled with the lords and ladies in waiting; and then a long train of little covered waggons, formed of some kind of nut, drawn by slow, hard working beetles; Squirrel and Company were the Queen's cartwrights—(I just name it as a sort of advertisement for that active firm).

---

30 Mount Hecla: Hekla – a volcano in southern Iceland.

As soon as Fritz saw who was coming, he ran quickly to tell the Gnomes: and then there was a hurry-skurry to get everything in order for the reception of Her Majesty of Fairyland;—one ran to tell the King, who was taking his nap after dinner, and shake him awake, and then put on his crown properly, and straighten out his robe; others began to arrange the gold dinner-service for the Queen to *inspect*,—Royal people always inspect things, they do not *look* at them like ordinary men and women, at least the newspapers say so: some hurried away to put on their best clothes, and told Fritz to do the same: one or two tumbled over each other in their haste:—and what with running, tumbling, screaming, and laughing, there had not been such a hurley-burley in Gnomeland for many a day!

However, just as the out-riders came up to the door, with a buzz and a flourish, all was ready, and the dwarfs standing in two rows at the entrance, the King came to within six inches and a half of the archway, and stood until the carriage door was opened, and then advanced and offered his hand to lead the Queen to the throne prepared for her on the right side of his; you will wonder perhaps how they knew court ceremonial so correctly, living down in their underground country so much, and never having been presented at a drawing-room, but the Queen's Chamberlain had sent them a book of Court etiquette he had written,—it was considered by his friends a masterpiece, for it regulated to within half an inch the distance each person was to approach Her Majesty, and the number of words they might use in answering her questions. The Gnomes had much fun about the book, and sometimes one would pretend to be the Queen, and would say: "What do you think of the weather?" and then they would look in the book for the proper number of words to reply to it;—one would give too many, another too few, and then they laughed till the cavern echoed with their merriment, and then their jolly little King would call out to know what they were so merry about and they had to act it over again before him, and he would laugh as loudly as the rest: for you see they lived down there more like one family than like a Court and a King and subjects.

Well, at last the Queen was seated, and her people standing behind her; the King told the dwarfs to bring in the chests of plate, and after they had been inspected by Her Majesty, they were taken to the waggons and put in; then she very gracefully thanked the Gnomes for the trouble they had taken in making such beautiful things, and the King for his costly gift. After that she ate some preserved rose leaf, and tasted the conserve of violets, and sipped some dissolved dew drops, and then prepared to return to her own country; but before she left, the King sent for Fritz, whom the Queen recollected at once, and pointing to the bracelet, said: "Thou must keep that for many years yet,—I can bestow many gifts on mortals, but none equal to thine, Fritz." Then she and her long train departed.

And things went on as usual till Fritz had grown to be a tall, strong young man, and a very skilful workman. One day the King sent for him and all the dwarfs, and said: "It is time now that thou shouldest return to thy own land—we shall miss thee, good Fritz, but thou must come to see us sometimes, and bring us news of what the mortals are doing up there, and whether they are getting any wisdom into their dull heads!" Fritz was glad to hear that he might return to the upper world, though very sorry to leave his kind, merry little friends. "But how am I to find my way down to you again?" he asked. Then they told him that in a lonely place they described to him on the moor that he knew, there was a rock that looked like the tower of a castle, and behind it was a flat smooth stone, which, when struck with a hammer, gave out a metallic sound. "When you want to visit us," they said, "you must strike that stone with your hammer, and it will be lifted up like a trap door, and you will see a flight of stone steps: you must come down them, and you will arrive here:"—and they showed him a little opening in the King's dressing-room which he had never seen, because a curtain was always hung before it: "You need not bring a light," they said, "for the rock oil has been burning there for years, and lightens the passage beautifully." "And now," said the King, "let us have the best supper you can give, and some of our oldest wine to drink to the success of friend Fritz—otherwise Baron Von Arbeit."[31]

So they had a merry supper; and the next morning Fritz took his leave with tears in his eyes, and many thanks for all their goodness to him. Two of the Gnomes took him up the secret staircase, and when they got to the top, they struck the stone with their hammers, and it opened, and Fritz saw he was on the moor where the foundry was where he used to work;—when he looked round to say farewell to his good little friends, they were not to be seen, and the stone was in its place again: but he carefully observed everything around that he might know it again, for it would have made him very sad indeed to think he should never see the kind Gnomes and their merry crooked-legged King anymore; he sat down beside the rock thinking for a long time, and rather bewildered, for the earth and sky were unfamiliar to him now. At length, as he saw by the sun it was noonday, he rose and walked in the direction of the foundry; when he came in sight of it, he was surprised to see no smoke coming out of the chimneys, and on going up to it, he found it was deserted, the fires all gone out, and not a living thing to be seen. Fritz then went to find the hut in which the kind workman lived who had been his friend, when he had no other in the world; he found him digging in his little garden, but the place looked very desolate, there was scarcely any furniture in the hut, and no fire on the hearth, and the poor children were all huddled together on some straw, trying to keep each other warm. When Hans, that was the name of the father, saw Fritz, he took off his old cap and made a low bow: but Fritz ran up to him, and said: "Do you not know me, my dear old friend, I am Fritz?" The man stared, without speaking, he was so astonished at the change in Fritz, who had grown into a strong, handsome young man. At last Fritz convinced him who he was, and then, saying he would return soon, walked as fast as he could to the nearest town, where he hired a cart, and put into it plenty of food and clothing, and beds for the poor children, with a pile of wood for a fire, and a bottle of good wine for Hans, who was almost worn out with poverty and hard work. Oh! what rejoicing there was, when the cart stopped at the door, and one big basket after another was carried into the hut! The children helped to make the fire, and Hans cooked the supper, and Fritz poured out the wine into a cup of gold of his own designing that the dwarfs had given him at parting; and then they sat down: Fritz on a cask turned upside down, and Hans on an old wheelbarrow, the two boys and three girls on billets of fire-wood; and the huge fire they had made blazed up the chimney, and gave them plenty of light, and the big logs crackled, and the children laughed, and Hans and Fritz talked together; and I think they were as merry as the dwarfs and Fritz the first night he supped in the cavern. Then the children arranged their beds, and felt so deliciously comfortable in the warm blankets, that they soon went to sleep; but Fritz and Hans sat talking by the fire for many hours, for they had long histories to tell each other. Fritz told his wonderful adventures first, and then Hans told him how nothing at the foundry prospered after he was turned away: for the master believed all the lies the

---

31 Baron Von Arbeit: translates as Baron of Work.

bad workman told him, and all the best men and boys went away, and at last it had to be deserted, and was to be sold, but no one would buy it, and everything had gone to ruin. "I will purchase it," said Fritz, "and you shall be my partner."

The good little Gnomes had given Fritz plenty of gold, so the next day he bought the foundry, and all the moor round it, and Hans soon collected plenty of the old men and boys to work, and the great fires blazed again in the furnaces, and the workmen had nice cottages and gardens, and everyone was contented and happy.

And so things went on for many years, and Fritz married Gretchen with the golden hair and blue eyes,—the eldest daughter of Hans, and he built a beautiful chateau, and was called Baron Von Arbeit.

You must not think that he ever forgot his kind old friends in the mountain, he often went to see them, and never came back without some beautiful jewels for his wife, or a fine cup for his boys.

And so years passed, and Fritz and Gretchen were keeping their golden wedding, and all their children and grandchildren were assembled at the castle, and the workpeople were having a great feast at the works. The master and mistress sat in two high-backed chairs, on a dais at the end of the great hall: and their relations and friends stood near them, and in the middle of the hall was a large table, on which were put all the beautiful cups and dishes the Gnomes had given Fritz;—they had made him one for that day expressly: on one side was a young man working in a field, on the other an old man sitting under a tree, and round the rim of the cup was written: "At eventide rest."

When all were assembled, Fritz and Gretchen stood up, and their eldest son brought them the golden wedding cup full of wine, and they drunk the health of all their sons and daughters, and of their grandchildren, and their relations and friends,—and when they said friends they smiled to each other, for they remembered their kindest of all friends—the good little Gnomes of the mountain; and they knew by the designs and the motto on the cup that the time had come for Fritz to take off the bracelet he had worn so long, and that the Gnomes would fetch it that night, to return to the Fairy Queen.

So, dear beautiful old Gretchen, with silver hair now, unclasped the iron armlet, and laid it on the table: and they saw inside the words—

TRUTH AND INDUSTRY

Part II.

Change—not Death

There was a bright cloud in the West,
Rosy and golden, and at rest,
It seemed an island of the blest.

I gazed upon it as it lay,
And wished it there would ever stay,
And never, never, melt away:

But the sun went down, and each glorious dye,
Faded away from the darkening sky;
And I was sad, I knew not why.

There was a bird, whose pleasant song
All day had sounded the reeds among,
Where the still, deep river, flowed along:

But there came a time when it must fly
To warmer lands, or stay and die,
When wintry winds swept fiercely by.

And one soft, warm, autumnal day,
It stretched its wings and flew away;
And I heard no more its cheerful lay.

There was a plant whose snow-white flower,
Burst into splendour at twilight's hour,
And beauty and perfume filled the bower;

And when the gazers at midnight came,
The Queen of the Night was still the same,[32]
And to gather its blossoms they said, was shame!

So in its beauty they left it there,
To fill with scent the midnight air;
With the stars to gleam on its petals rare.

But in the morning they found it dead,
Beauty and perfume alike had fled:
And a withering mass was there instead.

---

32 The Queen of the Night: a fragrant flower which blooms for only one night.

But the glittering sunbeams, and the rain,
Many cloud isles will build again;
'Ere another moon shall wax and wane.

And the bird will come back from across the sea,
When the young buds are bursting on plant and tree,
And the air will be filled with its melody.

And the summer sun will revive the flower,
And beauty and perfume fill the bower,
From the soft, calm twilight, to midnight's hour.

Thus life and death go on for ever—
Nought may the two-fold cord dissever:
'Tis *change* unceasing—*destruction* never.

Earth's Waters

Which, of all earth's waters,
    Do'st thou love the best;
The stream that runneth softly
    By the water ouzel's nest;

Or the wide and solemn river,
    That telleth not of glee,
But of forces irresistible,
    Man cannot stop or flee;

Or the quiet pool, where groweth
    The lily and the reed,
And where the spotless water birds
    In the twilight come to feed;

Or the mountain lake, that mirroreth
    The eagle as he soars,
And the storm clouds as they gather,
    When the mighty thunder roars?

Oh! best of all earth's waters,
    I love the mountain stream;
It speaketh to me ever,
    Of the past's bright, tender dream.

When, by its dancing waters,
    Five happy children played;[33]
And their ringing laughter mingled
    With the music that it made.

Oh! mountain stream, thou babblest
    Still ever gaily on;
But the music of that laughter
    For me, and earth, has gone!

---

33 In referring to five children, Hawkshaw places this memory at a time between the death of Ada in 1845 and the death of Oliver in 1856.

The Birds of Passage

A sound of countless wings;
    A dark and wavy line across the sky;—
And then the birds of passage sped away
    Before the gazer's eye—

Over the rivers, and the pathless sea,
    O'er silent desert, and o'er treeless plain,
Where the scorched grass was crackling in the sun—
    Waiting for Autumn rain:

Onward, still on they go,
    Nor swerve, nor hesitate about their way;
And on the self-same path they will return
    Some coming day;—

And find their former haunts,
    And build their nests beneath the cottage thatch,
The harbingers of sunny days—for them
    Shall village children watch.

Oh! wondrous law!
    That, through unnumbered ages, nought hath broken;
Sure as the ebb and flow of ocean's wave:—
    Unwritten and unspoken!

Homes of the Flowers

Upon the mountain's bow,
    The bright blue Gentians have their home,[34]
Buried beneath the drifting snow
    Of many a winter's storm.

    Rooted in desert sand,
Or on the barren shore, and wet by spray,
    The Tamarisk to the lonely wanderer says:[35]
"Go hopeful on thy way."

---

34 Gentians: violet or blue trumpet-shaped flowers found in mountainous and temperate regions.
35 Tamarisk: shrub found in semi-arid regions, having blue-grey scale-like leaves and small white or pink flowers.

The Cocoa Palm-trees wave
Their pendant leaves, above the coral isle,
　　　While at their root, the insect-makers work—
Tomb and memorial pile.

　　　On Afric's arid plains,
A strange weird plant spreads out its tattered leaves,
　　　More like a monster of the deep, than aught
That life from earth receives.

　　　In the dim dripping cave,
Where sunbeams die in twilight's settled gloom:
　　　Where the shy seal finds for itself a home
Lulled by the sea wave's everlasting boom;—

　　　Grows the bright Fern, that will not bear a change,
Or other winds than ocean waves to fan
　　　Its glossy fronds; but slowly withering dies
Beside the haunts of man.

　　　Upon the ruined tower,
Where feudal banners waved in days of old,
　　　The scented Wall-flower opens to the sun
Its tufts of brown and gold:

　　　While on the chalky cliffs,
Its purple sister, shares the beetling height,
　　　With wearied swallows—resting, ere they take
To their old haunts, their flight.

　　　Scarcely a spot of earth
But is a home for you, fair, gentle things:
　　　To the sad exile, many a tender thought
Sight of your beauty brings.

　　　Oh! wise and gracious law,
That upon matter, nature hath imprest
　　　Awaking living beauty ceaselessly
From earth's dead breast!

In Memoriam[36]

Once in a far-off northern home,[37]
   Five happy children played:
They ran beside the mountain streams,
   And through the pine woods strayed,
Or watched the wild birds on the hills,
   From morn to evening's shade.

---

36 'In Memoriam' is the final poem in *Cecil's Own Book*, and in effect, Hawkshaw's final word. Just as *Poems for My Children* ends with a poignant elegy on childhood death from a mother's perspective ('Ada'), Hawkshaw draws this final collection to a close by reflecting on the deaths of her three children. Writing now as a mother and grandmother, the elegy looks back over her children's lives and expresses the cumulative effect of Ada, Oliver and Mary's deaths on a mother who could not have anticipated the agony of losing three of her cherished 'flowers'. A detailed analysis of the poem's references to the Hawkshaw children can be found in the biographical introduction. This is one of five poems to deal with the death of children. See also: 'To a Bereaved Father', 'To—— on the Death of Three of her Children', 'To—— after the Death of her Daughter' (*'Dionysius the Areopagite', with Other Poems*), 'Ada' (*Poems for My Children*).

37 northern home: a likely reference to Pitlochry in Scotland, where the family frequently holidayed.

One made a mill-wheel in a stream,[38]
    Another read his book—[39]
Stretched on the sweet thyme-covered bank:
    But oft away would look
To where his youngest brother fished
    For minnows in the brook.[40]

And ever by the brother's side
    Kept the two sisters dear,[41]
And borne upon the mountain breeze
    Their laugh came soft and clear—
To where the mother sat—her heart
    Had not then learned to fear:

For though within her distant grave,
    One fair young sister slept,[42]
Though softly still they breathed her name,
    Though still the mother wept—
And hid deep in her heart of hearts,
    That pure sweet memory kept.

"Death is contented with that one:"
    Such was the mother's dream,
"That bud of beauty, will it not
    "My other flowers redeem?"
Oh! foolish was that mother's thought,
    Beside the mountain stream.

But then these young lives were so glad,
    Their hearts so good and pure,
They filled one home so full of love,
    It seemed it must endure:
For, to fill up such a void on earth,
    What solace, or what cure.

---

38 In this and the following stanza, Hawkshaw describes her five young children according to their interests. The budding engineer is John Clarke Hawkshaw (b. 1841); in later life John Clarke would be a civil engineer of some renown.
39 The middle brother, Henry Paul (b. 1843).
40 Hawkshaw's youngest son, Oliver (b. 1846).
41 Mary Jane Jackson (b. 1838) and Editha (b. 1845).
42 Ada: the reference to 'her distant grave' places the setting more securely in Scotland, as Ada (1840–45) had been buried in Manchester.

There came a change—through highland glen
    Walked quietly but *four*,[43]
Or talked with whispered words, within
    The heather covered bower,
Or gathered for the sick boy's room,
    Green fern or autumn flower.

There—with fair brow and sunny hair,
    Upon his couch he lay,
Patient and loving to the last:—
    And as he passed away,
Giving sweet words of love to her
    Who wept in wild dismay!

Amid the scenes he loved so well,
    There is a little grave:
The giant hills behind it tower,—
    Before it corn-fields wave,
And there, with bitter tears, they lay
    To rest, their good and brave.[44]

Time passed—and then there were but *three*:
    Who wept in speechless woe,
The young wife-mother, must she die!—[45]
    Oh! God,—must this be so?
It must be but a hideous dream!
    They could not let *her* go.

Beside the village church, a cross
    Tells where that dear one sleeps:
Her boy treads gently there,—and love,
    Untiring vigil keeps;
And years go by, of good and ill,
    But still that mother weeps!

---

43 Oliver Hawkshaw fell ill with typhoid fever and peritonitis during the family's holiday to Pitlochry in 1856. He lay ill for five weeks. His final days are remembered by Hawkshaw in her unpublished memoir 'Memories of My Childhood' which she began to write in the months after Oliver's death.

44 Oliver died at Inverchostie Lodge near Pitlochry on 15 September 1856. He is buried in Moulin churchyard.

45 The young wife-mother: reference to Ann's eldest daughter Mary, who contracted puerperal mania and died in the days following her son Cecil's birth at Hem Heath, the Wedgwood's home in Trentham, Stafford. Cecil was born on 28 March 1863 and Mary died on 7 April. It is to Mary's memory that *Cecil's Own Book* is dedicated.

Appendix A

The following contemporary reviews of Hawkshaw's work draw comparisons with other female writers and place her poetry in a literary and cultural context. Original spelling and punctuation is retained throughout.

Reviews of *'Dionysius the Areopagite', with Other Poems* (London: Jackson and Walford; Manchester: Simms and Dinham, 1842)

North of England Magazine 2, no. 11 (December 1842): 121–2.

> "Oh! to awake once more the love of song,
>   The love of nature, and of holier things
> Than crowd the visions of the busy throng:
>   Alas! the dust is on the angel's wings,
> And those who woke the lyre in days gone by
> Wake it no more, or touch it with a sigh."
> INTRODUCTORY STANZAS

We think not so, fair lady! and yourself are strong evidence in favour of our opinion that the elements of poetic feeling are more widely extending their influence, where so far they have been the least anticipated. Poetry is not dead but sleepeth, and though Shakesperes [sic] and Miltons are not to be met with in our daily walks, yet we have a long list of high names not discreditable to any age or country. There is much poetry in the prose of the present day, and we feel strongly inclined to believe that the love of the good and true, of nature, and of art as her faithful imitator, is strongly growing up among us. We have faith in the present age, and in the progress of humanity, and this little book has strengthened our belief.

Were we inclined to be severe, we might find fault with an occasional negligence, that other parts of the poem warrant us in supposing to be merely such, which, however, rarely as they occur, interfere with the otherwise natural flow of harmony running through these pages.

There is much picturesque beauty in the principal poem, with considerable force, and here and there a grandeur of thought very much beyond the common place.

> "The dust of ages is upon thee, Rome;
> Dark were thy deeds, and dark hath been thy doom.
> The blood of martyred saints bedewed thy sod,—
> Its voice ascended from thy hills to God;
> The winds took up their dying groans—the wave
> Back to the earth its answering echo gave.
> And o'er thy vine-clad shores, thy sunny sea,
> It brooded like the voice of prophecy.
> And vengeance heard its tones, and woke at last,—
> At the still midnight pealed the Gothic blast,
> And through thy streets the hosts of Alaric passed!"

We are not among those who believe "woman kind" intended solely to fulfil the natural offices of nurse, cook, and housekeeper, or that such duties interfere with a love for higher things; the greatest men have had the most intelligent of mothers, and we are glad to find the rising generation beginning to understand this truth, and women endeavouring to make themselves the companions rather than toys, or domestic servants to their lords and masters. The feelings of him, who cannot understand the following beautiful sonnet, are unenviable, and we may add, that this little volume is full of poetry, inculcating such sentiments:—

Sonnet to——

"I love my country, for I love my kind—
   Man is my brother wheresoe'er he roam—
   I love my father's hearth, my childhood's home,
And all the hopes and memories round it twined:
I love the deep thoughts and the cares which bind
   The mother to her children—in my heart
   These, and the love of song have each their part:
But not a part for thee alone, I find,
   For 'tis all thine—as light that fills no space
And yet pervades all nature, and which gives
   All forms their beauty, loveliness, and grace,
And energy and hope to all that lives;
So unto me hath been thy love—then take
This song of mine, and keep it for my sake."

To which we most cordially say, Amen. It was our wish to notice this unpretending little work at more length, but time and space are not our masters. We shall recur to it again, if possible, in the mean time we recommend it to the perusal of our readers, containing as it does much that is beautiful in thought, feeling and expression, and altogether an honour to our good old Town.

Gentleman's Magazine 174 (January–June 1843): 621.

This volume of poetry is recommended by the elegance of the imagery, and the correctness and harmony of the language and versification; indeed the critic must look very closely to detect any errors except what are trifling, and such as are occasionally found in the highest productions of the art. The author has a command of elegant and impressive language, and is, what many of her sisters of the lyre are not, a poetical *artist*. When she next writes, we recommend any measure rather than the one she has chosen, for the exercise of her powers: it is too short for sufficient variety of harmony, and the rhymes recur too frequently—our common heroic verse would be preferable, or blank verse; but blank verse is a weapon that few can wield.

Court Magazine and Monthly Critic (June 1843): 60–61.

Here we have a poem of great length, containing passages of great beauty, and possessing touches of true poetic character. The Areopagite of itself is far too long to be introduced into our pages, but we have no doubt the perusal will afford satisfaction to persons possessing a poetic vein. We shall, therefore, content ourselves by introducing to our readers some of the authoress' minor poems. We think that, at a time when the right of search, a regular anti-slave question, is making such a noise in France, and when England, with native generosity, has taken from the national wealth so large a sum as twenty millions to set her own slaves free, that the following lines, "Why am I a slave!" must go deep—deep to our fair readers' hearts. The verses, "Why am I a Slave?" were occasioned by an occurrence in the Isle of France, where we are informed one poor wretch died broken hearted, constantly exclaiming, "Why am I a slave?"

WHY AM I A SLAVE?

"One poor wretch died here (Isle of France) broken hearted, constantly exclaiming, 'Why am I a slave?'" *Bennet and Tyerman's Voyage round the World*

> Why do I bear that cursed name?
>   Why, why am I a slave?
> Why doomed to drag a wretched life
>   In sorrow to the grave?
> Born 'mid the mountain solitudes,
>   And as the lion free,
> Who had a right to bind these limbs
>   And make a slave of me?
>
> I looked—there stood the white man's home,
>   'Mid pleasant founts and flowers,
> 'Mid waving woods and waters clear,
>   Green vines and rosy bowers;
> It had an air of loveliness
>   That suited not despair—
> I turned away, for well I knew
>   That happy hearts were there.
>
> I knew that happy hearts were there,
>   For voices full of glee
> Came on the air, and from their tone
>   I knew that they were free;
> Unlike the low faint murmuring sound,
>   That marks the wretched slave,
> Words wrung from misery's quivering lips,
>   That sound as from the grave.
>
> I turned—there stood my lonely hut,
>   I call it not my home,
> For no beloved face is there,
>   And no familiar form,

> No voice to break its solitude,
>   And none to soothe the woe
> Of him who was but born to sigh,
>   Whose tears must ever flow.
>
> Why does the rose bestrew his path,
>   And mine the pricking thorn?
> Why was the white man born to smile,
>   And I to sigh and mourn?
> I know not, only this I know,
>   Till in the silent grave
> There is no hope, no joy for me,
>   I am a slave—a slave!

We, too, have asked ourselves the question, why man, who has committed no crime, should be torn by *monsters*, Christian-infidels and murderers, from the home of his childhood, from his country beloved. Why he should be separated from his wife, or forced to endure slavery with them, were even such his good fortune. We are glad Christian England speaks in a language not to be misunderstood by unthinking, worse than heathen, nations, though they profess, but do not practise Christianity. We are on this occasion proud of our country; we rejoice that she has set a religious example to all the nations of the earth—to Spain, to Portugal, to America—even to America—the boasted, the free, with *her* millions of slaves!!—nay, to France herself. That there may be some bravado about the right of stealing human beings for gain, and in revenge murdering them for non-obedience to the hated application of the whip, alias slow death, and consequently, murder by torture, we consider highly probable: but, in the slave's cause, in defence of the rights of humanity, *now* so dearly interesting to all civilized states, let one or all together offer the least resistance; let them if they dare, in a cause so sacred, rouse the feeling and face the vengeance of the British lion, under our present able Conservative minister and strong Conservative government—though we offer our hearty thanks to the late government for their ever memorable carrying the great question of emancipation—and we dare stake our credit, as we often have, that the settlement will not long be doubtful. Yes! professing Christian nations, it is useless! You may get yourselves into difficulty, but under Peel you will never get out of it. Yours, the cruel and unjust cause, the end will be your utter discomfiture.

We must not, however, forget our authoress at parting, whose poetry, well matched in quality with the contents of two small volumes by Mr. Milne, M.P., has delighted us *exceedingly*.

Extract from the preface to Samuel Bamford's *Poems* (Manchester: published by the author, 1843).

In offering this volume of Poems to the public, the author cannot be unaware of some disadvantageous circumstances under which it is put forth. Since his last volume of poetry was published,—which is about eight years ago—the attention of the literati of Manchester, and its neighbourhood, has been justly claimed by the productions of a Swain, a Prince, a Rogerson, inhabitants of the town—of a Festus, the circumstance of whose first surprising essay in poetry, having been printed at Manchester, will one day be esteemed an honour to the town—and of Mrs. Hawkshaw, whose interesting poem, "The Areopagite," has added another name to those destined for immortality.

Perhaps the author would not—having been thus presented, and being at present, as it were, shadowed by talent of a high order—have ventured to offer his humble tribute to the public, had he not felt persuaded that his brother bards would welcome it to a place in the records of Lancashire Minstrelsy—that it might add a not altogether discordant strain to their harmonious numbers,—and that, being the expression of a mind of more mature years than theirs,—of feelings derived from, and springing up with, a somewhat harsher fate,—it might perhaps compensate, by originality and strong contrast, for want of smoothness of numbers, and exactness of rhythm.

Reviews of *Poems for My Children* (London: Simpkin and Marshall; Manchester: Simms and Dinham, 1847)

Manchester Times (20 July 1847), 3.

A pretty little volume, full of pretty verses. Better than any criticism will be a characteristic extract. Take the following:

MARY'S WISH

> I often wish that I could see,
> This country as it used to be;
> For where now busy cities stand,
> There once was moor and forest land,
> And the tall elk and freedom bounded,
> Ere hunter's bugle had been sounded!
>
> How quiet must those shores have been,
> Where now a thousand ships are seen!
> There was no sound of steam, or oar,
> Scarcely a foot-print on the shore,
> And the sea-eagle from the cliff,
> Soared, startled at the passing skiff.
>
> Where quay and warehouse crowd the edge
> Of rivers,—once, 'mid reeds and sedge,
> The otter watched his fishy prey,
> With none to frighten him away,
> Unless a tall grey heron came,
> Its share of booty, too, to claim.
>
> Where now the wavy cornfields spread,
> Once stood the Briton's mud-built shed;
> And round it savage children played,
> While stretched beneath the oak-tree's shade,

Their father strung his bow afresh,
Or in his fish-net wove a mesh.

Where now such peaceful dwellings are,
Were heard the sounds of barbarous war;
And mothers with their children fled
At midnight from the burning shed;
The smoke from engines now is seen,
Where blazing hamlets once had been.

I do not think that time was good,
For then men shed each other's blood,
Without a thought that it was wrong,
And the weak fell beneath the strong;
But still, I often wish to see
This country as it used to be!

Manchester Courier and Lancashire General Advertiser (21 July 1847), 3.

We select the following sweet poem from a volume just published, entitled *Poems for My Children*, by Mrs Hawkshaw, of this town. The work is excellently got up, illustrated with beautiful wood cuts, and contains some most delightful poetry; which, though written for juvenile readers, will not fail to give delight to "children of a larger growth." Mrs Hawkshaw is already known to the public by her poem of "Dionysius the Areopagite;" and we hope soon to welcome her again, when her muse shall have taken a bolder flight than in the little work now before us. These poems are in reality that which their title page imports, and were written for the authoress's own children; but we are not sorry that they should have been extended in their sphere of usefulness by this publication:—

ADA.

Ada, the flowers of spring are blooming now;
   The flowers we talked of in the wintry hours,
When at my feet thou sat'st, thy thoughtful brow
   And fair face turned to mine; we talked of flowers,
Spring's sunny days, and birds amid the trees,
Themes that thy gentle heart could ever please.

And they are here; but thou art gone my child;
   And even the sunshine seems a mournful thing
To my sad heart, that flattering hope beguiled,
   To look with gladness to the coming spring:
For in those hours I had no secret dread;
Gazing on *thee*, I thought not of the dead.

The snow was on the ground, the biting blast
    Swept the bare earth when in the ground we laid
Thee, our first smitten flower: but they have past,
    And earth again in beauty is arrayed:
Oh that the sunbeam could awake the flower
That withered by me in that bitter hour!

It cannot be!—ah me, how much of woe
    In the few words are hidden, "I shall see
Thee here no more," till now I did not know:
    Yet doth one thought bring comfort e'en to me,—
Thou art my child, my Ada still; not death
Can wither love e'en with his blighting breath:

No, he but purifies it—'t is no more
    Of earth or time but of eternity.
Time cannot now my hopes or joys restore,
    And earth can offer nought, dear one, to thee,
'T is love unmingled with all meaner dreams
Of pride, or selfishness, or earthly schemes.

Therefore I will not say to thee farewell:
    No, none shall fill thy place within my heart.
There love for thee, and thoughts of thee shall dwell
    Until we meet again to never part:
A spirit dwelling in a home above
It is a sweet and solemn thing to love!

Athenæum (15 January 1848), 57.

If our readers imagine that because we are in mid-winter there has been a suspension of the music of the song-bird whose name is Legion, they have extracted from the mere exigencies of our columns a speculative good in which we have not been permitted to share. With us, the singing "Million" have had for the time to give place to that speciality of the season the Christmas carollers, in verse and prose; but we have them about us, nevertheless,—caged in bindings of all gay forms and hues, and uttering every variety of note save the higher ones. Our library-table is vocal with the chirp of the small poets,—as in summer. "Alike to *them* all seasons and their change." The leaf falls not in the groves where they learn their singing,—and their Helicon is never frozen over. "No song no supper" is a threat which in the Little Britain of poetry implies a danger so remote as would make the term of proposition ridiculous. The rule of political economy is defied in that world—the supply is infinitely beyond the demand. Its population seem to grow and multiply upon neglect. They pipe though no man should dance—and the more you "won't come" the more they "call."—For him, however, who will listen with an ear not too nice, there are low sweet notes to be caught from time to time amid the chorus of the Million. The voices of the poultry-yard (to avoid unpleasant specification) have too great a preponderance, it is true, in their concert,—and set the world against listening: but here and there steals out the pipe of a spirit whose cheerfulness is song,—or the plaintive note that finds a way to the hearer's heart because the singer's own leans upon a real thorn.

We must, then, as our leisure will permit, devote a few articles to bring up our arrears with the Poetry of the Million. Scarcely yet, however, beyond the Christmas claim, we will begin with one or two volumes which, while they belong to the general category, have something in the form or manner of their presentment bringing them within the pretensions of the classes with which we have recently been dealing—of Christmas and of Children's Books.

Of all the many ladies who have in our day undertaken to write verse for children, in our opinion Mrs. Hawkshaw is the happiest. Whoever this lady may be, she has been found out by the very Muse who has charge of this gentle ministry. The little volume by her now before us, *Poems for My Children*, is the pleasantest gift of its kind that we have yet seen offered for the young mind's acceptance. Its engraved borders and pretty vignettes begin by conciliating the childish fancy through the eye; and then its other attractions make their way through the fancy to the heart. The morals are not a bit more profound than the childish mind can fathom—and are conveyed in a music well calculated to train the infant spirit to poetry. The union of melody and simplicity applied to the rendering of every-day morals is remarkable. The absence of cant is a charming feature in the seriousness of these little songs—as that of affectation is in their sweetness. Truths are gathered for the child, like roses, where they grow wild in its daily paths—and offered with the dew and fragrance of Nature fresh upon them. A specimen or two will be welcome to many of our readers, for repetition to their children by the winter's fire—and will probably send them to the book itself for more, on the juvenile demand.—

The Oak Tree

The oak it is a noble tree,
  The monarch of the wood;
Through winter's storms a thousand years,
  Its hardy trunk hath stood.

It is not stately, like the beech;
  The elm more tall may be;
And gracefuller the lovely lime;
  Yet 't is a noble tree.

An acorn, by a squirrel dropped
  Amid a tuft of grass,
May be an oak, on which we look
  With wonder as we pass.

But then it years, long years, must grow,
  And this may teach to all,
What mighty things in after times
  May come from means now small.

How little did they think who saw
    A green oak sapling spring
In some old forest long ago,
    That it would float a king!

Perhaps some ancient Druid came
    To pluck from it a bough;
'T is now a gallant ship—but *he*,
    Where is that Druid now?

Perhaps an acorn from that tree
    Dropped on his nameless grave,
And o'er it now in summer green,
    Dark, tangled branches wave.

How beautiful the oak's young leaves,
    In the bright days of Spring;
Or, when a richer tint the skies
    Of early autumn bring:

And all upon the dewy ground
    The acorn-cups are laid,
Like richly chasèd spoons are they,
    For fairy banquets made.

So, monarch of all forest trees,
    On every English plain;
We crown thee still, thou brave old oak,
    And long, long be thy reign!

The City Child's Complaint

"The trees and flowers are beautiful,
    The sky is blue and high,
And the small streams make pleasant sounds,
    As they run swiftly by.

"But all these things are not for me,
    I live amid dark walls;
And scarcely through these dusty panes
    A single sunbeam falls.

"I never hear the wild bird's song,
    Or see the graceful deer
Go trooping through the forest glades:
    What can I learn from here?

"They say *God's works* are wonderful,
    In sea, and sky, and land;
I never see them for *men's works*
    Are here on every hand."

Oh murmur not, thou little one,
    That *here* thy home must be,
And not amid the pleasant fields,
    Or by the greenwood tree.

There is a voice can speak to thee,
    Amid the works of men;
Speak, with a sound as loud and clear
    As in the lonely glen.

Do not the works thou seest around
    Spring from man's thoughtful mind,
And in *that*, is there nought of God,
    For thee, for all, to find?

The earth, with all its varied blooms,
    Will have to pass away;
But man's immortal mind will live
    Through everlasting day:

And without mind these sheltering walls
    Around thee had not been,
These busy engines had not moved,
    Nor whirling wheels been seen!

The Wind

The wind it is a mystic thing,
    Wandering o'er ocean wide,
And fanning all the thousand sails
    That o'er its billows glide.

It curls the blue waves into foam,
    It snaps the strongest mast,
Then like a sorrowing thing it sighs,
    When the wild storm is past.

And yet how gently do
    At evening through
As if it said a kind "goo
    To all the closing flowers.

It bears the perfume of the rose,
    It fans the insect's wing;
'T is round me, with me everywhere,
    Yet 't is an unseen thing.

How many sounds it bears along,
    As o'er the earth it goes;
The songs of many joyous hearts,
    The sounds of many woes!

It enters into palace halls,
    And carries thence the sound
Of mirth and music;—but it creeps
    The narrow prison round.

And bears away the captive's sigh,
    Who sits in sorrow there;
Or from the martyr's lonely cell
    Conveys his evening prayer.

It fans the reaper's heated brow;
    It through the window creeps,
And lifts the fair child's golden curls,
    As on her couch she sleeps.

'T is like the light, a gift to all,
    To prince, to peasant given;
Awake, asleep, around us still,
    There is this gift of heaven:

This strange, mysterious thing we call
    The breeze, the air, the wind;
We call it so, but know no more,—
    'T is mystery, like our mind.

Think not the things most wonderful
    Are those beyond our ken,
For wonders are around the paths,
    The daily paths of men!

We have so rarely the opportunity of catering to our own satisfaction for the class especially addressed in the little poetical moralities that we are tempted to one extract more.—

Common Things

The sunshine is a glorious thing,
    That comes alike to all,
Lighting the peasant's lowly cot,
    The noble's painted hall.

The moonlight is a gentle thing,
    It through the window gleams,
Upon the snowy pillow, where
    The happy infant dreams.

It shines upon the fisher's boat,
    Out on the lonely sea;
Or where the little lambkins lie,
    Beneath the old oak-tree.

The dew-drops on the summer morn,
    Sparkle upon the grass;
The village children brush them off,
    That through the meadows pass.

There are no gems in monarchs' crowns,
    More beautiful than they;
And yet we scarcely notice them,
    But tread them off in play.

Poor Robin on the pear-tree sings,
    Beside the cottage-door;
The heath-flower fills the air with sweets,
    Upon the pathless moor.

There are as many lovely things,
    As many pleasant tones,
For those who sit by cottage hearths,
    As those who sit on thrones!

John Evans's Review of Hawkshaw as a 'Lancashire' Poet

Lancashire Authors and Orators: A Series of Literary Sketches of Some of the Principle Authors, Divines, Members of Parliament, etc, Connected with the County of Lancaster (London: Houlston and Stoneman, 1850), 127–32.

In the "Introductory Stanzas" to the first volume Mrs. Hawkshaw presented to the world, we think, with all due and polite deference, she commits a slight error. In the following beautiful language, she tells us—

> "This is no time for song: there is a strife
>   For wealth or for existence all around;
> And all the sweet amenities of life,
>   And all the gentle harmonies of sound,
> Die like the flowers upon a beaten path,
> Or music midst the noise of toil and wrath."

The mere fact of Mrs. Hawkshaw's presenting us with a series of poems like those in which this stanza occurs, proves beyond all doubt that this *is* a time for song, and one that will make us the lovers of song to which ever way our inclinations may have tended. We are of those who, despite the mechanical and utilitarian character generally ascribed to our age, deem it fully as much alive to the soft sensibilities of poetic feeling, as any other period of our existence, as a civilized community. Poetic feeling, when once infused in a nation's breast, though it may be harassed with care and turmoil, never can die. The same principles that its sublime precepts taught in the meridian reign of Shakespere [sic] and Milton, or of Homer, Virgil, and Petrarch, are taught and acknowledged now; and though we may have grown more perfectly alive to the ways and means of our daily subsistence, still all this care and toil but adds to the beauty and eloquence of poetic feelings and sentiments. No man knows or feels what poetry is until he has had some little contention with the world; and he who works the hardest, will always find its smooth and silvery sounds the more exquisite means of raising his soul from the dust, and unburdening his mind from care.

We dwell at this length in our observations upon this passage, because it introduces us to one who has proved by her writings alone that this is a time for song; for if any of our fair *literati* in Lancashire ever did show the gift of song, it is certainly in the highly gifted lady before us. Did we want a proof of the existence of the spirit of poetry in this noisy locality, we do not think we could select a more befitting one than a volume of the poems of Mrs. Hawkshaw. And we do not say this out of mere gallantry, or the courtesy that is generally expected to meet any female effort. Setting all this aside, Mrs. Hawkshaw's poetry will stand a fair critical test. Here we find none of those namby-pamby, milk-and-water sentimentalisms that are so frequently identified with the early efforts of many young authors or poetesses; all her effusions manifest something of a genuine character, something that you feel and know to be real poetry in the most enlarged acceptation of the word. You cannot peruse her effusions without being sensibly affected by the high poetic feelings they convey. They always indicate the true genius—the *summum bonum* of poetic inspiration and poetic sentiment. Viewed in a comparative point of view, we think we may safely assign Mrs. Hawkshaw the chief seat among our present line of Lancashire poetesses. She has much of the graceful feeling of Mrs. Hemans, and no inconsiderable portion of the tasteful beauty and artistic polish of Mrs.

Norton; schools in which she has doubtless well studied, and undoubtedly with much success. We think we have perused most of the writings of our lady-authors of Lancashire, but none have given us such a complete satisfaction, as the effusions of the one before us. They possess such an amount of real poetic emotion, such a degree of beautiful poetic imagery, such an expansion of ideas and thought conveyed in so chaste and elegant a style, that anybody perusing them must acknowledge their claims to poetry of a very high order.

But a closer inspection of Mrs. Hawkshaw's productions will more clearly justify our remarks. In 1842 appeared the first collection of poems by our fair author, entitled *Dionysius the Areopagite*. The leading poem of *Dionysius* is in all respects a fine poetic conception, and is sustained, from first to last, with a vigour and energy that must captivate every reader. Replete as it is with great artistic power, an almost Eastern magnificence of style and language, a flow of thought, and ideas of high poetic beauty and imagery, that sometimes almost leads us to think we are holding converse with "Queen Mab." We cannot be too warm in our encomiums upon this meritorious production. The tale itself, with the few characters introduced into it, is well sustained throughout. The eloquence with which Mrs. Hawkshaw expatiates on ancient Greece, the elegant language in which she describes its thousand relics of decayed beauty and grandeur, the artistic beauty in which she enrobes the scenes into which she introduces the reader, infuses into the poem a captivating grace and elegance that fills us with emotions, that do not lie within our reach to describe. Her address to Greece, beginning

> "I love the beautiful where'er
> 'Tis found"

exhibits considerable resources of beautiful imagery and elegant verbiage. "Dionysius" to "Myra," on the immortality of the soul, is another equally fine passage. But, we are led to think, it is in the great artistic picturing Mrs. Hawkshaw displays, lies her principle power. Here is a beautiful line or two—

> "And still on Grecian hills and plains
> Are roofless temples, priestless fanes,
> All beautiful; as though decay
> But touched them with a pencilled ray:"

And here, the Plague—

> "Unseen its form of mystery,
> As on it sped!
> It spared not beauty in its pride;
> It snatched the bridegroom from the bride;
> It breathed upon the sleeping child,
> While in its mother's arms it smiled;
> And as the mother o'er it wept,
> Throughout her veins the poison crept;
> And while she caught its dying sigh,
> Death darkened o'er her tearful eye."

We might add numerous illustrations of this power of artistic picturing that is generally identified with Mrs. Hawkshaw's poems. It is nothing but just, however, to remark that they are all truthful and consistent, and rarely savour of anything approaching extravagance or over-colouring. A few minor pieces are attached to *Dionysius*, which, for the most part, exhibit much fervency of feeling and beauty of sentiment. Two somewhat fine poems, the one entitled "The Past," and the other, "The Future," are deserving of high commendation. A few stanzas on "Wild Flowers," and some entitled "Spring to the Flowers," are very sweet and tripping. "The Mother to her Starving Child" is replete with pathetic eloquence, and the "Line on a Friend lost at Sea" are of the same character. Mrs. Hawkshaw's "Sonnet to America" is, we may justly say, powerfully written, developing, as it does, sentiments of the highest character expressed in language of equal force. To give the reader, however, a proper specimen of Mrs. Hawkshaw's powers, we cannot resist quoting a piece, which, for the expression of an earnest and intense feeling in language of consistent beauty and power, we have rarely seen surpassed.

SONNET
To———

"I love my country, for I love my kind—
   Man is my brother wheresoe'er he roam—
   I love my father's hearth, my childhood's home,
And all the hopes and memories round it twined:
I love the deep thoughts and the cares which bind
   The mother to her children—in my heart
   These, and the love of song have each their part:
But not a part for thee alone, I find,
   For 'tis all thine—as light that fills no space
And yet pervades all nature, and which gives
   All forms their beauty, loveliness, and grace,
And energy and hope to all that lives;
So unto me hath been thy love—then take
This song of mine, and keep it for my sake."

Although the last in the book, this is certainly not the least of Mrs. Hawkshaw's productions.

In 1847, the fair author of *Dionysius* issued another small production entitled, *Poems for My Children*; as pretty and felicitous a collection of original poems for the youthful mind we have met with for a long period. Space forbids us entering into their merits minutely; but we may casually observe that they fully evince all that tenderness of feeling and beauty of expression so characteristic of her former productions. The series of poems are grave and gay, lively and solid; and though written in a beautifully poetical vein, are rendered sufficiently simple and familiar for the minds to which she addresses herself. We shall just take one charming little extract.

COMMON THINGS

"The sunshine is a glorious thing,
    That comes alike to all,
Lighting the peasant's lowly cot,
    The noble's painted hall.

The moonlight is a gentle thing,
    It through the window gleams,
Upon the snowy pillow, where
    The happy infant dreams.

It shines upon the fisher's boat,
    Out on the lonely sea;
Or where the little lambkins lie,
    Beneath the old oak-tree.

The dew-drops on the summer morn,
    Sparkle upon the grass;
The village children brush them off,
    That through the meadows pass.

There are no gems in monarchs' crowns,
    More beautiful than they;
And yet we scarcely notice them,
    But tread them off in play.

Poor Robin on the pear-tree sings,
    Beside the cottage-door;
The heath-flower fills the air with sweets,
    Upon the pathless moor.

There are as many lovely things,
    As many pleasant tones,
For those who sit by cottage hearths,
    As those who sit on thrones!"

With this extract we close our notice of Mrs. Hawkshaw, sincerely trusting that she may long continue to sing with all the beauty of sentiment and sound which she has hitherto thrown into her numerous effusions.

Reviews of *Sonnets on Anglo-Saxon History* (London: John Chapman, 1854)

Blackburn Standard (10 May 1854), 3.

Among the works announced as in preparation are two by Manchester ladies—one a novel by Miss Jewsbury,[1] the other a historical work by Mrs Hawkshaw.

Westminster Review (July–October 1854), 615.

We have two small volumes of poems to mention, both considerably above average merit. The first is a book of "Sonnets on Anglo-Saxon History;" the past has been faithfully consulted and interpreted in their production; the versification is good, and the language pure. Much benefit may be gained from perusing these modest, well-designed frescoes of Anglo-Saxon life.

Manchester Guardian (8 November 1854), 10.

It is seldom that an English poet resorts to the sonnet for the embodiment of his thoughts; and it has been held that the deficiency of English rhymes is adverse to the culture of this class of poetry, for which the Italian and the Spanish languages are much more facile. Still we recollect with pleasure that three of our true poets have indulged to some extent in this form of short poem—a quarterzain of two quatrains and two tercets—we mean Shakspere [*sic*], Milton, and Wordsworth. But they have poured forth in it individual emotions of love and sorrow, of deep thought and feeling, or of holy and elevated contemplation. Shakspere [*sic*], especially, seems to have made the sonnet the vehicle for the expression of feelings and emotions of intense poignancy, or of touching sadness; but which lose half their charm to the reader, lacking the key to the mysterious passion, to the griefs and complaints they sing. Beautiful as some of the more intelligible of these sonnets are, how infinitely more precious they would have been to all time, had the poet embalmed in them a series of historical pictures in miniature, instead of addresses to a friend persuading him to marry, or forgiving him for having robbed him of his mistress, or complaining of his coldness, and that he prefers another poet's praises, or disclaiming his own inconstancy to his friend, or reproaching his mistress with infidelity. But these are idle regrets; we must accept Shakspere's [*sic*] 154 sonnets as they reach us, with all their obscurity and mystery.

Mrs. Hawkshaw, who is already favourably known to the literary public by former poetic works, has given us, in the little volume under notice, a hundred sonnets, each upon some interesting passage of Anglo-Saxon history, and arranged in chronological sequence, from the aboriginal period of Britain down to the memorable battle of Hastings, and the extinction of Anglo-Saxon rule in England. Here then we have a charming little gallery of poetic historiettes, not merely a turning of facts into rhythm, but embalmed in amber thoughts and reflections which have a charm of their own. Few living writers have more concentrativeness than Mrs. Hawkshaw; she penetrates the outward husk of fact to the central idea kernelled within, and hence her poems are not merely descriptive but

---

1 Miss Jewsbury: Geraldine Jewsbury (1812–80), novelist. A likely reference to *Constance Herbert*, which was published in 1855.

suggestive; they instruct and refine, while they gratify the ear by the smoothness of their versification. Take her introductory sonnet:—

> 'T is a hard thing to judge the past aright,
>   Harder to judge the present, though it be
>   Before our eyes in stern reality:
> Nought of the beautiful, the ideal, the bright,
> Haloes the things that meet the common sight:
>   To find the lovely in the walks of life,
>   The music of humanity in strife,
> Kindness in sternness, gentleness in might,
> May try the mind as much as to unfold
>   The mouldering records of departed times,
> And more shall try the heart; too warm, too cold,
>   To judge of present hopes, and schemes, and crimes;
> How changed will they appear throughout the gloom
> Of coming years—our life seen from our tomb!

Here is a picture of aboriginal Britain:—

I.—THE BEGINNING.

> Man to our island came; but from what land
>   Were the first wanderers? Driven by adverse wind,
>   And mourning for the homes they left behind,
> Perchance they came; and on the silent strand
> They stood a lonely and deserted band:
>   The startled eagle, screaming, left the shore,
>   From the thick forest looked the tusky boar,
> While in the vale the stately elk reclined.
> Oblivion's stream hath swept all deeper trace,
>   They lived, toiled, died, and on the fertile plain
> The rude descendent took his father's place,
>   And felt his wants, and lived his life again:
> Saplings chance rooted in the mountain cleft,
> Seeds that the winds of time bore there and left.

We will even give a third sonnet in the order in which it occurs:—

II.—PROGRESS.

> Progress is nature's stamp on man; the mark
>   Of his divine and his humanity;
>   And dimly through the night of years we see
> Britain's first impulse onward: that strange bark
> Making its way across the billows dark

>   Of unknown seas, from far Phenicia's shore,
>   Another treasure bears than eastern store;
>   Thoughts that the heart shall feel, words that the ear shall hark.
>   E'en as the tropic stream bears through the tide
>   Of icy seas the seed-grains of its home,
>   Man hath his conscious schemes of wealth and pride,
>   But his unconscious ones, where'er he roam,
>   Work through the outer; o'er all life there lies
>   The soft, deep colouring of the heavenly skies.

The next which attracts us relates to the early introduction of Christianity into Britain, for it was in A.D. 525 that St. Deiniol is said to have founded a college at Bangor, which was raised to a bishopric about 550:—

>   Oh! beautiful as light when down it streams
>   Through cloudless ether, was the truth when taught
>   By the Great Master; but how soon it caught
>   A tinge of earthly colouring; Grecian dreams,
>   The Eastern's slavish fear, the mystic gleams
>   Of light through darkness struggling in the soul
>   That could not break an earlier creed's control,
>   Obscured, though never quenched, its heavenly beams.
>   But purer far was that beclouded light
>   Than aught before e'er seen in Britain's isle:
>   Oft the lone wanderer in the wintry night
>   Sought shelter in old Bangor's monkish pile,
>   And by the wood-heaped fire then waning dim,
>   Heard from the low-roofed church the Christian's hymn.

We take the first of three sonnets dedicated to Bede:—

XXI.—THE VENERABLE BEDE.—I.

>   Once by thy ruined but time-honoured cell
>   In years gone by I stood; I thought not then,
>   For I was but a child, that ever pen
>   Of mine should write thy name, or mine eyes dwell
>   In interest on thy antique page,—yet well
>   Hath memory kept that picture; the mossed stones
>   In the dull churchyard—e'en the north wind's tones,
>   As from the distant past, seem round me still to swell.
>   A book like thine is a most precious thing
>   By mind bequeathed to mind; it hath outlived
>   Thousands that much of fame and wealth could bring
>   For a brief space; for he who wrote, believed,
>   Aye, and believing words, whate'er they be,
>   Have on them stamped an immortality.

The next is a favourite with us:—

XXVI.—UNDER-CURRENTS.

But silently beneath this noise and strife,
    Worked countless energies of heart and head,
    And men, the glooms of time have overspread,
Nor left a single annal of their life;
Who tells what savage shaped from ore the knife?
    Toil for the good of man, but ask not fame,
    Ages may bless thy work, not know thy name,
No good once done time in the dust can tread.
The marsh is drained, the yellow harvest waves
    Where the lone heron watched the lazy stream,
Wood-lighted hearths were there, flower-sprinkled graves,
    And love and hope; 't was life, and not a dream,
And that blest gift to wearied man from heaven
Came to the toil-worn serf—one day of rest in seven.

Here is another vigorous picture:—

XXVII.—THE SERF.

Master and slave! strange words are those to hear
    Among a family of brethren named,
    Within a world a father's goodness framed,
Harsh 'mid its harmonies upon the ear
They fall; conjuring up every shape of fear
    That haunts the oppressor or the oppressed's path,
    Pride, avarice, cruelty, revenge, and wrath;
All that from misery wrings the bitterest tear;
All that brings into human hearts the blight
    Of selfishness, before whose poisonous breath
Love's flowers droop withering, and day fades to night,
    And the great gift of life turns to a death;
War's hurricane sweeps past, but while we sleep
Slavery's dark vapours poison as they creep.

We must not omit a portrait of the greatest of our Anglo-Saxon monarchs; but as all the great events of his life are familiar to us, we select a sonnet on his adversity and physical suffering:—

L.—ALFRED THE GREAT.—III. ADVERSITY.

We wish to those we love skies ever clear,
    Long summer-days, and pathways strewed with flowers:
    Best lessons are not learn'd in such bright hours;
The dark must teach them; through the dimming tear

The spirit-land looks beautiful and near;
    Such hours the soul does to itself reveal,
    And we the mystery of our being feel,
And shapes of beauty from the gloom appear.
No true and noble heart was ever reared
    Amid soft things; it may be pain or want,
Or sorrow o'er the grave of those endeared,
    Or that mysterious woe the soul can plant
Within itself,—but sorrow there must be,
Ere it can struggle to the high and free.

A summary of his character and rule:—

LVIII.—THE HERO-KING.

One hero fills a century, and the age
    An Alfred filled might well be satisfied;
    He slept within his tomb the Saxon's pride,
And History writ his name upon her page,
And hailed him patriot, statesman, poet, sage,
    And Nature, in his children, bade him still
    Live for the land he loved, and guard from ill
The shores round which the northern sea-steeds rage;
Son, daughter, grandson, echoes of his fame,
    Bore on to after years, until they died
On coward hearts, and not that hero name
    Could rouse to manly hope or noble pride;
Priest-ridden, slavish, down they bow the head
To the proud churchman, or the despot's tread.

As early as the year 692, missionaries left England to preach Christianity to the Pagan nations of the continent, and the following sonnet commemorates their labours:—

XLI.—TRUE WORKERS.

Forth from their homes they went, a simple band,
    To toil in heathendom; no cumbrous plan
    Fettered the movements of the earnest man;
Faith had he in his soul, and in his hand,
And needed not to work what others planned:
    It is a living soul, and not a thing
    Of mechanism, to which hearts will cling,
Or that to life can rouse a dying land.
There is more power in one deep truthful word,
    One honest, noble deed, than in all schemes
That men have planned, whose hearts no faith hath stirred,—
    More power in one great poet's glorious dreams

Than in a thousand systems hard and cold,
That but the mortal, not the man unfold.

A portrait of Alfred's noble daughter will interest:—

LIV.—WOMAN.—I. ETHELFLEDA, THE DAUGHTER OF ALFRED.

Woman hath trodden every path of life,
   Though to her nature strange; priestess or queen,
   To whom men looked in reverence, she hath been;
Leader of armies in heroic strife,
Champion for truth when error hath been rife,—
All these, and more, she hath been, and may be,
And out of these may work in harmony
   That deeper life of hers, the life unseen:
And that true life, how doth the outer touch,
   And make or mar it!—'t is a gift to all,
A solemn gift, that equalises much
   That we think differing, and call great or small.
What are the things that give thee inner might?
These are the great, the rest are rust and blight.

We should like to quote Dunstan the Boy, Godwin the Boy, the Forest, and various other sonnets, but we must stay our hand, The following are thoughts suggested by the Battle of Hastings:—

XCVII.—NIGHT AFTER BATTLE.

Silence and death! how hideous or how fair
   These two may be; soft as in angel's sleep
   The dead may look, and grief forget to weep;
And on the mountains there are moments, rare
And precious, when the earth, and sky, and air,
   Are hushed in breathless stillness, as if God
   Amid their mighty solitudes had trod.
And not a tone did awe-struck nature dare;
And death, and night, and silence settled down
   Upon that field of fatal fight; and not
A requiem sighed the wind; with sullen frown
   The clouds hung moveless o'er the accursed spot,
But bursting storms, less fearful, had seemed there
The death was doom, the silence was despair.

We close our extracts with the last sonnet in the volume:—

CONCLUSION.

And now the task I planned in days gone by
  Is finished; and I turn mine eyes once more
  From their long looking on the things of yore
Unto the future's veiléd mystery,
Or the all-pressing present, wherein lie
  The truth-grains of that past—atoms enwrought
  With stately forms, or household words and thought,
And mixed for aye with England's destiny.
Farewell, then, country of my Saxon sires!
  By Edward's shrine I bid thee now farewell;
  In thee were lighted first those household fires
    Where loving hearts and truthful spirits dwell;
  Each summer glade beneath the forest tree,
To me, old Saxon-land, shall speak of thee!

Living Age 44, no. 554 (6 January 1855), 142.

In a series of about a hundred sonnets, the accomplished author gives a comprehensive and interesting sketch of Anglo-Saxon history. Few of the facts of importance recorded by the old chroniclers are here omitted; and references occur to traditional tales, which, if less authentic, are now inseparable from our early English annals. Prefixed to each sonnet is an extract from some author of note, or some explanatory remarks by which the thread of the metrical story is sustained. Some of the sonnets are written with spirit and force, and the poetry is pleasantly made the vehicle of historical facts and allusions. Here is one, with its introductory explanation:—"When he (Edwin, King of Northumbria) inquired of the high priest (Coifi) who should first profane the altars and temples of their idols, with the enclosures that were about them, he answered, 'I; for who can more properly than myself destroy those things which I worshipped through ignorance?' ... As soon as he drew near the temple he profaned the same, casting into it the spear which he held; ... the place where the idols were is still shown, not far from York, to the eastward, beyond the River Derwent, and is now called Godmundingham." See Bede's *Ecclesiastical History*.

CHRISTIANITY RECEIVED BY THE SAXONS.

'T is easy on the accustomed path to tread,
  Worn by the feet of generations past;
  But he who treads it first, or treads it last,
Venturing where all is silent as the dead—
Or lingering there when all besides are fled—
  These are the lofty spirits who unfold
  New views of greatness, or preserve the old.
Both noble, but by different natures led.
The Saxon story tells of one who flung

>   His fateful arrow at the idol's shrine,
>   While others round the mouldering ruins hung,
>   Whose desolation was to them divine:
>   Types of two classes who must ever be
>   Within a land that would be strong, yet free.

We give also the last of six sonnets on King Alfred:—

>   One hero fills a century, and the age
>   An Alfred filled might well be satisfied;
>   He slept within his tomb the Saxon's pride,
>   And History writ his name upon her page,
>   And hailed him patriot, statesman, poet, sage,
>   And Nature, in his children, bade him still
>   Live for the land he loved, and guard from ill
>   The shores round which the northern sea-steeds rage;
>   Son, daughter, grandson, echoes of his fame,
>   Bore on to after years, until they died
>   On coward hearts, and not that hero name
>   Could rouse to manly hope or noble pride;
>   Priest-ridden, slavish, down they bow the head
>   To the proud churchman, or the despot's tread.

From some of the historical readings and reflections of the author we may be disposed to dissent; but we commend her book as much for its historical information as its poetical merit.

Athenæum (20 January 1855), 76–7.

This book has at least two merits,—it has no Preface and it has a purpose. We hear no venial nonsense about the entreaties of friends, and no foolish, vapouring defiance of critics and criticism. The work has an artistic shape; and is, in reality, not a bundle of sonnets, but one long poem, rather loosely connected, on the chief events of Anglo-Saxon history. As sonnets they do not rank very high, for, though metrical and not wanting in vigour, they require the full diapason that should consummate the fourteen lines,— and instead of one thought fully worked out they often contain two or three thoughts crowded and unelaborated. We can scarcely class Miss Hawkshaw as an addition to our female writers, for though tender, polished, pious, and sincere, she aims more at the manly excellencies of Wordsworth than the plaintive cadence of Mrs. Hemans or the Byronism of L.E.L. A careful equality (rather unprogressive and past growing) is the peculiar feature of her writing. The following sonnet is sufficient to show her style:—

>   *Alfred the Great.—V. Romney Marsh, Kent.*
>
>   The fisher's boat rocks idly on the sea,
>   The sheep are resting on the grassy hill,
>   Where village children wander at their will,

> Blithe as the singing birds, almost as free;
> And are these all the thoughtful man can see
> > Where once intrepid Alfred and his band
> > Drove the fierce Northman from the Kentish strand?
> Fair is the scene, yet other things there be
> Than meet the eye; and with this seeming good
> > How much of evil mingles, who may say?
> Rightly we shudder at those days of blood;
> > But ignorance and crime still bar the way,
> And avarice hugs his bags of golden dust,
> And long repose brings idlesse and false trust.

Miss Hawkshaw's subjects are well selected, and chosen, with poetical taste, rather for their suggestiveness than for the pictures they present.

Monthly Christian Spectator 5 (January–December 1855), 55.

Sonnets on Anglo-Saxon History, by Ann Hawkshaw (J. Chapman), is the title of an extremely interesting and very meritorious collection of original sonnets on incidents of our early national history, and, we are afraid we must say, early myths. We are not very partial to the sonnet, but Miss Hawkshaw's pen glides gracefully round the stiff settings of this very artificial form of poetical composition.

Eclectic Review 10 (July–December 1855): 376.

Sonnets on Anglo-Saxon History, by Ann Hawkshaw (John Chapman), exhibit industry and considerable vigour, but the authoress possesses no adequate power for rendering the soul of history 'rhythmically visible.'

Obituary

Manchester Guardian (1 May 1885), 8.

Death of Lady Hawkshaw.—We much regret to announce the death, which took place on Wednesday evening, at her residence, Belgrave Mansions, Grosvenor Gardens, London, of Ann, wife of Sir John Hawkshaw, F.R.S. Among many accomplished women who have made their home in Manchester during the past half century, none secured a deeper regard than the gifted lady whose death we now record. Lady Hawkshaw was the daughter of the Rev. James Jackson, of Green Hammerton, Yorkshire, where she was born in 1813 [sic]. Soon after her marriage (in 1835) her husband was appointed engineer to the Manchester and Bolton Canal and Railway, and subsequently to the Lancashire and Yorkshire Railway; and they took up their residence in the first instance in Sandy Lane, Pendleton; afterwards in Islington Square, Salford; and for some years at Broughton Lodge, Higher Broughton. It was during her fifteen to twenty years' residence in Manchester that Mrs Hawkshaw gave to the world strong evidence of being possessed of the poetic gift. If we remember rightly, some of her earliest effusions appeared in the Manchester Guardian—a corner of which at that period was supplied by the muse of some of our best-known local poets. In 1842 appeared "Dionysius the Areopagite, with other Poems. By Ann Hawkshaw." The little volume, which was issued by a firm of local publishers—Messrs. Simms and Dinham, of Exchange-street,—attracted considerable attention and was very favourably received both in London and the provinces. In 1847 she published another volume of verse, called "Poems for My Children," which showed much tenderness of feeling and beauty of expression. In 1854 she published a series of 98 "Sonnets on Anglo-Saxon History," and in 1871 a series of prose and poetical sketches for children entitled "Cecil's Own Book".

Posthumous Review

Notes and Queries: Northern Notes, 'A Yorkshire Poetess', *Yorkshire Herald* (16 July 1892), 4.

Lady Ann Hawkshaw was the daughter of the Rev. James Jackson, minister of the Independent congregations at Great Ouseburn and Green Hammerton, near York. Her parents were descended from old well-to-do Yorkshire yeomen families. Born in the year 1813 [sic], Lady Ann began early to give evidence of a poetic sense, and at 15 had written several stories in verse, which, however, were not published. *'Dionysius the Areopagite', with other poems* was the earliest work she published. This came out exactly fifty years ago, and was followed by *Sonnets on Saxon History* [sic] and *Poems for My Children*, and more recently by a small volume for her grandchild, Cecil Wedgwood. In 1840 [sic] Miss Jackson was married to the then rising engineer Mr John Hawkshaw (afterwards Sir John Hawkshaw, F.R.S.), the designer and constructor of many great works both in England and abroad. Lady Hawkshaw died in 1887 [sic]. There is such a faculty of expression with sweet music of rhythm in some of her verse that it is difficult to say why her works have not been more popular.

Appendix B

Since single poems published in newspapers and magazines, and often unattributed, are difficult to trace, this list of poems republished in Hawkshaw's lifetime, and reprinted after her death, is inevitably incomplete. As the list shows, the poems Hawkshaw wrote for her children were widely anthologised and appear in educational readers in the United Kingdom, the Republic of Ireland and the United States over a number of years during the nineteenth and twentieth centuries. Research into the republishing of Hawkshaw's poetry has raised an interesting misappropriation of authorship. Early twentieth-century anthologies of children's poetry frequently identify Ann Hawkshaw as the author of *Aunt Effie's Rhymes for Little Children* (1852) and *Aunt Effie's Gift to the Nursery* (1854). Since 1906, poems from these collections have been included in several anthologies and educational readers in England and the United States, with Hawkshaw named as the author. Indeed, volume one of the first edition of Halkett and Laing's *Dictionary of the Anonymous and Pseudonymous Literature of Great Britain*, published in 1882 and whilst Hawkshaw was still alive, ascribes *Aunt Effie's Rhymes for Little Children* and *Aunt Effie's Gift to the Nursery* to 'Mrs Hawkshaw'. However, ten years later, John Julian's *Dictionary of Hymnology* (1892) correctly credits Jane Euphemia Saxby (née Browne) with the authorship of *Aunt Effie's Gift to the Nursery*. Thereafter, in volume one of the new edition of Halkett and Laing, published in 1926, the *Aunt Effie* collections are again ascribed to 'Mrs Hawkshaw', but now with the note 'Ascribed also to Mrs Saxby, née Jane Euphemia Browne'.

Any confusion of authorship is dispelled in a publisher's advertisement in the back pages of *Aunt Effie's Gift to the Nursery*, which begins 'By the same Author, *The Dove on the Cross*'. James Nisbett & Co. had first published this book of devotional verse by Jane Euphemia Browne in 1849, with poems from the collection, many of which were later set to music as hymns, attracting the attention of John Julian, who included several in his 1892 hymnology. 'Mrs Saxby's hymns are very plaintive and tender', Julian notes, citing Saxby herself in explanation: "I wrote many of my published hymns during a very long and distressing illness, which lasted many years. I thought probably that I was then in the 'Border Land', and wrote accordingly" (Julian's *Hymnology*, 998).

The publication in 1905 of the diary of Jane Euphemia Browne's fourteen-year-old sister Mary (*The Diary of a Girl in France in 1821*) makes the identity of Aunt Effie explicit. An editor's note identifies sister 'Euphemia' of Mary's narrative as the future Aunt Effie: 'In after years [Euphemia] published a clever children's book, *Aunt Effie's Nursery Rhymes* (illustrated), which ran through many editions; also a volume of sacred poems, *The Dove on the Cross*'.[1] Even without these biographical and bibliographical clues, the style of the poets is distinct enough to separate authorship. The overtly didactic poems of *Aunt Effie's Rhymes for Little Children* and the pious, devotional and God-fearing tone of *Aunt Effie's Gift to the Nursery* have little in common with Hawkshaw's poetry written for children, in which intimate dialogue between mother and child leads to a more subtle brand of moral education.

It is not entirely clear how these early misattributions occurred, but after 1906 Hawkshaw becomes routinely credited as the author of poems from the *Aunt Effie* volumes, particularly in American anthologies. In 1906, the poem 'Dame Duck's First Lecture on

---

1 Mary Browne, *The Diary of a Girl in France in 1821* (London: John Murray, 1905), 14.

Education' from *Aunt Effie's Rhymes for Little Children* is included under the name of 'Ann Hawkshaw' in the Hill Readers series of educational readers, published in Boston by Ginn & Co. Prior to this, Hawkshaw's poems for children had been reprinted and correctly attributed in several nineteenth-century children's anthologies and educational readers published in England and the United States between 1848 and 1891 (see listings below). Indeed, in *Easy Rhymes and Simple Poems for Young Children* (London: Routledge, 1864), 'Mrs Hawkshawe [sic]' and 'Aunt Effie' are listed as separate contributors. Sometime in the latter half of the nineteenth-century, Hawkshaw becomes confused with Aunt Effie – and a second misappropriation may hold a clue to this confusion. On several occasions between 1851 and 1919, Hawkshaw's poems for children are anthologised under the name of 'Elizabeth Hawkshaw', which can be dated back to 1851, and the publication in Ireland of *Selections from the British Poets*, compiled by the Commissioners of National Education in Ireland. Volume one of the collection includes 'A City Child's Complaint', by 'Mrs E. Hawkshaw', which as the footnote indicates, is taken from 'an interesting and valuable little work, entitled "Poems for My Children"'.[2] Volume two features 'The Wind', by 'Elizabeth Hawkshaw'. Both poems are Ann Hawkshaw's, published in 1847 in *Poems for My Children* under the name of 'Mrs Hawkshaw'. Around the time that *Selections from the British Poets* was compiled, the Hawkshaws were a prominent Dublin family that included an 'Elizabeth Hawkshaw'. Although the family was not connected to Ann Hawkshaw, it is likely that with only 'Mrs Hawkshaw' listed as the author of *Poems for My Children*, an assumption of authorship was made that linked Elizabeth Hawkshaw of Dublin to the poetry of Ann Hawkshaw. After this date, Hawkshaw's poems for children were published in several anthologies under the name of 'Elizabeth Hawkshaw' or 'Mrs E Hawkshaw'. With anthologies listing poems under the name of 'E' rather than 'A' Hawkshaw, it is conceivable that later anthologists connected Hawkshaw to the name Effie, and from there to the *Aunt Effie* collections.

---

2 *Selections from the British Poets, chronologically arranged from Chaucer to the present time, under separate divisions, with introductions explaining the different species of poetry*, vol. 1 (Dublin: Director of the Commissioners of National Education in Ireland, 1851), 313.

Reprinted Poems

'Sonnet—To America' (final two lines), John Hawkshaw, *Reminiscences of South America: From Two and a Half Years' Residence in Venezuela* (London: Jackson and Walford, 1838), 52.

'Dionysius the Areopagite', 28 lines from part 2, section 5, retitled 'The Same, yet Changed', *Cork Examiner* (23 December 1842), 4.

'Life's Dull Reality', *Athenæum Souvenir; original Poems, &c., contributed by various Authors, in aid of the Funds of the Athenæum Bazaar, held in the Town Hall, MANCHESTER, October 1843* (Manchester: J. Gadsby, 1843), 3.

'Life's Dull Reality', *Manchester Guardian* (11 October 1843), 3.

'The Past' (stanzas 22–5), *Carlisle Journal* (9 May 1846), 4.

'Common Things', *Manchester Guardian* (24 July 1847), 3.

'Mary's Wish', *Derby Mercury* (8 September 1847), 4.

'The History of a Coral Islet', *Leicestershire Mercury* (27 November 1847), 4.

'Common Things', *Reading Mercury, Oxford Gazette, Newbury Herald, and Berks County Paper* (22 January 1848), 4.

'The Wind', *Dundee Courier* (26 January 1848), 4.

'Common Things', *Hereford Journal* (26 January 1848), 4.

'The City Child's Complaint', *Hereford Journal* (23 February 1848), 4.

'The City Child's Complaint', *Leicester Journal* (3 March 1848), 4.

'Common Things', *Eclectic Magazine*, vol. 13 (March 1848), 428.

'Common Things', *Cambridge Chronicle and Journal, and Huntingdonshire Gazette* (22 April 1848), 4.

'Common Things', *Family Economist; a Penny Monthly Magazine, Devoted to the Moral, Physical, and Domestic Improvement of the Industrious Classes*, vol. 1 (London: Groombridge and Sons, 1848), 46.

'Common Things', *The Friend: A Religious and Literary Journal*, vol. 21 (Philadelphia, 1848), 284.

'The Wind', *Magazine for the Young*, vol. 7 (London, 1848), 239–40.

'Common Things', [Mrs Hawkshawe], *Lessons on Industrial Education, for the Use of Female Schools* (London: Longman, Brown, Green & Longmans, 1849), 5.

'Common Things', *Tales and Readings for the People*, vol. 1 (London: George Vickers, 1849), 69.

'The Wind', *Pleasant Pages*, vol. 5 (London: Houlston and Stoneman, 1850), 271.

'A City Child's Complaint', [Mrs E Hawkshaw], *Selections from the British Poets, chronologically arranged from Chaucer to the present time, under separate divisions, with introductions explaining the different species of poetry*, vol. 1 (Dublin: Director of the Commissioners of National Education in Ireland, 1851), 313–14.

'The Wind', [Mrs E Hawkshaw], *Selections from the British Poets, chronologically arranged from Chaucer to the present time, under separate divisions, with introductions explaining the different species of poetry*, vol. 2 (Dublin: Director of the Commissioners of National Education in Ireland, 1851), 199–201.

'Common Things', *Jackson's Oxford Journal* (24 January 1852), 4.

'Common Things', *Berrow's Worcester Journal* (29 January 1852), 4.

'Common Things', *Stirling Observer* (22 December 1852), 2.

'Common Things', *Kendal Mercury* (25 December 1852), 3.

'Common Things' (final stanza), 'The Bawdsey Lectures', *Essex Standard* (25 March 1853), 3.

'Common Things' (extract), Seacome Ellison, *A Grammar of the English Language for the Use of Schools and Students: With Copious Examples and Exercises* (London: Nathaniel Cooke, 1854), 92.
'Common Things', *Gems of Thought and Flowers of Fancy*, ed. Richard Wright Procter (London: Partridge and Oakey, 1855), 311–12.
'Alfred the Great' (from *Sonnets on Anglo-Saxon History*), *Taunton Courier and Western Advertiser* (5 March 1856), 6.
'Common Things', [Mrs Hawkshawe], Kenelm Henry Digby, *The Lover's Seat: Kathemérina or Common Things in Relation to Beauty, Virtue and Truth*, vol. 1 (London: 1856), 29–30.
'Common Things', [Mrs Hawkshawe], Edward Hughes, *Select specimens of English Poetry, with prose introductions, notes, and questions: to which is added, an etymological appendix of Greek, Latin and Saxon roots*, 5th ed. (London: Longman, Brown, Green & Longmans, 1856), 296.
'Common Things', *The Progressive Third Reader, for public and private schools: containing the elementary principles of elocution, illustrated by examples and exercises in connection with the tables and rules, and a series of lessons in reading; with original designs and engravings* (Boston: Sanborn, Bazin and Ellsworth, 1857), 88–9.
'The Wind', *Huddersfield Chronicle* (6 February 1858), 3.
'Common Things', [Mrs Hawkshawe], A.W. Buchan, *The Advanced Prose and Poetical Reader, being a collection of select specimens in English with explanatory notes and questions on each lesson to which are appended lists of prefixes and affixes with an etymological vocabulary*, 2nd ed. (Edinburgh: Adam and Charles Black, 1859), 190.
'The City Child's Complaint', [Mrs E Hawkshawe], *The Book of Children's Hymns and Rhymes, Collected by the Daughter of a Clergyman* (London: James Hogg and Sons, 1859), 305.
'The Wind', *Popular Poetry: A Selection of Pieces Old and New, Adapted for General Use* (London: Burns and Lambert, 1862), 36–7.
'The Wind' (final stanza), William Houlston, *The Circle secerned from the Square, and its area gauged in terms of a triangle common to both; and an original, simple, and exact method pointed out, of approximating as closely as possible to the numeral value of this triangle, and the consequent veritable content of the inscribed circle, in relation to any given square* (London: Simpkin, Marshall & Co., 1862), 11.
'The Wind' (final stanza), used in a review of Houlston's *The Circle secerned from the Square*, in *Athenæum* (18 January 1862), 81.
'Common Things' (final stanza), 'Happy Homes, and How to Make Them', *Bury Times* (15 March 1862), 3.
'Common Things', [Mrs Hawkshawe], *Easy Rhymes and Simple Poems for Young Children* (London: Routledge, Warne, and Routledge, 1864), 37–8.
'Common Things' (listed as 'Common To All'), [Mrs Hawkshawe], *Life-Lights of Song: Songs of Life and Labour*, ed. David Page (Edinburgh: William P. Nimmo, 1864), 204–5.
'The Wind', [Elizabeth Hawkshaw], *Book of Juvenile Poetry: Containing Historical, Narrative, Descriptive, and Sacred Pieces, Selected from the Best Authors* (London: T. Nelson and Sons, 1864), 218–19.
'The Wind', [Elizabeth Hawkshaw], *The Casquet of Gems: Choice Selections from the Poets* (Edinburgh: William P. Nimmo, 1864), 477.
'Common Things', *The Children's Prize*, no. 11 (November 1864), 167.

'The Wind', [Mrs Ann Hawkshawe], John Hugh H… Composition in a series of familiar letters, with num… Examination Papers; chapters on précis writing, etc. (L… …8), 126–7.
'The Wind', [Elizabeth Hawkshaw], The Useful Knov… …ing Books, ed. Edward Thomas Stevens (London, 1872), 45.
'The City Child's Complaint', [Mrs. E. Hawkshawe], Grantham Journal (14 June 1873), 7.
'Common Things', [Mrs. Hawkshawe], The Onward Reciter, ed. W. Darrah (London, 1877), 141.
'Common Things', Gleeson's Monthly Companion, vol. 8 (1879), 333–4.
'The Wind', [Elizabeth Hawkshaw], Army and Navy Magazine, vol. 6 (1882), 86.
'The Wind', [E Hawkshaw], entry for 19 September, 'Through All the Varying Year': A Calendar of Nature, Mary Jeaffreson (Orpington, 1884).
'King Alfred and His Mother', 'The Hermit, the Chieftain and the Child', 'Editha', 'Ada', [Lady Hawkshaw], The Children's Casket: Favourite Poems for Recitation, compiled by Annie M. Hone (London: Griffith, Farran, Okeden and Welsh, 1891), 26–8, 124–7, 132–4, 260–261.
'Common Things' (final stanza), 'Conservative Opinion of Working Men', Portsmouth Evening News (22 June 1892), 3.
'The Wind' (final stanza), The Preacher's Complete Homiletical Commentary on the Old Testament, vol. 4 (New York and London: Fune & Wagnalls, 1892), 346.
'Common Things' (final stanza), précised in an advertisement in the Western Gazette (1 July 1898), 5.
'Common Things', Walter Lorenzo Sheldon, Lessons in the Study of Habits: For Use in School and Home (Chicago: W. M. Welch, 1903), 167.
'Common Things', Geoffrey Buckwalter, The Third Reader (New York: P. P. Simmons, 1907), 59.
'The Wind', [Elizabeth Hawkshaw], The Sea's Anthology, from the Earliest Times Down to the Middle of the Nineteenth Century, ed. J. E. Patterson (London, 1913), 23.
'Common Things', reader's contribution to 'Children's Circle' in the Southern Reporter (21 September 1922), 2.
'Common Things', reader's contribution to 'Children's Circle' in the Southern Reporter (15 February 1923), 2.
'The Wind' (stanza ten), Derby Daily Telegraph (13 February 1925), 6.
'The Wind' (final stanza), reader's contribution to 'Thoughts of the Week', Bath Chronicle and Weekly Gazette (19 September 1936), 13.
'The Wind' (final stanza), J. Maurus, Just a Moment Please (Bombay Saint Paul Society, 1988), 193.
'The City Child's Complaint', Winged Words: An Anthology of Victorian Women's Poetry and Verse, ed. Catherine W. Reilly (London: Enitharmon Press, 1994), 74.
'The Mother to her Starving Child', Nineteenth-Century Women Poets: An Oxford Anthology, eds Isobel Armstrong, Joseph Bristow and Cath Sharrock (Oxford: Clarendon Press, 1996), 346–7.
'Why am I a Slave?', Nineteenth-Century Women Poets: An Oxford Anthology, eds Isobel Armstrong, Joseph Bristow and Cath Sharrock (Oxford: Clarendon Press, 1996), 347–8.
'The Anglo-Saxons' (from Sonnets on Anglo-Saxon History), Paul Hill, The Anglo-Saxons: The Verdict of History (Stroud: Tempus Publishing, 2006), 146.

Bibliography

Primary

Bamford, Samuel. *Poems*. Manchester: published by the author, 1843.

Barthélemy, Jean Jacques. *The Travels of Anacharsis the Younger in Greece During the Middle of the Fourth Century before the Christian Era*, 7 vols. London, 1794.

Bennet, George, and the Rev. Daniel Tyerman. *Journal of Voyages and Travels*, 2 vols. London: Frederick Westley and A. H. Davis, 1831.

British Museum: Egyptian Antiquities, The, vol. 1. London: Charles Knight, 1832.

Browne, Mary. *The Diary of a Girl in France in 1821*. London: John Murray, 1905.

Carlyle Letters Online [CLO], ed. Brent E. Kinser: http://carlyleletters.org (accessed 25 May 2013).

Chateaubriand, François-René de. *La Génie du christianisme*, 3 vols, trans. Frederic Shoberl. London: Henry Colburn, 1813.

Cowper, William. *The Complete Poetical Works of William Cowper*. Edinburgh: Gall and Inglis, 1855.

Diary of John Clarke Hawkshaw of Hollycombe, The, vol. 1. Unpublished manuscript, 1913. Transcribed from the manuscript notebooks by Martin Beaumont. Original notebooks retained by Dr Christabel Barran.

Evans, John. *Lancashire Authors and Orators: A Series of Literary Sketches of Some of the Principle Authors, Divines, Members of Parliament, etc, Connected with the County of Lancaster*. London: Houlston and Stoneman, 1850.

Gaskell, Elizabeth. *The Life of Charlotte Brontë*, vol. 1. London: Smith, Elder, 1857.

Gibbon, Edward. *The History of the Decline and Fall of the Roman Empire*, 6 vols. London: Strachan and Cadell, 1776–89.

Giles, John Allen. *The Venerable Bede's Ecclesiastical History of England, also The Anglo-Saxon Chronicle*. London: Henry G. Bohn, 1847.

———. *The Life and Times of Alfred the Great*. London: George Bell, 1848.

———. *Six Old English Chronicles*. London: Henry G. Bohn, 1848.

Gordon, George, Lord Byron. *Childe Harold's Pilgrimage: A Romaunt*. London: John Murray, 1812.

Hawkshaw, Ann. *'Dionysius the Areopagite', with Other Poems*. London: Jackson and Walford; Manchester: Simms and Dinham, 1842.

———. 'Life's Dull Reality'. In *Athenæum Souvenir; original Poems, &c., contributed by various Authors, in aid of the Funds of the Athenæum Bazaar, held in the Town Hall, MANCHESTER, October 1843*. Manchester: J. Gadsby, 1843.

———. *Poems for My Children*. London: Simpkin and Marshall; Manchester: Simms and Dinham, 1847.

———. *Sonnets on Anglo-Saxon History*. London: John Chapman, 1854.

———. *Cecil's Own Book*. Printed for private circulation, 1871.

———. 'Memories of my Childhood'. Unpublished manuscript, 1856. From the private papers of Mrs Diane Whitehead.

———. Letters to John Relly Beard. Woodhouse Collection. John Rylands University Library. Manchester: reference A2/1, shelf 22.8.

———. Letters to Henry Hawkshaw. Staffordshire and Stoke-on-Trent Archive Service. Staffordshire Records Office: reference D4347.

Hawkshaw, John. *Reminiscences of South America: From Two and a Half Years' Residence in Venezuela*. London: Jackson and Walford, 1838.

Hemans, Felicia. *The Siege of Valencia: A Dramatick Poem; The Last Constantine: With Other Poems*. London: John Murray, 1823.

Hollycombe visitors' book (1873–1935). From the private papers of Mrs Diane Whitehead.

Kemble, John Mitchell. *The Saxons in England: A History of the English Commonwealth till the Period of the Norman Conquest*, 2 vols. London: Longman, Brown, Green & Longmans, 1849.

Landon, Letitia. E. *The Improvisatris, and Other Poems*. London: Hurst, Robinson; Edinburgh: A. Constable, 1824.

Palgrave, Francis. *History of the Anglo-Saxons*. London: John Murray, 1831.

Pausanias. *The Description of Greece*, 3 vols, trans. Thomas Taylor. London: R. Faulder, 1794.

Penny Cyclopædia of the Society for the Diffusion of Useful Knowledge, The, 30 vols, ed. George Long. London: Charles Knight, 1833–43.

Penny Magazine of the Society for the Diffusion of Useful Knowledge, The, 14 vols, London: Charles Knight, 1832–45.

Richardson, George. *Patriotism, in Three Cantos, and Other Poems*. London: W. J. Adams; Manchester: G. & A. Falkner, 1844.

Rogerson, John Bolton, ed. *The Festive Wreath: A Collection of Original Contributions Read at a Literary Meeting Held in Manchester March 24th 1842*. Manchester: Bradshaw and Blacklock, 1842.

Rossetti, Christina. *Sing-Song*. London: Routledge and Sons, 1872.

Southey, Caroline A. *Ellen Fitzarthur: A Metrical Tale, in Five Cantos*. London: Longman, Hurst, Rees, Orme & Brown, 1820.

Taylor, Ann, Jane Taylor and Isaac Taylor, Jr. *Hymns for Infant Minds*. Bucklersbury, 1810.

Turner, Sharon. *A Vindication of the Genuineness of the Ancient British Poems of Aneurin, Taliesin, Llywarch Hen and Merdhin with Specimens of Their Poems*. London: E. Williams, 1803.

———. *The History of England during the Middle Ages*, 4 vols. London: Longman, Hurst, Rees, Orme, Brown & Green, 1825.

———. *The History of the Anglo-Saxons: From the Earliest Period to the Norman Conquest*, 3 vols, 6th ed. Paris: Baudry's European Library, 1840.

Wheeler, James. *Manchester Poetry*. London: Charles Tilt, 1838.

Secondary

Armstrong, Isobel. *Victorian Poetry: Poetry, Poetics and Politics*. London: Routledge, 1993.

———. 'Msrepresentation [sic]: Codes of Affect and Politics in Nineteenth-Century Women's Poetry'. In *Women's Poetry, Late Romantic to Late Victorian: Gender and Genre, 1830–1900*, ed. Isobel Armstrong and Virginia Blain, 3–32. Basingstoke: Palgrave Macmillan, 1999.

Armstrong, Isobel, Joseph Bristow and Cath Sharrock, eds. *Nineteenth-Century Women Poets: An Oxford Anthology*. Oxford: Clarendon Press, 1996.

Bark, Debbie. 'Sight, Sound, and Silence: Representations of the Slave Body in Barrett Browning, Hawkshaw, and Douglass'. *Victorian Newsletter* 114 (Fall 2008): 51–68.

_____. 'Reconfiguring the Urban Child: Ann Hawkshaw's *Poems for My Children* (1847)'. In 'Victorian Childhoods', *Leeds Working Papers in Victorian Studies* 11 (2010): 19–29.

_____. 'Manchester and Early Victorian Literary Culture'. *Literature Compass* 8, no. 6 (2011): 404–14.

_____. 'Ann Hawkshaw'. In *British Writers Supplement XVIII*, ed. Jay Parini, 127–43. Farmington Hills: Charles Scribner's Sons, 2012.

_____. 'Mothers, Wives and Daughters Speak: The Recovery of Anglo-Saxon Women in Ann Hawkshaw's *Sonnets on Anglo-Saxon History*'. *Women's Writing* 19, no. 4 (December 2012): 404–16.

_____. 'Poetry of Social Conscience, Poetry of Transition: Ann Hawkshaw's "Introductory Stanzas" and "The Mother to Her Starving Child"'. In *Poetry, Politics and Pictures: Culture and Identity in Europe, 1840–1914*, ed. Ingrid Hanson, Jack Rhoden and Erin Snyder, 45–65. Oxford: Peter Lang, 2013.

Chrimes, Mike. 'Hawkshaw, Sir John (1811–1891)'. *Oxford Dictionary of National Biography*. Oxford: Oxford University Press, 2004; online ed. January 2013: http://www.oxforddnb.com/view/article/12690 (accessed 23 July 2013).

Delli Carpini, John. *History, Religion and Politics in William Wordsworth's 'Ecclesiastical Sonnets'*. Lewiston: The Edwin Mellen Press, 2004.

Easson, Angus. *Elizabeth Gaskell: The Critical Heritage*. London: Routledge and Kegan Paul, 1991.

Emma Darwin's Diary. Darwin Online: http://darwin-online.org.uk/content/frameset?itemID=CUL-DAR242%5B.27%5D&viewtype=image&pageseq=1 (accessed 15 May 2009).

Colley, Linda. *Britons: Forging the Nation, 1707–1837*. New Haven and London: Yale University Press, 2005.

Chapple, J. A. V., and Arthur Pollard, eds. *The Letters of Mrs Gaskell*. Manchester: Manchester University Press, 1966.

Chapple, John, and Alan Shelston, eds. *Further Letters of Mrs Gaskell*. Manchester: Manchester University Press, 2000.

Halkett, Samuel, and John Laing. *Dictionary of the Anonymous and Pseudonymous Literature of Great Britain*, 4 vols, ed. Catherine Laing. Edinburgh: W. Paterson, 1882–8; 7 vols, Edinburgh, 1926–34 (revised and enlarged by James Kennedy et al.).

Heywood, James. *Illustrations of the Manchester Meeting of the British Association for the Advancement of Science, June 1842*. Manchester: Thomas Forrest, 1843.

Hill, Paul. *The Anglo-Saxons: The Verdict of History*. Stroud: Tempus Publishing, 2006.

Julian, John D. *Dictionary of Hymnology: Origin and History of Christian Hymns and Hymnwriters of All Ages and Nations, Together with Biographical and Critical Notices of Their Authors and Translators*. London: John Murray; New York: Charles Scriber's Sons, 1892.

Langlands, A. W. *Dionysius the Areopagite: A Tragedy*. London: Elliot Stock, 1910.

Maidment, Brian. 'Class and Cultural Production in the Industrial City: Poetry in Victorian Manchester'. In *City, Class and Culture: Studies of Social Policy and Cultural Production in Victorian Manchester*, ed. Alan J. Kidd and K. W. Roberts, 148–66. Manchester: Manchester University Press, 1985.

Porter, Val. *Milland: The Book*. Milland: Milland Memories Group, 2003.

Richards, Bernard. *English Poetry of the Victorian Period 1830–1890*, 2nd ed. Harlow: Longman, 2001.

Secord, James A. *Victorian Sensation: The Extraordinary Publication, Reception, and Secret Authorship of 'Vestiges of the Natural History of Creation'*. Chicago: University of Chicago Press, 2000.

Shaen, Margaret J., ed. *Memorials of Two Sisters: Susanna and Catherine Winkworth*. London: Longman, Green, 1908.

Smyth, George Lewis. *The Monuments and Genii of St. Paul's and of Westminster Abbey*. London: John Williams, 1826.

Styles, Morag. *From the Garden to the Street: Three Hundred Years of Poetry for Children*. London: Cassell, 1998.

Swindells, Thomas. *Manchester Streets and Manchester Men*. Manchester: J. E. Cornish, 1908.

Vicinus, Martha. 'Literary Voices of an Industrial Town: Manchester, 1810–1870'. In *The Victorian City: Images and Realities*, vol. 2, ed. H. J. Dyos and Michael Wolff. 739–61. London: Routledge and Kegan Paul, 1973.

Index of Titles

Ada *164*
Alfred of Northumbria.—I. Retirement *237*
Alfred of Northumbria.—II. Self-Reliance *239*
Alfred the Great.—I. The Child *267*
Alfred the Great.—II. Remembrances *269*
Alfred the Great.—III. Adversity *271*
Alfred the Great.—IV. Releasing the Wife and Children of Hastings the Northman *273*
Alfred the Great.—V. Romney Marsh, Kent *275*
A Little Girl's Wish *153*
Anglo-Saxon Patriots *265*
A Talk in Furness Abbey—to J.C.H *152*
Athelstan.—II *293*
Caedmon the Anglo-Saxon Poet *209*
Canute the Great *325*
Cecil's Own Book *369*
Change *185*
Change—not Death *417*
Christianity *181*
Christianity in Britain *183*
Christianity received by the Saxons.—I *193*
Christianity received by the Saxons.—II *195*
Common Things *114*
Conclusion *368*
Death-Shadowings.—I. Edward the Etheling *345*
Death-Shadowings.—II. Leofric *347*
Death-Shadowings.—III. Leofric *349*
Denulf *277*
Destruction of the Abbey of Peterborough by the Northmen *221*
Dionysius the Areopagite *6*
   Part I *6*
   Part II *43*
   Part III *61*
'Dionysius the Areopagite', with Other Poems *1*

Disunion *299*
Dunstan.—I. The Boy *301*
Dunstan.—II. The Dream *303*
Dunstan.—III. The Youth's aspirings *305*
Dunstan.—IV. The Trial *307*
Dunstan.—V. Love *309*
Dunstan.—VI. The Fall *311*
Dunstan.—VII. Nature's Revenge *313*
Dunstan.—VIII. Refusing to crown Ethelred *315*
Earth's Waters *418*
Editha *131*
Editha in the Monastery at Wherwell *343*
Edmund Ironside *323*
Edward the Confessor.—I *351*
Edward the Confessor.—II *353*
Edwin of Northumbria.—II *205*
Edwy and Elfgiva *295*
Egbert *257*
Ethelberga *243*
Ethelbert embraces Christianity *201*
Ethelbert examining the Christian Doctrines *199*
Ethelred the Unready *317*
Ethelwulph.—II *261*
Ethelwulph leaving the Cloister.—I *259*
God is Love *148*
Godwin.—I. Childhood *329*
Godwin.—II. The meeting with Ulfr *331*
Godwin.—III. The Flight *333*
Godwin.—IV. The Earl *335*
Godwin.—V. The Death-Feast *337*
Harold.—I *359*
Harold.—II *361*
Homes of the Flowers *420*
I do not love the Night *134*
Ina resigning his Crown *229*
Introductory *171*
Introductory Stanzas *3*
In Memoriam *422*
King Alfred and His Mother—a Scene in the Time of the Saxons *137*
Land of my Fathers *90*

Life's Dull Reality   105
Lines on a Friend lost at Sea   96
Little Prince Bepettedbyall   390
Mary's Wish   111
Massacre of the Danes   319
Merlin   197
Night after Battle   365
Palestine   89
Poems for My Children   107
Progress   175
Saxon Mythology   191
Scene in the Time of the Romans   126
Sir Oswald's Return—a Scene in the Time of the Crusades
   Part I   155
   Part II   158
Song   98
Sonnets on Anglo-Saxon History   167
Sonnet to——   103
Sonnet—To America   88
Spring is Coming   110
Spring to the Flowers   87
Sweyne, the Outlawed   339
The Ambitious Water-Lily   398
The Angel Friend   139
The Anglo-Saxons   367
The beginning   173
The benighted Ceorl   245
The Birds of Passage   420
The Captive King   100
The Chronicler   211
The City Child's Complaint   128
The death of Bede.—III   217
The Discontented Stream   387
The Druids   177
The Eventide.—I   355
The Eventide.—II   357
The Exile Song   92
The Fairy Gift; or, The Iron Bracelet   403
The Festival of the Last of October—Scene in the Time of the Druids   112
The First Spring Flowers   129
The Forest   327
The Future   77

The great Edwin of Northumbria.—I   203
The Greek Girl's Song   99
The Hermit, the Chieftain, and the Child—a Tale about Happiness   145
The Hero-King   287
The History of a Coral Islet   143
The Land of my Dreams   142
The Little Wanderers   115
   Part I. The Resolve   115
   Part II. The Avalanche   118
   Part III. The Cave in the Mountains   122
The Markman's Cottage.—I   249
The Markman's Cottage.—II   251
The Monastery   241
The Monk of Chester—a Scene in the Time of the Normans   149
The Mother of Egbert   255
The Mother of Harold   363
The Mother to her Starving Child   93
The Noontide Dream   393
The Northmen   219
The Oak Tree   132
The Past   69
The Pilgrim.—I   231
The Pilgrim.—II   233
The Pilgrim.—III   235
The Poet   321
The Poor Fly—for my little Harry   141
The Prophet's Lament   97
The remorse of Athelstan.—I   291
The Romans   179
The Saxons.—I   187
The Saxons.—II   189
The Selfish Toad   383
The Serf   225
The Serf Freed   227
The Squirrel that forgot that it would be Winter   395
The Stream   140
The Thane Lilla saving Edwin.—III   207
The Thane's Fireside   289
The three Pilgrims   285
The Tomb of Ethelberga   263

Index of Titles

The Town *297*
The Venerable Bede.—I *213*
The Venerable Bede.—II *215*
The Visit *341*
The Welsh Bard's Last Song *86*
The Wind *125*
The Witena meeting at Easter *247*
The Wonderful Adventures of Hassan the Younger, the Son of Hassan-el-Alfi the Camel Driver *371*
Thinking and Dreaming *135*
To a Bereaved Father *91*
To Editha *130*
To Fountain's Abbey *90*
To—— after the Death of her Daughter *96*
To—— on the Death of Three of her Children *95*
True Workers *253*
Under-Currents *223*
Why am I a Slave? *102*
Wild Flowers *85*
Woman.—I. Ethelfleda, the daughter of Alfred *279*
Woman.—II. Ethelfleda *281*
Woman.—III. Ethelgiva the Nun *283*

Index of First Lines

A boy through that old forest wends his way *329*
Ada, the flowers of spring are blooming now *164*
Ages ago, beneath the deep *143*
A little child sat on the grass *393*
All is not lost, for Nature still survives *309*
Amid the bloody haze of Hastings' fight *361*
And now there rises from the shadowy past *359*
And now the task I planned in days gone by *368*
And so he did, nor weakly bowed his mind *239*
And soon the polish and the splendour fled *189*
And what art thou?—an ideal of the great *197*
Around that grief-struck woman silently *363*
Arouse thee, Ethelwulph, it is no time *261*
Art thou too gone? the loved, the kind, the young *96*
A sound of countless wings *420*
At length they leave, those masters of the world *185*
Avaunt! thou hideous spectre—hence—avaunt *291*
A wish, an unsubstantial hope—a beam *347*
Before his powerful genius had bowed down *257*
"Be free," they said, and placed within his hand *227*
Believe not him whose creed thy heart denies *307*
Bowed down with years, but unsubdued in will *315*
Bring me a nosegay? Where shall I go *129*

But silently beneath this noise and strife *223*
But the death-struggles of that fiery soul *313*
Canute the Great!—the great in what? in crime *325*
Conquered, but unsubdued in spirit still *367*
Dark clouds are glooming o'er the Saxon land *317*
Dear to the Briton was his island home *179*
Did he do well and wisely, who resigned *229*
Exile, thou tread'st thy native shores again *345*
Far away amid the mountains *387*
First of the Saxon kings whom learning led *237*
Fling on oblivion's wave *99*
Forth from their homes they went, a simple band *253*
From a small lamp a single thread of light *277*
Hadst thou been Greek, thy name had been enshrined *207*
Have I done well the priest alone to hear *233*
He came an honoured and a peaceful guest *341*
He had been thinking how, in earth's first day *303*
He sat beside an antique shrine and thought *205*
He thought his hero-soul could animate *323*
He would be great, and hard he toiled for fame *305*
Home, love, and faith in God and man were gone *243*
I call thee great—as such, would honour thee *203*

I do not know thee, but one
    kindred tie   95
"I do not love the night, mamma   134
"I know there are sunny lands that lie   142
I live upon the memory of the past   92
I love my country, for I love my
    kind—   103
"I need not that—take back thy glittering
    bribe   333
In Chester's ancient convent dim   149
In massive chair of oak-wood, rudely
    made   211
In monkish cowl, or in the hermit's
    cell   351
In the rude ages, earth had shrines,
    where men   285
In the soft melody of winds and
    streams   191
I often wish that I could see   111
Is this Judea? this the promised land   89
It could not be that he had trod in
    vain   269
It is a common record   90
It was a summer's evening   145
It was a wearied man, and that gave
    claim   251
It was a winter's evening   137
I will resign thee to the earth
    again   235
I wish I had wings to fly away   153
Land of my fathers, isle of the free   90
"Life's dull reality!"—ah! say not so   105
Long years, long years ago   100
Love God the more by loving
    man the less   311
"Mamma, my sister's gone   152
Man to our island came; but from what
    land   173
Man's heart could listen then, as now, and
    hear   177
Master and slave! strange words are those
    to hear   225
Mending his hunting-spear before the
    fire   249
Mother, do angels ever come   139
My hand is on my harp   86

Nature hath mighty things, and what are
    they   199
No neutral character will nature
    own   353
Not from indifference, not with hasty
    tread   201
Not useless, in that age of war and
    strife   241
Oh! beautiful as light when down it
    streams   183
Oh! is there ought more beautiful   140
Oh! sleep I dread to see
    those eyes   93
Oh! tell me not the loved and lost
    forget   96
Oh, that I know, indeed, is true   148
Once by thy ruined but time-honoured
    cell   213
Once embosomed by high
    mountains   398
Once in a far-off northern home   422
Once there was a little fly   141
One evening little Editha   131
One hero fills a century, and
    the age   287
Pale famine, with her nerveless hand, had
    stood   357
Pause for a while upon those gentler
    things   327
Peace, peace, is what I crave, the last, best
    gift   231
Primrose bud, be thou the child   87
Progress is nature's stamp on man; the
    mark   175
Proudly she stood before him, but her
    eye   273
Queen of the western world, upon thy
    brow   88
Rome's clarion-blast had thundered
    through the air   181
Rust gather on that harp from aye that
    rings   321
Silence and death! how hideous or how
    fair   365
Simple and saintly as the histories
    told   217

Index of First Lines

Sprung from a Saxon stock, by bigot zeal *219*
That care-worn man, amid his stately sons *335*
The daws are wheeling round the minster roof *297*
The dew is on the grass *130*
The Druid's time had passed away *126*
The fisher's boat rocks idly on the sea *275*
The forest echoes to another tread *331*
The morning sun crept through the quiet room *343*
The music of the vesper hymn had died *221*
The night was closing round the Saxon's throne *355*
The oak it is a noble tree *132*
The ocean billows, and the rock-bound shore *209*
The polished Roman left how slight a trace *187*
"The trees and flowers are beautiful *128*
There is a whisper in the woods *110*
There was a bright cloud in the West *417*
There was a little Squirrel once *395*
There was once an old Toad *383*
The Saxon sun had reached its noontide height *299*
The sunshine is a glorious thing *114*
The time for change had come! what once had might *193*
The times have changed since of a Kentish king *295*
The wind it is a mystic thing *125*
They had one home, they saw one mother's smile *283*
The yule log crackles in the ample grate *289*
Think not thy crooked policy will save *319*
Though a smile is on my lip *98*

Through the bare forest rushes past the wind *245*
Thy story conjures up a thousand things *263*
True, he was but a child, but a child's heart *267*
'T is a hard thing to judge the past aright *171*
'T is easy on the accustomed path to tread *195*
'T was a rude pile, although a noble dame *255*
'T was an old chapel, and a sunny ray *259*
'T was early spring, the yellow catkins waved *247*
'T was morning—and the valleys lay *115*
'T was winter, and the snow fell fast *155*
Upon a wide and lonely moor *112*
Upon the mountain's bow *420*
We call them childish fables that he tells *215*
Weep, lonely daughter of Judea, weep *97*
Weep,—for the silent grave *91*
We wish to those we love skies ever clear *271*
What more will be thy prey *6*
When on the fields of fight he braved his foes *337*
Where is the record of the past inscribed *69*
Where are the strains like solemn music stealing *3*
Which, of all earth's waters *418*
Who shall unveil the future—who unfold *77*
Who sleep beneath thy earth, my native land *265*
Why do I bear that cursed name *102*
Wild flowers, wild flowers, ye are sweeter far *85*
Wise, moderate, reverent!—when he died, a tie *349*

Within an ancient church's ruined aisles *301*
Within the cloister feebler men had sought *293*
Within the garden where the Saviour prayed *339*

Woman hath trodden every path of life *279*
Working 'mid humble cares and petty strife *281*
"You tell me I must think—I thought *135*